MOUNT MARY
Milwaukee, Wisconsin

P9-CBH-557

WOMAN
IN WESTERN
THOUGHT

MOUNT MARY COLLEGE LIBRARY
Milwaukee, Wisconsin 53222

WOMAN IN WESTERN THOUGHT

Edited by

Martha Lee Osborne
The University of Tennessee at Knoxville

80-1056

RANDOM HOUSE *New York*

First Edition

987654321

Copyright © 1979 by Random House, Inc.

All rights reserved under International and Pan-American Copyright Conventions. No part of this book may be reproduced in any form or by any means, electronic or mechanical, including photocopying, without permission in writing from the publisher. All inquiries should be addressed to Random House, Inc., 201 East 50th Street, New York, N.Y. 10022. Published in the United States by Random House, Inc., and simultaneously in Canada by Random House of Canada Limited, Toronto.

Library of Congress Cataloging in Publication Data
Main entry under title:
Woman in Western thought.

Bibliography: p.
1. Women—Addresses, essays, lectures. 2. Women—Social conditions—Addresses, essays, lectures. 3. Women—History—Addresses, essays, lectures.
I. Osborne, Martha Lee, 1928–
HQ1121.W88   301.41'2   78-16116
ISBN 0-394-32112-X

Manufactured in the United States of America

Cover illustration and design by Brenda Kamen
Text design by Brenda Kamen

ACKNOWLEDGMENTS

Meno and *Republic* V excerpted from *The Dialogues of Plato*, 3rd edition, translated by Benjamin Jowett. Published by the Oxford University Press, 1892.

"Plato's *Republic* and Feminism" by Julia Annas, from *Philosophy* 51 (July 1976). Reprinted by permission of the author and the publisher.

De Generatione Animalium, Politica, and *Oeconomica* excerpted from *The Oxford Translation of Aristotle,* edited by W. D. Ross. Reprinted by permission of the Oxford University Press.

"Can a Woman Be Good in the Same Way As a Man?" by Christine Garside Allen excerpted from *Dialogue* 10, 3 (1971). Reprinted by permission of the author and the publisher.

St. Augustine's *Confessions,* translated by J. G. Pilkington; *On the Trinity,* translated by Arthur West Haddan; and *The City of God,* translated by Marcus Dods, excerpted from *A Select Library of the Nicene and Post-Nicene Fathers of the Christian Church,* edited by Philip Schaff. Published by the Christian Literature Company, 1887.

"Misogynism and Virginal Feminism in the Fathers of the Church" by Rosemary Radford Ruether excerpted from *Religion and Sexism,* edited by Rosemary Radford Ruether. Copyright © 1974 by Rosemary Radford Ruether. Reprinted by permission of Simon & Schuster, a Division of Gulf & Western Corporation.

"Part 1, Question 92," "Part 3, Question 67," "Part 3 (Supplement), Question 39," and "Part 3 (Supplement), Question 81" excerpted from *The Summa Theologica of St. Thomas Aquinas,* translated by the Fathers of the English Dominican Province. Published in London and New York, 1922. Reprinted by permission.

"Equality of Souls, Inequality of Sexes: Women in Medieval Theology" by Eleanor Commo McLaughlin excerpted from *Religion and Sexism,* edited by Rosemary Radford Ruether. Copyright © 1974 by Rosemary Radford Ruether. Reprinted by permission of Simon & Schuster, a Division of Gulf & Western Corporation.

"Of Democracy" excerpted from *Tractatus Politicus* by Benedict de Spinoza, translated by R. H. M. Elwes. Published by George Routledge and Sons, Ltd., 1895. Reprinted by permission of Routledge & Kegan Paul.

301.412
W844

"The Natural Superiority of Queens" excerpted from *The First Sex* by Elizabeth Gould Davis. Copyright © 1971 by Elizabeth Gould Davis. Reprinted by permission of G. P. Putnam's Sons.

"Book 1, Chapter 5" and "Book 2, Chapter 7" excerpted from *Two Treatises of Civil Government* by John Locke, 2nd edition. Published by George Routledge and Sons, 1887.

"Letter XIII" excerpted from *Letters on the Equality of the Sexes and the Condition of Woman* by Sarah M. Grimké. Published by Lenox Hill Pub. and Dist. Co., 1838.

"Sophia" excerpted from *Emilius; or, A New System of Education* by Jean-Jacques Rousseau, translated by "the translator of Eloisa." Published by J. Potts, 1779.

"On the Future of Love: Rousseau and the Radical Feminists" by Elizabeth Rapaport. Reprinted by permission of G. P. Putnam's Sons from *Women and Philosophy: Toward a Theory of Liberation,* edited by Carol C. Gould and Marx W. Wartofsky. Copyright © 1976 by Carol C. Gould and Marx W. Wartofsky.

"Chapter 1" and "Chapter 2" excerpted from *A Vindication of the Rights of Woman* by Mary Wollstonecraft. Published by Walter Scott, 1891.

"Reason and Morals in the Early Feminist Movement: Mary Wollstonecraft" by Carolyn W. Korsmeyer. Reprinted by permission of G. P. Putnam's Sons from *Women and Philosophy: Toward a Theory of Liberation,* edited by Carol C. Gould and Marx W. Wartofsky. Copyright © 1976 by Carol C. Gould and Marx W. Wartofsky.

"Observations on the Feeling of the Beautiful and Sublime" excerpted from *Essays and Treatises on Moral, Political, and Various Philosophical Subjects* by Immanuel Kant, translated anonymously. Published by William Richardson, 1799.

"The Rights of the Family As a Domestic Society" excerpted from *The Philosophy of Law: An Exposition of the Fundamental Principles of Jurisprudence As the Science of Right* by Immanuel Kant, translated by W. Hastie. Published by T. and T. Clark, 1887.

"The Woman Question: The Philosophy of Liberation and the Liberation of Philosophy" by Carol C. Gould. Reprinted by permission of G. P. Putnam's Sons from *Women and Philosophy: Toward a Theory of Liberation,* edited by Carol C. Gould and Marx W. Wartofsky. Copyright © 1976 by Carol C. Gould and Marx W. Wartofsky.

"The Ethical World" and "Guilt and Destiny" excerpted from *The Phenomenology of Mind* by G. W. F. Hegel, translated by J. B. Baillie. Published by Swan Sonnenschein and Macmillan, 1910. Reprinted by permission of George Allen & Unwin.

"Woman in the Nineteenth Century" by Margaret Fuller and "Margaret Fuller Ossoli, A Representative Woman" by Elizabeth Dorcas Livermore excerpted from *Woman in the Nineteenth Century, and Kindred Papers Relating to the Sphere, Condition, and Duties of Woman,* edited by Arthur B. Fuller. Published by the Tribune Association, 1859; Roberts Brothers, 1874.

"Subjective Dread" excerpted from Søren Kierkegaard, *The Concept of Dread,* translated by Walter Lowrie. Copyright © 1944, 1957 by Princeton University Press. Reprinted by permission of Princeton University Press.

"The Relationship of Dread to Spirit in Man and Woman, According to Kierkegaard" by Howard P. Kainz, Jr., from *The Modern Schoolman* 47 (November 1969). Reprinted by permission of the publisher.

"On Women" excerpted from *Studies in Pessimism,* a selection of essays from *Parerga and Paralipomena* by Arthur Schopenhauer, translated by T. Bailey Saunders. Published by George Allen & Unwin, 1890. Reprinted by permission of the publisher.

"The Natural Superiority of Women" by Ashley Montagu from *The Saturday Review* 35 (March 1, 1952). Reprinted by permission of the publisher.

"Our Virtues" excerpted from *Beyond Good and Evil* by Friedrich Nietzsche, translated by Helen Zimmern. Published by T. N. Foulis and the Darien Press, 1907; reissued in 1964 by Russell & Russell, New York. Reprinted by permission of Russell & Russell.

"Nietzsche and Moral Change" by Kathryn Pyne Parsons excerpted from *Nietzsche,* edited by Robert C. Solomon. Published by Doubleday-Anchor, 1973. Reprinted by permission of the editor and the publisher. This essay has also been reprinted in *Feminist Studies* 2 (1974), pp. 57–74.

Preface to *The Catechism of Positive Religion* by Auguste Comte, translated by Richard Congreve, 3rd edition. Published by Kegan Paul, Trench, Trubner, 1891.

"The Compassion Trap," by Margaret Adams, in *Woman in Sexist Society: Studies in Power and Powerlessness,* edited by Vivian Gornick and Barbara K. Moran. Copyright © 1971 by Basic Books, Inc., Publishers, New York, as excerpted in *Psychology Today.* Reprinted by permission of Basic Books, Inc.

Chapter 4 of *The Subjection of Women* by John Stuart Mill. Published by D. Appleton, 1869.

"Sentiment and Intellect" by Alice S. Rossi excerpted from *Essays on Sex Equality,* edited by Alice S. Rossi. Copyright © 1970 by University of Chicago Press. Reprinted by permission of the publisher.

"Preface" and "The Family" excerpted from *The Origin of the Family, Private Property, and the State* by Friedrich Engels, translated by Ernest Untermann. Published in Chicago by Charles Kerr & Co., 1902.

"Political Ramifications of Engels' Argument on Women's Political Subjugation" by Eleanor Burke Leacock from the Introduction to Friedrich Engels' *The Origin of the Family, Private Property, and the State,* edited, with an introduction, by Eleanor Burke Leacock. Copyright © 1972 by International Publishers. Reprinted by permission of the publisher.

"Liberalism and Women's Suffrage" by Bertrand Russell from *Contemporary Review* 94 (July–December 1908). Reprinted by permission of the publisher.

"Woman Suffrage" by Emma Goldman from *Anarchism and Other Essays,* 2nd revised edition, by Emma Goldman. Published by the Mother Earth Publishing Association and A. C. Fifield, 1911.

"Doing and Having" excerpted from *Being and Nothingness* by Jean-Paul Sartre, translated by Hazel E. Barnes. Copyright © 1956 by Philosophical Library, Inc. Reprinted by permission of the publisher.

"Holes and Slime: Sexism in Sartre's Psychoanalysis" by Margery L. Collins and Christine Pierce. Reprinted by permission of G. P. Putnam's Sons from *Women and Philosophy: Toward a Theory of Liberation,* edited by Carol C. Gould and Marx W. Wartofsky. Copyright © 1976 by Carol C. Gould and Marx W. Wartofsky.

"Myth and Reality" from *The Second Sex* by Simone de Beauvoir, translated by H. M. Parshley. Copyright © 1952 by Alfred A. Knopf, Inc. Reprinted by permission of the publisher.

"The Dialectic of Sex" by Shulamith Firestone. Reprinted by permission of William Morrow & Co., Inc. from *The Dialectic of Sex: The Case for Feminist Revolution* by Shulamith Firestone. Copyright © 1970 by Shulamith Firestone.

To a couple who,
long before it was fashionable to do so,
brought up two daughters to pay little heed to traditional sex roles,
this book is gratefully dedicated.

Preface

Woman in Western Thought grew out of a course on the philosophy of woman, which I have been teaching since 1975. Student reaction to the course and to the philosophers examined in it has been most gratifying. The goal of the teacher of philosophy, of course, is not to provide the student with a vast array of discrete facts, or to advocate any particular philosophical system, but to stimulate the student to think independently about the problems that have always preoccupied philosophers. In many respects, the study of the various concepts of woman has proved an almost ideal way to achieve this goal. For one thing, philosophers' concepts of woman (and their ways of arriving at them and, in some cases, defending them) usually reflect their other philosophical views— their political philosophy, their ethics, their views on religion, and, most strikingly perhaps, their concept of the male of the species. For another, the problem of the nature of woman is one that transcends both time and place and, more important, is one to which nearly every person—male and female, adolescent and adult—brings definite ideas and preconceptions. Some people may go through life without giving a thought to their relationship to God, to the state, to existing value systems, to existence itself; but virtually every human being, from puberty to maturity and even (as some of the philosophers represented here demonstrate) into the last years of life, is confronted by and preoccupied with the problem of sex differentiation. And nearly everyone, no matter how disinclined to speculate or philosophize, has formed judgments—and prejudices—on the subject.

This anthology is arranged more or less chronologically, not because it is intended to show any historical development in the concept of woman—for indeed, in my opinion there is almost none. Just as Aristotle and Plato, St. Thomas Aquinas and St. Augustine, Rousseau and Wollstonecraft, took opposite sides on the question in their time, so today do Jean-Paul Sartre and Simone de Beauvoir. Rather, this organization has been chosen because it is the most neutral arrangement and the one least likely to obscure the relevancy of philosophical concepts of woman to other branches of philosophy and to the arts and sciences. As an aid to a better understanding of these relationships a syntopicon has been included—an alternative table of contents in which the subject matter is organized into various related areas.

I cannot conclude these remarks without expressing my sincere thanks to those who have assisted and supported me in preparing this work: the faculty and staff of the Department of Philosophy at The University of Tennessee, Knoxville, my family, and particularly my students.

June 1978
Knoxville, Tennessee

Martha Lee Osborne

Contents

Syntopicon

WOMEN AND WORK

WOMEN AND THE STATE

WOMEN AND MARRIAGE

WOMEN AND RELIGION

WOMEN AND EDUCATION

WOMEN AND MORALITY

WOMEN AND THE ARTS

WOMEN'S DRESS AND ADORNMENT

WOMEN IN OTHER CULTURES

WOMAN'S BODY / WOMAN'S MIND

WOMAN IN WESTERN THOUGHT

✦1 *Introduction*

A book concerned with the role of woman in Western philosophy might reasonably be expected to be a slender volume indeed. Few women's names are found in the index to *The Encyclopedia of Philosophy*, very few anthologies of philosophy include any excerpts from the works of women, and the women mentioned in the standard histories of philosophy are seldom philosophers. And yet it seems that women were active in philosophy as early as the fifth century B.C., when Theano, wife of Pythagoras and onetime student in his school, took it upon herself to see that his doctrines were not misinterpreted after his death. In the late fourth and early fifth centuries A.D., Hypatia won great fame as a leading representative of the Alexandrian school of Neoplatonism. Hildegard von Bingen may quite appropriately be regarded as a medieval philosopher, and something of a feminist at that. In the eighteenth century Mary Wollstonecraft refers to herself as a philosopher, although she is doubtless more frequently thought of as a literary figure. The works of Margaret Fuller, written a half-century later, are also generally classified as literary, although they exhibit the same characteristics as those of Emerson and Thoreau, both of whom are recognized American philosophers. In our own time Simone de Beauvoir is generally regarded as a novelist, presumably because her existentialist philosophy is most frequently expressed in fictional form. But more and more women's names are listed in each new volume of the *Directory of American Philosophers*; more and more articles by women are appearing in philosophical journals; more and more books by women philosophers are coming off the press; and more and more thoughtful people, both male and female, are evincing interest in the problem of woman and philosophy.

This anthology, however, is primarily concerned not with woman as philosopher but with woman as the subject of philosophy. Philosophy, according to Aristotle, begins in wonder, and just as philosophers have wondered about the nature of ultimate reality, the process of cognition, the good, the true, the beautiful, and the just, they have in almost every instance wondered about woman, about the nature of sexuality, about the extent of sexual differentiation. And just as philosophers' answers to metaphysical questions have ranged from materialism to dualism to idealism, so have their answers to questions regarding woman ranged from the predominant male-supremacy position to the modified male-supremacy view to partial critiques of male-supremacy thinking.

To assess philosophers' theories of woman properly, we must take into account three distinguishable but related matters: their personal experiences, the time and place in which they lived, and the other theories they embraced. These three ingredients are blended in varying proportions to form the various philosophical views of woman presented in this volume.

Traditionally the philosopher has been regarded as an impersonal thinker who develops views dispassionately and remains virtually free of the prejudices that beset the unphilosophical soul. Johann Gottlieb Fichte was perhaps the first to suggest otherwise: "What sort of philosophy one chooses," Fichte observed in his *Wissenschaftslehre*, "depends on what sort of man [*sic*] one is; for a philosophical system is not a dead piece of furniture that we can reject or accept as we wish; it is rather a thing animated by the soul of the person who holds it."[1] William James more or less echoed these sentiments when he proposed that one selects one's philosophy largely on the basis of one's temperament: "tender-minded" philosophers tend to be rationalists, idealists, optimists, monists, dogmatists, and believers in the freedom of the will, while "tough-minded" philosophers tend to embrace the opposite set of beliefs—empiricism, materialism, pessimism, pluralism, skepticism, fatalism.

If it can be plausibly maintained that personality, temperament, and experience can affect philosophers' beliefs in such abstract areas as metaphysics, how much more likely it is that these same factors would affect their thinking about woman. Friedrich Nietzsche admitted to a great deal of subjectivity in his views on every "cardinal problem." He opened a series of apothegms on woman by admitting that they embodied only "his truths." Plato, on the other hand, presumably followed the dictates of reason rather than his own predilections in assigning women a place among the guardian class of his ideal republic.

Closely connected with philosophers' personal experiences are the attitudes and customs of the time and place in which they live. While a philosopher's earliest personal experiences with women in all probability occur within the family, the family itself is a social unit, and its structure is determined to a great extent by the larger society of which it is a part.

The relationship between philosophy and the cultural milieu of a society has been noted by Alfred North Whitehead, who contends that certain types of intellectual activity within the cultural setting—such as the interest in and pursuit of mathematics—are conducive to the development of philosophy, while others are not. Hegel, on the other hand, seems to have held that personal experience is unimportant and society is all-important in the evolution of a philosopher's thought. What the philosopher does and says is insignificant, Hegel maintained; a philosophy is neither more nor less than the reflection of the *Zeitgeist*, the spirit of the age in which it is written. To be sure, philosophers may react to contemporary society either affirmatively or negatively. They may, like Aristotle, respect the views of ordinary people and use them as premises for their ethics, or, like Bertrand Russell, they may cry out against them. Only very rarely will they ignore them.

While personal experiences and social influences may have an unconscious or subconscious effect on a philosopher's "gynology," as philosophical views on woman might be called, the relationship between those views and views on other subjects is much more likely to be conscious. Philosophers will frequently turn to science or theology for premises upon which to construct arguments about the nature of woman, and often they follow their views on woman to a logical conclusion in their ethical and political theories. Other areas of their

---

[1] Johann Gottlieb Fichte, *Science of Knowledge (Wissenschaftslehre)*, ed. and tr. by Peter Heath and John Lachs (New York, 1970), p. 16.

philosophy will affect or be affected by their philosophy of woman, for a blatant contradiction between it and their metaphysics, epistemology, or axiology would mar the consistency of whatever system they elaborate.

Aristotle turned to biology for principles upon which to construct his philosophy of woman. Using as premises the propositions that (1) female animals are normally smaller and weaker than male animals, (2) the human being is a rational animal, and (3) psychological development is in direct proportion to physical development, Aristotle concluded that women were not only smaller and weaker than men but rationally inferior to them as well. This conclusion, of course, had repercussions on his ethics and his philosophy of politics; because he concluded that women were by nature inferior, he endorsed the Athenian practice of keeping them under the tutelage of men, both in the home and in the state.

Auguste Comte drew the premises for his gynology from his psychology, more specifically from his cerebral theory. According to Comte, the human brain is divided into three parts: affective, active, and speculative. He held that while women are so little suited for work that men must support them, and while the speculative part of their brains has all but atrophied, the development of the affective sector of a woman's cerebrum is far superior to that of a man's. Furthermore, he thought, within the affective section of the brain are two subdivisions, egoistic and altruistic, and whereas in men the development of the egoistic segment is superior to that of the altruistic, in women the opposite is the case. Since Comte deplored the decline of altruism in nineteenth-century Europe, he pinned his hopes for the restitution of society on women. He envisioned a society in which men would not only maintain women but would free them of all conjugal obligations as well, so as to enable them to devote themselves completely to maternity and to becoming a means by which men might arrive at happiness and moral perfection.

It was anthropology that provided Friedrich Engels with the foundation for his views on woman. Drawing on Lewis Henry Morgan's *Ancient Society,* Engels traced the enslavement of woman to man back to the appearance of private property and suggested that with the disappearance of private property and the advent of communism, sexual equality would be restored.

Christian philosophers such as St. Augustine and St. Thomas Aquinas turned, of course, to theology as a basis for their views on woman's nature. Inasmuch as conflicting testimony about it may be found in the Bible, these philosophers not only had to come to grips with various accounts of the Creation and the fall from grace, they had to explain St. Paul's misogynism as well. And the consequences of their theories were extended from the here to the hereafter.

The relationship between gynology and other branches of philosophy is analogous to the relationship between it and other disciplines. Metaphysics and epistemology are just as fertile fields for premises as are science and theology. Plato's idealism, for instance, entails a belief that reality is essentially mental or spiritual rather than material. Thus he could consistently embrace a sexist position—one in which discrimination among individuals is based on sex—only if he could find a significant distinction between the souls of men and those of women; and since his theory of transmigration or reincarnation expressly precludes that possibility, the egalitarianism he proposed in the *Republic* is the logical extension of two metaphysical convictions.

John Stuart Mill, on the other hand, claimed to have no metaphysics, and yet his epistemology led him to a position not unlike Plato's. Knowledge comes only from experience, Mill asserted. This thesis, coupled with the premise—borrowed from psychology—that the human character is enormously malleable, leads to the conclusion that it is impossible to ascertain woman's "true nature"; to know, in other words, what she might have been like had she not been subjected to the centuries of oppression that she has suffered. In keeping with his laissez-faire economic policy, then, Mill advocated opening the job market to all women as well as to all men, and letting the fittest survive.

Ethics is perhaps even more relevant than epistemology to Mill's position on women's rights. A utilitarian, Mill defined the rightness of an act in terms of its consequences. Thus he justified his proposal to open to women almost all fields of endeavor—educational, professional, political—on the grounds of the good that would result from doing so; for not only would women themselves benefit from the action he proposed, society at large would reap the rewards, even—or perhaps especially—the male half.

Kant's gynology is the development of a different branch of his value theory, his aesthetics. He made the distinction between the beautiful, that which is pleasing, and the sublime, that which is so immense or so powerful as to be awe-inspiring, and then he proceeded to relegate woman, the fair sex, to the sphere of the beautiful, and to place man, whom he considered noble, into the category of the sublime. Nevertheless, Kant asserted, man and woman are not so disparate in nature as to preclude a marriage of reciprocity, and upon this he insisted.

Many other examples could be given that show how philosophers' personal experiences, environment, and espousal of particular philosophical systems helped to determine their views on woman, but merely understanding why and how these views arose cannot satisfy the serious student of philosophy. Some knowledge of Nietzsche's relationships with the women in his life, of the Greek attitude toward women in Aristotle's Athens, and of Kant's views on aesthetics will certainly help us to put these philosophers' gynologies into proper perspective and to make them more intelligible, and perhaps in some measure even pardonable. But it will not enable us to determine whether these philosophers' views on woman are sound. While philosophy may indeed begin in wonder, it aspires to end in truth. And for that reason the truly inquiring mind will not only seek to comprehend the sources of and influences on a given philosophical view of woman, it will also strive to evaluate dispassionately and critically the arguments brought in support of that view.

In general, arguments may be divided into two types: deductive and inductive. The premises of deductive arguments are taken from various disciplines, such as science or theology or philosophy. If those premises are true and if the philosopher reasons validly, the conclusions drawn from them must then be true. If one or more of the premises are false or if the reasoning is invalid, the conclusion, while it may happen to be true, may just as easily be false. A deductive argument may be found in the concluding paragraph of *A Political Treatise* by Benedictus de Spinoza. Having posed the question "whether women are under men's authority by nature or institution," Spinoza answered with an argument that rests on two premises: (1) If men and women were equal in nature, in addition to patriarchies there would be matriarchies and societies in which men and women ruled together as equals; and (2) there are no matriarchies and no egalitarian societies. Therefore, Spinoza concluded, men and women are not equal in nature. This argument is of the form: (1) If *p*, then *q*; (2) *q* is not the case; therefore, *p* is not the case. It is a perfectly valid argument form known as *modus tollens* (the method of denying), and all arguments of this form are valid, for the conclusion follows from the two premises. In other words, it is impossible for both premises to be true without the conclusion being true as well. Conversely, if the conclusion of a valid argument is not true, then something must be wrong with one or both of the premises. Perhaps the absence of matriarchies and egalitarian societies can be accounted for by something other than female inferiority. Or perhaps human society has boasted of matriarchies and egalitarian communities of which Spinoza was ignorant. Or perhaps Spinoza was using the word "equal" equivocally, giving it one meaning in the premise and another in the conclusion. In the latter case the validity of the argument would be only apparent, not real.

Another deductive argument may be found in the second chapter of Mary Wollstonecraft's *A Vindication of the Rights of Woman*:

. . . if man did attain a degree of perfection of mind when his body arrived at maturity, it might be proper, in order to make a man and his wife *one,* that she should rely entirely on his understanding . . . But alas! husbands, as well as their helpmates, are often only overgrown children; . . . and if the blind lead the blind, one need not come from heaven to tell us the consequence.[2]

The premises of the argument may be paraphrased as follows: (1) If men's minds matured when their bodies do, it might be appropriate for them to guide their wives in matters of judgment; (2) many men never attain mental maturity. This argument is enthymematic; that is, one of its propositions, in this case the conclusion, is left implicit rather than being stated. That conclusion is, of course, that wives should not rely on the understanding of their husbands. This argument has a form that is quite different from that of Spinoza's. The form of Wollstonecraft's argument is: (1) If *p*, then *q*; (2) *p* is not the case; therefore, *q* is not the case. The argument is not valid. Even if the premises were true (and it is clear from the context that she does not consider the first one to be so), the conclusion would not necessarily be true, for it does not follow from the premises. The mistake Wollstonecraft makes here is a common one. She does not take into account the possibility that there might be occasions on which it would be appropriate for one to rely upon the

---

[2] Mary Wollstonecraft, *A Vindication of the Rights of Woman* (London, 1891), pp. 18–19.

judgment of someone mentally immature—if one were oneself even less mature mentally, for example. In the event that Wollstonecraft should wish to preclude that possibility (as well she might), she would have to do so explicitly, since the argument she has constructed does not do so for her.

Neither Spinoza's argument nor Wollstonecraft's is acceptable. Spinoza's appears to be valid, but it leads to a conclusion that the contemporary reader would probably not regard as true; and so we must look for a false premise or the equivocal use of a word. Wollstonecraft's argument is obviously invalid, but it yields a conclusion that the reader would probably accept; and so we might wish to set about deriving it validly from similar premises.

The validity of a deductive argument resides in its form. Thus its invalidity may often become apparent when it is juxtaposed to an argument of the same form that is obviously unsound. Plato used this device in the *Republic* when he showed Socrates putting the following argument into the mouths of imaginary opponents to his proposal concerning women guardians:

They will say: 'Socrates and Glaucon, no adversary need convict you, for you yourselves, at the first foundation of the State, admitted the principle that everybody was to do the one work suited to his own nature. . . . And do not the natures of men and women differ very much indeed?' . . . Then we shall be asked, 'Whether the tasks assigned to men and to women should not be different, and such as are agreeable to their different natures?'[3]

This is another enthymematic argument. In this case, however, it is the second premise that is suppressed: (1) Men and women have different natures [(2) men may be guardians]; therefore, women may not be guardians. To prove the invalidity of this argument, Socrates constructs a preposterous one that is analogous to it:

. . . Suppose that by way of illustration we were to ask the question whether there is not an opposition in nature between bald men and hairy men; and if this is admitted by us, then, if bald men are cobblers, we should forbid the hairy men to be cobblers, and conversely?[4]

This passage contains two related arguments combined into one: I. (1) Bald men and hairy-headed men have different natures; (2) bald men may be cobblers; therefore, hairy-headed men may not be cobblers; and II. (1) Bald men and hairy-headed men have different natures; (2) hairy-headed men may be cobblers; therefore, bald men may not be cobblers. That the presence or absence of hair on the head is not relevant to skill at shoemaking is obvious. Socrates is suggesting that sex is equally irrelevant to the ability to govern, although perhaps less obviously so.

Of course, the kind of approach used above cannot be applied to all arguments. Indeed, another type of argument, the inductive, requires a completely different kind of analysis. A deductive argument is either valid or not valid; there are no degrees of deductive validity. But in the case of an inductive

---

[3] Plato, *Republic* 453 B–C.
[4] Ibid., 454 B.

argument, no matter how good the reasoning employed may be, the premises do not *entail* the conclusion; they merely make it more or less probable that the conclusion is true. The better the argument, the higher the degree of probability that the conclusion is true.

Inductive arguments are therefore much more difficult to evaluate than are deductive ones, but they are also much more interesting. For whereas the conclusion of a deductive argument merely makes explicit what is already implicit in the premises, the inductive argument can lead to new knowledge. There is no dearth of inductive arguments in philosophers' assessments of the nature of women, because, after all, every philosopher, indeed every human being, experiences at first hand, in one way or another, the problem of sexuality and sexual differentiation.

One of the most common types of inductive argument is the argument by analogy. Mary Wollstonecraft, who was particularly felicitous in her use of it, employed such an argument in the penultimate paragraph of Chapter II of *A Vindication of the Rights of Woman*:

> . . . The many have always been enthralled by the few; and monsters, who scarcely have shewn any discernment of human excellence, have tyrannized over thousands of their fellow-creatures. Why have men of superior endowments submitted to such degradation? For, is it not universally acknowledged that kings, viewed collectively, have ever been inferior, in abilities and virtue, to the same number of men taken from the common mass of mankind . . . ? . . . *Men* have submitted to superior strength to enjoy with impunity the pleasure of the moment—*women* have only done the same, and therefore till it is proved that the courtier, who servilely resigns the birthright of a man, is not a moral agent, it cannot be demonstrated that woman is essentially inferior to man because she has always been subjugated.[5]

The argument may be summarized as follows: The fact that subjects have always been ruled by monarchs does not indicate their inferiority to those monarchs; therefore, the fact that women have always been ruled by men should not be considered a sign of women's inferiority. The analogy that Wollstonecraft draws is between women and the citizenry of a monarchy. The greater the number of relevant respects in which the two are alike and the fewer the number of dissimilarities between them, the better the argument will be.

Another familiar type of inductive argument is the inductive generalization. Examples of this type abound in philosophical treatises on women, although the arguments leading to them are, for obvious reasons, seldom detailed. A statement such as the one Schopenhauer made to the effect that "the female character . . . has no *sense of justice*" is obviously an inductive generalization, arrived at, presumably, after a series of judgments concerning the lack of justness in the characters of a number of women whom he knew: his mother, perhaps, whom he obviously regarded as unjust because of the way in which she spent her inheritance from his father; his sister, perhaps, who, like his mother, exhibited little regard for justice in settling for partial reimbursement

---

[5] Wollstonecraft, p. 40.

for funds invested in a company that went bankrupt (Schopenhauer himself demanded full reimbursement, and, after two years of litigation, got it—plus interest); and, perhaps, some of the many women with whom he was erotically involved and who, in his opinion, exhibited no sense of justice. Whatever the identity of the individuals upon whom his inductive generalization was based, there seems little doubt that it was hastily made. Any generalization should be made on a sufficient number of individuals, and while the number of Schopenhauer's brief encounters with members of the opposite sex was impressive, there may be some doubt that it was vast enough to warrant a generalization concerning all women. Furthermore, a generalization should be based on a fair sampling of individuals. Perhaps the very fact that the individuals sampled by Schopenhauer were all women of his acquaintance and in many cases victims of his charm would be sufficient to call into question the fairness of his sample. Moreover, one might well doubt the objectivity of his judgments concerning their sense of justice. John Stuart Mill, by contrast, was careful not to make a hasty inductive generalization about women in history—he mentioned Queen Elizabeth, Deborah, Joan of Arc—for he was well aware that they were too few and too atypical. Mill merely indicated that their achievements were indicative of what women could do.

The hasty generalization and the weak analogical argument, frequently referred to as the false analogy, are generally classified as material or informal fallacies. The material fallacy, unlike the mistake in reasoning which constitutes an error in a deductive argument, resides not in the form, but in the content of the inductive agrument. Numerous other material fallacies may be found in gynological literature. One, the *petitio principii* (begging the question), appears repeatedly in *The Concept of Dread* as Søren Kierkegaard continually assumes what he has set out to prove. In the following passage he turns to classical and neoclassical art for proof that facial expression is more essential to beauty in man than in woman:

... in manly beauty the face and its expression are more essential than in feminine beauty ... I will indicate this difference by a single suggestion. Essentially Venus remains equally beautiful whether she is represented sleeping or waking—indeed, she is perhaps most beautiful sleeping. ... On the other hand, if Apollo is to be represented, it would not do to let him sleep. ... This would detract from the beauty of Apollo. . . .[6]

Quite apart from the question of how accurately the artist mirrors reality, this argument is circular. Kierkegaard uses two premises: (1) The Greek goddess of beauty, Venus, is depicted as just as beautiful asleep as awake, if not more so; (2) the Greek god of beauty, Apollo, should not be depicted asleep because he would be less beautiful that way. The argument seems inconclusive. For the desired conclusion to follow, the second premise would have to indicate that representations of Apollo sleeping are less beautiful than those of him awake. As the argument stands, it is circular for Kierkegaard's assumption and his conclusion are identical.

[6] Søren Kierkegaard, *The Concept of Dread,* trans. Walter Lowrie (Princeton, 1957), pp. 58–59.

A flagrant example of the *non sequitur* (an argument in which the conclusion simply does not follow from the premises) occurs in Schopenhauer's essay "On Women": "You need only to look at the way in which she is formed to see that woman is not meant to undergo great labour, whether of the mind or of the body."[7] While Schopenhauer might have been able to make a case for his allegation that woman's physical build makes her unfit for strenuous physical labor, what possible relevance could her physique have to her mental prowess?

In the fifth book of *Émile*, Rousseau, instead of refuting views opposed to his, dismissed those who held them as idle woolgatherers. In other words, he employed the *argumentum ad hominem*, an attack not on an idea but on the person holding it: ". . . To maintain indiscriminately that the two sexes are equal, and that their reciprocal duties and obligations are the same is to indulge ourselves in idle declamations unworthy of a serious answer."[8]

These are but a few examples of deductive and inductive arguments and material fallacies. In the selections included in this book the careful and thoughtful reader will find many others, including a number of examples of the fallacy called the *argumentum ad populum* (appeal to popular prejudice).

In order to stimulate thinking about the various views of woman presented here, each selection is preceded by a brief introduction that discusses the factors that influence various philosophical views: the philosophers' personal experiences, their social and temporal environment, and the other theories they embraced. Further, each selection is followed by a response by a modern or contemporary commentator, in nearly every case a professional philosopher. In some cases the comment is directed specifically at the philosopher represented, sometimes at the very passage excerpted. In other cases the general topic that the philosopher addresses is further explored, usually from a different perspective. Rarely do philosopher and commentator hold a common view. The introductions to the selections, it should be noted, do not consider the arguments and fallacies contained in the selections of the philosophers and their commentators. It is left to the reader to subject what both philosopher and commentator say to careful and critical scrutiny, and in so doing, it is hoped, to develop an independent, well-founded, and fair personal philosophical view of woman.

[7] Arthur Schopenhauer, *Studies in Pessimism*, trans. T. Bailey Saunders (London, 1890), p. 105.

[8] Jean-Jacques Rousseau, *Emilius and Sophia; or, A New System of Education*, trans. "by the translator of *Eloisa*" (Dublin, 1779), p. 13.

part one: THE INITIAL DEBATE

. . . all the pursuits of men are the pursuits of women also . . .
    —Plato

Plato's argument . . . is not valid . . . , it is irrelevant to facts about women's desires, and it is irrelevant to the injustice of sexual inequality.
    —Julia Annas

. . . the woman has {the deliberative faculty}, but it is without authority . . .
    —Aristotle

. . . a systematic study of the nature of woman in Aristotle . . . reveals . . . an attitude which ultimately bars women from being good in the full sense in which men can be good.
    —Christine Garside Allen

The contemporary women's liberation movement, as is becoming increasingly clear, marks a qualitatively new stage in the struggle for equality between the sexes. The struggle itself, however, is an old one. From the beginning of its recorded history, Western civilization has boasted its feminists as well as its antifeminists. As early as the fourth century B.C., Plato deplored the conditions that prevailed in his native Athens, where women were not educated, not enfranchised, and not permitted outside their homes unescorted. In the *Republic* he not only suggests the removal of these restrictions, he also advocates the inclusion of women in the highest class of the ideal state he envisions— the class charged with enacting and enforcing the laws governing the remainder of the citizenry. Yet, as Julia Annas points out, liberal though Plato's proposals may have been in the context of his own era, in many respects they would be unacceptable by contemporary standards.

13

It is generally believed that Plato submitted his dialogues to the scrutiny of the pupils of his Academy. At least one of those pupils, Aristotle, was strongly opposed to the suggestions for the emancipation of women that were made by Plato in his famous dialogue. In the *Politics,* in which Aristotle depicts his own ideal state, he explicitly criticizes Plato's logic and strongly supports the practices of the Athenian state. He conceives of women as being so limited in nature that, according to Christine Garside Allen, his own moral theories cannot be stretched to embrace her. One can readily imagine master and pupil, then, conversing under "Plato's tree" just outside the Academy, perhaps anticipating some of the very arguments used by contemporary opponents.

❦ 2 *Plato*

Plato was born in Athens in 427 B.C., the youngest son of wealthy parents. When he was still a child, his father died, and his mother, in conformance with Athenian custom, married her closest kinsman, an uncle, Pyrilampes. As the maternal branch of Plato's family included a number of members who were prominent politically, Plato himself may well have been expected to follow a political career. That he did not do so was very likely due to the influence of Socrates, a controversial figure who was popular with young Athenian intellectuals largely because he went about preaching moral excellence and criticizing corruption wherever he found it. When he found it in the Athenian government and as a result was brought to trial and executed—unjustly, Plato was convinced—his young friend was bitterly disillusioned and spent a dozen years in self-imposed exile. Upon his return to Athens, Plato founded his Academy and set about writing dialogues commemorating the man he had admired so profoundly. He continued teaching and writing until his death in 347 B.C., at the age of eighty.

In the Athens of Plato's day woman lived in virtual seclusion. Except when attending women's religious festivals, she was not allowed to leave her home unescorted. Within the home she was confined to women's quarters and was not permitted to attend social gatherings even when they were held in her own house and presided over by her own husband. She was not educated, nor did she have control over her own property. She was unenfranchised and ineligible for public office. Her betrothal was arranged by a "guardian," her nearest male relative, who gave her in marriage.

Plato denounced many of the practices of his native city. In an ideal state, he suggested in the Republic, women would not only vote, they would serve in the highest echelons of the government as well. And in the Laws, in which he depicted a state that fell somewhat short of the ideal but was more practicable than the one described in the Republic, Plato proposed that women as well as men should serve as magistrates and priests.

Plato's idealistic philosophy was sufficient to assure his sexual egalitarianism. A dualist, he believed that the human being is constituted of body and soul. But in that union the two were in his eyes extremely unequal. The body served largely as a hindrance to the soul, at times distracting it from its serious business, the acquisition of knowledge, and at times preventing it from attaining the truth by deceiving it with optical illusions and other misleading sensory data. The body was unimportant in Plato's philosophy. It was the soul that mattered. Therefore any significant difference between the sexes would, in his opinion, be spiritual rather than physical.

But souls do not come in two sexes; they come in varying degrees of excellence or virtue. Gorgias, a century earlier, had suggested that virtues were different in kind rather than in degree. There is one virtue peculiar to man, he thought, running a state, and another and inferior virtue appropriate to woman, managing a house. Plato disagreed. He held that virtue is virtue, and one and the same wherever it might appear—in a man, in a woman, in a child—and that the notion that virtue means one thing when it appears in

*a man and another when it is found in a woman makes about as much sense
as the idea that health or strength or size means one thing in reference to
one sex and something else in relation to the other. Furthermore, he pointed
out, the masculine virtue of heading a state and the feminine capacity for
supervising a house involve identical qualities, temperance and justice,
qualities that are exhibited alike by men and women.*

*Plato did recognize sexual differences, to be sure, and he did presume,
generally speaking, that males were superior in all areas of endeavor, but he
believed that distinctions between the sexes are by far outweighed by individual differences. To Plato what mattered was the degree of excellence
that the individual soul attained, not the sex of the body in which it was
imprisoned. And women, like men, have not only varying degrees of virtue,
but varying tastes and capacities as well. One woman will have a predilection
for medicine, another for music, a third for gymnastics, a fourth for philosophy, just as is the case with men. Thus, in an ideal state, he suggested,
the activities and the educational and professional opportunities for men and
women would be identical. Men and women would exercise together in the
gymnasium, partake of meals at a common table, and serve together as
guardians of the state.*

From *Meno*

"THE SAMENESS OF VIRTUE"

. . .

Soc. By the gods, Meno, be generous, and tell me what you say that virtue
is; for I shall be truly delighted to find that I have been mistaken, and that you
and Gorgias do really have this knowledge; although I have been just saying
that I have never found anybody who had.

Men. There will be no difficulty, Socrates, in answering your question. Let
us take first the virtue of a man—he should know how to administer the state,
and in the administration of it to benefit his friends and harm his enemies; and
he must also be careful not to suffer harm himself. A woman's virtue, if you
wish to know about that, may also be easily described: her duty is to order her
house, and keep what is indoors, and obey her husband. Every age, every
condition of life, young or old, male or female, bond or free, has a different
virtue: there are virtues numberless, and no lack of definitions of them; for
virtue is relative to the actions and ages of each of us in all that we do. And
the same may be said of vice, Socrates.

Soc. How fortunate I am, Meno! When I ask you for one virtue, you
present me with a swarm of them, which are in your keeping. Suppose that I
carry on the figure of the swarm, and ask of you, What is the nature of the bee?
and you answer that there are many kinds of bees, and I reply: But do bees
differ as bees, because there are many and different kinds of them; or are they
not rather to be distinguished by some other quality, as for example beauty,
size, or shape? How would you answer me?

Men. I should answer that bees do not differ from one another, as bees.

Soc. And if I went on to say: That is what I desire to know, Meno; tell me what is the quality in which they do not differ, but are all alike—would you be able to answer?

Men. I should.

Soc. And so of the virtues, however many and different they may be, they have all a common nature which makes them virtues; and on this he who would answer the question, 'What is virtue?' would do well to have his eye fixed: Do you understand?

Men. I am beginning to understand; but I do not as yet take hold of the question as I could wish.

Soc. When you say, Meno, that there is one virtue of a man, another of a woman, another of a child, and so on, does this apply only to virtue, or would you say the same of health, and size, and strength? Or is the nature of health always the same, whether in man or woman?

Men. I should say that health is the same, both in man and woman.

Soc. And is not this true of size and strength? If a woman is strong, she will be strong by reason of the same form and of the same strength subsisting in her which there is in the man. I mean to say that strength, as strength, whether of man or woman, is the same. Is there any difference?

Men. I think not.

Soc. And will not virtue, as virtue, be the same, whether in a child or in a grown-up person, in a woman or in a man?

Men. I cannot help feeling, Socrates, that this case is different from the others.

Soc. But why? Were you not saying that the virtue of a man was to order a state, and the virtue of a woman was to order a house?

Men. I did say so.

Soc. And can either house or state or anything be well ordered without temperance and without justice?

Men. Certainly not.

Soc. Then they who order a state or a house temperately or justly order them with temperance and justice?

Men. Certainly.

Soc. Then both men and women, if they are to be good men and women, must have the same virtues of temperance and justice?

Men. True.

Soc. And can either a young man or an elder one be good, if they are intemperate and unjust?

Men. They cannot.

Soc. They must be temperate and just?

Men. Yes.

Soc. Then all men are good in the same way, and by participation in the same virtues?

Men. Such is the inference.

Soc. And they surely would not have been good in the same way, unless their virtue had been the same?

Men. They would not.

. . .

From *Republic*

"WOMEN ARE BUT LESSER MEN"

. . .

Well, I replied, I suppose that I must retrace my steps and say what I perhaps ought to have said before in the proper place. The part of the men has been played out, and now properly enough comes the turn of the women. Of them I will proceed to speak, and the more readily since I am invited by you.

For men born and educated like our citizens, the only way, in my opinion, of arriving at a right conclusion about the possession and use of women and children is to follow the path on which we originally started, when we said that the men were to be the guardians and watchdogs of the herd.

True.

Let us further suppose the birth and education of our women to be subject to similar or nearly similar regulations; then we shall see whether the result accords with our design.

What do you mean?

What I mean may be put into the form of a question, I said: Are dogs divided into hes and shes, or do they both share equally in hunting and in keeping watch and in the other duties of dogs? or do we entrust to the males the entire and exclusive care of the flocks, while we leave the females at home, under the idea that the bearing and suckling of their puppies is labour enough for them?

No, he said, they share alike; the only difference between them is that the males are stronger and the females weaker.

But can you use different animals for the same purpose, unless they are bred and fed in the same way?

You cannot.

Then, if women are to have the same duties as men, they must have the same nurture and education?

Yes.

The education which was assigned to the men was music and gymnastic.

Yes.

Then women must be taught music and gymnastic and also the art of war, which they must practise like the men?

That is the inference, I suppose.

I should rather expect, I said, that several of our proposals, if they are carried out, being unusual, may appear ridiculous.

MOUNT MARY COLLEGE LIBRARY
Milwaukee, Wisconsin 53222

PLATO 10

No doubt of it.

Yes, and the most ridiculous thing of all will be the sight of women naked in the palaestra, exercising with the men, especially when they are no longer young; they certainly will not be a vision of beauty, any more than the enthusiastic old men who in spite of wrinkles and ugliness continue to frequent the gymnasia.

Yes, indeed, he said: according to present notions the proposal would be thought ridiculous.

But then, I said, as we have determined to speak our minds, we must not fear the jests of the wits which will be directed against this sort of innovation; how they will talk of women's attainments both in music and gymnastic, and above all about their wearing armour and riding upon horseback!

Very true, he replied.

Yet having begun we must go forward to the rough places of the law; at the same time begging of these gentlemen for once in their life to be serious. Not long ago, as we shall remind them, the Hellenes were of the opinion, which is still generally received among the barbarians, that the sight of a naked man was ridiculous and improper; and when first the Cretans and then the Lacedaemonians introduced the custom, the wits of that day might equally have ridiculed the innovation.

No doubt.

But when experience showed that to let all things be uncovered was far better than to cover them up, and the ludicrous effect to the outward eye vanished before the better principle which reason asserted, then the man was perceived to be a fool who directs the shafts of his ridicule at any other sight but that of folly and vice, or seriously inclines to weigh the beautiful by any other standard but that of the good.

Very true, he replied.

First, then, whether the question is to be put in jest or in earnest, let us come to an understanding about the nature of woman: Is she capable of sharing either wholly or partially in the actions of men, or not at all? And is the art of war one of those arts in which she can or can not share? That will be the best way of commencing the enquiry, and will probably lead to the fairest conclusion.

That will be much the best way.

Shall we take the other side first and begin by arguing against ourselves; in this manner the adversary's position will not be undefended.

Why not? he said.

Then let us put a speech into the mouths of our opponents. They will say: 'Socrates and Glaucon, no adversary need convict you, for you yourselves, at the first foundation of the State, admitted the principle that everybody was to do the one work suited to his own nature.' And certainly, if I am not mistaken, such an admission was made by us. 'And do not the natures of men and women differ very much indeed?' And we shall reply: Of course they do. Then we shall be asked, 'Whether the tasks assigned to men and to women should not be

80-1056

different, and such as are agreeable to their different natures?' Certainly they should. 'But if so, have you not fallen into a serious inconsistency in saying that men and women, whose natures are so entirely different, ought to perform the same actions?'—What defence will you make for us, my good Sir, against any one who offers these objections?

That is not an easy question to answer when asked suddenly; and I shall and I do beg of you to draw out the case on our side.

These are the objections, Glaucon, and there are many others of a like kind, which I foresaw long ago; they made me afraid and reluctant to take in hand any law about the possession and nurture of women and children.

By Zeus, he said, the problem to be solved is anything but easy.

Why yes, I said, but the fact is that when a man is out of his depth, whether he has fallen into a little swimming bath or into mid ocean, he has to swim all the same.

Very true.

And must not we swim and try to reach the shore: we will hope that Arion's dolphin or some other miraculous help may save us?

I suppose so, he said.

Well then, let us see if any way of escape can be found. We acknowl-edged—did we not?—that different natures ought to have different pursuits, and that men's and women's natures are different. And now what are we saying?—that different natures ought to have the same pursuits,—this is the inconsistency which is charged upon us.

Precisely.

Verily, Glaucon, I said, glorious is the power of the art of contradiction!

Why do you say so?

Because I think that many a man falls into the practice against his will. When he thinks that he is reasoning he is really disputing, just because he cannot define and divide, and so know that of which he is speaking; and he will pursue a merely verbal opposition in the spirit of contention and not of fair discussion.

Yes, he replied, such is very often the case; but what has that to do with us and our argument?

A great deal; for there is certainly a danger of our getting unintentionally into a verbal opposition.

In what way?

Why we valiantly and pugnaciously insist upon the verbal truth, that different natures ought to have different pursuits, but we never considered at all what was the meaning of sameness or difference of nature, or why we distinguished them when we assigned different pursuits to different natures and the same to the same natures.

Why, no, he said, that was never considered by us.

I said: Suppose that by way of illustration we were to ask the question whether there is not an opposition in nature between bald men and hairy men; and if this is admitted by us, then, if bald men are cobblers, we should forbid the hairy men to be cobblers, and conversely?

That would be a jest, he said.

Yes, I said, a jest; and why? because we never meant when we constructed the State, that the opposition of natures should extend to every difference, but only to those differences which affected the pursuit in which the individual is engaged; we should have argued, for example, that a physician and one who is in mind a physician may be said to have the same nature.

True.

Whereas the physician and the carpenter have different natures?

Certainly.

And if, I said, the male and female sex appear to differ in their fitness for any art or pursuit, we should say that such pursuit or art ought to be assigned to one or the other of them; but if the difference consists only in women bearing and men begetting children, this does not amount to a proof that a woman differs from a man in respect of the sort of education she should receive; and we shall therefore continue to maintain that our guardians and their wives ought to have the same pursuits.

Very true, he said.

Next, we shall ask our opponent how, in reference to any of the pursuits or arts of civic life, the nature of a woman differs from that of a man?

That will be quite fair.

And perhaps he, like yourself, will reply that to give a sufficient answer on the instant is not easy; but after a little reflection there is no difficulty.

Yes, perhaps.

Suppose then that we invite him to accompany us in the argument, and then we may hope to show him that there is nothing peculiar in the constitution of women which would affect them in the administration of the State.

By all means.

Let us say to him: Come now, and we will ask you a question:—when you spoke of a nature gifted or not gifted in any respect, did you mean to say that one man will acquire a thing easily, another with difficulty; a little learning will lead the one to discover a great deal; whereas the other, after much study and application, no sooner learns than he forgets; or again, did you mean, that the one has a body which is a good servant to his mind, while the body of the other is a hindrance to him?—would not these be the sort of differences which distinguish the man gifted by nature from the one who is ungifted?

No one will deny that.

And can you mention any pursuit of mankind in which the male sex has not all these gifts and qualities in a higher degree than the female? Need I waste time in speaking of the art of weaving, and the management of pancakes and preserves, in which womankind does really appear to be great, and in which for her to be beaten by a man is of all things the most absurd?

You are quite right, he replied, in maintaining the general inferiority of the female sex: although many women are in many things superior to many men, yet on the whole what you say is true.

And if so, my friend, I said, there is no special faculty of administration in a state which a woman has because she is a woman, or which a man has by virtue of his sex, but the gifts of nature are alike diffused in both; all the pursuits of men are the pursuits of women also, but in all of them a woman is inferior to a man.

Very true.

Then are we to impose all our enactments on men and none of them on women?

That will never do.

One woman has a gift of healing, another not; one is a musician, and another has no music in her nature?

Very true.

And one woman has a turn for gymnastic and military exercises, and another is unwarlike and hates gymnastics?

Certainly.

And one woman is a philosopher, and another is an enemy of philosophy; one has spirit, and another is without spirit?

That is also true.

Then one woman will have the temper of a guardian, and another not. Was not the selection of the male guardians determined by differences of this sort?

Yes.

Men and women alike possess the qualities which make a guardian; they differ only in their comparative strength or weakness.

Obviously.

And those women who have such qualities are to be selected as the companions and colleagues of men who have similar qualities and whom they resemble in capacity and in character?

Very true.

And ought not the same natures to have the same pursuits?

They ought.

Then, as we were saying before, there is nothing unnatural in assigning music and gymnastic to the wives of the guardians—to that point we come round again.

Certainly not.

The law which we then enacted was agreeable to nature, and therefore not an impossibility or mere aspiration; and the contrary practice, which prevails at present, is in reality a violation of nature.

That appears to be true.

We had to consider, first, whether our proposals were possible, and secondly whether they were the most beneficial?

Yes.

And the possibility has been acknowledged?

Yes.

The very great benefit has next to be established?

Quite so.

You will admit that the same education which makes a man a good guardian will make a woman a good guardian; for their original nature is the same?

Yes.

I should like to ask you a question.

What is it?

Would you say that all men are equal in excellence, or is one man better than another?

The latter.

And in the commonwealth which we were founding do you conceive the guardians who have been brought up on our model system to be more perfect men, or the cobblers whose education has been cobbling?

What a ridiculous question!

You have answered me, I replied: Well, and may we not further say that our guardians are the best of our citizens?

By far the best.

And will not their wives be the best women?

Yes, by far the best.

And can there be anything better for the interests of the State than that the men and women of a State should be as good as possible?

There can be nothing better.

And this is what the arts of music and gymnastic, when present in such manner as we have described, will accomplish?

Certainly.

Then we have made an enactment not only possible but in the highest degree beneficial to the State?

True.

Then let the wives of our guardians strip, for their virtue will be their robe, and let them share in the toils of war and the defence of their country; only in the distribution of labours the lighter are to be assigned to the women, who are the weaker natures, but in other respects their duties are to be the same. And as for the man who laughs at naked women exercising their bodies from the best of motives, in his laughter he is plucking

'A fruit of unripe wisdom,'

and he himself is ignorant of what he is laughing at, or what he is about;—for that is, and ever will be, the best of sayings, *That the useful is the noble and the hurtful is the base.*

Very true.

Here, then, is one difficulty in our law about women, which we may say that we have now escaped; the wave has not swallowed us up alive for enacting that the guardians of either sex should have all their pursuits in common; to the utility and also to the possibility of this arrangement the consistency of the argument with itself bears witness.

. . .

◆§◆ *Julia Annas*

Julia Annas, Fellow of St. Hugh's College, Oxford, is well known for her work on ancient Greek philosophers, especially for her translation, introduction, and annotation of Aristotle's Metaphysics: Books M and N. *In the following excerpt she turns her attention to Plato, arguing that although his proposal to allow women to become philosopher-rulers is hailed by champions of women's liberation, the grounds he offers for the proposal are unacceptable to contemporary feminists. First, his argument is not valid against the anti-feminist; second, he ignores the needs and desires of women; and third, he does not consider the question of the injustice of sexual inequality.*

Plato's *Republic* and Feminism

Not many philosophers have dealt seriously with the problems of women's rights and status, and those that have, have unfortunately often been on the wrong side.[1] In fact Plato and Mill are the only great philosophers who can plausibly be called feminists. But there has been surprisingly little serious effort made to analyse their arguments; perhaps because it has seemed like going over ground already won.

This paper is concerned only with Plato. I shall maintain what may surprise some: that it is quite wrong to think of Plato as 'the first feminist'.[2] His arguments are unacceptable to a feminist, and the proposals made in *Republic* V are irrelevant to the contemporary debate.

The idea that Plato is a forerunner of Women's Liberation has gained support from the fact that in *Republic* V Plato proposes not only that women should share men's tasks but also that the nuclear family should be abolished.[3] This idea is put forward by some radical feminists today as an essential part of any programme for the liberation of women. But I shall argue that Plato's grounds for the proposal are so different from the modern ones that he is in no sense a forerunner of them. Furthermore, where they differ, empirical evidence suggests that it is Plato who is wrong.

---

[1] Rousseau, *Émile*, ch. 5, and Schopenhauer, 'On Women', in *Parerga and Paralipomena*, are the most striking examples.

[2] J. R. Lucas, 'Because You Are a Woman', *Philosophy* (1973). The claim that Plato was a feminist is very common in discussions of *Republic* V, and also in recent feminist discussions. Cf. A. Rosenthal, 'Feminism Without Contradictions', *Monist* (1973): 'The feminism of Plato is exemplary and unparalleled in philosophy or political theory'.

[3] The term 'nuclear family' may be found dislikable, but it is useful in avoiding the suggestion that Plato wants to abolish the family in favour of impersonal institutions of a 1984 type. He stresses that family affection will remain, though spread over a wider class of people (463d–e).

Plato's proposals about women[4] come at the beginning of Book V, where Socrates is represented as having to surmount three waves of opposition. The first wave concerns the admission of women as Guardians; the second concerns the communal life of the Guardians; the third concerns the practicability of the ideal state, and this leads into the discussion which occupies the rest of Books V–VII. The figure of separate 'waves' is constantly brought before us; for Plato the capacity of women to be Guardians is a separate question from the replacement of nuclear family life.[5]

Plato begins his treatment of the first problem (451) by extending the metaphor he has used already. Female watchdogs do just what the male ones do, except that they are weaker, and their lives are interrupted by giving birth. By analogy, the same is true of women; though they are weaker than men and their lives are interrupted by childbirth, they are otherwise the same, and so should be given the same upbringing and tasks as men, however distasteful the sight of ugly old women exercising in the gymnasium may be.

Now this is only metaphor—and in fact it does not pretend to be serious argument. Plato wants to give us a picture first, perhaps so that we have a vivid idea of what the arguments are about before they are presented, perhaps also so that he can meet and deflect mere ridicule right at the start, before the serious discussion. Still, the initial metaphor is important, for it continues to influence Plato in the actual argument.

Plato now (453b–c) puts forward what he regards as a serious objection to the idea of women being Guardians. The opponent is made to say that it contradicts the principle on which the ideal state is constructed—namely, that each person is to do his own work, according to his nature (453b5). As women differ greatly in nature from men, they should surely have different functions in the city (453b10–11).

Plato dismisses this objection as merely captious. Of course it is true that different natures should do different things, but it does not follow that men and women should do different things unless it can be shown that they have natures that are different in the important respect of affecting their capacity for the same pursuit. Otherwise it would be like letting bald men, but not hairy men, be cobblers. Plato now claims that men and women differ only in their sexual roles: men impregnate, women give birth (454d–e). The objector fails to show that there is any capacity that is peculiar to women, and Plato claims to show that there are no civic pursuits which belong to a woman as such or to a man as such (this is the part of the argument we shall come back to).

---

[4] And children, though I shall not be considering them in this paper. In modern discussions the question of children's rights is often raised along with that of women's rights, but significantly no one has ever tried to see Plato as a precursor of these ideas.

[5] Plato justifies the abolition of the nuclear family solely on grounds of eugenics and of the unity of the state . . . and there seems no reason why these grounds should not hold even if women were not full Guardians and had a subordinate status; Plato's second proposal is thus in principle independent of his first.

Since there are no specific male or female competences, men and women should follow the same pursuits, and women who have natures suitable to be Guardians should therefore be appropriately trained.

This is how Plato deals with the first 'wave'. There are three important points to be made about his argument.

1. Firstly, there is something very odd about the actual course of the argument from 455a–d. Plato has established the undeniable point that while women are different from men in some ways and similar in others, discussion at that level is sterile; the interesting question is whether the undisputed differences matter when we decide whether women should be able to hold certain jobs. This is the crucial point not only for Plato but for any sensible discussion of the topic. But Plato's argument is seriously incomplete.

At 455a9–b2 he poses the question, 'Are there any occupations which contribute towards the running of the state which only a woman can do?' Very swiftly he claims to show that there are none. Men are better equipped both mentally and physically (455b4–c6). So in every pursuit men can do better than women, though it is not true that all men do better than all women (455d3–5). Women, he says, are ridiculed when men do such traditional feminine tasks as cooking and weaving better than they do; still, it follows from what has been said that if men bothered to turn their attention to these tasks they would do them better. 'The one sex is, so to speak, far and away beaten in every field by the other' (455d2–3).

Now it is hardly a feminist argument to claim that women do not have a special sphere because men can outdo them at absolutely everything. What is more important in the present context, however, is that Plato sums up his argument at 455d6–e1 by saying that there is no civic pursuit which belongs to a woman as such *or to a man as such*. But while he has argued that there are no pursuits appropriate for a woman as such, because men could do them all better, where is the argument that there are no specifically *male* competences? There is not a trace of any such argument in the text, nor of any materials which could be used for one.

This is a serious gap, both because it is the point that the objector, if he were not being shepherded by Socrates (cf. 455a5–b2), would in fact press and because what Plato says about male and female capacities actually provides material for such an objector.

Anyone acquainted with the modern literature will realize at once that someone objecting to the idea that men and women should share all roles is not very worried about whether there are some jobs that only *women* are suited for. The reason for this is obvious enough: jobs that women usually do are badly paid or unpaid and lack status, and men are generally not interested in doing them. What really interests the objector is the claim that there are some occupations in society which only *men* are suited for: being doctors, lawyers, judges, taking part in politics by voting or holding office, owning and managing property. In the Athens of Plato's day women were not allowed to do any of these things, and the average Athenian would no doubt have simply assumed that they could not do them (as we can see from Aristophanes' *Ecclesiazusae*).

Any feminist must take this objection seriously and meet it, simply because it has been historically the main objection to attempts by women to enter hitherto male professions or obtain hitherto male rights like the vote.[6] Yet Plato not only does nothing to meet this overwhelmingly obvious objection, he even provides materials for the objector. At 455b4–c6 he distinguishes three ways in which a gifted nature differs from an ungifted one. The gifted learn quickly, the ungifted only with difficulty. The gifted do not have to be taught very long before they can go on to make discoveries of their own; the ungifted need long instruction and are hard put to it to retain what they have learnt. The gifted can put their thoughts into action; the ungifted are clumsy. Plato then asks rhetorically, 'Do you know of any human pursuit in which men do not greatly excel women in all these qualities?' Clearly the answer is, 'No'. But if men always excel women in these very important respects, the objector has all he wants: surely there are some pursuits (e.g. generalship) where these qualities are needed in a high degree and which it is therefore not reasonable to open to women. It is no good saying, as Plato at once does, that, 'many women are better than many men at many things' (455d3–4). The objector does not need to claim that all men are always better than all women in a specific respect. If only men excel in a quality, then if efficiency is our aim[7] surely that makes it reasonable to regard a pursuit that requires a high degree of that quality as suited specially to men. The fact that women will not invariably come bottom is neither here nor there. In Plato's fiercely specialized state, the aim will be the maximum number of alpha performances.

This is an important argument. Scientific research into sex differences is an area of great controversy precisely because its results do have important social consequences; if men and women did have different types of intelligence, for example, then different types of education would surely be appropriate. But why does Plato not even notice the gap in his argument, or the ammunition he is handing to the opposition? Of course he does not want to make the opponent's case seem strong. But it is possible that he genuinely does not see the disastrous relevance of his claims about men's superior intellectual gifts to his point about distinct fields of activity. He may be doing here what Aristotle often criticizes him for—taking metaphor for argument.

The metaphor of male and female watchdogs with which the subject was introduced would naturally lead Plato to think predominantly of human tasks which are analogous. And this is what we find. At 455e1, after the argument just discussed, he mentions that women are weaker than men at all pursuits. This suits his use of the analogy with the dogs, for there the difference in

---

[6] Mill in *The Subjection of Women* deals with this type of argument as an objection to women having political rights. Nowadays the idea that women differ intellectually from men is directed rather against women having serious careers comparable to men's; cf. C. Hutt, *Males and Females*, ch. 9.

[7] As it certainly is Plato's aim. He does not use the patronizing argument that on grounds of 'respect for persons' women should have equal pay and status with men even if their contribution is recognized to be inferior.

strength between male and female was not sufficient reason to give them different tasks. And in the whole discussion that follows he simply shelves the question of intellectual differences between men and women. He never seriously discusses activities where these differences would matter and which are nevertheless to be open to women in the ideal state. There is only one reference to women officials (460b9–10) and even then they have a traditionally 'feminine' role (inspecting newborn children). There is possibly a reference to women doctors at 454d1–3 (but the text is very uncertain), and some women are said to be capable of being doctors at 455e6–7. Against these two (or possibly three) meagre and offhand references to women doing jobs requiring some intellectual capacity, there are at least nine references[8] to women fighting, serving in the army and doing gymnastics. On this topic Plato's discussion is full and emphatic. He is taking seriously the idea that the life of the human female is like that of any other female animal, with reproduction making only short breaks in physical activity otherwise like the male's. No doubt this is because he is mainly interested in the eugenic possibilities for his 'herd'.[9] The picture of the female watchdog diverts him from the problems he faces given his beliefs about female intellectual capacities.

So Plato's argument here is not one which a feminist would find useful or even acceptable. In any case, it has a serious gap, and it is not clear that Plato could repair it except by abandoning his beliefs about the intellectual inferiority of women.[10]

2. Secondly, the argument is not based on, and makes no reference to, women's desires or needs. Nothing at all is said about whether women's present roles frustrate them or whether they will lead more satisfying lives as Guardians than as house-bound drudges.

This is rather striking, since women in fourth-century Athens led lives that compare rather closely to the lives of women in present-day Saudi Arabia. The place of women in Athenian life is summed up forcibly in the notorious statement, 'We have courtesans for our pleasure, concubines for the requirements of the body, and wives to bear us lawful children and look after the home faithfully' (Pseudo-Demosthenes, *Against Neaera*, 122). The contrast between this and the life of the Guardians is so striking that one would have thought some comparison inevitable. Yet Plato shows no interest in this side of the picture. Later on in Book V (465b12–c7) he talks about the liberating effect of communal life in freeing people from the struggle to make ends meet and the need to hand one's money over to women and slaves to take care of it. Here the woman's position in the household is presented as something that the *man*

---

[8] 452a4–5, a10–b3, b8–c2, 453a3–4, 457a6–9, 458d1–2, 466c6–d1, 467a1–2, 468d7–e1.

[9] The word is used literally at 459e1, e3, and (possibly) as a metaphor at 451c7–8.

[10] It is, however, true that Plato's argument breaks some ground at least, in making it possible to consider women as individuals and not as a class with fixed capacities; at 455e–456a, after the argument just considered, women are compared with other women in various ways, not with men. Hence Plato has removed objections to considering his proposals at all on the ground that women as a class are incompetent.

is to be liberated from. There is nothing about the effect on *her* of communal living.

Of course Plato is not bound to be interested in the psychology of women, but his complete lack of interest underlines the fact that his argument does not recommend changing the present state of affairs on the ground that women suffer from being denied opportunities that are open to men.

His argument has quite different grounds, in fact. The state benefits from having the best possible citizens, and if half the citizens sit at home doing trivial jobs then usable talent is being wasted. Here Mrs Huby gets the point exactly right: 'There was nothing worth while for a woman to do at home; she should therefore share in man's work outside the home' (*Plato and Modern Morality*, p. 23). Plato's sole ground for his proposals is their usefulness to the state; the point is repeated several times.[11]

Of course there is nothing non-feminist about this argument.[12] But Plato's argument gains rather different significance from the fact that this is his *only* ground. His argument is authoritarian in spirit rather than liberal; if a woman did not want to be a Guardian, Plato would surely be committed to compelling her to serve the state. Though this question never arises in the *Republic*, at *Laws* 780a–c the Athenian says openly that women are to be compelled to attend the communal meals (all that is left of the communal life of the *Republic*), because most women will be shy and used to seclusion and so will not want to take part. This is rather far from modern liberal arguments that women should have equal opportunities with men because otherwise they lead stunted and unhappy lives and lack the means for self-development.

This point may have been missed because at 456c1–2 Plato says that the present set-up of society is 'contrary to nature' (*para phusin*). We are not, however, entitled to claim that for Plato confinement to the home thwarts the nature of women. What is 'contrary to nature' surely has to be understood as the opposite of what has just been said to be 'according to nature' (*kata phusin*, 456c1), and this is the principle that similar natures should follow similar pursuits. The present set-up is contrary to nature only in the sense that women do not in fact do jobs that they are capable of doing. There is no suggestion in the present passage that by 'contrary to nature' Plato means anything stronger, such as for example that women's present roles are imposed on them in a way which deforms their lives. (This is not a point peculiar to the discussion of

---

[11] 456c4–9: the question is, are the proposals best, *beltista* (Jowett translates this and similar phrases by 'most beneficial'). At 457a3–4 the proposals are 'best for the city', *ariston polei*. At 457b1–2 women's nakedness in the gymnasium will be 'for the sake of what is best', *tou beltistou heneka*, and people who find it ludicrous will be foolish, because 'what is useful (*ōphelimon*) is fair and what is harmful (*blaberon*) is ugly', and the proposals are useful as well as possible (c1–2). Cf. 452d3–e2, where the supposed analogy of men exercising naked is justified in terms of benefit.

[12] It is found even in Firestone (*The Dialectic of Sex*, pp. 206–210), though her main argument is not utilitarian. Interestingly, it is not the main argument in the utilitarian Mill, for whom the main objection to sexual inequality is the curtailment of the freedom, and hence the happiness, of women. Mill causes confusion, however, by also including utilitarian arguments.

women. The arguments in Book II that each person should have one occupation make no appeal to people's happiness or satisfaction in doing only one thing. Cf. 370b–c, 374b–d.)

In the *Laws* also (805a–b) Plato says that it is stupid not to train and bring up boys and girls in the same way to have the same pursuits and purposes, and adds that nearly every state is half a state as things are, whereas it could double its resources (cf. 806c). For Plato the reason why housewifery is not a real occupation is that it makes no irreplaceable contribution to the state, and absorbs time and energy that could be put to publicly beneficial use. He is completely unconcerned with the sort of objection which is nowadays familiar, namely that housewifery is incapable of providing an intelligent woman with a satisfying life, and leads to boredom, neurosis and misery.[13]

3. The third point leads on naturally from the second, since it is also a consequence of the fact that Plato justifies his proposals solely in terms of benefit to the state. The proposals for women are not a matter of their *rights*. There is nothing in *Republic* V that one could apply to the question of women's rights; the matter is simply not raised.

Of course Plato nowhere discusses men's rights either, and notoriously has no word for 'rights', any more than he has for 'duty' or 'obligation'. But the point is not lost if we abandon talk of rights and merely notice instead that Plato nowhere says that his proposals for women are *just*. It is remarkable in a work which makes proposals about women as radical as the *Republic*'s, and which has as much to say about justice as the *Republic* has, that inequality of the sexes is not presented as an injustice, and that the proposals to treat the sexes equally are not presented as measures which will make the state more just than its rivals. Yet the ideal state is just for reasons, explained in Books II–IV, which have nothing to do with the position of women in it. Nothing is said about any connection between the decline to the various forms of unjust state and the position of women in them.[14]

In fact it is rather unclear how the proposals of Book V relate to justice at all, whether in the state or in the soul. If women are to be Guardians, they must have just souls. We know from Book IV that the just soul has rightly organized parts—the *logistikon* or rational element, *epithumētikon* or desiring element, and *thumoeides*, the part usually called 'spirit' or the like. If the Guardian women are just, presumably they have these parts of soul. But do women's souls have a thumoeidic part? As it is introduced in Book IV, *thumoeides* appears to be a capacity for aggressive and violent behaviour, visible even in animals, but, one would have thought, notably lacking in fourth-century Athenian women. It is true that *thumoeides* is not limited to unthinking aggression, but even the more developed forms of behaviours that Plato regards as

---

[13] Of course there are other objections to housewifery as an occupation for women, e.g. that it is hard, unpleasant and unpaid, and these may well be more important from the viewpoint of practical reforms, but the charge that it does not satisfy a woman's capacities is the most relevant to discussion of Plato's argument.

[14] However, the equal and free association of men and women appears as one of the *bad* effects of the completely democratic state (563b7–9)....

typically thumoeidic display what Gosling[15] calls 'admiration for manliness', what we might call *machismo*. Unless the account of the just soul is to be done all over again for women Guardians to take account of female psychology, Plato must assume that women have the same aggressive tendencies as men. And in Book V he does make this assumption, and says that some women at any rate will be of the predominantly thumoeidic type (456a1–5). But this seems to conflict with his statements elsewhere which say or imply that women's psychology differs from men's precisely in that they lack the thumoeidic qualities of courage and 'guts'; by contrast with men they are weak, devious and cowardly.[16]

I have argued so far that for Plato his proposals about women are justified entirely by the resulting benefit to the state and not at all by women's needs or rights. It is important that the state in question is the ideal state. As far as I can see, there is nothing in *Republic* V which would commit Plato to the view that it was unjust for fourth-century Athenian women to be treated as they were. The proposals for women arise when the just constitution of the ideal state has been determined. There seems no reason why analogous proposals should be made in an unreformed state. Why should women be able to do men's jobs where this will merely have the result that instead of operating in a private sphere in the home, they will be operating in a private sphere at work? Plato would have no grounds for arguing that it would be best and useful for the state for this to happen.

Is this an ungenerous way to take the spirit of Plato's proposals? We should notice that even in the ideal state Plato limits his proposals for women to the Guardian class. There is nothing to suggest that the worker class do not live like fourth-century Greeks, with the women at home doing the cooking and weaving. This seems to show that whether women should do men's jobs depends, for Plato, on the nature of the jobs. The ideal state might contain many discontented potters' wives wanting to be potters; but presumably the Guardians (male and female) would only tell them to stay at home and learn *sophrosunē* in carrying out their appointed tasks.

If Plato's argument applies only to the performance of tasks which contribute towards the public good in the direct way that the Guardians' tasks do, it is clearly irrelevant to modern arguments for equality of opportunity. No modern feminist would argue that women should be able to do men's jobs

---

[15] *Plato,* ch. 3, 'Admiration for Manliness'. As the title suggests, Gosling conducts the discussion wholly in terms of male ideals, and does not remark on any difficulty arising from the fact that half the Guardians will be women.

[16] *Laws* 802e declares that pride and courage are characteristic of men (and should be expressed in their music) whereas what is characteristic of women is restraint and modesty. Plato seems to endorse in the *Meno* the idea that the scope of men's and women's virtue is different—that of a man is to manage his own and the city's affairs capably, that of a woman is to be a good and thrifty housewife and to obey her husband (71e, 73a). This makes it hard to see how women can possess the thumoeidic part of the soul necessary for the complete justice of a Guardian. The *Laws* concludes, consistently, that a woman has less potentiality for virtue than a man (781b2–4): Plato says that it is women's weakness and timidity that makes them sly and devious.

when this will result in greater direct benefit to the state, and otherwise stay at home. The moment it could be shown that the state did not need the extra women public servants, there would be no grounds for letting them have the jobs.

It would in fact be surprising if Plato's argument were relevant to women's rights, because it is a purely utilitarian argument. This is, however, precarious ground for a feminist, for once more efficient means to the desired end are found, women can at once be thrust back into the home. Mill begins *The Subjection of Women* with the statement that 'the legal subordination of one sex to the other is wrong in itself'. Plato is not committed to this by the *Republic,* and I see no reason whatsoever to believe that he thought that it was true. He thinks only that the present situation is wasteful and inefficient, and, *under ideal conditions*, should be changed.

This makes it easier to understand what seemed puzzling earlier, namely that Plato should combine a belief that the jobs of (Guardian) men should be open to women with a belief that women are physically and mentally inferior to men. It has always been difficult for those who see Plato as a feminist to understand why he stresses so much the comparative feebleness of women's contribution, for it is not usual to combine proposals like Plato's with extreme contempt for women. But on a purely utilitarian argument, since women represent a huge pool of untapped resources, it does not matter in the least if their contribution is not as good as that of men; and that is just what Plato seems to think.

Throughout Plato's works there are scattered examples of conventional contempt for women. At *Cratylus* 392b1–d10, for example, we are told that the Trojan men called Hector's son Astyanax and the Trojan women called him Scamandrius, and that this means that the former is the right name, as men are more intelligent than women. Of course nothing can be built on this kind of remark, and it would be unprofitable as well as depressing to comb Plato's works for such passages. Nevertheless they are significant in that taken together they build up a consistent tone which is hard to reconcile with an attitude that could be called feminist. Even in Book V itself Plato remarks that the practice of despoiling the dead shows a 'small and womanish mind' (469d7)—this in a context where half of the army doing the killing and despoiling are women. This might be put down to carelessness were it not for the *Timaeus*, where Plato not only says (42e), 'Human nature being twofold, the better sort was that which should thereafter be called man', but says twice (42b3–c4, 90e6–91a4) that evil and cowardly men are reborn as women, that being the first step downwards to rebirth as animals. There could hardly be a more open declaration that women are inferior to men. If the *Timaeus* was written at roughly the same time as the *Republic*, this embarrasses those who want to see Plato in the *Republic* as a feminist. But if what I have argued is right, then the *Timaeus* is quite compatible with the *Republic*. Even if women are inferior to men, it will still be of advantage to the state to have women do what men do if it is of public benefit. The argument in the *Republic* does not need, or claim, more than this.

There is one striking and revealing passage which shows that even in the *Republic* Plato holds the view of women's inferiority which has its uglier expression in the *Timaeus*. At 563b7–9 equality (*isonomia*) and freedom between men and women turns up as one of the deplorable corruptions of the democratic state. Now what is wrong with the democratic state, in Plato's view, is that unequals are treated equally—young and old, for example, and slave and free. The only possible inference is that Plato himself holds that women are naturally inferior to men,[17] and that any actual state where they are on terms of equality has corrupted the natural hierarchy. It is true that in his hostile portrait of the democratic state Plato carries over some details from contemporary Athens (for example, the fact that slaves cannot be distinguished at sight from free men by their clothes) and so not all features of his description embody serious theses. But even at his most careless Plato could hardly have thought of fourth-century Athens as an example of a place where men and women were on terms of freedom and equality. The passage must, then, be taken as a deliberate and important statement of what Plato believes, and it shows conclusively that the *Republic* does not differ on this point from the *Timaeus*. Even in the *Republic*, Plato never advocates the view that men and women are equal.

It comes as no surprise, then, that when Plato stops believing that the ideal state can be realized, he also stops thinking that women should do the same jobs as men, even in a greatly improved state. In the *Laws* he has abandoned the idea that men and women might be totally devoted to the state as the Guardians were. And the *Republic*'s radical proposals about women lapse. Although women are still educated and forced into public to some extent, this is merely so that they can be controlled, since their potential for virtue is less than man's and they would get up to mischief (780d9–781b6). They are still to learn how to fight, but only so as to defend their homes and children in the last resort (804–806, 813e–814c). The only office they hold seems to be that of organizing a kind of women's moral vigilante group. Otherwise they are left in the position of fourth-century Greek women. They take no part in any political process, they are unable to own or inherit property in their own right, and they are perpetual legal minors always under the authority of male relatives or guardians. Women are married off by their fathers or brothers, and an heiress passes with the property to the nearest male relative,[18] as was the normal Greek practice of the time.[19]

Plato's argument that women should be Guardians thus has three crucial defects: it is not valid against an anti-feminist, it is irrelevant to facts about women's desires, and it is irrelevant to the injustice of sexual inequality.

· · ·

[17] Cf. *Laws* 917a4–6, where this is clearly brought out.

[18] A woman can choose her own husband, if she is an heiress, only in the extremely unlikely situation of there being absolutely no suitable male relative available; and even then her choice is to be in consultation with her guardians.

[19] Even so, a limited amount of gymnastic activity and fighting is left open for women in the *Laws*; this shows how little this has to do with real liberation of women from traditional roles, in spite of the fuss made over it in the *Republic*.

⊷⊷3 *Aristotle*

Aristotle, born in Stagira in 384 B.C., went to Athens at the age of seventeen to study in Plato's Academy. Upon the death of the master in 347 and the appointment of Plato's nephew, Speusippos, to succeed him as head of the Academy, Aristotle left Athens for a twelve-year sojourn in Assos and Macedonia, where he taught, engaged in biological research, and ultimately served as tutor to the prince who was to become known later as Alexander the Great. In 335, shortly after Alexander had attained his majority, Aristotle returned to Athens, bringing with him a wife, Pythias, who was the niece and adopted daughter of the tyrant Hermias of Atarneus. Soon after his return Aristotle opened his own school, the Lyceum, in competition with the Academy. He remained there, absorbed in his teaching, until 323, when Alexander's death caused the political tide to turn. Aristotle fled to Chalcis, where he died the following year.

As a resident alien in Athens, Aristotle suffered a number of restrictions not unlike those imposed upon Athenian women. He had no voice in the government, for example, and he had to lease the property on which his school was established, because foreigners were not allowed to acquire land in Attica. But this sort of discrimination by no means moved Aristotle to cry out for reform in Athenian legislation concerning women. He had great respect for prevailing opinion. It has been remarked that he spoke not to but for his readers. Many of the shortcomings of the Spartan state he attributed to the license afforded Spartan women; in the ideal state, as he conceived it, not only would husbands command their wives but male rule would be institutionalized in the form of a magistry for the control of women. The difference between Aristotle's views on woman and those of his master may be attributed in part to the fact that Aristotle had a much livelier interest in the body than Plato had. He regarded sexual differentiation as a primary distinction among individuals. The fact that sex is deeply rooted, Aristotle thought, is indicated by the changes that follow the castration of an animal. Its entire character is altered, he found, so that ultimately it resembles the female more closely than it does members of its own sex.

Furthermore, Aristotle considered sexual differentiation to be more than merely physical. Body and soul are very closely connected in his philosophy—so closely, in fact, as to prompt him to contend that physical distinction in living things is everywhere accompanied by a psychological distinction. In Aristotle's view, all living things—plants and animals as well as human beings—have souls. In the plant the soul is simple. It is the life of the plant, one might say. It is what enables the plant to receive nourishment, assimilate food, grow, and reproduce. The animal soul is sensitive as well as nutritive in function, for the animal is not fixed in the ground and cannot merely absorb nourishment through its roots: it must seek out its food. To do so it needs sight, smell, taste, touch, and hearing. In both plant and animal the soul is mortal and dies with the body; but the human soul includes a third faculty, reason, which Aristotle suggested, may survive the death of the body. Reason has two functions: to guide one's actions and to contemplate the truth.

Aristotle believed that woman's soul differs from man's in all three of its divisions. As far as the nutritive soul is concerned, woman requires less nourishment than man (due, one would presume, though Aristotle nowhere says so, to her smaller size). As regards the sensitive soul, woman is deficient in desire, which is attendant on sensation—indeed, she is devoid of sexual desire, Aristotle thought, as is evidenced by the passive role she plays in copulation. But her memory, which is also a function of sensation, is superior to man's. This is a mark not of strength but of weakness, however, for Aristotle distinguished between memory and recollection, maintaining that the former attends inferior intellect, the latter superior intellect. But it is in the rational soul that woman's deficiency is most marked. The deliberative authority that enables one to regulate one's own actions is inoperative in a woman, Aristotle contended. And while he was silent about her contemplative ability, it would seem unlikely that woman would be more richly endowed with the higher than the lower of the soul's rational faculties.

In Aristotle's view the human being is by nature a social animal. Since neither sex is able to reproduce itself without the other, he believed marriage to be a necessity for the survival of the species. Not only does that institution provide for procreation, it is also requisite for what Aristotle referred to as the good life. For the difference between the sexes makes it appropriate for man to go out and acquire the goods and chattels for the entire household and for woman to remain at home and preserve what man has provided. Within the household, consisting of husband, wife, children, and slaves, it is the husband, superior in reason, who rules. The wife, like the child and the slave, obeys. And as the household unites with others to form a village and eventually a state, an office is created whose express function is to supervise the activities of women.

From *De Generatione Animalium*, Book I

CHAPTER 2

. . .

Male and female differ in their essence by each having a separate ability or faculty, and anatomically by certain parts; essentially the male is that which is able to generate in another, as said above; the female is that which is able to generate in itself and out of which comes into being the offspring previously existing in the parent. And since they are differentiated by an ability or faculty and by their function, and since instruments or organs are needed for all functioning, and since the bodily parts are the instruments or organs to serve the faculties, it follows that certain parts must exist for union of parents and production of offspring. And these must differ from each other, so that consequently the male will differ from the female. (For even though we speak of the animal as a whole as male or female, yet really it is not male or female in virtue of the whole of itself, but only in virtue of a certain faculty and a certain part—just as with the part used for sight or locomotion—which part is also plain to sense-perception.)

Now as a matter of fact such parts are in the female the so-called uterus, in the male the testes and the penis, in all the sanguinea; for some of them have testes and others the corresponding passages. There are corresponding differences of male and female in all the bloodless animals also which have this division into opposite sexes. But if in the sanguinea it is the parts concerned in copulation that differ primarily in their forms, we must observe that a small change in a first principle is often attended by changes in other things depending on it. This is plain in the case of castrated animals, for, though only the generative part is disabled, yet pretty well the whole form of the animal changes in consequence so much that it seems to be female or not far short of it, and thus it is clear that an animal is not male or female in virtue of an isolated part or an isolated faculty. Clearly, then, the distinction of sex is a first principle; at any rate, when that which distinguishes male and female suffers change, many other changes accompany it, as would be the case if a first principle is changed.[1]

. . .

From *Historia Animalium,* Book IX

CHAPTER 1

Of the animals that are comparatively obscure and short-lived the characters or dispositions are not so obvious to recognition as are those of animals that are longer-lived. These latter animals appear to have a natural capacity corresponding to each of the passions: to cunning or simplicity, courage or timidity, to good temper or to bad, and to other similar dispositions of mind.

Some also are capable of giving or receiving instruction—of receiving it from one another or from man: those that have the faculty of hearing, for instance; and, not to limit the matter to audible sound, such as can differentiate the suggested meanings of word and gesture.

In all genera in which the distinction of male and female is found, Nature makes a similar differentiation in the mental characteristics of the two sexes. This differentiation is the most obvious in the case of human kind and in that of the larger animals and the viviparous quadrupeds. In the case of these latter the female is softer in character, is the sooner tamed, admits more readily of caressing, is more apt in the way of learning; as, for instance, in the Laconian breed of dogs the female is cleverer than the male. Of the Molossian breed of dogs, such as are employed in the chase are pretty much the same as those

---

[1] Turning Aristotle's phraseology about 'first principles' into modern language, we should say that the phenomenon of secondary sex-characteristics varying in consequence of injury to the primary proves that the primary sex-distinction is deeply rooted in the organism, and that the secondary characteristics have been acquired later in consequence of and in connexion with it. The physical cause of the secondary characteristics is probably certain chemical substances called 'hormones' which are secreted by the testes and getting into the blood act as a stimulus upon the other parts concerned, making the beard to grow, etc.

elsewhere; but the sheep-dogs of this breed are superior to the others in size, and in the courage with which they face the attacks of wild animals.

Dogs that are born of a mixed breed between these two kinds are remarkable for courage and endurance of hard labour.

In all cases, excepting those of the bear and leopard, the female is less spirited than the male; in regard to the two exceptional cases, the superiority in courage rests with the female. With all other animals the female is softer in disposition than the male, is more mischievous, less simple, more impulsive, and more attentive to the nurture of the young; the male, on the other hand, is more spirited than the female, more savage, more simple and less cunning. The traces of these differentiated characteristics are more or less visible everywhere, but they are especially visible where character is the more developed, and most of all in man.

The fact is, the nature of man is the most rounded off and complete, and consequently in man the qualities or capacities above referred to are found in their perfection. Hence woman is more compassionate than man, more easily moved to tears, at the same time is more jealous, more querulous, more apt to scold and to strike. She is, furthermore, more prone to despondency and less hopeful than the man, more void of shame or self-respect, more false of speech, more deceptive, and of more retentive memory. She is also more wakeful, more shrinking, more difficult to rouse to action, and requires a smaller quantity of nutriment.

As was previously stated, the male is more courageous than the female, and more sympathetic in the way of standing by to help. Even in the case of molluscs, when the cuttle-fish is struck with the trident the male stands by to help the female; but when the male is struck the female runs away.

. . .

From *Oeconomica*, Book I

CHAPTER 2

The component parts of a household are man and property. But since the nature of any given thing is most quickly seen by taking its smallest parts, this would apply also to a household. So, according to Hesiod, it would be necessary that there should be

First and foremost a house, then a wife[1] . . . ,

for the former is the first condition of subsistence, the latter is the proper possession of all freemen. We should have, therefore, as a part of economics to make proper rules for the association of husband and wife; and this involves providing what sort of a woman she ought to be.

In regard to property the first care is that which comes naturally. Now in the course of nature the art of agriculture is prior, and next come those arts

[1] *Works and Days,* 405.

which extract the products of the earth, mining and the like. Agriculture ranks first because of its justice; for it does not take anything away from men, either with their consent, as do retail trading and the mercenary arts, or against their will, as do the warlike arts. Further, agriculture is natural; for by nature all derive their sustenance from their mother, and so men derive it from the earth. In addition to this it also conduces greatly to bravery; for it does not make men's bodies unserviceable, as do the illiberal arts, but it renders them able to lead an open-air life and work hard; furthermore it makes them adventurous against the foe, for husbandmen are the only citizens whose property lies outside the fortifications.

CHAPTER 3

As regards the human part of the household, the first care is concerning a wife; for a common life is above all things natural to the female and to the male. For we have elsewhere[2] laid down the principle that nature aims at producing many such forms of association, just as also it produces the various kinds of animals. But it is impossible for the female to accomplish this without the male or the male without the female, so that their common life has necessarily arisen. Now in the other animals this intercourse is not based on reason, but depends on the amount of natural instinct which they possess and is entirely for the purpose of procreation. But in the civilized and more intelligent animals the bond of unity is more perfect (for in them we see more mutual help and goodwill and co-operation), above all in the case of man, because the female and the male co-operate to ensure not merely existence but a good life. And the production of children is not only a way of serving nature but also of securing a real advantage; for the trouble which parents bestow upon their helpless children when they are themselves vigorous is repaid to them in old age when they are helpless by their children, who are then in their full vigour. At the same time also nature thus periodically provides for the perpetuation of mankind as a species, since she cannot do so individually. Thus the nature both of the man and of the woman has been preordained by the will of heaven to live a common life. For they are distinguished in that the powers which they possess are not applicable to purposes in all cases identical, but in some respects their functions are opposed to one another though they all tend to the same end. For nature has made the one sex stronger, the other weaker, that the latter through fear may be the more cautious, while the former by its courage is better able to ward off attacks; and that the one may acquire possessions outside the house, the other preserve those within. In the performance of work, she made one sex able to lead a sedentary life and not strong enough to endure exposure, the other less adapted for quiet but well constituted for outdoor activities; and in relation to offspring she has made both share in the procreation of children, but each render its peculiar service towards them, the woman by nurturing, the man by educating them.

[2] Cp. *Eth. Nic.* 1162ª 16 ff.; *Pol.* 1252ª 26 ff.

CHAPTER 4

First, then, there are certain laws to be observed towards a wife, including the avoidance of doing her any wrong; for thus a man is less likely himself to be wronged. This is inculcated by the general law, as the Pythagoreans say, that one least of all should injure a wife as being 'a suppliant and seated at the hearth'. Now wrong inflicted by a husband is the formation of connexions outside his own house. As regards sexual intercourse, a man ought not to accustom himself not to need it at all nor to be unable to rest when it is lacking, but so as to be content with or without it. The saying of Hesiod is a good one:

A man should marry a maiden, that habits discreet he may teach her.[3]

For dissimilarity of habit tends more than anything to destroy affection. As regards adornment, husband and wife ought not to approach one another with false affectation in their person any more than in their manners; for if the society of husband and wife requires such embellishment, it is no better than play-acting on the tragic stage.

. . .

From *Politica,* Book I

CHAPTER 1

Every state is a community of some kind, and every community is established with a view to some good; for mankind always act in order to obtain that which they think good. But, if all communities aim at some good, the state or political community, which is the highest of all, and which embraces all the rest, aims at good in a greater degree than any other, and at the highest good.

Some people think that the qualifications of a statesman, king, householder, and master are the same, and that they differ, not in kind, but only in the number of their subjects. For example, the ruler over a few is called a master; over more, the manager of a household; over a still larger number, a statesman or king, as if there were no difference between a great household and a small state. The distinction which is made between the king and the statesman is as follows: When the government is personal, the ruler is a king; when, according to the rules of the political science, the citizens rule and are ruled in turn, then he is called a statesman.

But all this is a mistake; for governments differ in kind, as will be evident to any one who considers the matter according to the method which has hitherto guided us. As in other departments of science, so in politics, the compound should always be resolved into the simple elements or least parts of the whole. We must therefore look at the elements of which the state is composed, in order that we may see in what the different kinds of rule differ from one another, and whether any scientific result can be attained about each one of them.

---

[3] *Works and Days,* 699.

CHAPTER 2

He who thus considers things in their first growth and origin, whether a state or anything else, will obtain the clearest view of them. In the first place there must be a union of those who cannot exist without each other; namely, of male and female, that the race may continue (and this is a union which is formed, not of deliberate purpose, but because, in common with other animals and with plants, mankind have a natural desire to leave behind them an image of themselves), and of natural ruler and subject, that both may be preserved. For that which can foresee by the exercise of mind is by nature intended to be lord and master, and that which can with its body give effect to such foresight is a subject, and by nature a slave; hence master and slave have the same interest. Now nature has distinguished between the female and the slave. For she is not niggardly, like the smith who fashions the Delphian knife for many uses; she makes each thing for a single use, and every instrument is best made when intended for one and not for many uses. But among barbarians no distinction is made between women and slaves, because there is no natural ruler among them: they are a community of slaves, male and female. Wherefore the poets say,—

'It is meet that Hellenes should rule over barbarians';

as if they thought that the barbarian and the slave were by nature one.

Out of these two relationships between man and woman, master and slave, the first thing to arise is the family, and Hesiod is right when he says,—

'First house and wife and an ox for the plough',

for the ox is the poor man's slave. The family is the association established by nature for the supply of men's everyday wants, and the members of it are called by Charondas 'companions of the cupboard', and by Epimenides the Cretan, 'companions of the manger'. But when several families are united, and the association aims at something more than the supply of daily needs, the first society to be formed is the village. And the most natural form of the village appears to be that of a colony from the family, composed of the children and grandchildren, who are said to be 'suckled with the same milk'. And this is the reason why Hellenic states were originally governed by kings; because the Hellenes were under royal rule before they came together, as the barbarians still are. Every family is ruled by the eldest, and therefore in the colonies of the family the kingly form of government prevailed because they were of the same blood. As Homer says:

'Each one gives law to his children and to his wives.'

For they lived dispersedly, as was the manner in ancient times. Wherefore men say that the Gods have a king, because they themselves either are or were in ancient times under the rule of a king. For they imagine, not only the forms of the Gods, but their ways of life to be like their own.

When several villages are united in a single complete community, large enough to be nearly or quite self-sufficing, the state comes into existence, originating in the bare needs of life, and continuing in existence for the sake of a good life. And therefore, if the earlier forms of society are natural, so is the state, for it is the end of them, and the nature of a thing is its end. For what each thing is when fully developed, we call its nature, whether we are speaking of a man, a horse, or a family. Besides, the final cause and end of a thing is the best, and to be self-sufficing is the end and the best.

Hence it is evident that the state is a creation of nature, and that man is by nature a political animal. And he who by nature and not by mere accident is without a state, is either a bad man or above humanity; he is like the

'Tribeless, lawless, heartless one,'

whom Homer denounces—the natural outcast is forthwith a lover of war; he may be compared to an isolated piece at draughts.

Now, that man is more of a political animal than bees or any other gregarious animals is evident. Nature, as we often say, makes nothing in vain, and man is the only animal whom she has endowed with the gift of speech. And whereas mere voice is but an indication of pleasure or pain, and is therefore found in other animals (for their nature attains to the perception of pleasure and pain and the intimation of them to one another, and no further), the power of speech is intended to set forth the expedient and inexpedient, and therefore likewise the just and the unjust. And it is a characteristic of man that he alone has any sense of good and evil, of just and unjust, and the like, and the association of living beings who have this sense makes a family and a state.

Further, the state is by nature clearly prior to the family and to the individual, since the whole is of necessity prior to the part; for example, if the whole body be destroyed, there will be no foot or hand, except in an equivocal sense, as we might speak of a stone hand; for when destroyed the hand will be no better than that. But things are defined by their working and power; and we ought not to say that they are the same when they no longer have their proper quality, but only that they have the same name. The proof that the state is a creation of nature and prior to the individual is that the individual, when isolated, is not self-sufficing; and therefore he is like a part in relation to the whole. But he who is unable to live in society, or who has no need because he is sufficient for himself, must be either a beast or a god: he is no part of a state. A social instinct is implanted in all men by nature, and yet he who first founded the state was the greatest of benefactors. For man, when perfected, is the best of animals, but, when separated from law and justice, he is the worst of all; since armed injustice is the more dangerous, and he is equipped at birth with arms, meant to be used by intelligence and virtue, which he may use for the worst ends. Wherefore, if he have not virtue, he is the most unholy and the most savage of animals, and the most full of lust and gluttony. But justice is the bond of men in states, for the administration of justice, which is the determination of what is just, is the principle of order in political society.

CHAPTER 3

Seeing then that the state is made up of households, before speaking of the state we must speak of the management of the household. The parts of household management correspond to the persons who compose the household, and a complete household consists of slaves and freemen. Now we should begin by examining everything in its fewest possible elements; and the first and fewest possible parts of a family are master and slave, husband and wife, father and children. We have therefore to consider what each of these three relations is and ought to be:—I mean the relation of master and servant, the marriage relation (the conjunction of man and wife has no name of its own), and thirdly, the procreative relation (this also has no proper name). And there is another element of a household, the so-called art of getting wealth, which, according to some, is identical with household management, according to others, a principal part of it; the nature of this art will also have to be considered by us.

.   .   .

CHAPTER 12

Of household management we have seen that there are three parts—one is the rule of a master over slaves, which has been discussed already, another of a father, and the third of a husband. A husband and father, we saw, rules over wife and children, both free, but the rule differs, the rule over his children being a royal, over his wife a constitutional rule. For although there may be exceptions to the order of nature, the male is by nature fitter for command than the female, just as the elder and full-grown is superior to the younger and more immature. But in most constitutional states the citizens rule and are ruled by turns, for the idea of a constitutional state implies that the natures of the citizens are equal, and do not differ at all. Nevertheless, when one rules and the other is ruled we endeavour to create a difference of outward forms and names and titles of respect, which may be illustrated by the saying of Amasis about his foot-pan. The relation of the male to the female is of this kind, but there the inequality is permanent. The rule of a father over his children is royal, for he rules by virtue both of love and of the respect due to age, exercising a kind of royal power. And therefore Homer has appropriately called Zeus 'father of Gods and men', because he is the king of them all. For a king is the natural superior of his subjects, but he should be of the same kin or kind with them, and such is the relation of elder and younger, of father and son.

CHAPTER 13

Thus it is clear that household management attends more to men than to the acquisition of inanimate things, and to human excellence more than to the excellence of property which we call wealth, and to the virtue of freemen more than to the virtue of slaves. A question may indeed be raised, whether there is any excellence at all in a slave beyond and higher than merely instrumental and ministerial qualities—whether he can have the virtues of temperance, courage, justice, and the like; or whether slaves possess only bodily and ministerial qualities. And, whichever way we answer the question, a difficulty arises; for, if they have virtue, in what will they differ from freemen? On the other hand, since they are men and share in rational principle, it seems absurd to say that they have no virtue. A similar question may be raised about women and children, whether they too have virtues: ought a woman to be temperate and brave and just, and is a child to be called temperate, and intemperate, or not? So in general we may ask about the natural ruler, and the natural subject, whether they have the same or different virtues. For if a noble nature is equally required in both, why should one of them always rule, and the other always be ruled? Nor can we say that this is a question of degree, for the difference between ruler and subject is a difference of kind, which the difference of more and less never is. Yet how strange is the supposition that the one ought, and that the other ought not, to have virtue! For if the ruler is intemperate and unjust, how can he rule well? if the subject, how can he obey well? If he be licentious and cowardly, he will certainly not do his duty. It is evident, therefore, that both of them must have a share of virtue, but varying as natural subjects also vary among themselves. Here the very constitution of the soul has shown us the way; in it one part naturally rules, and the other is subject, and the virtue of the ruler we maintain to be different from that of the subject;—the one being the virtue of the rational, and the other of the irrational part. Now, it is obvious that the same principle applies generally, and therefore almost all things rule and are ruled according to nature. But the kind of rule differs;—the freeman rules over the slave after another manner from that in which the male rules over the female, or the man over the child; although the parts of the soul are present in all of them, they are present in different degrees. For the slave has no deliberative faculty at all; the woman has, but it is without authority, and the child has, but it is immature. So it must necessarily be supposed to be with the moral virtues also; all should partake of them, but only in such manner and degree as is required by each for the fulfilment of his duty. Hence the ruler ought to have moral virtue in perfection, for his function, taken absolutely, demands a master artificer, and rational principle is such an artificer; the subjects, on the other hand, require only that measure of virtue which is proper to each of them. Clearly, then, moral virtue belongs to all of them; but the temperance of a man and of a woman, or the courage and justice of a man and of a woman, are not, as Socrates maintained, the same; the courage of a man is shown in commanding, of a woman in obeying. And this holds of all other virtues, as will be more clearly seen if we look at them in detail, for those who say generally that virtue consists in a good disposition of the soul, or in doing rightly, or the like, only deceive themselves. Far better than such definitions is their mode of speaking, who, like Gorgias, enumerate the virtues. All classes must be deemed to have their special attributes; as the poet says of women,

'Silence is a woman's glory',

but this is not equally the glory of man. The child is imperfect, and therefore obviously his virtue is not relative to himself alone, but to the perfect man and to his teacher, and in like manner the virtue of the slave is relative to a master. Now we determined that a slave is useful for the wants of life, and therefore he will obviously require only so much virtue as will prevent him from failing in his duty through cowardice or lack of self-control. Some one will ask whether, if what we are saying is true, virtue will not be required also in the artisans, for they often fail in their work through the lack of self-control. But is there not a great difference in the two cases? For the slave shares in his master's life; the artisan is less closely connected with him, and only attains excellence in proportion as he becomes a slave. The meaner sort of mechanic has a special and separate slavery; and whereas the slave exists by nature, not so the shoemaker or other artisan. It is manifest, then, that the master ought to be the source of such excellence in the slave, and not a mere possessor of the art of mastership which trains the slave in his duties. Wherefore they are mistaken who forbid us to converse with slaves and say that we should employ command only, for slaves stand even more in need of admonition than children.

So much for this subject; the relations of husband and wife, parent and child, their several virtues, what in their intercourse with one another is good, and what is evil, and how we may pursue the good and escape the evil, will have to be discussed when we speak of the different forms of government. For, inasmuch as every family is a part of a state, and these relationships are the parts of a family, and the virtue of the part must have regard to the virtue of the whole, women and children must be trained by education with an eye to the constitution, if the virtues of either of them are supposed to make any difference in the virtues of the state. And they must make a difference: for the children grow up to be citizens, and half the free persons in a state are women.

. . .

✑Christine Garside Allen

Christine Garside Allen, a specialist in metaphysics and epistemology, is an associate professor of philosophy at Concordia University in Montreal. Professor Allen has published a number of articles and essays in the field of women's studies as well as in her own discipline, among them "The Diary of the Seduced," "Women and Persons," and "A Contemporary Approach to Sex Identity." In "Can a Woman Be Good in the Same Way As a Man?" she points out that Aristotle's attitude toward women has serious repercussions on his ethical theory. If human virtue is dependent on reason, and if women are rationally inferior to men, the inescapable consequence is ethical relativism. The obvious answer to the question posed in the title of Professor Allen's critique is negative: in Aristotle's view a woman cannot be good in the same way as a man.

Can a Woman Be Good
in the Same Way As a Man?

INTRODUCTION

Many philosophers would claim that sexual differentiation is irrelevant to philosophy. They would say that the philosopher is trying to understand the world and himself qua human being, not qua man or qua woman. While this may have been the intent, in ethics some curious results concerning women have occurred. In some cases, when one compares the analysis of what a philosopher considers to constitute a good person with what he says about the nature of woman, we must conclude that a woman cannot ultimately be good. In this paper I propose to show how Aristotle . . . maintained this.

ARISTOTLE'S CONCEPT OF WOMAN

For Aristotle the virtuous person (i.e., someone with practical wisdom) is one who has "a true and reasoned state of capacity to act with regard to things that are good or bad for man."[1] In other words, to be good a person must have the sort of understanding which issues in commands. (1143a8) Practical wisdom ultimately means being able to use one's rational faculties in such a way that true premises can be intuited and the consequences of these premises can be demonstrated with an action issuing from the deliberation. Since Aristotle conceives of the rational faculty as the essence or nature of a person (1168b33), we can say that the virtuous person is one who uses his rational faculty well or who lives in accordance with his nature.

The first question we have to ask about Aristotle's ethics is this: does everyone become virtuous in the same way? On the surface it would seem as though the answer would have to be affirmative. If there is a common nature among human beings, and if being a good person means living in accordance with this nature, it would follow that any person wishing to acquire practical wisdom would seek to exercise his rational faculty in the same way. In the *Politics* Aristotle realizes the consequences of his ethics when he is considering whether slaves can be good:

Since they are men and share in rational principle, it seems absurd to say that they have no virtue. A similar question may be raised about women and children. (1259b27–30)

He resolves this problem by introducing an observation about the nature of things, namely that some things naturally rule while other things naturally obey. He notes that in the soul the rational part is more fit to rule the irrational part, and by analogy the rational part of society should rule the irrational part. By "irrational part of society" he means that part consisting of those individuals

---

[1] Aristotle, trans. W. D. Ross, 1140b 1–5.

whose irrational soul dominates. The irrational part of society is broken down into three sections, two of which are free (women and children) and one of which is not free (slaves). The three irrational parts of the society are able to be virtuous but "only that measure of virtue which is proper to each of them." (1260a20) So it turns out that only men of a particular nature can be good, i.e., those men who possess a developed rational faculty. Slaves have no deliberative faculty, and women have a deliberative faculty but it is without authority. (1260a12–14)

We can see that while Aristotle believes that his ethics is universal in the sense that all perfectly virtuous persons would be good in the same way, many people are not capable of perfect goodness. This incapacity is a psychological factor relating to one's ability to deliberate in a particular way. Woman has the capacity to deliberate, but not the authority. Presumably, this means that she lacks self control as her rational faculty is present in less proportion than her irrational faculty.

Although the parts of the soul are present in all of them [women, children and slaves], they are present in different degrees. (1260a10)

The result of all this is that a woman is virtuous by obeying not commanding (1260a24), by being silent (1260a30), by preserving not acquiring (1277b21), by having true opinion not wisdom (1277b27) and by entering into friendships of inequality not equality (1158b11–13). In short, a good woman lives very differently from a good man. For both, to be good is to live in accordance with one's nature; so the conclusion must be that man's nature is different from woman's nature. To understand Aristotle's views about the nature of man and woman we must turn to his statements in other than ethical or political sections.

In the *Metaphysics* we find:

But male and female, while they are modifications peculiar to 'animal', are so not in virtue of its essence but in the matter, i.e., the body. (1058b23)

We must remember that two men are distinguished by the fact that their matter is different, so there must be something more which explains the difference between a man and a woman. Aristotle tries to introduce this element by understanding body in terms of its function or purpose, and in the case of animals one of the functions is reproduction. It turns out that the male contributes the formal and efficient cause to reproduction while the female contributes the material cause. (729a11)

The female always provides the material, the male that which fashions it, for this is the power that we say they each possess, and *this is what is meant by calling them male and female.* (738b20, my italics)

The analogy between the biological and ethical relations of man and woman is evident. Aristotle does not say that woman's deliberative powers are derived from her biological powers, he merely describes her nature in such a way that she is understood as being defined by her ability to provide matter or, as seen in another way, as her inability to provide form. She is even referred to as an "impotent male" because she is incapable of contributing form to reproduction (728a17–21). The force of this description, however, is very powerful and the similarity to the ethical conclusion that woman has a kind of impotent mind is clear. In the second case the impotence is not one of lacking anything essential, as woman has a rational or deliberative faculty; rather she does not have enough of it. Her irrational soul dominates so that she is unable to exercise her rational faculty in the same way as a man of practical wisdom would do.

At this point we are led to the puzzling situation in which both the inability to deliberate and the inability to provide form in reproduction are characteristic of the female but not by virtue of her form. How does she get these characteristics? Aristotle tries to provide the answer by the use of the term "contrary."

Female and male are contrary and their difference is a contrariety. (1058a30)

This means that men and women belong to the same genus or species (in this case species), but that they are opposites in the sense that female is a privation of male. Men and women must have the same form, but they have a more radical difference than the color of hair, or height, or other differences obviously due to matter.

We still have not answered the question "Why is woman a privation?" and Aristotle gives us no more help. It is just the state of things. We can only speculate that it must be due to some defective aspect of vast quantities of matter so that the form does not adequately combine with matter at the conception of half of the human species. Needless to say, this speculation could not give much comfort to women who desire practical wisdom.

. . .

CONCLUSION

We have seen that a systematic study of the nature of woman in Aristotle . . . reveals . . . an attitude which ultimately bars women from being good in the full sense in which men can be good. A practical result of this attitude is that a woman who studies . . . Aristotle . . . with a desire to come to some conclusion about how she should live either has to accept [his] views of the nature of woman and reject [his] moral theories as applicable to her; or, if she accepts one of [his] moral theories then she must reject the corresponding views [he has] about the nature of woman.

My purpose in this paper was not to offer criteria for evaluating positions on the nature of woman, but to show that for women there is a dilemma which arises in the study of certain influential philosophers. A woman cannot, qua human being, appropriate their work, as it turns out in many ways to be a study of man.

NOTE: I am indebted to Lynda Lange of the University of Toronto for pointing out to me in an unpublished paper on Aristotle that he tries to explain the basis for sex differences on the difference in soul heat in women and men (726b30).—C. G. A.

THE IMPACT OF CHRISTIANITY

. . . the image of God may remain on that side of the mind of man on which it cleaves to the beholding or the consulting of the eternal reasons of things; and this, it is clear, not men only, but also women have.
—St. Augustine

. . . we must . . . find out how to pour {transcendence and spiritual personhood} back into a full-bodied Hebrew sense of creation and incarnation, as male and female, but who can now be fully personalized autonomous selves and also persons in relation to each other, not against the body, but in and through the body.
—Rosemary Radford Ruether

It was necessary for woman to be made, as the Scripture says, as a helper to man; not, indeed, as a helpmate in other works, as some say, since man can be more efficiently helped by another man in other works; but as a helper in the work of generation.
—St. Thomas Aquinas

However often the medieval commitment to spiritual equivalence was undermined by androcentric and patriarchal assumptions, the institution of monasticism was for the Christian woman a real and concrete option, a little world occasionally run by and for women.
—Eleanor Commo McLaughlin

In the Middle Ages a new dimension was added to the debate over the status of woman. Not only were there questions about her proper role within the household and in the state; there were also questions concerning the part she should play in the Christian community and the eternal life she might hope to enjoy. Although St. Augustine never questions the propriety of the subjection of wives to their husbands and never advocates the emancipation of women in the secular state, in spiritual matters he places woman on a par with man. Only in her mortal body is she inferior; her immortal soul is sexless. Although the egalitarianism of Augustine's ethical theories is grounded in the separation he makes between soul and body, it is a dichotomy that Rosemary Radford Ruether deplores. A fuller sexual equality, she suggests, may be attained through the reconciliation of body and soul.

On the major issues the views of St. Thomas Aquinas coincide with those of Augustine; but the misogynism of Aristotle is occasionally evident in the work of Aquinas, as numerous quotations from and references to "the Philosopher" will attest. Moreover, the very scope of the massive *Summa Theologica* leads Aquinas to consider a number of matters that Augustine never treats. Here he frequently prescribes against women: they are unfit for the priesthood, they may administer the rite of baptism only in cases of dire emergency, their sole function is procreation. To be sure, as Eleanor Commo McLaughlin points out, cloisters run by and for women flourished throughout the Middle Ages. But in the eyes of Aquinas, marriage is the institution designed for the female sex. Thus while Augustine constantly urges woman to rise above her physical being, Aquinas appears much more inclined to consider her a product of her corporeal condition.

⋗ 4 *St. Augustine*

Aurelius Augustinus was born in A.D. 354 in Tagaste, Africa, to a pagan father, Patricius, and a Christian mother, Monica. Patricius was primarily interested in his son's physical and mental development, but Monica was concerned almost exclusively with his immortal soul. She seems to have instilled in the boy such a sense of sinfulness that he later records in his Confessions as heinous crimes the fact that as a child he occasionally pilfered food from the family table and envied schoolmates who recited better than he did. As a young man Augustine appears to have been troubled by desires of the flesh. For a number of years he incurred his mother's displeasure by living with a mistress, who bore him a son, Adeodatus. But eventually Monica managed to break up the illicit union and to convert her son to Christianity. He soon was ordained a priest, then was installed as assistant bishop, and ultimately, in 395, became the bishop of Hippo. Augustine dedicated himself to writing attacks on various heresies, among them Manichaeanism, which had attracted him before his conversion. He died in 430 as the Vandals were storming the gates of Hippo.

In the fourth century A.D., both secular and ecclesiastical reform were effected to improve the rather lowly status of Christian woman. The state introduced legislation providing her with more and better protection against cruel and unjust treatment, and the church admitted her to the deaconry. It was perhaps only natural, then, that questions concerning woman's conduct and her basic nature should have come to the philosophical fore. The relatively secluded social position of woman had been deemed by St. John Chrysostom an ideal one from which to effect not only her own salvation but also that of her more beleaguered husband. St. Jerome, on the other hand, was impressed by her capacity for evil, describing her as "the gate of the devil, the path of wickedness, the sting of the serpent, in a word a perilous object."

As St. Augustine tries to adjudicate between woman's champions and her detractors, he encounters apparent inconsistencies in pertinent passages of the Bible itself. Genesis seems to suggest that woman, like man, was made in the image of the Creator. To St. Paul, however, woman appears to have been made in the image of an image, and thus to be a step further removed from the Divine Maker. St. Augustine's attempt to explain away the apparent contradiction only leads to further inconsistency.

In his life Augustine was perhaps less ambiguous in his attitude toward woman than he was in his philosophical works. Among his correspondents were a number of women, including his sister, who was the abbess of a convent, and Juliana Faltonia, to whom he addressed a treatise, The Excellence of Widowhood.

In Augustine's age gynology was focused on woman's Creator and her life in the hereafter and ignored her life on earth except insofar as it related to her divine origins and her ultimate end. St. Augustine devoted a great deal of attention to the creation of woman and the degree to which her nature reflects that of her Maker. Although all creatures bear some likeness to their

51

Creator, it is the last of God's creations that resembles him most perfectly. The author of Genesis explains the situation as follows: "God made man in the image of God. God made him; male and female He made them, and blessed them" (Genesis 1:27–28). This passage strongly implies that woman as well as man reflects the divine image. But St. Paul implies the contrary, calling man the glory of God, woman the glory of man, and prescribing on that basis different rules of conduct for the two sexes: "For man indeed ought not to cover his head, forasmuch as he is the image and glory of God; but the woman is the glory of the man" (I Corinthians 11:7).

It was St. Augustine's aim to reconcile the apparent conflict between those passages by developing a view of woman's nature compatible with both—a task that inevitably led to contradiction and paradox. It is in man considered together with woman that the divine image is reflected, Augustine concluded. But woman was created merely as man's helpmate. Considered as helpmate she is not in the divine image. And so, whereas man alone is in God's image just as much as are the two together, the same cannot be said of woman considered by herself.

More specifically, it is the human mind, and in particular reason, that constitutes the divine image, and in the Confessions Augustine declared woman to be man's mental equal, made inferior to him only by the sex of her body. Because of the inferiority of her body, he says in the essay "On Continence," woman may be said to symbolize the flesh, man reason. And On the Trinity contains a passage that suggests that woman symbolizes appetite, the portion of the human mind that should be controlled by reason, whereas man symbolizes reason itself.

The superiority of man to woman, then, Augustine explained as being partly figurative rather than completely literal. Thus he did not favor the view that after the resurrection everyone would assume the male sex. Nor did he adopt in his ethical works the double moral standard of his contemporary Pollentius. On the contrary, Augustine insisted that the laws of celibacy, marriage, remarriage, and divorce applied to both sexes equally. And yet he continually referred to the husband as head of the wife, and in a letter he advised Ecdicia, a married woman who had given away all her belongings to two monks, that a woman was "subject to her husband in all things" and that she had "no right to dispose of [her] clothing or of gold or silver or any money, or of any of [her] earthly property without his consent." Also, although he went so far as to censure men who considered themselves superior to women, in the very act of criticizing them he seemed to grant their actual superiority. In any realistic attempt to punish immoral behavior, he suggested, men ought to be judged by more, not less, severe standards than those used in judging their wives, for in view of their very manhood, it "befits them to surpass the virtue of their wives and to govern by their example."

Other passages in Scripture that lend themselves to conflicting interpretations may be found in two of the Gospels describing certain events that took place between Christ's resurrection and his ascension into heaven. Confronted in the gardens adjacent to his tomb by Mary Magdalene, who addressed him as "Master," Jesus cautioned her and the woman with her not to touch him, reminding them that he had not yet risen to his Father. Yet shortly afterward, according to another account, when appearing to doubting Thomas and the other disciples, all male, Jesus urged them to feel his wounds to prove to themselves that he was indeed he who had been crucified.

Eager to explain the apparent inconsistency of his Lord's words and actions and reluctant to write them off to antifeminism (that men could touch him but women could not), Augustine tried a metaphorical interpretation, taking "touch" to mean "believe." Thus, Augustine argued, although it was necessary that the disciples believe the apparition before them to be Jesus, it would have been unfitting for the women to believe Christ to be their ascended Lord before he had indeed ascended. The explanation is less than convincing, as are both the single moral standard that Augustine attempted to develop in his ethics and his efforts at compromise in the matter of the degree to which woman reflects the image of God.

From *Confessions*

CHAPTER 32—OF THE PARTICULAR WORKS OF GOD, MORE ESPECIALLY OF MAN

Thanks to Thee, O Lord. We behold the heaven and the earth, whether the corporeal part, superior and inferior, or the spiritual and corporeal creature; and in the embellishment of these parts, whereof the universal mass of the world or the universal creation consisteth, we see light made, and divided from the darkness. We see the firmament of heaven, whether the primary body of the world between the spiritual upper waters and the corporeal lower waters, or—because this also is called heaven—this expanse of air, through which wander the fowls of heaven, between the waters which are in vapours borne above them, and which in clear nights drop down in dew, and those which being heavy flow along the earth. We behold the waters gathered together through the plains of the sea; and the dry land both void and formed, so as to be visible and compact, and the matter of herbs and trees. We behold the lights shining from above—the sun to serve the day, the moon and the stars to cheer the night; and that by all these, times should be marked and noted. We behold on every side a humid element, fruitful with fishes, beasts, and birds; because the density of the air, which bears up the flights of birds, is increased by the exhalation of the waters. We behold the face of the earth furnished with terrestrial creatures, and man, created after Thy image and likeness, in that very image and likeness of Thee (that is, the power of reason and understanding) on account of which he was set over all irrational creatures. And as in his soul there is one power which rules by directing, another made subject that it might obey, so also for the man was corporeally made a woman, who, in the mind of her rational understanding should also have a like nature, in the sex, however, of her body should be in like manner subject to the sex of her husband, as the appetite of action is subjected by reason of the mind, to conceive the skill of acting rightly. These things we behold, and they are severally good, and all very good.

From *On the Trinity,* Book 12

CHAPTER 5—THE OPINION WHICH DEVISES AN IMAGE OF THE TRINITY IN THE MARRIAGE OF MALE AND FEMALE, AND IN THEIR OFFSPRING

Accordingly they do not seem to me to advance a probable opinion, who lay it down that a trinity of the image of God in three persons, so far as regards human nature, can so be discovered as to be completed in the marriage of male and female and in their offspring; in that the man himself, as it were, indicates the person of the Father, but that which has so proceeded from him as to be born, that of the Son; and so the third person as of the Spirit, is, they say, the woman, who has so proceeded from the man as not herself to be either son or daughter,[1] although it was by her conception that the offspring was born. For the Lord hath said of the Holy Spirit that He proceedeth from the Father,[2] and yet he is not a son. In this erroneous opinion, then, the only point probably alleged, and indeed sufficiently shown according to the faith of the Holy Scripture, is this,—in the account of the original creation of the woman,—that what so comes into existence from some person as to make another person, cannot in every case be called a son; since the person of the woman came into existence from the person of the man, and yet she is not called his daughter. All the rest of this opinion is in truth so absurd, nay indeed so false, that it is most easy to refute it. For I pass over such a thing, as to think the Holy Spirit to be the mother of the Son of God, and the wife of the Father; since perhaps it may be answered that these things offend us in carnal things, because we think of bodily conceptions and births. Although these very things themselves are most chastely thought of by the pure, to whom all things are pure; but to the defiled and unbelieving, of whom both the mind and conscience are polluted, nothing is pure;[3] so that even Christ, born of a virgin according to the flesh, is a stumbling-block to some of them. But yet in the case of those supreme spiritual things, after the likeness of which those kinds of the inferior creature also are made although most remotely, and where there is nothing that can be injured and nothing corruptible, nothing born in time, nothing formed from that which is formless, or whatever like expressions there may be; yet they ought not to disturb the sober prudence of any one, lest in avoiding empty disgust he run into pernicious error. Let him accustom himself so to find in corporeal things the traces of things spiritual, that when he begins to ascend upwards from thence, under the guidance of reason, in order to attain to the unchangeable truth itself through which these things were made, he may not draw with himself to things above what he despises in things below. For no one ever blushed to choose for himself wisdom as a wife, because the name of wife puts into a man's thoughts the corruptible connection which consists in begetting children; or because in truth wisdom itself is a woman in sex, since it is expressed in both Greek and Latin tongues by a word of the feminine gender.

[1] Genesis 2:22.
[2] John 15:26.
[3] Titus 1:15.

CHAPTER 6—WHY THIS OPINION IS TO BE REJECTED

We do not therefore reject this opinion, because we fear to think of that holy and inviolable and unchangeable Love, as the spouse of God the Father, existing as it does from Him, but not as an offspring in order to beget the Word by which all things are made; but because divine Scripture evidently shows it to be false. For God said, "Let us make man in our image, after our likeness;" and a little after it is said, "So God created man in the image of God."[4] Certainly, in that it is of the plural number, the word "our" would not be rightly used if man were made in the image of one person, whether of the Father, or of the Son, or of the Holy Spirit; but because he was made in the image of the Trinity, on that account it is said, "After our image." But again, lest we should think that three Gods were to be believed in the Trinity, whereas the same Trinity is one God, it is said, "So God created man in the image of God," instead of saying, "In His own image."

For such expressions are customary in the Scriptures; and yet some persons, while maintaining the Catholic faith, do not carefully attend to them, in such wise that they think the words, "God made man in the image of God," to mean that the Father made man after the image of the Son; and they thus desire to assert that the Son also is called God in the divine Scriptures, as if there were not other most true and clear proofs wherein the Son is called not only God, but also the true God. For whilst they aim at explaining another difficulty in this text, they become so entangled that they cannot extricate themselves. For if the Father made man after the image of the Son, so that he is not the image of the Father, but of the Son, then the Son is unlike the Father. But if a pious faith teaches us, as it does, that the Son is like the Father after an equality of essence, then that which is made in the likeness of the Son must needs also be made in the likeness of the Father. Further, if the Father made man not in His own image, but in the image of His Son, why does He not say, "Let us make man after Thy image and likeness," whereas He does say, "our;" unless it be because the image of the Trinity was made in man, that in this way man should be the image of the one true God, because the Trinity itself is the one true God? Such expressions are innumerable in the Scriptures, but it will suffice to have produced these. It is so said in the Psalms, "Salvation belongeth unto the Lord; Thy blessing is upon Thy people;"[5] as if the words were spoken to some one else, not to Him of whom it had been said, "Salvation belongeth unto the Lord." And again, "For by Thee," he says, "I shall be delivered from temptation, and by hoping in my God I shall leap over the wall;"[6] as if he said to some one else, "By Thee I shall be delivered from temptation." And again, "In the heart of the king's enemies; whereby the people fall under Thee;"[7] as if he were to say, in the heart of Thy enemies. For he had said to that King, that is, to our

---

[4] Genesis 1:26, 27.
[5] Psalms 3:8.
[6] Psalms 18:29.
[7] Psalms 45:5.

Lord Jesus Christ, "The people fall under Thee," whom he intended by the word King, when he said, "In the heart of the king's enemies." Things of this kind are found more rarely in the New Testament. But yet the apostle says to the Romans, "Concerning His Son who was made to Him of the seed of David according to the flesh, and declared to be the Son of God with power, according to the spirit of holiness, by the resurrection of the dead of Jesus Christ our Lord;"[8] as though he were speaking above of some one else. For what is meant by the Son of God declared by the resurrection of the dead of Jesus Christ, except of the same Jesus Christ who was declared to be Son of God with power? And as then in this passage, when we are told, "the Son of God with power of Jesus Christ," or "the Son of God according to the spirit of holiness of Jesus Christ," or "the Son of God by the resurrection of the dead of Jesus Christ," whereas it might have been expressed in the ordinary way, In His own power, or according to the spirit of His own holiness, or by the resurrection of His dead, or of their dead: as, I say, we are not compelled to understand another person, but one and the same, that is, the person of the Son of God our Lord Jesus Christ; so, when we are told that "God made man in the image of God," although it might have been more usual to say, after His own image, yet we are not compelled to understand any other person in the Trinity, but the one and selfsame Trinity itself, who is one God, and after whose image man is made.

And since the case stands thus, if we are to accept the same image of the Trinity, as not in one, but in three human beings, father and mother and son, then the man was not made after the image of God before a wife was made for him, and before they procreated a son; because there was not yet a trinity. Will any one say there was already a trinity, because, although not yet in their proper form, yet in their original nature, both the woman was already in the side of the man and the son in the loins of his father? Why then, when Scripture had said, "God made man in the image of God," did it go on to say, "God created him; male and female created He them: and God blessed them"?[9] (Or if it is to be so divided, "And God created man," so that thereupon is to be added, "in the image of God created He him," and then subjoined in the third place, "male and female created He them;" for some have feared to say, He made him male and female, lest something monstrous, as it were, should be understood, as are those whom they call hermaphrodites, although even so both might be understood not falsely in the singular number, on account of that which is said, "Two in one flesh.") Why then, as I began by saying, in regard to the nature of man made after the image of God, does Scripture specify nothing except male and female? Certainly, in order to complete the image of the Trinity, it ought to have added also son, although still placed in the loins of his father, as the woman was in his side. Or was it perhaps that the woman also had been already made, and that Scripture had combined in a short and comprehensive statement, that of which it was going to explain afterwards more carefully, how it was done; and that therefore a son could not be mentioned, because no son

8 Romans 1:3, 4.
9 Genesis 1:27, 28.

was yet born? As if the Holy Spirit could not have comprehended this, too, in that brief statement, while about to narrate the birth of the son afterwards in its own place; as it narrated afterwards in its own place, that the woman was taken from the side of the man,[10] and yet has not omitted here to name her.

CHAPTER 7—HOW MAN IS THE IMAGE OF GOD. WHETHER THE WOMAN IS NOT ALSO THE IMAGE OF GOD. HOW THE SAYING OF THE APOSTLE, THAT THE MAN IS THE IMAGE OF GOD, BUT THE WOMAN IS THE GLORY OF THE MAN, IS TO BE UNDERSTOOD FIGURATIVELY AND MYSTICALLY

We ought not therefore so to understand that man is made in the image of the supreme Trinity, that is, in the image of God, as that the same image should be understood to be in three human beings; especially when the apostle says that the man is the image of God, and on that account removes the covering from his head, which he warns the woman to use, speaking thus: "For a man indeed ought not to cover his head, forasmuch as he is the image and glory of God; but the woman is the glory of the man." What then shall we say to this? If the woman fills up the image of the trinity after the measure of her own person, why is the man still called that image after she has been taken out of his side? Or if even one person of a human being out of three can be called the image of God, as each person also is God in the supreme Trinity itself, why is the woman also not the image of God? For she is instructed for this very reason to cover her head, which he is forbidden to do because he is the image of God.[11]

But we must notice how that which the apostle says, that not the woman but the man is the image of God, is not contrary to that which is written in Genesis, "God created man: in the image of God created He him; male and female created He them: and He blessed them." For this text says that human nature itself, which is complete [only] in both sexes, was made in the image of God; and it does not separate the woman from the image of God which it signifies. For after saying that God made man in the image of God, "He created him," it says, "male and female:" or at any rate, punctuating the words otherwise, "male and female created He them." How then did the apostle tell us that the man is the image of God, and therefore he is forbidden to cover his head; but that the woman is not so, and therefore is commanded to cover hers? Unless, forsooth, according to that which I have said already, when I was treating of the nature of the human mind, that the woman together with her own husband is the image of God, so that that whole substance may be one image; but when she is referred separately to her quality of *help-meet*, which regards the woman herself alone, then she is not the image of God; but as regards the man alone, he is the image of God as fully and completely as when the woman too is

[10] Genesis 2:24, 22.
[11] I Corinthians 11:7, 5.

joined with him in one. As we said of the nature of the human mind, that both in the case when as a whole it contemplates the truth it is the image of God; and in the case when anything is divided from it, and diverted in order to the cognition of temporal things; nevertheless on that side on which it beholds and consults truth, here also it is the image of God, but on that side whereby it is directed to the cognition of the lower things, it is not the image of God. And since it is so much the more formed after the image of God, the more it has extended itself to that which is eternal, and is on that account not to be restrained, so as to withhold and refrain itself from thence; therefore the man ought not to cover his head. But because too great a progression towards inferior things is dangerous to that rational cognition that is conversant with things corporeal and temporal; this ought to have power on its head, which the covering indicates, by which it is signified that it ought to be restrained. For a holy and pious meaning is pleasing to the holy angels.[12] For God sees not after the way of time, neither does anything new take place in His vision and knowledge, when anything is done in time and transitorily, after the way in which such things affect the senses, whether the carnal senses of animals and men, or even the heavenly senses of the angels.

For that the Apostle Paul, when speaking outwardly of the sex of male and female, figured the mystery of some more hidden truth, may be understood from this, that when he says in another place that she is a widow indeed who is desolate, without children and nephews, and yet that she ought to trust in God, and to continue in prayers night and day,[13] he here indicates, that the woman having been brought into the transgression by being deceived, is brought to salvation by child-bearing; and then he has added, "If they continue in faith, and charity, and holiness, with sobriety."[14] As if it could possibly hurt a good widow, if either she had not sons, or if those whom she had did not choose to continue in good works. But because those things which are called good works are, as it were, the sons of our life, according to that sense of life in which it answers to the question, What is a man's life? that is, How does he act in these temporal things? which life the Greeks do not call ζωή but βίος; and because these good works are chiefly performed in the way of offices of mercy, while works of mercy are of no profit, either to Pagans, or to Jews who do not believe in Christ, or to any heretics or schismatics whatsoever in whom faith and charity and sober holiness are not found: what the apostle meant to signify is plain, and in so far figuratively and mystically, because he was speaking of covering the head of the woman, which will remain mere empty words, unless referred to some hidden sacrament.

For, as not only most true reason but also the authority of the apostle himself declares, man was not made in the image of God according to the shape of his body, but according to his rational mind. For the thought is a debased and empty one, which holds God to be circumscribed and limited by the lineaments

[12] I Corinthians 11:10.
[13] I Timothy 5:5.
[14] I Timothy 2:15.

of bodily members. But further, does not the same blessed apostle say, "Be renewed in the spirit of your mind, and put on the new man, which is created after God;"[15] and in another place more clearly, "Put off the old man," he says, "with his deeds; put on the new man, which is renewed to the knowledge of God after the image of Him that created him"?[16] If, then, we are renewed in the spirit of our mind, and he is the new man who is renewed to the knowledge of God after the image of Him that created him; no one can doubt, that man was made after the image of Him that created him, not according to the body, nor indiscriminately according to any part of the mind, but according to the rational mind, wherein the knowledge of God can exist. And it is according to this renewal, also, that we are made sons of God by the baptism of Christ; and putting on the new man, certainly put on Christ through faith. Who is there, then, who will hold women to be alien from this fellowship, whereas they are fellow-heirs of grace with us; and whereas in another place the same apostle says, "For ye are all the children of God by faith in Christ Jesus; for as many as have been baptized into Christ have put on Christ: there is neither Jew nor Greek, there is neither bond nor free, there is neither male nor female; for ye are all one in Christ Jesus"?[17] Pray, have faithful women then lost their bodily sex? But because they are there renewed after the image of God, where there is no sex; man is there made after the image of God, where there is no sex, that is, in the spirit of his mind. Why, then, is the man on that account not bound to cover his head, because he is the image and glory of God, while the woman is bound to do so, because she is the glory of the man; as though the woman were not renewed in the spirit of her mind, which spirit is renewed to the knowledge of God after the image of Him who created him? But because she differs from the man in bodily sex, it was possible rightly to represent under her bodily covering that part of the reason which is diverted to the government of temporal things; so that the image of God may remain on that side of the mind of man on which it cleaves to the beholding or the consulting of the eternal reasons of things; and this, it is clear, not men only, but also women have.

.   .   .

CHAPTER 13—THE OPINION OF THOSE WHO HAVE THOUGHT THAT THE MIND WAS SIGNIFIED BY THE MAN, THE BODILY SENSE BY THE WOMAN

Nor does it escape me, that some who before us were eminent defenders of the Catholic faith and expounders of the word of God, while they looked for these two things in one human being, whose entire soul they perceived to be a sort of excellent paradise, asserted that the man was the mind, but that the woman was the bodily sense. And according to this distribution, by which the

[15] Ephesians 4:23, 24.
[16] Colossians 3:9, 10.
[17] Galatians 3:26–28.

man is assumed to be the mind, but the woman the bodily sense, all things seem aptly to agree together if they are handled with due attention: unless that it is written, that in all the beasts and flying things there was not found for man an helpmate like to himself; and then the woman was made out of his side.[18] And on this account I, for my part, have not thought that the bodily sense should be taken for the woman, which we see to be common to ourselves and to the beasts; but I have desired to find something which the beasts had not; and I have rather thought the bodily sense should be understood to be the serpent, whom we read to have been more subtle than all beasts of the field.[19] For in those natural good things which we see are common to ourselves and to the irrational animals, the sense excels by a kind of living power; not the sense of which it is written in the epistle addressed to the Hebrews, where we read, that "strong meat belongeth to them that are of full age, even those who by reason of use have their senses exercised to discern both good and evil;"[20] for these "senses" belong to the rational nature and pertain to the understanding; but that sense which is divided into five parts in the body, through which corporeal species and motion is perceived not only by ourselves, but also by the beasts.

But whether that the apostle calls the man the image and glory of God, but the woman the glory of the man,[21] is to be received in this, or that, or in any other way; yet it is clear, that when we live according to God, our mind which is intent on the invisible things of Him ought to be fashioned with proficiency from His eternity, truth, charity; but that something of our own rational purpose, that is, of the same mind, must be directed to the using of changeable and corporeal things, without which this life does not go on; not that we may be conformed to this world,[22] by placing our end in such good things, and by forcing the desire of blessedness towards them, but that whatever we do rationally in the using of temporal things, we may do it with the contemplation of attaining eternal things, passing through the former, but cleaving to the latter.

From *The City of God,* Book 22

CHAPTER 17—WHETHER THE BODIES OF WOMEN SHALL RETAIN THEIR OWN SEX IN THE RESURRECTION

From the words, "Till we all come to a perfect man, to the measure of the age of the fullness of Christ,"[1] and from the words, "Conformed to the image

---

[18] Genesis 2:20–22.
[19] Genesis 3:1.
[20] Hebrews 5:14.
[21] I Corinthians 11:7.
[22] Romans 12:2.
[1] Ephesians 4:13.

of the Son of God,"[2] some conclude that women shall not rise women, but that all shall be men, because God made man only of earth, and woman of the man. For my part, they seem to be wiser who make no doubt that both sexes shall rise. For there shall be no lust, which is now the cause of confusion. For before they sinned, the man and the woman were naked, and were not ashamed. From those bodies, then, vice shall be withdrawn, while nature shall be preserved. And the sex of woman is not a vice, but nature. It shall then indeed be superior to carnal intercourse and child-bearing; nevertheless the female members shall remain adapted not to the old uses, but to a new beauty, which, so far from provoking lust, now extinct, shall excite praise to the wisdom and clemency of God, who both made what was not and delivered from corruption what He made. For at the beginning of the human race the woman was made of a rib taken from the side of the man while he slept; for it seemed fit that even then Christ and His Church should be foreshadowed in the event. For that sleep of the man was the death of Christ, whose side, as He hung lifeless upon the cross, was pierced with a spear, and there flowed from it blood and water, and these we know to be the sacraments by which the Church is "built up." For Scripture used this very word, not saying "He formed" or "framed," but "built her up into a woman;"[3] whence also the apostle speaks of the *edification* of the body of Christ,[4] which is the Church. The woman, therefore, is a creature of God even as the man; but by her creation from man unity is commended; and the manner of her creation prefigured, as has been said, Christ and the Church. He, then, who created both sexes will restore both. Jesus Himself also, when asked by the Sadducees, who denied the resurrection, which of the seven brothers should have to wife the woman whom all in succession had taken to raise up seed to their brother, as the law enjoined, says, "Ye do err, not knowing the Scriptures nor the power of God."[5] And though it was a fit opportunity for His saying, She about whom you make inquiries shall herself be a man, and not a woman, He said nothing of the kind; but "In the resurrection they neither marry nor are given in marriage, but are as the angels of God in heaven."[6] They shall be equal to the angels in immortality and happiness, not in flesh, nor in resurrection, which the angels did not need, because they could not die. The Lord then denied that there would be in the resurrection, not women, but marriages; and He uttered this denial in circumstances in which the question mooted would have been more easily and speedily solved by denying that the female sex would exist, if this had in truth been foreknown by Him. But, indeed, He even affirmed that the sex should exist by saying, "They shall not be given in marriage," which can only apply to females; "Neither shall they marry," which applies to males. There shall therefore be those who are in this world accustomed to marry and be given in marriage, only they shall there make no such marriages.

[2] Romans 8:29.
[3] Genesis 2:22.
[4] Ephesians 4:12.
[5] Matthew 22:29.
[6] Matthew 22:30.

❦Rosemary Radford Ruether

Rosemary Radford Ruether, a scholar of some renown in the fields of theology and church history, occupies the Georgia Harkness chair in Applied Theology at the Garrett-Evangelical Theological Seminary in Evanston, Illinois. Her recent books include The Church Against Itself, The Radical Kingdom, Liberation Theology, New Woman/New Earth, *and* Mary, the Feminine Face of the Church. *In the following excerpt from an article in* Religion and Sexism, *which she edited, Professor Ruether finds Augustine's views on woman typical of patristic theology insofar as they exhibit misogyny on the one hand and celebrate virginity on the other. This duality, she asserts, stems from the sharp contrast made by the fathers of the church between the soul and the body.*

Misogynism and Virginal Feminism in the Fathers of the Church

The usual image of the Fathers of the Church, especially among those promoting women's liberation, is that of fanatical ascetics and woman haters. Hatred of sex and hatred of women are identified.[1] But this view tends to ignore the high praise of women, in their new role as "virgins," in patristic theology. It also fails to explain the rise of that veneration of Mary that is characteristic of patristic thought in the fourth century A.D. In this chapter I wish to show that this ambivalence between misogynism and the praise of the virginal woman is not accidental. One view is not more "characteristic" than the other. Both stand together as two sides of a dualistic psychology that was the basis of the patristic doctrine of man.

.   .   .

. . . The crucial biblical text for the creation of man was Genesis 1:27: "God created man in His own image; in the image of God he created him; male and female He created them." If the Fathers could have had the first part of the text without the final phrase, they would have been happier. Indeed, they often quote only the first part of this text without alluding to the second.[2] About the character of the image of God in man they had no doubts. This referred to man's soul or reason. The Hellenistic Jew Philo had

---

[1] William Phipps, *Was Jesus Married?* (New York: Harper & Row, 1970), pp. 142–163.

[2] For example, Athanasius' *De Incarnatione* and Origen's *De Principiis* develop an anthropology built on the doctrine of the "image" without any mention of bisexuality.

already established this interpretation by the first century A.D.[3] The problem came with reconciling this spiritual interpretation of the image of God with the subsequent reference to bisexuality, which they saw as a bodily characteristic. Since God was wholly spiritual and noncorporeal, this appeared to mix contraries and imply either a sexed spirituality or a bodily God. Since it was anathema to think of God as bodily, with male and female characteristics, the two parts of the text must be separated so that the "image" could be defined in a monistic, spiritual way, and bisexuality could refer to something other than the nature of God as reflected in man.

For Greek thought it was axiomatic that spiritual reality was unitary (monistic, from which the words "monk" and "monastic" derive). Duality appears only with matter. So God cannot be dual, nor can man's spiritual image be bisexual. This does not mean an "androgynous" view of God and the original humanity, as some recent commentators have thought. The guiding view of the Fathers was not an androgyny that preserved bisexuality on a psychic level, but rather that monism which, alone, is appropriate to spirit.[4] This could be stated by identifying maleness with monism, making femaleness secondary, or else by a nonsexual monism, but not by a true androgyny. Gregory Nyssa chose the latter course, and Augustine the former.

. . .

. . . For Augustine, man as the image of God was summed up in Adam, the unitary ancestor of humanity. But Adam is compound, containing both male spirit and female corporeality. When Eve is taken from Adam's side, she symbolizes this corporeal side of man, taken from him in order to be his helpmeet. But she is a helpmeet solely for the corporeal task of procreation, for which alone she is indispensable.[5] For any spiritual task another male would be more suitable than a female as a helpmeet.

Inexplicably, Augustine must also affirm that Eve, too, has a rational nature, being likewise a compound of spirit and body. Yet in relation to man she stands for body vis-à-vis male spirit.[6] Moreover, Augustine persists in calling this latter her "nature," not only with a view to sin but in the order of nature as well. Augustine defines the male as, alone, the full image of God. Woman, by herself, is not this image, but only when taken together with the male, who is her "head." Augustine justifies this view by fusing the Genesis text with I Corinthians 11:3–12.

How then did the apostle tell us that the man is the image of God and therefore he is forbidden to cover his head, but that the woman is not so, and therefore she is commanded to cover hers? Unless forsooth according to that which I have said already, when I was treating of the nature of the human mind, that the woman, together with her own husband, is the image of God, so that the whole substance

---

[3] Philo, Leg. All. I, 31–32; De Conf. 62–63; also see De Migr. Abr. 174.

[4] M. N. Maxey, "Beyond Eve and Mary," Dialog. X (Spring 1971), 112 ff.

[5] Augustine, De Grat. Ch. et de Pecc. Orig. II, 40.; De Genesi ad Lit. 9.5.

[6] Augustine, Confessiones 13.32; De Opere Monach. 40.

may be one image, but when she is referred to separately in her quality as a help-meet, which regards the woman alone, then she is not the image of God, but, as regards the man alone, he is the image of God as fully and completely as when the woman too is joined with him in one.[7]

This assimilation of male–female dualism into soul–body dualism in patristic theology conditions basically the definition of woman, both in terms of her subordination to the male in the order of nature and her "carnality" in the disorder of sin. The result of this assimilation is that woman is not really seen as a self-sufficient, whole person with equal honor, as the image of God in her own right, but is seen, ethically, as dangerous to the male. Augustine works this out explicitly, but patristic theology makes use of the same assumptions of woman's subordination to man in the order of nature, and her special "carnality" in the disorder of sin, which imply the same attitudes, however unjustified by the contrary assumption of the equivalence of male and female in the original creation. This definition of femaleness as body decrees a natural subordination of female to male, *as flesh must be subject to spirit in the right ordering of nature.*[8] It also makes her peculiarly the symbol of the Fall and sin, since sin is defined as the disordering of the original justice wherein the bodily principle revolts against its ruling spirit and draws the reason down to its lower dictates.

This double definition of woman, as submissive body in the order of nature and "revolting" body in the disorder of sin, allows the Fathers to slide somewhat inconsistently from the second to the first and attribute woman's inferiority first to sin and then to nature. In Augustine the stress falls decidedly on the side of woman's natural inferiority as body in relation to mind in the right ordering of nature, and thus he is somewhat temperate in his polemics against Eve as the original cause of the Fall. For him, the Fall could only occur, not when the body tempts, but when the male ruling principle agrees to "go along." This, however, does not imply a milder view of sin, only a more contemptuous view of Eve's capacity to cause the Fall "by herself."[9] In other Fathers, ... Eve is made to sound as though she bore the primary responsibility.

. . .

This assimilation of woman into bodiliness allows Augustine to explain why woman's subjugation is "natural" within the order of creation, but it makes for some contradiction when it comes time to defend woman's redeemability and her ability, like that of the man, to become "virgin" and return to the monistic incorporeal nature. This conflict does not appear in Nyssa in the same way, because he makes bisexuality, rather than femaleness, the symbol of corporeality, and thus makes woman and man equivalent, both in their spiritual natures and in their sexed bodily natures. But, then, the Greeks had the cor-

[7] Augustine, *De Trinitate* 7.7, 10.

[8] Augustine, *De Contin.* I.23; Augustine parallels the supra- and subordinations of Christ and the Church; man and woman and the soul and the body. On the ambivalence between an equivalent and a subordinate view of women in the Fathers, especially Augustine, see Kari Elizabeth Børresen, *Subordination et Équivalence; Nature et rôle de la femme d'après Augustin et Thomas d'Aquin* (Oslo: Universitets-forlaget, 1968).

[9] Augustine, *De Civitate Dei* 14, 11; *De Genesi ad Lit.* 11, 42.

responding conflict of an inexplicable use of language which suggested that woman was subordinate to man in nature and peculiarly identified with "carnality"—a language to which they, too, were addicted.

Augustine attempts to explain this contradiction by distinguishing between what woman is, as a rational spirit (in which she is equivalent to the male), and what she "symbolizes" in her bodily nature, where she stands for the subjection of body to spirit in nature and that debasing carnality that draws the male mind down from its heavenly heights. But he thinks that what she thus symbolizes, in the eye of male perception, is also what she "is" in her female nature! It never occurs to him that defining woman as something other than what she is, and placing her in subjugation in the order of nature *from the perspective of the male visual impression of her as a "body"* is nothing else than an expression, in the male himself, of that disorder of sin, and thus, in no way a stance for the definition of woman's nature! For Augustine, however, this androcentric perspective is never questioned, but presupposed. Yet he, too, must admit that woman has "another" possibility beyond this androcentrically conceived bodiliness. She, too, has a rational nature and can be saved by overcoming the body and living according to the spirit. Augustine cannot deny this since he, along with all the Church Fathers, believes that woman can become "virgin" and live the monistic, angelic life.

. . .

In this twilight period of antiquity, we see . . . the image of the virginal woman appearing as a new cultural ideal, raising up the possibility of woman as capable of the highest spiritual development, which could lead to the *summum bonum* of communion with the divine, intellectual nature of the Divine itself. Such heights had previously been reserved for men in antiquity . . .

. . . Virginal woman was thus bound for heaven, and her male ascetic devotees would stop at nothing short of this prize for her. But they paid the price of despising all real physical women, sex and fecundity, and wholly etherealizing women into incorporeal phantasms in order to provide love objects for the sublimated libido and guard against turning back to any physical expression of love with the dangerous daughters of Eve.

Perhaps the task of Christians today, as they take stock of this tradition and its defects, is not merely to vilify its inhumanity but rather to cherish the hard-won fruits of transcendence and spiritual personhood, won at such a terrible price of the natural affections of men and the natural humanity of women. Without discarding these achievements, we must rather find out how to pour them back into a full-bodied Hebrew sense of creation and incarnation, as male and female, but who can now be fully personalized autonomous selves and also persons in relation to each other, not against the body, but in and through the body.

❧5 St. Thomas Aquinas

Thomas Aquinas was born to a noble family in Roccasecca, near Naples, late in 1224 or early in 1225. As an infant he managed to acquire a reputation for great piety by seizing a piece of parchment on which the Hail Mary was written and refusing to let it go. Perhaps as a result of this precocity, but more likely because, as the youngest of seven sons, he was destined to follow an ecclesiastical career, he was sent to a Benedictine monastery as an oblate at the age of five. There he impressed the abbot with his constant inquiries into the nature of God, and at fourteen he was sent to the University of Naples for further study. Conforming to parental expectations, he announced his intention of taking holy orders; to the consternation of his family, however, it was not the established Benedictine order that Thomas proposed to join, but the new Dominican order of mendicant friars. His mother, by then widowed, arranged for two of his brothers to kidnap him and hold him prisoner at Aquino for a year while the family tried to dissuade him from his intent. His sisters pleaded with him, and his brothers even sent a young girl to his bedroom in an attempt to turn him from his purpose. They all failed. Thomas joined the order of his choice and became a pupil of Albert the Great. He lectured extensively, and he wrote the massive Summa Theologica, in which he attempted to encompass all of human knowledge. He died in 1274 en route to an ecclesiastical council.

Among the topics that Aquinas addressed in the Summa are the nature of woman and her proper role in the life of the church. A century before, a German abbess, Hildegard von Bingen, had blamed the decadent condition of society generally and that of the church specifically on the weakness of men, particularly the clergy. What the world needed, she claimed, was a tempus muliebre—an era of woman. She envisioned armies of women marching up and down the Rhine, making converts. The twelfth century, which came almost as close as any era ever has come to fulfilling Hildegard's dream, witnessed an unprecedented outburst of feminine activity, both temporal and spiritual, and produced such women as Eleanor of Aquitaine, the Empress Matilda, Blanche of Castile, Marie de France, and, of course, Hildegard herself. But by the end of the century this wave of feminism had subsided. Aquinas might well be considered a spokesman for the masculine age which followed, for he looked upon woman as an incomplete male and rigidly restricted her activities in the church as well as in society at large.

The following passages are taken from the Summa Theologica, which employs a method introduced in the twelfth century by Peter Abelard. First Aquinas poses a question and lists a number of erroneous answers to it, each supported by argument and defended by authority. Then he cites a counterauthority with whom he more or less agrees, elaborates his own answer, and proceeds to reply, one by one, to each of the erroneous arguments. A number of his answers to questions concerning the nature of woman are little more than restatements of arguments used by Aristotle, whom Aquinas refers to as "the Philosopher." Others show the obvious influence of Augustine. All of them relegate woman to second-class citizenship in the Christian community.

Aquinas has been accused of having expressed Augustine's philosophy in Aristotelian terms and of having interpreted Aristotle so as to make his views consistent with those of Augustine. Antifeminism tempered with ambivalence is still antifeminism, only very slightly mitigated.

Aquinas agreed with Aristotle's dictum that woman is a decidedly inferior creature, a "misbegotten male." Her creation, however was demanded for the greater perfection of the universe. She is "misbegotten," he believed, because the male seed tends to try to reproduce itself as perfectly as possible. When it produces not a male but a female, obviously something has gone wrong. Although designated man's helpmate, woman is of real assistance to him only in the procreation and care of offspring, for in all other things, Aquinas maintained, man is better served by other men.

In considering woman's creation Aquinas made the point that the substance of which she was made, Adam's rib, was ideally situated, since it implied neither her superiority to him (as would have been the case had she been made from his head) nor her inferiority to him (as her creation from his feet would have done). Yet, in the church, woman's place is decidedly below that of man. Aquinas never questioned her fitness to receive the sacrament of baptism, but he made abundantly clear that she might confer it only in the most extreme cases—in the absence of any and all members of the male sex: bishop, priest, clerk, layman. After carefully examining the question of whether woman should be confirmed, he concluded that her confirmation was indeed appropriate. But matrimony is the one sacrament of the church that was designed for woman, partly because it secures for her a provider, but mainly because it is only through that institution that she can fulfill her one purpose in life, to have children.

In her relationship to her husband woman is definitely subservient, according to Aquinas. She must meet his demands even when they are immoral. For example, she must "pay the marriage debt" upon demand, even during the menses when she is "unclean" and when there is danger of "harm . . . to the offspring of such intercourse." The man should try to anticipate her needs when it may reasonably be feared that the awareness of her lowly position might result in shame, which would prevent her from making these needs known to him; but she can demand nothing. Aquinas, it is clear, did not adopt the single moral standard for which Augustine was striving, but he was equally strict on the two sexes with regard to chastity, marriage, remarriage, and divorce.

Finally, Aquinas pursued the matter of woman's inferiority even to her resurrection. If human beings are to be resurrected in idealized form, he asked, would it not be likely that they all should be resurrected as males? Although he eventually answered in the negative, the length and care with which he considered the question indicate the seriousness with which he entertained the idea. Augustine's treatment of the matter had been a bit more perfunctory.

From *Summa Theologica*

PART 1, QUESTION 92

The Production of the Woman

We must next consider the production of the woman. Under this head there are four points of inquiry: (1) Whether the woman should have been made in that first production of things? (2) Whether the woman should have been made from man? (3) Whether of man's rib? (4) Whether the woman was made immediately by God?

First Article
Whether the Woman Should Have Been Made in the
First Production of Things?
We proceed thus to the First Article:—

Objection 1. It would seem that the woman should not have been made in the first production of things. For the Philosopher says (*De Gener. Animal.* ii. 3), that the *female is a misbegotten male.* But nothing misbegotten or defective should have been in the first production of things. Therefore woman should not have been made at that first production.

Obj. 2. Further, subjection and limitation were a result of sin, for to the woman was it said after sin (Gen. iii. 16): *Thou shalt be under the man's power;* and Gregory says that, *Where there is no sin, there is no inequality.* But woman is naturally of less strength and dignity than man; *for the agent is always more honourable than the patient,* as Augustine says (*Gen. ad lit.* xii. 16). Therefore woman should not have been made in the first production of things before sin.

Obj. 3. Further, occasions of sin should be cut off. But God foresaw that the woman would be an occasion of sin to man. Therefore He should not have made woman.

On the contrary, It is written (Gen. ii. 18): *It is not good for man to be alone; let us make him a helper like to himself.*

I answer that, It was necessary for woman to be made, as the Scripture says, as *a helper* to man; not, indeed, as a helpmate in other works, as some say, since man can be more efficiently helped by another man in other works; but as a helper in the work of generation. This can be made clear if we observe the mode of generation carried out in various living things. Some living things do not possess in themselves the power of generation, but are generated by some other specific agent, such as some plants and animals by the influence of the heavenly bodies, from some fitting matter and not from seed: others possess the active and passive generative power together; as we see in plants which are generated from seed; for the noblest vital function in plants is generation. Wherefore we observe that in these the active power of generation invariably accompanies the passive power. Among perfect animals the active power of generation belongs to the male sex, and the passive power to the female. And as among animals there is a vital operation nobler than generation, to which their life is principally directed; therefore the male sex is not found in continual union with the female in perfect animals, but only at the time of coition; so that we may consider that by this means the male and female are one, as in plants they are always united; although in some cases one of them preponderates, and in some the other. But man is yet further ordered to a still nobler vital action, and that is intellectual operation. Therefore there was greater reason for the distinction of these two forces in man; so that the female should be produced separately from the male; although they are carnally united for generation. Therefore directly after the formation of woman, it was said: *And they shall be two in one flesh* (Gen. ii. 24).

Reply Obj. 1. As regards the individual nature, woman is defective and misbegotten, for the active force in the male seed tends to the production of a perfect likeness in the masculine sex; while the production of woman comes from defect in the active force or from some material indisposition, or even from some external influence; such as that of a south wind, which is moist, as the Philosopher observes (*De Gener. Animal.* iv. 2). On the other hand, as regards human nature in general, woman is not misbegotten, but is included in nature's intention as directed to the work of generation. Now the general intention of nature depends on God, Who is the universal Author of nature. Therefore, in producing nature, God formed not only the male but also the female.

Reply Obj. 2. Subjection is twofold. One is servile, by virtue of which a superior makes use of a subject for his own benefit; and this kind of subjection began after sin. There is another kind of subjection, which is called economic or civil, whereby the superior makes use of his subjects for their own benefit and good; and this kind of subjection existed even before sin. For good order would have been wanting in the human family if some were not governed by others wiser than themselves. So by such a kind of subjection woman is naturally subject to man, because in man the discretion of reason predominates. Nor is inequality among men excluded by the state of innocence, as we shall prove (Q. XCVI., A. 3).

Reply Obj. 3. If God had deprived the world of all those things which proved an occasion of sin, the universe would have been imperfect. Nor was it fitting for the common good to be destroyed in order that individual evil might be avoided; especially as God is so powerful that He can direct any evil to a good end.

Second Article
Whether Woman Should Have Been Made from Man?
We proceed thus to the Second Article:—
Objection 1. It would seem that woman should not have been made from man. For sex belongs both to man and animals. But in the other animals the

female was not made from the male. Therefore neither should it have been so with man.

Obj. 2. Further, things of the same species are of the same matter. But male and female are of the same species. Therefore, as man was made of the slime of the earth, so woman should have been made of the same, and not from man.

Obj. 3. Further, woman was made to be a helpmate to man in the work of generation. But close relationship makes a person unfit for that office; hence near relations are debarred from intermarriage, as is written (Lev. xviii. 6). Therefore woman should not have been made from man.

On the contrary, It is written (Eccli. xvii. 5): *He created of him,* that is, out of man, *a helpmate like to himself,* that is, woman.

I answer that, When all things were first formed, it was more suitable for the woman to be made from the man than (for the female to be from the male) in other animals. First, in order thus to give the first man a certain dignity consisting in this, that as God is the principle of the whole universe, so the first man, in likeness to God, was the principle of the whole human race. Wherefore Paul says that *God made the whole human race from one* (Acts xvii. 26). Secondly, that man might love woman all the more, and cleave to her more closely, knowing her to be fashioned from himself. Hence it is written (Gen. ii. 23, 24): *She was taken out of man, wherefore a man shall leave father and mother, and shall cleave to his wife.* This was most necessary as regards the human race, in which the male and female live together for life; which is not the case with other animals. Thirdly, because, as the Philosopher says (*Ethic.* viii. 12), the human male and female are united, not only for generation, as with other animals, but also for the purpose of domestic life, in which each has his or her particular duty, and in which the man is the head of the woman. Wherefore it was suitable for the woman to be made out of man, as out of her principle. Fourthly, there is a sacramental reason for this. For by this is signified that the Church takes her origin from Christ. Wherefore the Apostle says (Eph. v. 32): *This is a great sacrament; but I speak in Christ and in the Church.*

Reply Obj. 1 is clear from the foregoing.

Reply Obj. 2. Matter is that from which something is made. Now created nature has a determinate principle; and since it is determined to one thing, it has also a determinate mode of proceeding. Wherefore from determinate matter it produces something in a determinate species. On the other hand, the Divine Power, being infinite, can produce things of the same species out of any matter, such as a man from the slime of the earth, and a woman from a man.

Reply Obj. 3. A certain affinity arises from natural generation, and this is an impediment to matrimony. Woman, however, was not produced from man by natural generation, but by the Divine Power alone. Wherefore Eve is not called the daughter of Adam; and so this argument does not prove.

Third Article
Whether Woman Was Fittingly Made
from the Rib of Man?

We proceed thus to the Third Article:—

Objection 1. It would seem that the woman should not have been formed from the rib of man. For the rib was much smaller than the woman's body. Now from a smaller thing a larger thing can be made only—either by addition (and then the woman ought to have been described as made out of that which was added, rather than out of the rib itself);—or by rarefaction, because, as Augustine says (*Gen. ad lit.* x.): *A body cannot increase in bulk except by rarefaction.* But the woman's body is not more rarefied than man's—at least, not in the proportion of a rib to Eve's body. Therefore Eve was not formed from a rib of Adam.

Obj. 2. Further, in those things which were first created there was nothing superfluous. Therefore a rib of Adam belonged to the integrity of his body. So, if a rib was removed, his body remained imperfect; which is unreasonable to suppose.

Obj. 3. Further, a rib cannot be removed from man without pain. But there was no pain before sin. Therefore it was not right for a rib to be taken from the man, that Eve might be made from it.

On the contrary, It is written (Gen. ii. 22): *God built the rib, which He took from Adam, into a woman.*

I answer that, It was right for the woman to be made from a rib of man. First, to signify the social union of man and woman, for the woman should neither *use authority over man,* and so she was not made from his head; nor was it right for her to be subject to man's contempt as his slave, and so she was not made from his feet. Secondly, for the sacramental signification; for from the side of Christ sleeping on the Cross the Sacraments flowed—namely, blood and water—on which the Church was established.

Reply Obj. 1. Some say that the woman's body was formed by a material increase, without anything being added; in the same way as our Lord multiplied the five loaves. But this is quite impossible. For such an increase of matter would either be by a change of the very substance of the matter itself, or by a change of its dimensions. Not by change of the substance of the matter, both because matter, considered in itself, is quite unchangeable, since it has a potential existence, and has nothing but the nature of a subject, and because quantity and size are extraneous to the essence of matter itself. Wherefore multiplication of matter is quite unintelligible, as long as the matter itself remains the same without anything added to it; unless it receives greater dimensions. This implies rarefaction, which is for the same matter to receive greater dimensions, as the Philosopher says (*Phys.* iv.). To say, therefore, that the same matter is enlarged, without being rarefied, is to combine contradictories—viz., the definition with the absence of the thing defined.

Wherefore, as no rarefaction is apparent in such multiplication of matter, we must admit an addition of matter: either by creation or, which is more probable, by conversion. Hence Augustine says (*Tract.* xxiv., *in Joan.*) that *Christ filled five thousand men with five loaves, in the same way as from a few seeds He produces the harvest of corn*—that is, by transformation of the nourishment. Nevertheless, we say that the crowds were fed with five loaves, or that woman was made from the rib, because an addition was made to the already existing matter of the loaves and of the rib.

Reply Obj. 2. The rib belonged to the integral perfection of Adam, not as an individual, but as the principle of the human race; just as the semen belongs to the perfection of the begetter, and is released by a natural and pleasurable operation. Much more, therefore, was it possible that by the Divine power the body of the woman should be produced from the man's rib.

From this is it clear how to answer the third objection.

Fourth Article
Whether the Woman Was Formed Immediately by God?
We proceed thus to the Fourth Article:—

Objection 1. It would seem that the woman was not formed immediately by God. For no individual is produced immediately by God from another individual alike in species. But the woman was made from a man who is of the same species. Therefore she was not made immediately by God.

Obj. 2. Further, Augustine (*De Trin.* iii. 4) says that corporeal things are governed by God through the angels. But the woman's body was formed from corporeal matter. Therefore it was made through the ministry of the angels, and not immediately by God.

Obj. 3. Further, those things which pre-exist in creatures as to their causal virtues are produced by the power of some creature, and not immediately by God. But the woman's body was produced in its causal virtues among the first created works, as Augustine says (*Gen. ad lit.* ix. 15). Therefore it was not produced immediately by God.

On the contrary, Augustine says, in the same work: *God alone, to Whom all nature owes its existence, could form or build up the woman from the man's rib.*

I answer that, As was said above (A. 2, *ad* 2), the natural generation of every species is from some determinate matter. Now the matter whence man is naturally begotten is the human semen of man or woman. Wherefore from any other matter an individual of the human species cannot naturally be generated. Now God alone, the Author of nature, can produce an effect into existence outside the ordinary course of nature. Therefore God alone could produce either a man from the slime of the earth, or a woman from the rib of man.

Reply Obj. 1. This argument is verified when an individual is begotten, by natural generation, from that which is like it in the same species.

Reply Obj. 2. As Augustine says (*Gen. ad lit.* ix. 15), we do not know whether the angels were employed by God in the formation of the woman; but it is certain that, as the body of man was not formed by the angels from the slime of the earth, so neither was the body of the woman formed by them from the man's rib.

Reply Obj. 3. As Augustine says (*ibid.* 18): *The first creation of things did not demand that woman should be made thus; it made it possible for her to be thus made.* Therefore the body of the woman did indeed pre-exist in these causal virtues, in the things first created; not as regards active potentiality, but as regards a potentiality passive in relation to the active potentiality of the Creator.

PART 3, QUESTION 67

Of the Ministers who Confer Baptism

· · ·

Fourth Article
Whether a Woman Can Baptize?
We proceed thus to the Fourth Article:—

Objection 1. It seems that a woman cannot baptize. For we read in the acts of the Council of Carthage (iv.): *However learned and holy a woman may be, she must not presume to teach men in the church, or to baptize.* But in no case is a woman allowed to teach in church, according to I Cor. xiv. 35: *It is a shame for a woman to speak in the church.* Therefore it seems that neither is a woman in any circumstances permitted to baptize.

Obj. 2. Further, to baptize belongs to those having authority; wherefore baptism should be conferred by priests having charge of souls. But women are not qualified for this; according to I Tim. ii. 12: *I suffer not a woman to teach, nor to use authority over man, but to be subject to him* (Vulg.—*but to be in silence*). Therefore a woman cannot baptize.

Obj. 3. Further, in the spiritual regeneration water seems to hold the place of the mother's womb, as Augustine says on John iii. 4, *Can* a man *enter a second time into his mother's womb, and be born again?* While he who baptizes seems to hold rather the position of father. But this is unfitting for a woman. Therefore a woman cannot baptize.

On the contrary, Pope Urban (II.) says (*Decreta* xxx.): *In reply to the questions asked by your beatitude, we consider that the following answer should be given: that the baptism is valid when, in cases of necessity, a woman baptizes a child in the name of the Trinity.*

I answer that, Christ is the chief Baptizer, according to John i. 33: *He upon Whom thou shalt see the Spirit descending and remaining upon Him, He it is that baptizeth.* For it is written in Coloss. iii. (*cf.* Gal. iii. 28), that in Christ there is neither male nor female. Consequently, just as a layman can baptize, as Christ's minister, so can a woman.

But since *the head of the woman is the man,* and *the head of . . . man, is Christ* (I Cor. xi. 3), a woman should not baptize if a man be available for the purpose; just as neither should a layman in the presence of a cleric, nor a cleric in the presence of a priest. The last, however, can baptize in the presence of a bishop, because it is part of the priestly office.

Reply Obj. 1. Just as a woman is not suffered to teach in public, but is allowed to instruct and admonish privately; so she is not permitted to baptize publicly and solemnly, and yet she can baptize in a case of urgency.

Reply Obj. 2. When Baptism is celebrated solemnly and with due form, it should be conferred by a priest having charge of souls, or by one representing him. But this is not required in cases of urgency, when a woman may baptize.

Reply Obj. 3. In carnal generation male and female co-operate according to the power of their proper nature; wherefore the female cannot be the active, but only the passive, principle of generation. But in spiritual generation they do not act, either of them, by their proper power, but only instrumentally by the power of Christ. Consequently, on the same grounds either man or woman can baptize in a case of urgency.

If, however, a woman were to baptize without any urgency for so doing; there would be no need of rebaptism: as we have said in regard to laymen (A. 3 *ad* 1). But the baptizer herself would sin, as also those who took part with her therein, either by receiving Baptism from her, or by bringing someone to her to be baptized.

. . .

PART 3 (SUPPLEMENT), QUESTION 39

Of the Impediments to this Sacrament

. . .

First Article
Whether the Female Sex Is an Impediment
to Receiving Orders?
We proceed thus to the First Article:—

Objection 1. It would seem that the female sex is no impediment to receiving Orders. For the office of prophet is greater than the office of priest, since a prophet stands midway between God and priests, just as the priest does between God and people. Now the office of prophet was sometimes granted to women, as may be gathered from 4 Kings xxii. 14. Therefore the office of priest also may be competent to them.

Obj. 2. Further, Just as Order pertains to a kind of pre-eminence, so does a position of authority as well as martyrdom and the religious state. Now authority is entrusted to women in the New Testament, as in the case of abbesses, and in the Old Testament, as in the case of Debbora, who judged Israel (Judges ii.). Moreover martyrdom and the religious life are also befitting to them. Therefore the Orders of the Church are also competent to them.

Obj. 3. Further, The power of Orders is founded in the soul. But sex is not in the soul. Therefore difference in sex makes no difference to the reception of Orders.

On the contrary, It is said (I Tim. ii. 12): *I suffer not a woman to teach* (*in the Church*),* nor to use authority over the man.

Further, The crown is required previous to receiving Orders, albeit not for the validity of the sacrament. But the crown or tonsure is not befitting to women according to I Cor. xi. Neither therefore is the receiving of Orders.

* The words in parentheses are from I Cor. xiv. 34, *Let women keep silence in the churches.*

I answer that, Certain things are required in the recipient of a sacrament as being requisite for the validity of the sacrament, and if such things be lacking, one can receive neither the sacrament nor the reality of the sacrament. Other things, however, are required, not for the validity of the sacrament, but for its lawfulness, as being congruous to the sacrament; and without these one receives the sacrament, but not the reality of the sacrament. Accordingly we must say that the male sex is required for receiving Orders not only in the second, but also in the first way. Wherefore even though a woman were made the object of all that is done in conferring Orders, she would not receive Orders, for since a sacrament is a sign, not only the thing, but the signification of the thing, is required in all sacramental actions; thus . . . in Extreme Unction it is necessary to have a sick man, in order to signifiy the need of healing. Accordingly, since it is not possible in the female sex to signify eminence of degree, for a woman is in the state of subjection, it follows that she cannot receive the sacrament of Order. Some, however, have asserted that the male sex is necessary for the lawfulness and not for the validity of the sacrament, because even in the Decretals (cap. *Mulieres,* dist. 32; cap. *Diaconissam,* 27, qu. i.) mention is made of deaconesses and priestesses. But deaconess there denotes a woman who shares in some act of a deacon, namely who reads the homilies in the Church; and a priestess (*presbytera*) is a widow, for the word 'presbyter' means elder.

Reply Obj. 1. Prophecy is not a sacrament but a gift of God. Wherefore there it is not the signification, but only the thing which is necessary. And since in matters pertaining to the soul woman does not differ from man as to the thing (for sometimes a woman is found to be better than many men as regards the soul), it follows that she can receive the gift of prophecy and the like, but not the sacrament of Orders.

And thereby appears the *Reply* to the *Second* and *Third Objections.* However, as to abbesses, it is said that they have not ordinary authority, but delegated as it were, on account of the danger of men and women living together. But Debbora exercised authority in temporal not in priestly matters, even as now woman may have temporal power.

. . .

PART 3 (SUPPLEMENT), QUESTION 81

Quality after Resurrection

. . .

Third Article
Whether All Will Rise Again of the Male Sex?
We proceed thus to the Third Article:—
Objection 1. It would seem that all will rise again of the male sex. For it is written (Ephes. iv. 13) that we shall all meet *unto a perfect man,* etc. Therefore there will be none but the male sex.

Obj. 2. Further, In the world to come all pre-eminence will cease, as a gloss observes on I Cor. xv. 24. Now woman is subject to man in the natural order. Therefore women will rise again not in the female but in the male sex.

Obj. 3. Further, That which is produced incidentally and beside the intention of nature will not rise again, since all error will be removed at the resurrection. Now the female sex is produced beside the intention of nature, through a fault in the formative power of the seed, which is unable to bring the matter of the fetus to the male form: wherefore the Philosopher says (*De Animal.* xvi., i.e. *De Generat. Animal.* ii.) that *the female is a misbegotten male.* Therefore the female sex will not rise again.

On the contrary, Augustine says (*De Civ. Dei,* xxii.): *Those are wiser, seemingly, who doubt not that both sexes will rise again.*

Further, At the resurrection God will restore man to what He made him at the creation. Now He made woman from the man's rib (Gen. ii. 22). Therefore He will also restore the female sex at the resurrection.

I answer that, Just as, considering the nature of the individual, a different quantity is due to different men, so also, considering the nature of the individual, a different sex is due to different men. Moreover, this same diversity is becoming to the perfection of the species, the different degrees whereof are filled by this very difference of sex and quantity. Wherefore just as men will rise again of various stature, so will they rise again of different sex. And though there be difference of sex there will be no shame in seeing one another, since there will be no lust to invite them to shameful deeds which are the cause of shame.

Reply Obj. 1. When it is said: We shall all meet *Christ unto a perfect man,* this refers not to the male sex but to the strength of soul which will be in all, both men and women.

Reply Obj. 2. Woman is subject to man on account of the frailty of nature, as regards both vigour of soul and strength of body. After the resurrection, however, the difference in those points will be not on account of the difference of sex, but by reason of the difference of merits. Hence the conclusion does not follow.

Reply Obj. 3. Although the begetting of a woman is beside the intention of a particular nature, it is in the intention of universal nature, which requires both sexes for the perfection of the human species. Nor will any defect result from sex as stated above (*ad* 2).

⊸ટ⊱ *Eleanor Commo McLaughlin*

Eleanor Commo McLaughlin is an associate professor of church history at the Andover Newton Theological School in Newton Center, Massachusetts. A specialist in the late Middle Ages, she points out that, however sexist medieval theory concerning woman's nature might have been, the convent provided a genuine alternative to the home as a setting in which women could perform their Christian duty. The task of the modern theologian, she claims, is to recognize medieval sexism for what it is and to provide a new anthropology in which people are regarded primarily as individuals, and members of the two sexes are given equal opportunity for self-fulfillment.

Equality of Souls, Inequality of Sexes; Woman in Medieval Theology

Medievalists today are often sensitive to the issue of the "relevance" of their chosen field of study. When the topic is the theological definition of the female sex, there is apparently even more question as to the timeliness of the medieval perspective, for surely the years between the decline of antiquity and the Renaissance seem to have been a Dark Age for the woman. Because I suspect that this is a widely held view even among readers with some professional interest in the history of theology, I begin this paper with a note on the importance of the medieval period for the history of the woman. . . .

The student of the woman in the Christian tradition needs to look to the medieval centuries to discover what transformations occur in the biblical and patristic traditions during the period that saw the emergence of Western Christian civilization. The classical, antique Christian and Germanic components of that civilization merged and reformed each other into a new spiritual, intellectual, and sociopolitical reality that in many respects created the limits and possibilities of our own twentieth-century world. It is, therefore, a medieval reinterpretation of the antique and Christian heritage that we have inherited . . . By ["we"] I do not mean solely those who stand closer to a continuity with the medieval Christian tradition—Roman Catholics, Eastern Orthodox or Anglicans —but I refer also to our secularized society, which in its assumptions about the woman and all her works has deep and unconscious roots in medieval culture. True liberation from the androcentrism and misogyny of those assumptions can come only when that past is made explicit and clear in its implications. . . .

. . .

I

A representative theological framework for our study is appropriately drawn from the work of the Dominican Doctor of the Church Thomas Aquinas, not because he dominated the thirteenth-century theological scene (which he did not) but rather because of his mediation between the patristic and predominantly Augustinian inheritance, which had shaped theological speculation through the twelfth century, and the new naturalistic world view of Aristotelian metaphysics and natural science that became known to scholars in his lifetime. . . .

Thomas' discussion of the creation of the human being, focusing, as did the Fathers, on the Genesis 2 account, does depart from Augustine's in a way that has important implications for the nature of the female human being. In accord with Aristotelian hylomorphism, man (*homo*) is a composite of body and soul, in contrast to the Platonized patristic anthropology that defined the human being as a soul imprisoned in the materiality of the flesh.[1] This more integrated view of the relation of body and soul made possible for Thomas an escape from the patristic dualism that identified *vir,* the male, with spirit, and the female polarity with the earthward drag of the body. Thomas not only defines the human being (*homo*) as an integrity of body and soul, he gives a positive valuation to the body. The body has an excellence with respect to its end as long as it serves that end.[2] This view might have helped overcome the patristic pessimism about sex and the body, a pessimism that always fed a fear and denigration of women. However, Thomas followed Aristotle and his patristic authorities in their intellectualist definition of man, *homo,* so that the body-denying dualism and its associated androcentrism were reinvigorated. He did this by determining that the end for man, the final fulfillment of the human being, life with God, is achieved by the operation of the rational soul.[3] Ultimately, therefore, the body is again left out.

Furthermore, in his discussion of the bisexual creation of mankind, male and female, Thomas follows Aristotle in his view that the male is ordered to the more noble activity, intellectual knowledge, whereas the female, although possessing a rational soul, was created solely with respect to her sexuality, her body, as an aid in reproduction for the preservation of the species.[4] Thomas also follows Aristotelian biology in his assertion that the girl child represents a defective human being, the result of an accident to the male sperm, which was thought to contain the complete human being *in potentia* and to reproduce by nature the likeness of its origin, that is, another male.[5] This finality of the female as a mere instrumentality, an aid to reproduction, is the only explanation Thomas can offer for the existence of a "second sex," since for any other activity—work or play—man would have been better served by a male helpmate. Thomas asks reasonably why human beings were not created in pairs like the other animals, answering with the litany of female subordination familiar from our patristic sources: that it is appropriate to the dignity of the first man to be the principle of the totality of the species, as God is principle of the totality of the universe; that the monogamous marriage might be better preserved, for man will love the woman all the more if he knows her to have been made from his flesh; also, as man in society is the head of the family, "in which each has his or her particular duty," it is fitting that the woman be formed out of him.[6]

---

[1] Thomas Aquinas, *Summa Theologica,* ed. English Dominican Province, 3 vols. (New York, 1947), I, 76, 1. For the summary of Thomas' views that follows I am indebted to K. E. Børresen, *Subordination et équivalence.*

[2] *ST* I, 91, 3; Børresen, p. 126.

[3] *ST* I, 92, 1; Børresen, p. 129.

[4] Ibid.

[5] *ST* I, 92, 1, ad 1; "Woman is said to be a misbegotten male, as being a product outside the purpose of nature considered in the individual case: but not against the purpose of universal nature" (*ST* I, 99, 2, ad 1).

[6] *ST* I, 92, 2.

Finally, as the Church takes her origin from Christ, so sacramentally it is proper that woman be formed of man. Her creation from his side rather than his head is a reminder that she is not to be despised.[7] The subordination and inferiority of Eve—and therefore of all womankind—to the male are thus established before the Fall in the order of God's original creation: first, by reason of the primacy of Adam's creation, who was not only first in time and the founder of the human race but also the material source of the first woman; and second, by reason of finality, for Adam displays the peculiar end and essence of human nature, intellectual activity, whereas Eve's finality is purely auxiliary and summed up in her bodily, generative function.

Despite this natural prelapsarian subordination, the male and female do share an essential equivalence in that God created the human race to know and love Him, and both sexes are thus marked by the *imago dei* (the image of God) and the possession of a rational soul.[8] As soon as this is said one must quickly add that Thomas follows Augustine in the view that the male possesses the image of God in a way different from and superior to the image found in the woman, using the analogy of the differences in degree between superior and inferior angels.[9] Ultimately this difference resides in the fact that the rational faculties appear more strongly in the male than in the female, a proposition that Thomas supports with the Aristotelian notion that the inferior quality and finality of the female body inevitably works a deleterious effect on woman's soul.[10] Her sexuality, which is identified with her essence as a woman, involves a weaker and more imperfect body, which in turn affects the intelligence upon which moral discernment is based.[11] The inequality between male and female relates thus to the moral as well as physical and intellectual realms, and it seems to be the woman's body that is the ultimate source of her inferiority and subordination to the male. In addition, even that which is peculiarly the woman's, the generative function, is inferior to the male equivalent, for the man is the active and fecund force, the woman but a passive and receptive instrument. On every level she is subordinate and auxiliary. It is significant that nowhere does Thomas discuss in an extended and complete fashion the inferior and subordinate nature of the female, simply because he assumes this state of affairs and therefore makes little effort to prove what all perceive as given.

The role of the prototypical woman Eve in the Fall of man worsens this natural subordination into the punishment of male domination. Yet a careful examination of Eve's role in the Fall deprives her even of the dignity of clear responsibility for her own situation. The essential sin of the first parents, pride, the desire to be like God, is the same for both, but the motivation was different, and the course of events assigns differing responsibility. Eve, rather than Adam,

---

[7] *ST* I, 92, 3.

[8] Børresen, p. 136.

[9] Børresen, p. 137.

[10] *ST* II–II, 70, 3, concl.; *ST* II–II, 156, 1, ad 1; Børresen, p. 143.

[11] Børresen, p. 143; e.g., the woman, like a child or a fool, may not take a valid judicial oath.

was approached by the serpent, for she was recognized as more credulous, easier to seduce and, as his mate, more capable of seducing the male.[12] Eve's inferior reasoning ability accounts for her actual belief that she could equal God, whereas Adam never really believed the serpent's promise, but acceded to the temptation out of hope that he might attain the knowledge of good and evil, and out of love for and solidarity with his spouse.[13] Adam's loyalty to Eve diminishes the gravity of his sin; his superior intellectual powers, however, make him more responsible for his act than Eve. Furthermore, in Adam the species of the human race fell, for Thomas feels that if Eve had fallen to the snake's temptation and Adam had resisted, there would have been no expulsion from Paradise.[14] Eve's role was instrumental but not decisive. On the other hand, Thomas argues that Eve's pride was more serious, her sin more grave, for she actually believed the snake, and she sinned against her neighbor as well as God in occasioning Adam's fall.[15] It would seem that Eve's sin was more grave than that of Adam, but somehow less effectual. From our perspective, she is denied even the "dignity" of being successful and independent in evil.

The punishment for the Fall which relates to human bisexuality differs according to the proper function of each sex. The male of the species, who in the original creation was responsible as the head of the family for its material support, must now procure bread by the sweat of his brow. The woman, whose punishment Thomas considered the more grave, suffered an aggravation of her natural state of subordination.[16] After the Fall she became subject to male domination, under which she must obey her husband even against her own will. Also, her peculiar function as aid in generation becomes a painful burden, with the introduction of the fatigue of pregnancy and the pain of childbearing. Even the woman who by reason of sterility avoids that pain is punished by the opprobrium brought on the female who does not fulfill her natural purpose.[17]

. . .

II

Marriage always gave the Christian Church great difficulty insofar as it empirically involved physical sex. Despite Thomas' Aristotelian naturalism, the married state never quite escaped the Pauline/patristic brush of dualist pessimism, for coitus was associated with concupiscence and irrationality—a disorder from both Greek and Christian viewpoints. Thus Thomas felt it necessary to insist that marriage was not a result of the Fall, but existed as an institution at creation for the purpose of fecundity, the multiplication of souls

---

[12] ST II–II, 165, 2, ad 1.

[13] ST II–II, 163, 4, concl.

[14] ST I–II, 81, 5, ad 2; Børresen, p. 174.

[15] ST II–II, 163, 4, concl.

[16] ST II–II, 163, 4, concl.

[17] ST II–II, 164, 2; Børresen, pp. 169–170. This punishment appropriate to each sex is, in addition to the general effect of the Fall, the loss of the gift of original justice, which entails mortality and a diminishing of the natural inclination to virtue.

to know and love God.[18] However, he agreed with Augustine that prelapsarian sexuality was rational, without passion, the man implanting his semen as the farmer sows his seed. But within this hypothetical prelapsarian marriage the female was still subordinate to the male, her end auxiliary, procreation. Only the extent and harshness of her submission was less; and as noted, the absence of lust in the procreative act was balanced by an absence of pain in childbirth. Significantly, Thomas follows Augustine in speculating that this paradisical copulation would occur without destroying the woman's hymen: her virginity would remain undisturbed. In this Thomas follows the patristic view that defloration is a corruption of the female body.[19]

It must first be noted that in this fallen world marriage was the least acceptable of the three states of life open to the woman, the first being the virginal religious life, the second continent widowhood, the third "if you must" marriage.[20] After the Fall, marriage became a remedy for the sin of lust, in addition to being the natural institution for the procreation and education of children to love and honor God. . . .

It must be remembered that the woman, defined with reference to her ultimate reason for being as an aid in reproduction, is more essentially involved in marriage than is the male. Her position in the marriage relationship is, however, subordinate and auxiliary . . .

. . .

III

We turn now to that better life through which the woman can in theory escape the natural subordination and inferiority to which she is ordained by her sex. That option is the virginal life, to which both males and females may be called by God for the pursuit of religious perfection while on earth. The monastic life, which is the highest institutional expression of the call to virginity, is also the single institutional reflection of the religious equivalence of the sexes. . . .

. . .

. . . Ultimately the Fathers of the early Christian centuries agreed that both sexes are created with a rational soul in the image of God, and accordingly, that both are called to the same end, life with God. Despite subordination on the level of creation, the order of salvation offers equality between the sexes. This was a new ideal in the late Hellenistic world, in which religion and philosophy often limited the heights of spiritual perfection to males. The startlingly prominent public role taken by women in the New Testament Church is probably reflective of the impact of this revolutionary Christian attitude in the first century of the Church's life. However, it is important to see how that theoretical

[18] *ST* I, 98, 1 and 2; Børresen, pp. 150–151.

[19] *ST* I, 98, 2, ad 4; Børresen, p. 153.

[20] Within the first two states the woman can escape the special penalty laid on the daughters of Eve—direct subordination to a male.

equivalence between the sexes on the religious level was from the first undercut by fundamentally androcentric conceptions. In the patristic world the very idealization of virginity, which made it possible for a woman to pursue a religious life equal to that of the male, free of male domination, contained within itself the heavy burden of fear of the female as the ever-present threat to continence that underlies much of patristic misogyny.[21] The association of the mind/flesh dualism with the male/female bipolarity . . . lays the groundwork for a different and unequal definition of virginity as it is applied to the female. Thus only the female, whose whole existence and finality are bound up in her auxiliary procreative function, must deny what the society defined as her nature in order to follow the religious life. . . . For the female, virginity is not an affirmation of her being as a woman but an assumption of the nature of the male, which is identified with the truly human: rationality, strength, courage, steadfastness, loyalty. . . . One might object that the ideal of virginity demanded of both men and women a denial of their sexuality, of fatherhood as well as motherhood. That is of course correct, but what I am saying is that the male, already defined in terms of a superior rationality, with its possibility of self-transcendence, was upon entering the religious life, in contrast to the woman, denying something quite literally external to his being. . . .

In another aspect of the theoretical realm the religious equivalence of male and female is fundamentally undermined by the Church's development of a rationale for the denial to the woman of Holy Orders. Here the maleness of God and the Incarnation provide the foundations for this aspect of female insufficiency, for as Christ's humanity was of necessity male, the instrument of his grace, the priest, corresponding to the instrumentality of His flesh, must also be male. Furthermore, ordination confers a superiority of rank that cannot be received by one who is by the order of creation in a state of subjection. Thus the woman, like the slave, may not validly receive Holy Orders.[22] As the Church lives in the world, it properly follows the laws of society with respect to the subordinate status of the female. These arguments reflect the fundamentally sociological character of much of Thomas' discussion of the prohibition of women in Holy Orders. They presuppose the patriarchal and hierarchical structures of a premodern society. Thomas never explicitly forbids the priesthood to women, nor does he say directly, as Bonaventura did, that because Christ was male, so also his priests must be men.[23] Indeed, in Thomas' discussion of baptism, in an emergency he allows a laywoman as well as a layman to baptize validly as Christ's minister, citing Galatians 3 that in Christ there is neither male nor

[21] *Reallexikon für Antike und Christentum* (Stuttgart, 1941 ff.), Lfrg. 58 (1970), "Frau," p. 258. It would be useful to explore comparatively instructions to male and female religious ascetics to determine if the female ascetic perceived the opposite sex with the same fear and even horror that is found in ascetic literature addressed to men.

[22] *ST* Suppl., 39, 1, concl.; Børresen, pp. 183–184. For a recent discussion of this position, see Joseph A. Wahl, *The Exclusion of Women from Holy Orders*, Studies in Sacred Theology, 2d Ser., No. 110. Catholic University of America (Washington, D.C., 1959).

[23] Børresen, p. 188.

female. However, a woman performs this office instrumentally, by virtue of Christ's power, not by virtue of her spiritual equivalence to a layman, and her subordinate status is symbolized by the fact that she can baptize without incurring sin only privately and in the absence of an available male.[24] Without doubt for many reasons, having perhaps most of all to do with ancient and subconscious cultic taboos, Thomas would have abhorred the idea of female priests, but given the overwhelmingly androcentric character of thirteenth-century society and theology, he was less insistent on the theological necessity of a male priesthood than he might have been.

. . .

V

. . . Medieval misogyny had many sources: for example the antifemale rationalist bias of classical antiquity, the strongly patriarchal traditions of a Germanic warrior society, sexual and cultic taboos common to many civilizations, and the sexual projections Freud has taught us to recognize. The deeply androcentric and misogynist character of the medieval concept of the woman cannot be wholly accounted for by reference to the realm of theological ideas, for society, psychology, and experience also played their roles. Comparative studies of medieval and other premodern societies reveal, despite important differences in religious ideology, extensive similarities in attitudes toward women, sex-role differentiation, and sexuality in general. Yet the evidence is overwhelming that the medieval Christian theological tradition and the symbols that it generated, many of which are still with us, did provide important stimuli and a convenient ideology for the dehumanization of the female sex. Despite the truly revolutionary implications of the biblical admonition, "There is neither male nor female, for ye are all one in Christ Jesus" (an equivalence graphically illustrated by the single initiation rite, baptism, alike for men and women), at every level, theological, legal, institutional, popular piety, that paradisical equivalence of souls was undermined by a deeply felt androcentrism and misogyny.

. . .

What is to be done? The first task is to make explicit the assumptions received from this tradition about male/female difference and hierarchy, and to expose with the help of historical understanding the now patently invalid intellectual foundations of these typologies. For example, have not the insights of the social sciences already called into question the implicitly rationalist definition of human nature by which the feeling and responding side of our being is denigrated and perceived as specifically feminine? The twentieth-century person may well believe himself to be free of Adam and Eve mythologies and the monastic imperative to virginity, yet still think and feel in terms of an identification of the mind/body dualism with the male/female bipolarity which supports our stereotypes of the passive, emotional, and seductive woman and

---

[24] *ST* III, 67, 4.

the rational, idealistic, and active male. Behind the recently popular discussion of male and female complementarity lie some very traditional symbolism and feelings about the "eternal feminine" which need to be brought into the open.[25] The woman and the man must be demythologized.

More difficult, and ultimately more important, will be the constructive work, the evolution of a new Christian anthropology that first takes seriously the biblical affirmation of the goodness of creation and affirms the positive role of human sexuality as a vehicle of human love and true mutuality. This anthropology for human liberation calls for the building of a new model of sex identity which permits individual personality to flourish without the constraints of sex stereotypes or hierarchical power relationships.

For this reconstruction it will be necessary to affirm the fundamental moral equivalence of the sexes, not simply within the sexual relationship, as did the medieval church, but also in the world beyond the family, in which world, with fewer children and longer life spans, modern men and women are destined to spend more than half of their lives. This means that a new anthropology will be grounded in a recognition of the role of work in human self-fulfillment and the right, therefore, of women as well as men to meaningful work. In the medieval tradition work was a punishment for the Fall, assigned particularly to the sons of Adam; in Protestant capitalist societies work has become an alienating exploitive mode for dominating nature, both human and inanimate. The women's movement could well encourage the basic reconstitution of both economic structures and attitudes toward work, which would make possible a new balance between familial nurturing and socially productive work in the lives of women and men who share these roles and are not limited by their sex to a life of the hearth or the hunt.

A third aspect of a new anthropology will reside in the recognition that the categories underlying the theologians' or the psychologists' accounts of sex difference and role can be as time-bound as the dogmas of Aristotelian biology. A Christian view of the nature of woman and man needs to be dynamic and prophetic, not antiscientific, but also not taken in by the faith systems of the Freudians or their successors.

The medieval theological tradition does have, as we have seen, a positive core that can contribute to a new anthropology for free people, female and male. The medieval Church insisted in theory on a true mutuality and moral equivalence between the sexes in the area of sexual fidelity within marriage. In this regard the Church opposed the then newly emergent ethic of courtly love and condemned the romantic view of a sexual relationship based on "feelings" rather than on mutual commitment and self-giving. Some careful thought will reveal that the idea of the woman as sex object—idealized, even unattainable, but existing ultimately for the gratification of the male sense of

---

[25] See, for example, F. X. Arnold, *Woman and Man, Their Nature and Mission* (Freiburg and London, 1963), p. 50: "The focal point of woman's nature is her heart, her affections and emotions. Man's focal point on the other hand is more in his intelligence."

well-being—has important origins in the medieval courtly love tradition.[26] That tradition was condemned by the Church out of the conviction that mutual fidelity, reflecting the ultimate value of each partner as a child of God, is the only basis for the relationship between man and woman in marriage. In some sense, a woman never belonged wholly to her husband, was never completely defined in terms of her sexuality, for there was always the prior bond of the soul to God, in the context of which all other commitments were judged, the practice of medieval canonists notwithstanding. This medieval condemnation of the romantic ethic is a strong instance within the tradition of the rejection of the concept of woman as a purely sexual being. Insofar as the "new morality" sanctions the abandonment of a relationship when it ceases to please, or feel good, the medieval tradition opposes that reduction of the human being to a sensual instrumentality with an insistence that neither partner, female or male, exists to be used for the gratification of the other.

The eschatological dimension of the medieval theology of the sexes could also be of interest to those who seek to formulate a new anthropology. In the simplest of terms Thomas tells us that in Paradise all the inequalities and subordination of the order of creation shall be overcome. There will still be hierarchy, but it will be an ordering by merit, rather than by sex or status. So much of Christian eschatology has been secularized and brought down to earth. If one must have superiors and subordinates, why not on the basis of merit?

But is this hierarchical universe, with its fixed and ranked functions and orders, a positive basis for a new anthropology? Is it not rather of our inheritances from the past the most pervasive and difficult to bring into line with the needs of twentieth-century persons in their individuality and society? It is easy to find recent literature within the Christian theological tradition that insists on a nondualist anthropology and on an unambiguous moral equivalence of the sexes, but dwells at the same time upon the differences between women and men that imply not only separate function but also an unambiguous superordination and subordination, grounded paradigmatically in the relationship of God to his creatures. Thus Karl Barth has spoken of man and woman as an A and a B; in respect of order woman is B, ". . . and therefore behind and subordinate to man."[27] The problem here is not a medieval anthropology but a medieval doctrine of creation and sociology, by which a specific order of precedence was assigned by divine fiat to man and woman, which order we are yet bound to maintain. There is indeed implied an inadequate definition of human nature: static, ahistorical, hierarchical, Platonizing in its assumption of ontologically fixed relationships between the sexes. The reader will pardon me if under every bush of "complementarity" I espy this hierarchical cosmos, this Great Chain of Being, in which difference becomes rationalized subordination.

[26] John F. Benton, "Clio and Venus: An Historical View of Medieval Love," *The Meaning of Courtly Love*, ed. F. X. Newman (Albany, N.Y., 1968), p. 35: "Courtesy was created by men for their own satisfaction, and it emphasized a woman's role as an object, sexual or otherwise."

[27] Karl Barth, *Church Dogmatics* (Edinburgh, 1961), III, Part 4, p. 171.

In conclusion, despite this ambiguous legacy, the medieval Christian tradition did not only speak of the woman's spiritual equivalence with her brother. The Church provided an institution, and a calling, the monastic life, which symbolized and often gave concrete opportunity to exercise that spiritual equivalence in which all persons, female and male, are called alike to Christian perfection. Only within those portions of Christendom which after the sixteenth century renounced the dual ethic of monasticism and celibacy was the woman wholly limited in her Christian vocation to the home, to her role as procreator and nurturer. However often the medieval commitment to spiritual equivalence was undermined by androcentric and patriarchal assumptions, the institution of monasticism was for the Christian woman a real and concrete option, a little world occasionally run by and for women. She had an alternative to the authority of father and husband. She had a choice.

part three:

THE APPEAL TO REASON AND EXPERIENCE

... women have not by nature equal right with men ...
—Benedictus de Spinoza

... the very idea of queendoms fulfills an ancient need in man and answers an atavistic longing for the old days of feminine authority ...
—Elizabeth Gould Davis

... the Rule ... naturally falls to the Man's share, as the abler and the stronger.
—John Locke

O that woman may arise in her dignity as an immortal creature, and speak, think and act as unto God, and not unto man!
—Sarah M. Grimké

Nature herself has decreed that woman, both for herself and her children, should be at the mercy of man's judgment.
—Jean-Jacques Rousseau

There is a paradox at the heart of Rousseau's account of social relations. To be humanly happy we need others. But if we need others we are lost.
—Elizabeth Rapaport

> *Women, I allow, may have different duties to fulfill; but they are* human *duties, and the principles that should regulate the discharge of them, I sturdily maintain, must be the same.*
> —Mary Wollstonecraft

> *Mary Wollstonecraft's arguments, dated though they should be, have more than historical importance, for her particular battle has not altogether been won.*
> —Carolyn W. Korsmeyer

As the Middle Ages blend into modern times, biblical authority gives way to reason and experience as the final arbiters in the matter of woman's alleged inferiority. Spinoza's approach is essentially rational. He decides *a priori* the conditions that would prevail if woman were man's equal and then proceeds to consult experience, which reveals an absence of those conditions. The experience of Elizabeth Gould Davis, interestingly enough, in the wake of several centuries of anthropological research and speculation, causes her to question some of the very matters that Spinoza takes for granted.

Although John Locke refers extensively to the Bible in elaborating his views on woman, his main thrust is political. His aim is to protest against prevailing practices, both domestic and civil. Most of what Locke says about the sexes is found in *Two Treatises of Government,* intended primarily as a response to a lesser-known work, *Patriarcha non Monarcha,* by Sir Robert Filmer, who relies heavily on biblical authority. Locke's use of biblical allusions appears to be at least partially an attempt to meet his opponent on his own ground. And many of the passages that Filmer cites most frequently are interpreted in a decidedly different manner by Locke—a manner much more like that of one of America's earliest feminists, Sarah M. Grimké.

It has been suggested that Rousseau's views on woman may have stemmed not from experience but from a lack of it—that in Sophia, the ideal wife for the ideal man in his novel *Émile,* he is depicting the woman for whom he had always longed in vain. But had he found her, he might have been little better off. For as Elizabeth Rapaport suggests, the dependence that characterizes the love relation as Rousseau conceives it invariably brings unhappiness.

In contrast to Rousseau's arguments, Mary Wollstonecraft's are well grounded in experience and therefore, in her own view, are superior to his. Carolyn W. Korsmeyer finds Wollstonecraft's views to be still quite timely.

✦6 *Benedictus de Spinoza*

Baruch de Spinoza (1632–1677) was born in Amsterdam, his Jewish ancestors having been driven out of the Iberian peninsula by the Spanish Inquisition. Desiring a broader education than that traditionally given to boys of his faith, young Baruch enrolled in the school of one Francis van den Ende for the purpose of studying Latin. Legend has it that the young man fell in love with the van den Ende daughter, Clara Maria, who, the account goes, rejected him for a fellow pupil named Kerkering, who had found the way to her heart with a string of pearls. However that may have been, at the van den Ende school Spinoza did become acquainted with the works of Descartes and other philosophers whose views, to the consternation of his Jewish associates, led him to modify his orthodoxy. He was reported to the synagogue authorities, by whom he was eventually expelled for his heretical notions. He left Amsterdam for various Dutch villages and ultimately The Hague, he assumed the Latinized version of his given name, he ground lenses for a living, and he devoted himself as completely as possible to philosophy. In 1677 he died of consumption, a condition aggravated if not caused by the dust from the grinding of the lenses.

If it was the reassessment of Spinoza's views on religion that led the Jewish community to expel him, it was doubtless, at least in part, his expulsion that led him to reassess his views on woman. Traditionally Judaism has taught that woman is inferior to man and that conjugal union is a duty, not a pleasure. Jewish women sat—as the Orthodox still do—in a separate section of the synagogue, behind lattices, with veiled heads and downcast eyes. But in some of the Protestant circles in seventeenth-century Holland a new breed of woman was emerging. Women were becoming religious leaders, authors, educators. Antoinette Bourignon, the Flemish Quietist, was attracting followers not only in the Netherlands but in France and Scotland as well. Anna Maria van Schurman, having espoused the views of Jean de Labadie, was writing the definitive exposition of his ideas. And Clara Maria van den Ende was teaching in her father's school. It is little wonder that, attracted to his pedagogue's daughter as Spinoza later claims to have been, he might have wished to examine more fully the question of woman's proper role in society.

Although in the end his conservatism won out, Spinoza's approach to the problem of woman was typically historical and logical, not emotional. His major work, the Ethics, is developed like a series of geometric proofs, complete with axioms, definitions, and theorems. This method of exposition, also used to a lesser extent in other works, including the unfinished Tractatus Politicus, he believed to be the only means of arriving at the certitude that he wished to claim for his system. By this means he sought to explain the nature of God, the makeup of the world, the constitution of the human being. By this means he probed the question of woman's allegedly inferior nature.

89

From *A Political Treatise*

OF DEMOCRACY

. . .

But, perhaps, someone will ask, whether women are under men's authority by nature or institution? For if it has been by mere institution, then we had no reason compelling us to exclude women from government. But if we consult experience itself, we shall find that the origin of it is in their weakness. For there has never been a case of men and women reigning together, but wherever on the earth men are found, there we see that men rule, and women are ruled, and that on this plan, both sexes live in harmony. But on the other hand, the Amazons, who are reported to have held rule of old, did not suffer men to stop in their country, but reared only their female children, killing the males to whom they gave birth. But if by nature women were equal to men, and were equally distinguished by force of character and ability, in which human power and therefore human right chiefly consist; surely among nations so many and different some would be found, where both sexes rule alike, and others, where men are ruled by women, and so brought up, that they can make less use of their abilities. And since this is nowhere the case, one may assert with perfect propriety, that women have not by nature equal right with men: but that they necessarily give way to men, and that thus it cannot happen, that both sexes should rule alike, much less that men should be ruled by women. But if we further reflect upon human passions, how men, in fact, generally love women merely from the passion of lust, and esteem their cleverness and wisdom in proportion to the excellence of their beauty, and also how very ill-disposed men are to suffer the women they love to show any sort of favour to others, and other facts of this kind, we shall easily see that men and women cannot rule alike without great hurt to peace. But of this enough.

❧Elizabeth Gould Davis

Elizabeth Gould Davis, a graduate of Randolph-Macon College and of the University of Kentucky, was at the time of her death in 1974 a librarian in Sarasota, Florida. In The First Sex she undertook a major task: the proof that the contribution of women to history has been more significant than that of men. She was dedicated to the proposition that women are neither inferior nor equal to men, but superior to them. Davis approached the matter of sovereignty not quantitatively, as Spinoza had, but qualitatively, arguing empirically that women make the best rulers inasmuch as two of their attributes, lenity and moderation, make them naturally superior to male monarchs.

From *The First Sex*

THE NATURAL SUPERIORITY OF QUEENS

John Stuart Mill took note of the fact of the superiority of queens over kings and asked why female monarchs, although they had been a minority in historical times, had invariably proved better rulers than kings. Even that eighteenth-century misogynist Montesquieu conceded that women made the best rulers: "Their very weaknesses [*sic*] generally give them more lenity and moderation, qualifications fitter for good administration than severity and roughness."

This strikes one as somewhat odd reasoning, but it shows that in the eighteenth century, just as today, women's virtues, "lenity and moderation," are characterized as "weaknesses" rather than as the strong and desirable qualities they really are, while men's "severity and roughness" are made virtues—which they are not. As Ashley Montagu says, unless men forego aggressive severity and roughness and adopt some of woman's "weaknesses," civilization is doomed.

As an example of woman's natural talent for rulership and administration in modern times we need go no further than Mill's own land, England. In the history of that great country the greatest eras bear women's names: the Elizabethan Age of Discovery and Expansion, both geographical and intellectual; the age of Queen Anne, when "reason" triumphed in the rapid advancement of the sciences, arts, and letters; and the Victorian Age of the Pax Britannica.

Russia's greatest period prior to the Revolution of 1917 coincided with the reign of a queen, Catherine the Great. And Spain under Isabella achieved the position of world leadership it held in the fifteenth and sixteenth centuries. It was during the long regency of Queen Catherine de Medici in the sixteenth century that France rose to her status as the cultural and intellectual center of the world—a status maintained down to our own time. "Women rulers," writes Montesquieu, "succeed alike in moderate and despotic governments, as the example of England and Russia show; and in Africa and the Indies they are very easy under female administration."

Many writers have begrudgingly noted this phenomenon and have attributed it to the fact that queens have better advisers than kings!—which at least merits them a high rating, as adviser-pickers, if nothing else. The more likely answer, however, as Graves, Briffault, Bachofen, James, Fuller, and others have observed, is that men respond better to women's rule—that the very idea of queendoms fulfills an ancient need in man and answers an atavistic longing for the old days of feminine authority, the golden age of queendoms, when peace and justice prevailed on earth and the gods of war had not been born.

☙☚7 *John Locke*

John Locke was born in Somerset in 1632. Bereft of his mother at an early age, he was brought up very strictly by his Puritan father, whom he loved and respected. Locke was educated first at Westminster, then at Christchurch, Oxford, where he formed his first sentimental attachments to young women. Chief among these women was Anne Evelegh, the niece or daughter of an Oxford clergyman; then came someone identified in the correspondence only as P. E. But John Locke never married.

A man of diversified interests, Locke became active in medicine, in education, in diplomacy, and in politics. He was befriended by Anthony Ashley Cooper, later the Earl of Shaftesbury, who entrusted to him the education of his son and appointed him to high public offices. As a result of his participation in various preparations for the Glorious Revolution of 1688, Locke was forced to go into exile soon after Shaftesbury died in 1683. During his stay in Holland he devoted himself to philosophy, completing his major work, An Essay Concerning Human Understanding. In 1689, after the Revolution, he was able to return to England and resume his political career. When his health failed he retired to Oates, the Essex estate of Sir Francis Masham, where he received the tender care of Lady Masham and her stepdaughter, Esther. Locke died in 1704 at Oates.

In Two Treatises of Government, published in response to a work entitled Patriarcha non Monarcha by Sir Robert Filmer (more often referred to in the rebuttal as "our Author" or simply "our A"), Locke drew from the relationship between husband and wife a premise from which he argued against the doctrine of the divine right of kings. In Locke's day, although love matches were becoming increasingly popular, marriages were still usually arranged by the parents of the bride. But however the union may have been entered into, the end result was the same: the seventeenth-century Englishman was vested with full control over his wife and any properties she might have had before she entered into wedlock, even her dowry. His will was law, and he had the legal right to beat her at his pleasure—so long as he used a stick no thicker than his thumb. And whereas the normal punishment for murder was hanging, a woman who killed her husband was burned alive. Locke cried out against these inequities and urged a severe restriction on the power of a husband over his wife.

Locke was an empiricist. At birth, he held, the human mind is a tabula rasa, a blank slate, subsequently to be written on by sensation and reflection. There are no innate ideas, and authority, even that of the Bible, is suspect. One might expect, then, that Locke would arrive at the concept of woman's nature as he claimed that one arrives at any other general idea, by combining ideas of particular women, leaving out their peculiarities, separating, relating. In actual practice, however, Locke not infrequently relied on the authority of the Bible, his caution to his readers not to do so notwithstanding.

Inasmuch as Adam as well as Eve sinned in the Garden of Eden, Locke inferred that the superiority of man over woman is accidental, not essential. Thus *men and women have comparable conjugal rights, the authority going to the husband only on the presumably rare occasions when there is disagreement between the two. And by no means is a husband possessed of any real power over his wife—certainly not the power of life and death.*

From *Two Treatises of Government*

BOOK 1, CHAPTER 5

Of Adam's Title to Sovereignty by the Subjection of Eve

... [W]e find our author build his monarchy of Adam on ... Gen. iii. 26: "And thy desire shall be to thy husband, and he shall rule over thee." "Here we have," says he, "the original grant of government," from whence he concludes, in the following part of the page (O., 244) "that the supreme power is settled in the fatherhood, and limited to one kind of government—that is to monarchy;" for let his premises be what they will, this is always the conclusion; let but "rule" in any text be but once named, and presently "absolute monarchy" is by Divine right established. If any one will but carefully read our author's own reasoning from these words (O., 244), and consider, among other things, "the line and posterity of Adam," as he there brings them in, he will find some difficulty to make sense of what he says; but we will allow this at present to his peculiar way of writing, and consider the force of the text in hand. The words are the curse of God upon the woman for having been the first and forwardest in the disobedience; and if we will consider the occasion of what God says here to our first parents, that He was denouncing judgment and declaring His wrath against them both for their disobedience, we cannot suppose that this was the time wherein God was granting Adam prerogatives and privileges, investing him with dignity and authority, elevating him to dominion and monarchy; for though as a helper in the temptation as well as a partner in the transgression, Eve was laid below him, and so he had accidentally a superiority over her for her greater punishment; yet he, too, had his share in the Fall as well as the sin, and was laid lower, as may be seen in the following verses; and it would be hard to imagine that God, in the same breath, should make him universal monarch over all mankind, and a day-labourer for his life. Turn him out of Paradise "to till the ground" (ver. 23), and at the same time advance him to a throne and all the privileges and ease of absolute power.

This was not a time when Adam could expect any favours, any grant of privileges from his offended Maker. If this be the "original grant of government," as our author tells us, and Adam was now made monarch, whatever Sir Robert would have him, it is plain God made him but a very poor monarch, such an one as our author himself would have counted it no great privilege to be. God sets him to work for his living, and seems rather to give him a spade into his hand to subdue the earth, than a sceptre to rule over its inhabitants. "In the sweat of thy face thou shalt eat thy bread," says God to him (ver. 19). This was unavoidable, may it perhaps be answered, because he was yet without subjects, and had nobody to work for him; but afterwards, living as he did above 900 years, he might have people enough whom he might command to work for him. "No," says God, "not only whilst thou art without other help save thy wife, but as long as thou livest shalt thou live by thy labour." "In the sweat of thy face shalt thou eat thy bread, till thou return unto the ground, for out of it wast thou taken; for dust thou art, and unto dust shalt thou return" (ver. 19). It will perhaps be answered again in favour of our author, that these words are not spoken personally to Adam, but in him, as their representative to all mankind, this being a curse upon mankind because of the Fall.

God, I believe, speaks differently from men, because He speaks with more truth, more certainty; but when He vouchsafes to speak to men, I do not think He speaks differently from them in crossing the rules of language in use amongst them; this would not be to condescend to their capacities, when He humbles Himself to speak to them, but to lose His design in speaking what, thus spoken, they could not understand. And yet thus must we think of God, if the interpretations of Scripture necessary to maintain our author's doctrine must be received for good; for, by the ordinary rules of language, it will be very hard to understand what God says; if what He speaks here, in the singular number, to Adam, must be understood to be spoken to all mankind, and what He says in the plural number (Gen. i. 26 and 28), must be understood of Adam alone, exclusive of all others; and what He says to Noah and his sons jointly must be understood to be meant to Noah alone (Gen. ix.).

Further, it is to be noted, that these words here of Gen. iii. 16, which our author calls "the original grant of government," were not spoken to Adam, neither, indeed, was there any grant in them made to Adam, but a punishment laid upon Eve; and if we will take them as they were directed in particular to her, or in her, as a representative to all other women, they will at most concern the female sex only, and import no more but that subjection they should ordinarily be in to their husbands; but there is here no more law to oblige a woman to such a subjection, if the circumstances either of her condition or contract with her husband should exempt her from it, than there is that she should bring forth her children in sorrow and pain if there could be found a remedy for it, which is also a part of the same curse upon her, for the whole verse runs thus: "Unto the woman He said, I will greatly multiply thy sorrow and thy conception; in sorrow thou shalt bring forth children, and thy desire shall be to thy husband, and he shall rule over thee." It would, I think, have been a hard matter for anybody but our author to have found out a grant of "monarchical government to Adam" in these words, which were neither spoke to nor of him; neither will any one, I suppose, by these words think the weaker sex, as by a law so subjected to the curse contained in them, that it is their duty not to endeavour to avoid it. And will any one say that Eve, or any other woman, sinned if she were brought to bed without those multiplied pains God threatens her here with, or that either of our Queens, Mary or Elizabeth, had they married any of their subjects, had been by this text put into a political subjection to him, or that he thereby should have had "monarchical rule" over her? God in this text gives not, that I see, any authority to Adam over Eve, or men over their wives, but only foretells what should be the woman's lot, how by His Providence He would order it so that she should be subject to her husband, as we see that generally the laws of mankind and customs of nations have ordered it so, and there is, I grant, a foundation in Nature for it.

Thus when God says of Jacob and Esau that "the elder should serve the younger" (Gen. xxv. 23), nobody supposes that God hereby made Jacob Esau's sovereign, but foretold what should *de facto* come to pass.

But if these words here spoke to Eve must needs be understood as a law to bind her and all other women to subjection, it can be no other subjection than what every wife owes her husband, and then if this be the "original grant of government" and the "foundation of monarchical power," there will be as many monarchs as there are husbands. If therefore these words give any power to Adam, it can be only a conjugal power, not political—the power that every husband hath to order the things of private concernment in his family, as proprietor of the goods and land there, and to have his will take place in all things of their common concernment before that of his wife; but not a political power of life and death over her, much less over anybody else.

· · ·

BOOK 2, CHAPTER 7

Of Political or Civil Society

God, having made man such a creature that, in His own judgment, it was not good for him to be alone, put him under strong obligations of necessity, convenience, and inclination, to drive him into society, as well as fitted him with understanding and language to continue and enjoy it. The first society was between man and wife, which gave beginning to that between parents and children, to which, in time, that between master and servant came to be added. And though all these might, and commonly did, meet together and make up but one family, wherein the master or mistress of it had some sort of rule proper to a family, each of these, or all together, came short of "political society," as we shall see if we consider the different ends, ties, and bounds of each of these.

Conjugal society is made by a voluntary compact between man and woman, and though it consist chiefly in such a communion and right in one another's bodies as is necessary to its chief end, procreation, yet it draws with it mutual support and assistance, and a communion of interests too, as necessary not only to unite their care and affection, but also necessary to their common offspring, who have a right to be nourished and maintained by them till they are able to provide for themselves.

For the end of conjunction between male and female being not barely procreation, but the continuation of the species, this conjunction betwixt male and female ought to last, even after procreation, so long as is necessary to the nourishment and support of the young ones, who are to be sustained by those that got them till they are able to shift and provide for themselves. This rule, which the infinite wise Maker hath set to the works of His hands, we find the inferior creatures steadily obey. In those viviparous animals which feed on grass the conjunction between male and female lasts no longer than the very act of copulation, because the teat of the dam being sufficient to nourish the young till it be able to feed on grass, the male only begets, but concerns not himself for the female or young, to whose sustenance he can contribute nothing. But in beasts of prey the conjunction lasts longer, because the dam, not being able well to subsist herself and nourish her numerous offspring by her own prey alone (a more laborious as well as more dangerous way of living than by feeding on grass), the assistance of the male is necessary to the maintenance of their common family, which cannot subsist till they are able to prey for themselves, but by the joint care of male and female. The same is be observed in all birds (except some domestic ones, where plenty of food excuses the cock from feeding and taking care of the young brood), whose young, needing food in the nest, the cock and hen continue mates till the young are able to use their wings and provide for themselves.

And herein, I think, lies the chief, if not the only reason, why the male and female in mankind are tied to a longer conjunction than other creatures—viz., because the female is capable of conceiving, and, *de facto,* is commonly with child again, and brings forth too a new birth, long before the former is out of a dependency for support on his parents' help and able to shift for himself, and has all the assistance [that] is due to him from his parents, whereby the father, who is bound to take care for those he hath begot, is under an obligation to continue in conjugal society with the same woman longer than other creatures, whose young, being able to subsist of themselves before the time of procreation returns again, the conjugal bond dissolves of itself, and they are at liberty till Hymen, at his usual anniversary season, summons them again to choose new mates. Wherein one cannot but admire the wisdom of the great Creator, who, having given to man an ability to lay up for the future as well as supply the present necessity, hath made it necessary that society of man and wife should be more lasting than of male and female amongst other creatures, that so their industry might be encouraged, and their interests better united, to make provision and lay up goods for their common issue, which uncertain mixture, or easy and frequent solutions of conjugal society, would mightily disturb.

But though these are ties upon mankind which make the conjugal bonds more firm and lasting in a man than the other species of animals, yet it would give one reason to inquire why this compact, where procreation and education are secured and inheritance taken care for may not be made determinable, either by consent, or at a certain time, or upon certain conditions, as well as any other voluntary compacts, there being no necessity, in the nature of the thing, nor to the ends of it, that it should always be for life—I mean, to such as are under no restraint of any positive law which ordains all such contracts to be perpetual.

But the husband and wife, though they have but one common concern, yet having different understandings, will unavoidably sometimes have different wills too. It therefore being necessary that the last determination (*i.e.*, the rule) should be placed somewhere, it naturally falls to the man's share as the abler and the stronger. But this, reaching but to the things of their common interest and property, leaves the wife in the full and true possession of what by contract is her peculiar right, and at least gives the husband no more power over her than she has over his life; the power of the husband being so far from that of an absolute monarch that the wife has, in many cases, a liberty to separate from him where natural right or their contract allows it, whether that contract be made by themselves in the state of Nature or by the customs or laws of the country they live in, and the children, upon such separation, fall to the father or mother's lot as such contract does determine.

For all the ends of marriage being to be obtained under politic government, as well as in the state of Nature, the civil magistrate doth not abridge the right or power of either, naturally necessary to those ends—viz., procreation and mutual support and assistance whilst they are together, but only decides any controversy that may arise between man and wife about them. If it were otherwise, and that absolute sovereignty and power of life and death naturally belonged to the husband, and were necessary to the society between man and wife, there could be no matrimony in any of these countries where the husband is allowed no such absolute authority. But the ends of matrimony requiring no such power in the husband, it was not at all necessary to it. The condition of conjugal society put it not in him; but whatsoever might consist with procreation and support of the children till they could shift for themselves—mutual assistance, comfort, and maintenance—might be varied and regulated by that contract which first united them in that society, nothing being necessary to any society that is not necessary to the ends for which it is made.

. . .

✺Sarah M. Grimké

Sarah M. Grimké was the elder of the two famous Grimké sisters who were active in the Abolitionist movement in nineteenth-century America. Having taken the platform in opposition to slavery, they were soon compelled to defend this "unladylike" behavior and found themselves among the first generation of American feminists. In a series of letters addressed to the president of the Boston Female Anti-Slavery Society in 1837, Sarah Grimké aired many of the same problems that had concerned Locke more than a century before, and quite frequently she arrived at similar conclusions. Grimké regarded marriage primarily as a sacrament rather than a legal contract, and like Locke she relied on biblical authority to assert the basic equality of the sexes. She, too, regarded the "curse" placed on woman—that is, woman's subjection to her husband—as a prophecy, not a judgment, and insisted on an egalitarian interpretation of the marriage vows.

From *Letters on the Equality of the Sexes and the Condition of Woman*

LETTER XIII

Relation of Husband and Wife

Brookline, 9th Mo., 1837.

My Dear Sister,—Perhaps some persons may wonder that I should attempt to throw out my views on the important subject of marriage, and may conclude that I am altogether disqualified for the task, because I lack experience. However, I shall not undertake to settle the specific duties of husbands and wives, but only to exhibit opinions based on the word of God, and formed from a little knowledge of human nature, and close observation of the working of generally received notions respecting the dominion of man over woman.

When Jehovah ushered into existence man, created in his own image, he instituted marriage as a part of paradisiacal happiness: it was a *divine ordination,* not a civil contract. God established it, and man, except by special permission, has no right to annul it. There can be no doubt that the creation of Eve perfected the happiness of Adam; hence, our all-wise and merciful Father made her as he made Adam in his own image after his likeness, crowned her with glory and honor, and placed in her hand, as well as in his, the sceptre of dominion over the whole lower creation. Where there was perfect equality, and the same ability to receive and comprehend divine truth, and to obey divine injunctions, there could be no superiority. If God had placed Eve under the guardianship of Adam, after having endowed her, as richly as him, with moral perceptions, intellectual faculties, and spiritual apprehensions, he would at once have interposed a fallible being between her and her Maker. He could not, in simple consistency with himself, have done this; for the Bible teems with instructions not to put any confidence in man.

The passage on which the generally received opinion, that husbands are invested by divine command with authority over their wives, . . . is a prediction; and I am confirmed in this belief, because the same language is used to Cain respecting Abel. The text is obscure; but on a comparison of it with subsequent events, it appears to me that it was a prophecy of the dominion which Cain would usurp over his brother, and which issued in the murder of Abel. It could not allude to any thing but physical dominion, because Cain had already exhibited those evil passions which subsequently led him to become an assassin.

. . . [M]an has exercised the most unlimited and brutal power over woman, in the peculiar character of husband,—a word in most countries synonymous with tyrant. I shall not . . . adduce any . . . proofs of the fulfillment of that prophecy, 'He will rule over thee,' from the history of heathen nations, but just glance at the condition of woman in the relation of wife in Christian countries.

'Previous to the introduction of the religion of Jesus Christ, the state of society was wretchedly diseased. The relation of the sexes to each other had become so gross in its manifested forms, that it was difficult to perceive the pure conservative principle in its inward essence.' Christianity came in, at this juncture, with its hallowed influence, and has without doubt tended to lighten the yoke of bondage, to purify the manners, and give the spiritual in some degree an empire over the animal nature. Still, that state which was designed by God to increase the happiness of woman as well as man, often proves the means of lessening her comfort, and degrading her into the mere machine of another's convenience and pleasure. Woman, instead of being elevated by her union with man, which might be expected from an alliance with a superior being, is in reality lowered. She generally loses her individuality, her independent character, her moral being. She becomes absorbed into him, and henceforth is looked at, and acts through the medium of her husband.

In the wealthy classes of society, and those who are in comfortable circumstances, women are exempt from great corporeal exertion, and are protected by public opinion, and by the genial influence of Christianity, from much physical ill treatment. Still, there is a vast amount of secret suffering endured, from the forced submission of women to the opinions and whims of their husbands. Hence they are frequently driven to use deception, to compass their ends. They are early taught that to appear to yield, is the only way to govern. Miserable sophism! I deprecate such sentiments, as being peculiarly hostile to the dignity of woman. If she submits, let her do it openly, honorably, not to gain her point, but as a matter of Christian duty. But let her beware how she permits her husband to be her conscience-keeper. On all moral and religious subjects, she is bound to think and to act for herself. Where confidence and love exist, a wife will naturally converse with her husband as with her dearest friend, on all that interests her heart, and there will be a perfectly free interchange of sentiment; but *she is no more bound to be governed by his judgment,* than he is by hers. They are standing on the same platform of human rights, are equally under the government of God, and accountable to him, and him alone.

I have sometimes been astonished and grieved at the servitude of women, and at the little idea many of them seem to have of their own moral existence and responsibilities. A woman who is asked to sign a petition for the abolition of slavery in the District of Columbia, or to join a society for the purpose of carrying forward the annihilation of American slavery, or any other great reformation, not unfrequently replies, 'My husband does not approve of it.' She merges her rights and her duties in her husband, and thus virtually chooses him for a savior and a king, and rejects Christ as her Ruler and Redeemer. I know some women are very glad of so convenient a pretext to shield themselves from the performance of duty; but there are others, who, under a mistaken view of their obligations as wives, submit conscientiously to this species of oppression, and go mourning on their way, for want of that holy fortitude, which would enable them to fulfill their duties as moral and responsible beings, without reference to poor fallen man. O that woman may arise in her dignity as an immortal creature, and speak, think and act as unto God, and not unto man!

There is, perhaps, less bondage of mind among the poorer classes, because their sphere of duty is more contracted, and they are deprived of the means of intellectual culture, and of the opportunity of exercising their judgment, on many moral subjects of deep interest and of vital importance. Authority is called into exercise by resistance, and hence there will be mental bondage only in proportion as the faculties of mind are evolved, and woman feels herself as a rational and intelligent being, on a footing with man. But women, among the lowest classes of society, so far as my observation has extended, suffer intensely from the brutality of their husbands. Duty as well as inclination has led me, for many years, into the abodes of poverty and sorrow, and I have been amazed at the treatment which women receive at the hands of those, who arrogate to themselves the epithet of *protectors*. Brute force, the law of violence, rules to a great extent in the poor man's domicil; and woman is little more than his drudge. They are less under the supervision of public opinion, less under the restraints of education, and unaided or unbiased by the refinements of polished society. Religion, wherever it exists, supplies the place of all these; but the real cause of woman's degradation and suffering in married life is to be found in the erroneous notion of her inferiority to man; and never will she be rightly regarded by herself, or others, until this opinion, so derogatory to the wisdom and mercy of God, is exploded, and woman arises in all the majesty of her womanhood, to claim those rights which are inseparable from her existence as an immortal, intelligent and responsible being.

Independent of the fact, that Jehovah could not, consistently with his character as the King, the Lawgiver, and the Judge of his people, give the reins of government over woman into the hands of man, I find that all his commands, all his moral laws, are addressed to women as well as to men. When he assembled Israel at the foot of Mount Sinai, to issue his commandments, we may reasonably suppose he gave all the precepts, which he considered necessary for the government of moral beings. Hence we find that God says,—'Honor thy father and thy mother,' and he enforces this command by severe penalties upon those who transgress it: 'He that smiteth his father, or his mother, shall surely be put to death'—'He that curseth his father, or his mother, shall surely be put to death'—Ex. 21:15, 17. But in the decalogue, there is no direction given to women to obey their husbands: both are commanded to have no other God but Jehovah, and not to bow down, or serve any other. When the Lord Jesus delivered his sermon on the Mount, full of the practical precepts of religion, he did not issue any command to wives to obey their husbands. When he is speaking on the subject of divorce, Mark 16:11, 12, he places men and women on the same ground. And the Apostle, 1st Cor. 7:12, 13, speaking of the duties of the Corinthian wives and husbands, who had embraced Christianity, to their unconverted partners, points out the same path to both, although our translators have made a distinction. 'Let him not put her away,' 12—'Let her not leave him,' 13—is precisely the same in the original. If man is constituted the governor of woman, he must be her God; and the sentiment expressed to me lately, by a married man, is perfectly correct: 'In my opinion,' said he, 'the greatest excellence to which a married woman can attain, is to worship her husband.' He was a professor of religion—his wife a lovely and intelligent woman. He only spoke out what thousands think and act. Women are indebted to Milton for giving to this false notion, 'confirmation strong as proof of holy writ.' His Eve is embellished with every personal grace, to gratify the eye of her admiring husband; but he seems to have furnished the mother of mankind with just intelligence enough to comprehend her supposed inferiority to Adam, and to yield unresisting submission to her lord and master. Milton puts into Eve's mouth the following address to Adam:

'My author and disposer, what thou bidst,
Unargued I obey; so God ordains—
God is thy law, thou mine: to know no more,
Is woman's happiest knowledge and her praise.'

This much admired sentimental nonsense is fraught with absurdity and wickedness. If it were true, the commandment of Jehovah should have run thus: Man shall have no other gods before ME, and woman shall have no other gods before MAN.

The principal support of the dogma of woman's inferiority, and consequent submission to her husband, is found in some passages of Paul's epistles. I shall proceed to examine those passages, premising 1st, that the antiquity of the opinions based on the false construction of those passages, has no weight with me: they are the opinions of interested judges, and I have no particular reverence for them, *merely* because they have been regarded with veneration from generation to generation. So far from this being the case, I examine any opinions of centuries standing, with as much freedom, and investigate them with as much care, as if they were of yesterday. I was educated to think for myself, and it is a privilege I shall always claim to exercise. 2d. Notwithstanding my full belief, that the apostle Paul's testimony, respecting himself, is true, 'I was not a whit behind the chiefest of the apostles,' yet I believe his mind was under the influence of Jewish prejudices respecting women, just as Peter's and the apostles were about the uncleanness of the Gentiles. 'The Jews,' says Clarke, 'would not suffer a woman to read in the synagogue, although a servant, or even a child, had this permission.' When I see Paul shaving his head for a vow, and offering sacrifices, and circumcising Timothy, to accommodate himself to the prepossessions of his countrymen, I do not conceive that I derogate in the least from his character as an inspired apostle, to suppose that he may have been imbued with the prevalent prejudices against women.

In 1st Cor. 11:3, after praising the Corinthian converts, because they kept the 'ordinances,' or 'traditions,' as the margin reads, the apostle says, 'I would have you know, that the head of every man is Christ, and the head of the woman is the man; and the head of Christ is God.' Eph. 5:23, is a parallel passage. 'For the husband is the head of the wife, even as Christ is the head of the Church.' The apostle closes his remarks on this subject, by observing, 'This is a great mystery, but I speak concerning Christ and the Church.' I shall pass over this with simply remarking, that God and Christ are one. 'I and my Father are one,' and there can be no inferiority where there is no divisibility. The commentaries on this and similar texts, afford a striking illustration of the ideas which men entertain of their own superiority; I shall subjoin Henry's remarks on 1st Cor. 11:5, as a specimen: 'To understand this text, it must be observed, that it was a signification either of shame, or subjection, for persons to be veiled, or covered in Eastern countries; contrary to the custom of ours, where the being bare-headed betokens subjection, and being covered superiority and dominion; and this will help us the better to understand the reason on which he grounds his reprehension, "Every man praying, etc., dishonoreth his head," i.e. Christ, the head of every man, by appearing in a habit unsuitable to the rank in which God had placed him. The woman, on the other hand, that prays, etc., dishonoreth her head, i.e. the man. She appears in the dress of her *superior*, and throws off the token of her subjection; she might with equal decency cut her hair short, or cut it off, the common dress of the man in that age. Another reason against this conduct was, that the man is the image and glory of God, the representative of that glorious dominion and headship which God has over the world. It is the man who is set at the head of this lower creation, and therein bears the re-semblance of God. The woman, on the other hand, is the glory of the man: she is his representative. Not but she has dominion over the inferior creatures, and she is a partaker of human nature, and so far is God's representative too, but it is at second hand. She is the image of God, inasmuch as she is the image of the man. The man was first made, and made head of the creation here below, and therein the image of the divine dominion; and the woman was made out of the man, and shone with a *reflection of his glory,* being made superior to the other creatures here below, but in subjection to her husband, and deriving that *honor from him,* out of whom she was made. The woman was made for the man to be his help meet, and not the man for the woman. She was naturally, therefore, made subject to him, because made for him, for HIS USE AND HELP AND COMFORT.'

We see in the above quotation, what degrading views even good men entertain of women. Pity the Psalmist had not thrown a little light on this subject, when he was paraphrasing the account of man's creation. 'Thou hast made him a little lower than the angels, and hast crowned him with glory and honor. Thou madest him to have dominion over the works of thy hands; thou hast put all things under his feet.' Surely if woman had been placed below man, and was to shine only by a lustre borrowed from him, we should have some clear evidence of it in the sacred volume. Henry puts her exactly on a level with the beasts; they were made for the use, help and comfort of man; and according to this commentator, this was the whole end and design of the creation of woman. The idea that man, as man is superior to woman, involves an absurdity so gross, that I really wonder how any man of reflection can receive it as of divine origin; and I can only account for it, by that passion for supremacy, which characterizes man as a corrupt and fallen creature. If it be true that he is more excellent than she, as man, independent of his moral and intellectual powers, then every man is superior by virtue of his manship, to every woman. The man who sinks his moral capacities and spiritual powers in his sensual appetites, is still, as a man, simply by the conformation of his body, a more dignified being, than the woman whose intellectual powers are highly cultivated, and whose approximation to the character of Jesus Christ is exhibited in a blameless life and conversation.

But it is strenuously urged by those, who are anxious to maintain their usurped authority, that wives are, in various passages of the New Testament, commanded to obey their husbands. Let us examine these texts.

Eph. 5:22, 24. 'Wives, submit yourselves unto your own husbands as unto the Lord.' 'As the church is subject unto Christ, so let the wives be to their own husbands in every thing.'
Col. 3:18. 'Wives, submit yourselves unto your own husbands, as it is fit in the Lord.'
1st Pet. 3:2. 'Likewise ye wives, be in subjection to your own husbands; that if any obey not the word, they may also without the word be won by the conversation of the wives.'

Accompanying all these directions to wives are commands to husbands.

Eph. 5:25, 28. 'Husbands, love your wives even as Christ loved the Church, and gave himself for it.' 'So ought men to love their wives as their own bodies. He that loveth his wife, loveth himself.'
Col. 3:19. 'Husbands, love your wives, and be not bitter against them.'
1st Pet. 3:7. 'Likewise ye husbands, dwell with them according to knowledge, giving honor unto the wife as unto the weaker vessel, and as being heirs together of the grace of life.'

I may just remark, in relation to the expression 'weaker vessel,' that the word in the original has no reference to intellect: it refers to physical weakness merely.

The apostles were writing to Christian converts, and laying down rules for their conduct towards their unconverted consorts. It no doubt frequently happened, that a husband or a wife would embrace Christianity, while their companions clung to heathenism, and husbands might be tempted to dislike and despise those, who pertinaciously adhered to their pagan superstitions. And wives who, when they were pagans, submitted as a matter of course to their heathen husbands, might be tempted knowing that they were superior as moral and religious characters, to assert that superiority, by paying less deference to them than heretofore. Let us examine the context of these passages, and see what are the grounds of the directions here given to husbands and wives. The whole epistle to the Ephesians breathes a spirit of love. The apostle beseeches the converts to walk worthy of the vocation wherewith they are called, with all lowliness and meekness, with long suffering, forbearing one another in love. The verse preceding [Eph.] 5:22, is 'Submitting yourselves one to another in the fear of God.' Colossians 3, from 11 to 17, contains similar injunctions. The 17th verse says, 'Whatsoever ye do in word, or in deed, do all in the name of the Lord Jesus.' Peter, after drawing a most touching picture of Christ's sufferings for us, and reminding the Christians, that he had left us an example that we should follow his steps, 'who did no sin, neither was guile found in his mouth,' exhorts wives to be in subjection, etc.

From an attentive consideration of these passages, and of those in which the same words 'submit,' 'subjection,' are used, I cannot but believe that the apostles designed to recommend to wives, as they did to subjects and to servants, to carry out the holy principle laid down by Jesus Christ, 'Resist not evil.' And this without in the least acknowledging the right of the governors, masters, or husbands, to exercise the authority they claimed. The recognition of the existence of evils does not involve approbation of them. God tells the Israelites, he gave them a king in his wrath, but nevertheless as they chose to have a king, he laid down directions for the conduct of that king, and had him anointed to reign over them. According to the generally received meaning of the passages I have quoted, they directly contravene the laws of God, as given in various parts of the Bible. Now I must understand the sacred Scriptures as harmonizing with themselves, or I cannot receive them as the word of God. The commentators on these passages exalt man to the station of a Deity in relation to woman. Clarke says, 'As the Lord Christ is the head, or governor of the church, and the head of the man, so is the man the head, or governor of the woman. This is God's ordinance, and should not be transgressed. 'As unto the Lord.' The word church seems necessarily to be understood here: that is, act under the authority of your husbands, as the church acts under the authority of Christ. 'As the church submits to the Lord, so let wives submit to their husbands.' Henry goes even further—'For the husband is the head of the wife. The metaphor is taken from the head in the natural body, which being the seat of reason, of wisdom and of knowledge, and the fountain of sense and motion, is more excellent than the rest of the body.' Now if God ordained man the governor of woman, he must be able to save her, and to answer in her stead for all those sins which she commits by his direction. Awful responsibility. Do husbands feel able and willing to bear it? And what becomes of the solemn affirmation of Jehovah? 'Hear this, all ye people, give ear all ye inhabitants of the world, both low and high, rich and poor.' 'None can by any means redeem his brother, or give to God a ransom for him, for the redemption of the soul is precious, and man cannot accomplish it.'—*French Bible.*

Thine in the bonds of womanhood,

SARAH M. GRIMKÉ.

⋘8 Jean-Jacques Rousseau

Jean-Jacques Rousseau was born in Geneva in 1712, the youngest son of Isaac Rousseau, a watchmaker, and his wife, Suzanne Bernard, who died a week or so later of puerperal fever. Until he was ten the boy was brought up by "the best of fathers," as he styled him in the Confessions, with whom he would sit up all night reading novels, and by an aunt who sought to bring some semblance of order into the home. In 1722 Isaac Rousseau left Geneva to avoid a sentence passed against him as a result of a scuffle over an alleged act of trespass, and Jean-Jacques was placed under the tutorship of a country minister at Boissy. Two years later he was apprenticed, first to a notary and later to an engraver who treated him so badly that he ran away. When Rousseau was sixteen years old his wanderings took him to the home of Mme. de Warens, a twenty-nine-year-old divorcée of fairly substantial means, who became his patron and in time, it seems, his mistress.

In 1741 Rousseau parted company with Mme. de Warens, his maman (mamma), as he called her, and proceeded to Paris armed with letters of introduction that eventually led to his acquaintance with a number of Parisiennes of considerable influence. But it was with a woman of lowly birth that he formed a liaison: Thérèse le Vasseur, a seamstress at the boardinghouse where he roomed, lived with him, cared for him, and nursed him until his death, thirty-five years later. He claims that five children were born to this union and that each was sent to the foundling hospital upon its birth.

Although he led a simple life with a semiliterate concubine, Rousseau lived on the fringes of the haut monde. He frequented the most fashionable salons and was lionized by the ladies because of the sentimentality of La Nouvelle Héloïse, because of his interest in the education of their children, and because in the character of Sophia in his novel Emile he tried to portray them not from their husbands' point of view but from their own.

The ideal woman depicted by Rousseau in Emile provides quite a contrast to the real French women with whom he actually consorted—especially to the salonnières, who upon his arrival in Paris had been amused at his gaucherie, and who later, although they had bestowed their friendship and their patronage upon him, had denied him the love for which he had always yearned. It is significant that Emile encounters Sophia not in Paris but in the provinces. Eschewing the high heels, high hairdos, low necklines, and corsets popular among Parisian ladies, the ideal woman will choose to dress simply and modestly. Innocent of all philosophy, she will not aspire to the salon, but will devote herself entirely to the comfort and pleasure of her spouse. Her nature, her education, and her role in society are totally different from those of the ideal man. It is interesting to note that in Emile et Sophie, the sequel to Emile, the destruction of the ideal marriage occurs in Paris, where the bridegroom, distracted by urban pleasures, neglects his bride.

Jean-Jacques Rousseau developed his views on woman not in conjunction with his social and political theories but in Emile, a treatise on education. Although he addressed himself specifically to "those who regard woman as an imperfect man," Rousseau's own view is distinguished from the one he is repudiating by little more than a verbal quibble. Before puberty, he claimed, boys and girls are virtually indistinguishable. In face, in form, in complexion, in voice, there is little if any observable difference between them. Even after puberty, which Rousseau referred to as a "second birth," men and women are alike in all respects except those pertaining to sex, and in sex-linked characteristics, he contended, they exhibit similarities as well as differences. One soon realizes, however, that in his eyes all traits are sex-linked, and one searches in vain for the similarities to complement the differences, for Rousseau claimed that men and women are basically unlike in physique, in temperament, in behavior, in understanding, and in intellect. Moreover, he found that many of these differences antedate puberty. And furthermore, while carefully avoiding such words as "equality" and "superiority," while insisting that men and women are alike in their common characteristics and simply incomparable in all others, and while chiding those who call female traits defects, he was quick to add that those traits which are characteristic of women are traits that would be considered defects in a man.

Physically, women are weaker than men. Perhaps it is this weakness that leads to those temperamental and behavioral differences that precede puberty, girls preferring—almost from infancy, Rousseau thought—quiet play with dolls, mirrors, jewelry, and clothes, leaving to their brothers noisy, active games with drums and tops and hobbyhorses. Women's reason, he believed, is also inferior; consequently it may be used only indirectly to induce men to employ their reason to right ends, rather than directly to affect situations by its own power.

These basic differences between men and women Rousseau seemed to ascribe to the different functions for which the two sexes were designed, woman being intended merely to serve as man's helpmate. But rather than leaving her the ignorant bedmate and housekeeper of Aristotelian-Thomistic tradition, Rousseau suggested educating her carefully so that she might delight and complement man in every respect, and in the fifth chapter of Emile he carefully outlined such a program.

Although the rational capacity of woman is limited, it is adequate to her needs. It apprises her of her duty: the fidelity and obedience that she owes to her husband and the care and tenderness that she should lavish on her children. It also serves as a means of obtaining the approval, esteem, respect, and love of that husband upon whom she depends. Although these duties are easily seen, they are, according to Rousseau, less easily fulfilled. Since women are made to please men and be useful to them, the entire education of the female should be directed toward that end. Since the body is "born, in a manner, before the soul," it should be trained first. Woman needs little physical strength: only enough to enable her to bear strong children and to rear and educate them (especially the boys among them, one might presume). It is grace that her physical training should seek to cultivate—grace in demeanor, in attitude, in bearing, in gesture, in step, and in tone. To this end she should be given lessons in singing and dancing, especially dancing. Any elocution lessons given to a girl might also be considered physical rather than mental training and would probably be intended to enhance her grace as well, for Rousseau found the speech of men to differ from that of women in substance, in requisite, and in aim, that of men being based on knowledge and intended for use, and that of women grounded in whim and calculated to please.

Perhaps more important than the training of a girl's body, however, is the molding of her temperament. The restrictions to be imposed on her when she is grown make it mandatory, in Rousseau's estimation, to condition her to them early. The very restricted amount of liberty that is permitted a girl is likely to make her prize the little that she does have all the more dearly and to lead her ultimately to abuse it. To counteract this tendency in young girls, Rousseau recommends stern measures: interrupt them in the middle of their play, he says, and make them return to their work; if, on the other hand, they are absorbed in their work, make them stop. Such practices, he thinks, will cultivate docility and good temper in women, for they soon must accustom themselves to putting up with whatever their husbands choose to inflict upon them.

A woman's understanding matures earlier than a man's; therefore while it is important to show a boy the utility of what he learns, it is even more essential to do so in the case of a girl. Rousseau noted that girls dislike reading and suggested no remedy for this disaffection, for reading has little to do with household management, but he urged an emphasis on arithmetic because of its utilitarian value.

Woman's physical and mental weakness Rousseau believed to be compensated for by a sort of "experimental morality," which is her province and hers alone. This quality involves the manipulation of men and results in women's controlling, in the last analysis, the manners, passions, tastes, pleasure, even happiness of the world. They rear men in their boyhood, advise them in their maturity, and comfort them in their old age. They are, in Rousseau's words, "that sex which governs and doth honour to ours."

From *Emilius; or, A New System of Education*

SOPHIA

. . .

In every thing, which does not regard the sex, woman is the same as man; she has the same organs, the same necessities, the same faculties: the corporeal machine is constructed in the same manner, its component parts are alike, their operation the same, and the figure similar in both. In whatever light we regard them, they differ from each other only in degree.

On the other hand, in every thing immediately respecting sex, the woman differs entirely from the man; the difficulty of comparing them together, lying in our inability to determine what are those particulars in the constitution of each that immediately relate to the sex. From their comparative anatomy, and even from simple inspection, we perceive some general distinctions between them, that do not appear to relate to sex; and yet there can be no doubt that they do, although we are not capable of tracing their modes of relation. Indeed we know not how far the difference of sex may extend. All that we know, of a certainty, is, that whatever is common to both is only characteristic of their species; and that every thing in which they differ, is distinctive of their sex. Under this twofold consideration we find so much resemblance and dissimilitude, that it appears even miraculous, that nature should form two beings so much alike, and, at the same time, so very different.

This difference and similitude must necessarily have an influence over their moral character; such an influence is, indeed, obvious, and perfectly agreeable to experience; clearly demonstrating the vanity of the disputes that have been held concerning the superiority or equality of the sexes; as if, in answering the different ends for which nature designed them, both were not more perfect than they would be in more nearly resembling each other. In those particulars which are common to both, they are equal; and as to those wherein they differ, no comparison is to be made between them. A perfect man and a complete woman should no more resemble each other in mind than in feature, nor is their perfection reducible to any common standard.

In the union of the sexes, both pursue one common object, but not in the same manner. From their diversity, in this particular, arises the first determinate difference between the moral relations of each. The one should be active and strong, the other passive and weak: it is necessary the one should have both the power and the will, and that the other should make little resistance.

This principle being established, it follows, that woman is expressly formed to please the man. If the obligation be reciprocal also, and the man ought to please in his turn, it is not so immediately necessary: his great merit lies in his power, and he pleases merely because he is strong. This, I must confess, is not one of the refined maxims of love; it is, however, one of the laws of nature, prior to love itself.

If woman be formed to please and to be subjected to man, it is her place, doubtless, to render herself agreeable to him, instead of challenging his passion. The violence of his desires depends on her charms: it is by means of these she should urge him to the exertion of those powers which nature hath given him. The most successful method of exciting them, is to render such exertion necessary by her resistance; as, in that case, self-love is added to desire, and the one triumphs in the victory which the other obliged him to acquire. Hence arise the various modes of attack and defence between the sexes, the boldness of one sex, and the timidity of the other, and, in a word, that bashfulness and modesty with which nature hath armed the weak, in order to subdue the strong.

. . .

Hence we deduce a third consequence from the different constitutions of the sexes; which is, that the strongest should be master in appearance, and be dependent in fact on the weakest; and that not from any frivolous practice of gallantry or vanity of protectorship, but from an invariable law of nature, which, furnishing woman with greater facility to excite desires than she has given man to satisfy them, makes the latter dependent on the good pleasure of the former, and compels him to endeavour to please in his turn, in order to obtain her consent that he should be strongest. On these occasions, the most delightful circumstance a man finds in his victory is, to doubt whether it was the woman's weakness that yielded to his superior strength, or whether her inclinations spoke in his favour: the females are also generally artful enough to leave this matter in doubt. The understanding of women answers, in this respect, perfectly to their constitution: so far from being ashamed of their weakness, they glory in it: their tender muscles make no resistance; they affect to be incapable of lifting the smallest burdens, and would blush to be thought robust and strong. To what purpose is all this? Not merely for the sake of appearing delicate, but through an artful precaution: it is thus they provide an excuse beforehand, and a right to be feeble when they think it expedient.

. . .

There is no parity between man and woman as to the consequences of their sex. The male is such only at certain momentary intervals: the female feels the consequences of her sex all her life, at least during youth, and, in order to answer the purposes of it, requires first a suitable constitution. She requires next careful management in her pregnancy, repose in child-bed, ease and a sedentary life during the time of suckling her children, and, to bring them up, such patience, good-humour, and affection, as nothing can disgust. She serves as the means of their connection with their father: it is she who makes him love them, and gives him the confidence to call them his own. What tenderness and solicitude ought she not to be possessed of, in order to maintain the peace and unity of a whole family! Add to this, that her good qualities should not be the effects of virtue, but of taste and inclination, without which the human species would soon be extinct.

The relative duties of the two sexes do not require an equally rigorous observance in both. When women complain, however, of this partiality as unjust, they are in the wrong: this inequality is not of human institution; at least, it is not the effect of prejudice, but of reason. It certainly belongs to that party which nature hath more immediately intrusted with the care of children, to be answerable for that charge to the other. Neither of them, indeed, is permitted to violate their mutual engagements. Every faithless husband, who deprives his wife of the only compensation for the severer duties of her sex, being guilty of cruelty and injustice. A faithless woman, however, does still more: she dissolves the union of her family, and breaks through all the ties of nature; in giving to a man children which are not of his begetting, she betrays both, and adds perfidy to infidelity. Such an action is naturally productive of the worst of crimes and disorders. If there be a situation in life truly horrid, it is that of an unhappy father, who, placing no confidence in his wife, cannot indulge himself in the most delightful sentiments of the heart; who doubts, while he is embracing his child, whether it be not the offspring of another, the pledge of his dishonour, and the usurper of the rights of his real children. What a scene doth a family in such a case present to us! Nothing but a community of secret enemies, whom a guilty woman arms one against the other, by compelling them to pretences of reciprocal affection.

It is not only of consequence, therefore, that a woman should be faithful to her husband, but also that he should think her so. It is requisite for her to be modest, circumspect, and reserved, and that she should bear, in the sight of others, as well as in her own conscience, the testimony of her virtue. If it be necessary for a father to love his children, it is first necessary for him to esteem their mother. Such are the reasons which place even the preservation of appearances among the number of female duties, and render their honour and reputation no less indispensible than chastity. From these principles is derived a new motive of obligation and convenience, which prescribes peculiarly to women the most scrupulous circumspection in their manners, conduct, and behaviour. To maintain indiscriminately that the two sexes are equal, and that their reciprocal duties and obligations are the same, is to indulge ourselves in idle declamations unworthy of a serious answer.

. . .

It being once demonstrated that man and woman are not, nor ought to be, constituted alike in temperament and character, it follows of course that they should not be educated in the same manner. In pursuing the directions of nature, they ought indeed to act in concert, but they should not be engaged in the same employments: the end of their pursuits should be the same; but the means they should take to accomplish them, and of consequence, their tastes and inclinations, should be different. Having endeavoured to lay down the principles of a natural education for a man, let us trace, in the same manner, the methods to form a woman answerable to him.

Are you desirous of being always directed aright? Observe constantly the indications of nature. Whatever is characteristic of the sex, should be regarded as a circumstance peculiarly established. You are always complaining that women have certain defects and failings; your vanity deceives you: such, indeed, would be defects and failings in you, but they are essential qualities in them, and women would be much worse without them. You may prevent these pretended defects from growing worse; but you ought to take great care not entirely to remove them.

The women, again, on their part, are constantly crying out, that we educate them to be vain and coquettish; that we constantly entertain them with puerilities, in order to maintain our authority over them; and attribute to us the failings for which we reproach them. What a ridiculous accusation! How long is it that the men have troubled themselves about the education of the women? What hinders mothers from bringing up their daughters just as they please? There are, to be sure, no colleges and academies for girls: a sad misfortune truly! Would to God there were none also for boys; they would be more sensibly and virtuously educated than they are. Who, ye mothers, compels your daughters to throw away their time in trifles? to spend half their lives, after your example, at the toilette? Who hinders you from instructing, or causing them to be instructed in the manner you choose? Is it our fault that they charm us when they are pretty, that we are seduced by their affected airs, that the arts they learn of you attract and flatter us, that we love to see them becomingly dressed, and that we permit them to prepare at leisure those arms with which they subdue us to their pleasure? Educate them, if you think proper, like the men; we shall readily consent to it. The more they resemble our sex, the less power will they have over us; and when they once become like ourselves, we shall then be truly their masters.

. . .

To cultivate in women, therefore, the qualifications of the men, and neglect those which are peculiar to the sex, would be acting to their prejudice: they see this very well, and are too artful to become the dupes of such conduct: they endeavour, indeed, to usurp our advantages, but they take care not to give up their own. By these means, however, it happens that, not being capable of both, because they are incompatible, they fail of attaining the perfection of their own sex, as well as of ours, and lose half their merit. Let not the sensible mother, then, think of educating her daughter as a man, in contradiction to nature; but as a virtuous woman; and she may be assured it will be much better both for her child and herself.

It does not hence follow, however, that she ought to be educated in perfect ignorance, and confined merely to domestic concerns. Would a man make a servant of his companion, and deprive himself of the greatest pleasure of society? To make her the more submissive, would he prevent her from acquiring the least judgment or knowledge? would he reduce her to a mere automaton? Surely not! Nature hath dictated otherwise, in giving the sex such refined and agreeable talents: on the contrary, she hath formed them for thought, for judgment, for love, and knowledge. They should bestow as much care on their understandings, therefore, as on their persons, and add the charms of the one to the other, in order to supply their own want of strength, and to direct ours. They should doubtless learn many things, but only those which it is proper for them to know.

Whether I consider the peculiar destination of the sex, observe their inclinations, or remark their duties, all things equally concur to point out the peculiar method of education best adapted to them. Woman and man were made for each other; but their mutual dependance is not the same. The men depend on the women, only on account of their desires; the women on the men, both on account of their desires and their necessities: we could subsist better without them than they without us. Their very subsistance and rank in life depend on us, and the estimation in which we hold them, their charms and their merit. By the law of nature itself, both women and children lie at the mercy of the men: it is not enough they should be really estimable, it is requisite they should be actually esteemed; it is not enough they should be beautiful, it is requisite their charms should please; it is not enough they should be sensible and prudent, it is necessary they should be acknowledged as such: their glory lies not only in their conduct, but in their reputation; and it is impossible for any, who consents to be accounted infamous, to be ever virtuous. A man, secure in his own good conduct, depends only on himself, and may brave the public opinion: but a woman, in behaving well, performs but half her duty; as what is thought of her, is as important to her, as what she really is. It follows hence, that the system of a woman's education should, in this respect, be directly contrary to that of ours. Opinion is the grave of virtue among the men; but its throne among the women.

On the good constitution of mothers depends originally that of their children; on the care of the women depends our earliest education; on the women also depend our manners, our passions, our tastes, our pleasures, and even our happiness itself. For this reason, the education of the women should be always relative to the men. To please, to be useful to us, to make us love and esteem them, to educate us when young, and take care of us when grown up, to advise, to console us, to render our lives easy and agreeable; these are the duties of women at all times, and what they should be taught in their infancy. So long as we fail to recur to this principle, we run wide of the mark, and all the precepts which are given them contribute neither to their happiness nor our own.

.   .   .

Girls are, from their earliest infancy, fond of dress. Not content with being pretty, they are desirous of being thought so; we see, by all their little airs, that this thought engages their attention: and they are hardly capable of understanding what is said to them, before they are to be governed by talking to them of what people will think of their behaviour. The same motive, however indiscreetly made use of with boys, has not the same effect: provided they are left to pursue their amusements at pleasure, they care very little what people think of them. Time and pains are necessary to subject boys to this motive.

Whencesoever girls derive this first lesson, it is a very good one. As the body is born, in a manner, before the soul, our first concern should be to cultivate the former; this order is common to both sexes, but the object of that cultivation is different. In the one sex, it is the development of corporeal powers; in the other, that of personal charms: not that either the quality of strength or beauty ought to be confined exclusively to one sex; but only that the order of the cultivation of both is in that respect reversed. Women certainly require as much strength as to enable them to move and act gracefully, and men as much address as to qualify them to act with ease.

.   .   .

Children of both sexes have a great many amusements in common; and so they ought; have they not also many such when they are grown up? Each sex hath also its peculiar taste to distinguish in this particular. Boys love sports of noise and activity; to beat the drum, to whip the top, and to drag about their little carts: girls, on the other hand, are fonder of things of show and ornament; such as mirrors, trinkets, and dolls: the doll is the peculiar amusement of the females; from whence we see their taste plainly adapted to their destination. The physical part of the art of pleasing lies in dress; and this is all which children are capacitated to cultivate of that art.

You shall see a little girl spend whole days about her waxen baby; be perpetually changing its clothes, dress and undress it an hundred times, and be for ever studying new combinations of ornament; well or ill-sorted, it is no matter: her fingers want dexterity, and her taste is not yet formed; but her inclinations are sufficiently evident. While thus occupied, her time slips insensibly away; she forgets even her meals, and has more appetite to dress than to food. You will say, perhaps, that she dresses up her baby, and not herself. Doubtless, it is her baby she sees, and not herself: she can do nothing as yet about her own person, all her concerns center in her doll, and in the management of this it is that she displays all her coquetry. This, however, will not be always the case; the time approaches when she will take the same pleasure in ornamenting herself.

.   .   .

Whatever may be sometimes said in raillery, good sense is equally the property of both sexes. Girls in general are more docile than boys, and, indeed, we ought to use more authority over them, as I observe hereafter; but it does not thence follow, that we should require them to do any thing, of which they do not see the utility: it is the art of a mother to show them the usefulness of whatever they are set to do; and this is by so much the more easy, as the understanding ripens much sooner in girls than boys. This rule frees their sex, as well as ours, not only from those indolent and useless studies, which answer no good purpose, nor even render those who cultivate them the more agreeable to others; but also all those whose utility is not adapted to their present age, nor perceptible in a future one. If I am against compelling boys to learn to read, it is with still greater reason that I oppose using any such compulsion with girls, at least till they are well instructed in the utility of reading: the manner, however, in which this utility is usually inculcated, is much better adapted to our own notions of things than to theirs. And, after all, where is the necessity for a girl's learning to read and write so early? does she so soon take on herself the management of a family? I am afraid there are but few who do not make rather a bad use than a good one of this fatal science; and I am certain they have all so much curiosity as to learn it without compulsion, whenever they have leisure and opportunity. Perhaps they ought to learn arithmetic, in preference to every thing else; for nothing can appear more useful at any time of life, nor requires longer practice, than the keeping of accounts. If a little girl should have no means of obtaining cherries or sugar-plums, but by resolving a question in arithmetic, I will answer for it she would soon learn to calculate for them.

.   .   .

Let there be propriety in all the injunctions you lay upon young girls, but take care always to impose on them something to learn or to do. Indolence and indocility are two of the most dangerous ill qualities they are subject to, and what they are the most seldom cured of, when they have once contracted them. Girls ought to be active and diligent; nor is that all; they should also be early subjected to restraint. This misfortune, if it really be one, is inseparable from their sex; nor do they ever throw it off but to suffer more cruel evils. They must be subject, all their lives, to the most constant and severe restraint, which is that of decorum: it is, therefore, necessary to accustom them early to such confinement, that it may not afterwards cost them too dear; and to the suppression of their caprices, that they may the more readily submit to the will of others. If, indeed, they are fond of being always at work, they should be sometimes compelled to lay it aside. Dissipation, levity and inconstancy are faults that readily spring up from their first propensities, when corrupted or perverted by too much indulgence. To prevent this abuse, we should learn them, above all things, to lay a due restraint on themselves. The life of a modest woman is reduced, by our absurd institutions, to a perpetual conflict with herself: not but it is just that this sex should partake of the sufferings which arise from those evils it hath caused us.

. . .

For the same reason that they have, or ought to have, but little liberty, they are apt to indulge themselves excessively in what is allowed them. Addicted in every thing to extremes, they are even more transported at their diversions than boys: this is the second inconvenience of which I spoke before. These transports ought to be moderated; being the cause of many vices peculiar to the women; such, among others, are the caprice and infatuation by which a woman is in raptures today with an object she may regard with coldness and indifference tomorrow. The inconstancy of their inclinations is as fatal to them as their excess; both one and the other also are derived from the same source. Deny them not the indulgence of their innocent mirth, their sports and pastimes; but ever prevent their sating themselves with one to run to another; permit them not for a moment to perceive themselves entirely freed from restraint. Use them to be interrupted in the midst of their play, and sent to work, without murmuring. Habit alone is sufficient to inure them to this, because it is only confirming the operations of nature.

There results from this habitual restraint a tractableness which the women have occasion for during their whole lives, as they constantly remain either under subjection to the men, or to the opinions of mankind; and are never permitted to set themselves above those opinions. The first and most important qualification in a woman is good-nature or sweetness of temper: formed to obey a being so imperfect as man, often full of vices, and always full of faults, she ought to learn betimes even to suffer injustice, and to bear the insults of a husband without complaint: it is not for his sake, but her own, that she should be of a mild disposition. The perverseness and ill-nature of the women only serve to aggravate their own misfortunes, and the misconduct of their husbands; they might plainly perceive that such are not the arms by which they gain the superiority. Heaven did not bestow on them the powers of insinuation and persuasion to make them perverse and morose; it did not constitute them feeble to make them imperious; it did not give them so soft and agreeable a voice to vent abuse, nor features so delicate and lovely to be disfigured with anger. When they give way to rage, therefore, they forget themselves: for, though they may often have reason to complain, they are always in the wrong to scold. Each sex should preserve its peculiar tone and manner; a meek husband may make a wife impertinent; but mildness of disposition on the woman's side will always bring a man back to reason, at least if he be not absolutely a brute, and will sooner or later triumph over him.

. . .

Whatever is, is right; nor can any general rule in nature be wrong. The superiority of address peculiar to the female sex, is a very equitable indemnification for their inferiority in point of strength: without this, woman would not be the companion of man, but his slave: it is by her superior art and ingenuity that she preserves her equality, and governs him while she affects to obey. . . .

Dress may make a woman fine, but personal charms only make her please. Our clothes are not ourselves: they often disfigure and are unbecoming, because they are too remarkable: and those which most distinguish the wearer, are often such as are least remarkable in themselves. The usual method of educating girls is, in this respect, quite absurd: they are promised fine clothes, etc., by way of rewards, and are taught to admire affected modes of dress. Again, they are themselves admired when finely dressed; whereas they ought to be given to understand, that so much care to deck them out is bestowed on them only to hide their defects, and that the real triumph of beauty lies in the display of its native charms. A fondness for fashions is thus a proof of bad taste, as the person and features do not change with the mode; what is becoming or unbecoming at one time, must therefore be always so.

. . .

The first thing which young persons observe, as they grow up, is, that all these foreign aids of dress are still insufficient, if they have no charms in their own persons. Beauty cannot be acquired by dress, and coquetry is an art not so early and speedily attained. While girls are yet young, however, they are in a capacity to study agreeable gesture, a pleasing modulation of voice, an easy carriage and behaviour; as well as to take the advantage of gracefully adapting their looks and attitudes to time, place, and occasion. Their application, therefore, should not be solely confined to the arts of industry and the needle, when they come to display other talents, whose utility is already apparent.

I know some persons are so severe, that they would not have girls taught singing, dancing, nor any of the agreeable arts. This seems to me, however, very absurd and ridiculous. Pray, on whom would they have these talents bestowed? On the boys? Do these accomplishments best become the men or the women? They will answer, perhaps, that they become neither: that profane songs are criminal: that dancing is the invention of the devil: and that girls ought to have no other amusements than their sampler and their prayers. Strange amusements, truly, for a girl of ten years of age! For my part, I am somewhat afraid that these little saints, in consequence of being thus compelled to spend their childhood in praying to God, will be tempted to spend their youth in very different employment; and that they will endeavour to make up, when they are married, for the time they will conceive they lost before-hand. It is, in my opinion, necessary to pay a regard to their age as well as their sex: a little miss ought not, surely, to lead the life of her grandmother, but, on the contrary, to be indulged in her vivacity and childish amusements; she should be permitted to sing, to dance, to play about as much as she pleases, and to enjoy all the innocent pleasures of her age: the time will come but too soon, when she must be more reserved, and put on a more constrained behaviour.

. . .

Industry and talents form the taste; by means of taste also it is that the mind insensibly acquires ideas of the truly beautiful, and, in time, of moral relations, which depend thereon. This is, perhaps, one of the reasons why the sentiments of modesty and decency take rise earlier in girls than boys: for to imagine that notions so premature are the effect of the lessons of the governess, argues but little acquaintance with the nature of those lessons, and the progress of the human mind. The talent of speaking holds the first rank in the art of pleasing: it is that alone which can give new attractions to those charms which have lost their power over the senses by habit. It is the mind which not only animates the body, but in some sense gives it a new form: it is by the succession of its sentiments and ideas, that it enlivens and diversifies the countenance: it is by the discourse it inspires, that attention is kept on the stretch, and preserves, for any long time, the same regard for the same object. I conceive it is for all these reasons that girls so early acquire an agreeable mode of prattle; that they are emphatic in their discourse, even before they well know what they say; and that men amuse themselves by listening to their talk, even before they can understand them.

The tongues of women are very voluble: they speak earlier, more readily and more agreeably than the men: they are accused also of speaking much more; but so it ought to be: and I should be very ready to convert this reproach into a compliment: their lips and eyes have the same activity, and for the same reason. A man speaks of what he knows, a woman of what pleases her: the one requires knowledge, the other taste. The principal object of a man's discourse should be what is useful, that of a woman's what is agreeable. There ought to be nothing in common between their different conversation but truth.

We ought not, therefore, to restrain the prattle of girls, in the same manner as we should that of boys, with that severe question, *To what purpose are you talking?* but by another, which is not less difficult to answer, *How will your discourse be received?* In infancy, while they are as yet incapable to discern good from evil, they ought to observe, as a law, never to say any thing disagreeable to those whom they are speaking to. What will render the practice of this rule also the more difficult, is, that it must ever be subordinate to the former, of never speaking falsely or telling an untruth.

. . .

If boys ought not to be indulged in asking indiscreet questions, much less should girls; whose curiosity, either satisfied or imprudently evaded, is of much greater consequence, on account of their penetration to foresee the mysteries which are concealed from them, and their address in discovering them. But, without permitting them to ask questions, I would have them be continually interrogated themselves; and excited to prattle, in order to accustom them to a fluency of speech, to make them quick at reply, and to refine their wit and their tongue as much as possible, without danger. Such conversations being always accompanied with gaiety, but managed with art and discretion, would be an amusement adapted to their years, and might be made the means of inculcating, in the innocent minds of such young persons, the first, and perhaps the most useful lessons of morality they may ever receive; teaching them, under the appearance of pleasure and vanity, what are the qualities for which men truly hold them in esteem, and in what consist the glory and happiness of a modest woman.

It is easy to be conceived, that if male children are not in a capacity to form any true notions of religion, those ideas must be greatly above the conception of the females: it is for this very reason, I would begin to speak to them the earlier on this subject; for if we were to wait till they were in a capacity to discuss methodically such profound questions, we should run a risk of never speaking to them on this subject as long as they lived. Reason in women is a practical reason, capacitating them artfully to discover the means of attaining a known end, but which would never enable them to discover that end itself. The social relations of the sexes are indeed truly admirable: from their union there results a moral person, of which women may be termed the eyes and man the hand, with this dependance on each other, that it is from the man that the woman is to learn what she is to see, and it is of the woman that man is to learn what he ought to do. If woman could recur to the first principles of things as well as man, and man was capacitated to enter into their *minutiae* as well as woman, always independent of each other, they would live in perpetual discord, and their union could not subsist. But in the present harmony which naturally subsists between them, their different faculties tend to one common end; it is difficult to say which of them conduces the most to it: each follows the impulse of the other; each is obedient, and both are masters.

As the conduct of a woman is subservient to the public opinion, her faith in matters of religion should for that very reason be subject to authority. Every daughter ought to be of the same religion as her mother, and every wife to be of the religion of her husband: for, though such religion should be false, that docility which induces the mother and daughter to submit to the order of nature, takes away, in the sight of God, the criminality of their error. As they are not in a capacity to judge for themselves, they ought to abide by the decision of the fathers and husbands as confidently as by that of the church.

. . .

As for the rest, it is proper to observe, that till girls arrive at the age, when their enlightened reason or growing sentiment gives use to the dictates of conscience, they should be governed in their notions of good and evil entirely by the decisions of those who are about them. Whatever they are commanded to do, should be thought right, and what they are forbidden to do, wrong: they ought at present to know nothing farther than this: hence we see of how much greater importance it is, that we should be careful in the choice of persons to educate girls than we are of those who take the charge of boys. At length, however, the time will come when even girls will begin to judge for themselves, and when it will be necessary to diversify our plan of education.

I have, indeed, hitherto, perhaps, said too much. How low should we reduce the women, if we gave them no other laws than those of public opinion? Let us not so far disparage that sex, which governs and doth honour to ours, when we do not debase it. There exists, for the whole species, a rule prior to opinion. It is to the fixed and certain direction of that rule we should subject all others; it is the judge of prejudice itself, and it is not that the esteem in which men hold it agrees therewith, so much as that such esteem ought to give it authority with them.

This rule is that of innate sentiment. I shall not repeat what I have already said on that subject: it is sufficient to observe here, that if these two rules do not concur in the education of women, it will be always defective. Sentiment, without regard to opinion, will not give them that delicacy of mind, which adds to virtue the approbation of the world; and a regard to opinion, without sentiment, will only make them false and deceitful, placing the appearances of virtue in the room of virtue itself.

It is of consequence to them, therefore, to cultivate a faculty which serves as an umpire between the two guides, preventing the mistakes of conscience, and correcting the errors of prejudice. This faculty is reason: but how many queries offer themselves at that word? Are women capable of solid reasoning? Is it of any use for them to cultivate their reason? Can they do it with any success? Is that cultivation expedient to the functions imposed on them? Is it compatible with that simplicity of manners which becomes the sex?

. . .

The motive which leads a man to the knowledge of his various duties is not very complicated; that which directs a woman to the knowledge of her duties is still more simple. That obedience and fidelity which she owes to her husband, that care and tenderness which is due to her children, are such natural and affecting consequences of her situation, that unless she is abandoned to an habitual depravity, she cannot revolt from those internal principles which influence her conduct; nor mistake her duty, while she retains that propensity which nature has implanted in her bosom.

I would not indiscriminately condemn the practice of confining a woman solely to the occupations of her sex, and leaving her in profound ignorance with respect to all other concerns: But in such case it is necessary that the public morals should be very pure and simple, or that her manner of living should be extremely retired. In large cities, and in the midst of licentious men, such a woman would be easily seduced; her virtue would, on many occasions, be merely accidental; but this philosophic age requires a virtue which is at all times a proof against temptation. A woman ought to be sensible, before-hand, what may be said to her, and in what light it becomes her to consider it.

Besides, being subject to the opinion of men, she should study to merit their esteem: and she ought to be particularly anxious to acquire that of her husband; she should not only endeavour to make him love her person, but engage him to approve her conduct; she ought, in the eyes of the world, to justify the choice he has made, and derive honour to her husband, in consequence of the respect which is paid to his wife. But how should she accomplish these ends, if she is a stranger to our institutions, if she is ignorant of our customs and rules of decorum, if she is not acquainted with the sources of human judgment, nor with the passions by which it is determined? When she becomes sensible that she must depend both on the dictates of her own conscience, and on the opinion of others, it is necessary that she should learn to compare these two rules of action, to reconcile them, and never to prefer the former but when they stand in opposition to each other. From hence she becomes a judge over her judges; she determines within herself when she ought to submit to them, and when she ought to reject their authority. Before she adopts or rejects their prejudices, she considers their weight; she learns to recur to their first source, to obviate them, and render them favourable to her principles: she is cautious never to incur censure, when her duty will allow her to avoid it. These purposes cannot be effected, without enlarging her mind, and cultivating her reason.

. . .

From these considerations, I believe, we may in general be able to determine what kind of culture is most suitable to female minds, and upon what objects we ought to turn their reflections during their infancy.

I have already observed, that the duties of their sex are more easily known than practised. The first thing they should learn, is to be in love with their duty from a principle of interest; which is the only means to render it easy. Every station and every age has its peculiar duties. We are easily acquainted with them, provided we do but love them. Respect your condition as a woman, and whatever station Providence thinks proper to allot you, you will always be a woman of virtue. The essential point is to be what nature formed us; we are always too propense to be what the world would wish us.

Researches into abstract and speculative truths, the principles and axioms of sciences, in short, every thing which tends to generalize our ideas, is not the proper province of women; their studies should be relative to points of practice; it belongs to them to apply those principles which men have discovered; and it is their part to make observations, which direct men to the establishment of general principles. All the ideas of women, which have not an immediate tendency to points of duty, should be directed to the study of men, and to the attainment of those agreeable accomplishments which have taste for their objects; for as to works of genius, they are beyond their capacity: neither have they sufficient precision or power of attention to succeed in sciences which require accuracy: and as to physical knowledge, it belongs to those only who are most active, most inquisitive; who comprehend the greatest variety of objects; in short, it belongs to those who have the strongest powers, and who exercise them most, to judge of the relations between sensible beings and the laws of nature. A woman who is naturally weak, and does not carry her ideas to any great extent, knows how to judge and make a proper estimate of those movements which she sets to work, in order to aid her weakness; and these movements are the passions of men. The mechanism she employs is much more powerful than ours; for all her levers move the human heart. She must have the skill to incline us to do every thing which her sex will not enable her to do of herself, and which is necessary or agreeable to her; therefore she ought to study the mind of man thoroughly, not the mind of man in general, abstractedly, but the disposition of the men about her, the disposition of those men to whom she is subject, either by the laws of her country, or by the force of opinion. She should learn to penetrate into their real sentiments from their conversations, their actions, their looks and gestures. She should also have the art, by her own conversation, actions, looks and gestures, to communicate those sentiments which are agreeable to them, without seeming to intend it. Men will argue more philosophically about the human heart; but women will read the heart of man better than they. It belongs to women, if I may be allowed the expression, to form an experimental morality, and to reduce the study of man to a system. Women have most wit, men have most genius; women observe, men reason; from the concurrence of both we derive the clearest light and the most perfect knowledge, which the human mind is, of itself, capable of attaining: in one word, from hence we acquire the most intimate acquaintance, both with ourselves and others, of which our nature is capable; and it is thus that art has a constant tendency to perfect those endowments which nature has bestowed.

The world is the book of women; if they do not read well it is their own fault, or some passion blinds them. Nevertheless, a true mistress of a family, is not less a recluse in her own house, than a nun in her convent. Therefore, before a young virgin is married, we ought to act with regard to her, as they do, or at least ought to do, towards those who are to be confined in nunneries; that is, we should show them the pleasures they are to quit, before we suffer them to renounce them, lest the false idea of pleasures to which they are strangers, should mislead their minds, and interrupt the felicity of their retirement. In France, young ladies live in nunneries, and wives go abroad in the world. Among the ancients it was just the reverse; the maidens, as I have observed, were indulged with entertainments and public festivals; but wives lived retired. This custom was more rational, and had a better tendency to preserve morals. A kind of coquetry is allowed to young girls who are unmarried; their grand concern is to amuse themselves. Wives have other employment at home, and they are no longer in pursuit of husbands; but such a reformation would not be for their interest, and unhappily they lead the fashion. Mothers, however, make companions of your daughters! cultivate in them a just understanding and an honest heart, and then hide nothing from them which a chaste eye may view without offence. Balls, entertainments, public sights, even theatres; every thing which, seen improperly, delights indiscreet youth, may without danger be presented to the eye of prudence. The more they are conversant with these tumultuous pleasures, the sooner they will be disgusted with them.

. . .

Parents impose an outward restraint on their daughters, in hopes to meet with dupes who will marry them from their appearance. But examine these young girls attentively for a moment. Under an affected air of constraint, they do but ill disguise the eager desires which prey upon them; and you may already read in their eyes their violent inclination to imitate their mothers. But they do not covet a husband; they only long for the licence of matrimony. What occasion can they have for a husband, when they may have so many lovers? But they stand in need of a husband as a cover to their intrigues. Modesty is in their looks, but licentiousness in their hearts: That affected modesty is a symptom of it. They affect it only to get rid of it the sooner. . . .

. . .

Would you inspire young girls with a love of morality? Instead of telling them continually, "Be discreet," show them that it is their interest to be so; make them acquainted with the value of discretion, and you will make them in love with it. It is not sufficient, however, to present this interest to their view at a distance; convince them of their present advantage, with regard to the circumstances of their age, and with respect to the characters of their lovers. Describe to them the man of worth, the man of merit; teach them to know him, to love him, and to love him for their own sakes; persuade them that such a man alone is capable of making them happy, either as friends, wives or mistresses. Introduce virtue under the guidance of reason; make them sensible that the dominion of their sex, and all their prerogatives, do not depend entirely on their own good conduct, their own morals, but likewise on those of the men; that they can have no sure dependance on mean and groveling souls, and that a man is only qualified to oblige his mistress, in proportion as he is subservient to virtue. Take care likewise that in describing the manners of the present age, you at the same time inspire your daughter with a sincere aversion to them: by giving her a true description of our modish people, you will teach her to despise them; you will render her averse to their maxims, give her a dislike to their sentiments, and a contempt for their idle gallantries; you will excite in her a more noble ambition, that of reigning over strong and vigorous minds, that which inspired the women of Sparta, who boasted that they ruled over *men.* A forward, audacious and intriguing woman, who knows no other method of alluring lovers, but by coquetry, nor of preserving them but by repeated favours, makes them obey her like lacqueys on trifling and servile occasions; but in serious and weighty matters, she has no authority over them. But a woman who is virtuous, amiable and discreet, who obliges her lover to respect her, one who has reserve and modesty, in a word, one who supports love by esteem, will, by a single motion, send them to the farthest part of the world, to battle, to glory, to death; in short, wherever she pleases: such an empire, in my opinion, is glorious, and is well worth the pains of purchasing.

❦ *Elizabeth Rapaport*

Elizabeth Rapaport is an associate professor of philosophy at Boston University, where she specializes in ethics and political philosophy. In the following excerpt, taken from an article in The Philosophical Forum, *Professor Rapaport points out that despite Rousseau's dedication to the belief in the essential difference between woman's nature and man's, he finds the effects of love to be equally disastrous to the two sexes. This pessimistic view she deems a product of Rousseau's conviction that the love relation is essentially a dependent one and his notion that autonomy is a requisite for happiness. If the fear of dependence could be mitigated, Rapaport suggests, love might be "rehabilitated."*

"On the Future of Love: Rousseau and the Radical Feminists"

. . .

ROUSSEAU ON LOVE

Rousseau's theory of love might be captured by the traditional adage of husbands, "I can't live with her and I can't live without her," were the adage not so wry. The climate of love for Rousseau is bathed in intense feeling. Sexual love is portrayed by Rousseau as mutually destructive to men and women. Sexual love is at the center of Rousseau's account of social relations. It is the first other-regarding emotion that the developing human individual experiences and the paradigm of social relations with others. Sexual love is an inescapable human need. But the pursuit of love inevitably leads to frustration and unhappiness. The way we love inevitably defeats the ends of love. Defeat in love engulfs our whole personality. It destroys not only love but the lovers as well. For Rousseau man's love is like his sociality. Man is naturally social. But social living, the condition of human development and self-realization, is the irredeemable cause of human misery. To be happy we must be self-sufficient. But because we are human we need others. We are therefore happy neither in isolation nor in company.

Love, according to Rousseau's psychology, is a natural but not an original human need or desire. The distinction between original and nonoriginal elements in the human constitution is crucial in Rousseau's psychology. For Rousseau ontogeny recapitulates phylogeny. The nature of the human species and the human individual can only be understood in terms of their identical developmental courses. Savage man is not natural man but natural man at the beginning stages of human development. He has the potential to develop intellectual and moral capacities which will carry the human race from the savage to the civilized state. The development of these capacities is necessary for the full realization of human possibilities. Savage man is an isolate, a self-sufficient creature, with minimal, peaceful and uneventful interactions with others of his kind. He develops the characteristic and essential human capacities of reason and conscience as his world becomes social. As human life becomes social, he comes to need and depend upon others. He gains his humanity but loses his self-sufficiency. The quality of his life depends on the quality of his society. The human personality requires social living for its development. Its contours and contents vary with different sorts of society, some of which suit the inborn features of human personality very much more comfortably than others. A bad fit produces much avoidable misery. But societies cannot be torn off and replaced like ill-fitting suits of clothes. Tragically the best fit is not nearly good enough to prevent human misery. Why this is so can be seen by tracing out the parallel ontogenetic developmental course.[1]

---

[1] Cf. Rousseau's *A Discourse on the Origin of Inequality*, for his phylogenetic account.

The human child like the human savage is an essentially asocial creature. Rousseau sees the human adult as ruled and motivated by two "sentiments" which organize and color his affective structure, *amour de soi*—rendered in English as "self-preservation," "self-love" or "proper self-love" and *amour propre*, rendered in English as "pride," "selfishness" or "egotism." *Amour propre* is not yet an active principle in the infant and child. He is wholly a creature of self-love. *Amour de soi*, in savage and child, Rousseau regards as a benign principle. *Amour propre* is regarded as a pernicious principle that always leads to personal unhappiness and interpersonal conflict. The whole strategy of childhood education that Rousseau sets out in his *Emile* revolves around allowing the child to develop the powers to satisfy the desires of self-love in such fashion as to be as far as possible autonomous and self-sufficient. Both the powers and desires are naturally given and naturally develop commensurately so that the powers are adequate for the satisfaction of desire. Of course the child will need adult help and guidance. But adult help and guidance should be aimed at increasing his autonomy as well as perhaps the illusion of a greater autonomy than he really has. "True happiness consists in decreasing the distance between our desires and our powers, in establishing a perfect equilibrium between power and will."[2] Happiness will therefore be possible for the well-educated child as it never will be for the man in any possible human society.

If the child is made to feel dependent on the will of others, whether they are generous with him, over-generous, or whether they deny him, he will develop hostile feelings towards those around him. Worse, his personality structure will be adversely affected. He will be by turns servile and domineering in his attempts to gain his will through those on whom he is forced to depend. Rousseau's doctrine is that both tyranny and servility stem from impotence and breed hatred for those with the power to satisfy and withhold satisfaction of our desires. Tyrannical or servile, the frustrated child is equally miserable.[3]

Amour propre, sexual desire and the capacity for sexual love, all develop at the same time, at puberty, and bring in their train the development of genuinely other-regarding emotions and social interactions which go beyond an awareness of others as simply helps or obstacles to the child's own ends.

As soon as man needs a companion he is no longer an isolated creature, his heart is no longer alone. All his relations with his species, all the affections of his heart, came into being along with this. His first passion soon arouses the rest.[4]

Sexual love is a natural but not an original desire. The sexual desire is original but can be satisfied indifferently by any one of the opposite sex. Savages meet and couple in passing. They form no sexual relationships which endure beyond the desires of the moment. Sexual love involves choice of a lover. This choice involves comparison and preference. These preferences require standards of beauty and virtue. These standards of beauty and virtue are products of social living and culture.

[2] *Emile*, Everyman Library, p. 44.
[3] Cf. *Emile*, Part II.
[4] *Ibid.*, p. 175.

All women would be alike to a man who had no idea of virtue and beauty, and the first comer would always be the most charming. Love does not spring from Nature, far from it; it is the curb and law of her desires; it is love that makes one sex indifferent to the other, the loved one alone excepted.[5]

But the lover desires to be loved in turn. And here is where *amour propre* enters, like the snake into the Garden of Eden.

We wish to inspire the preference we feel; love must be mutual. To be loved we must be worthy of love; to be preferred we must be more worthy than the rest, at least in the eyes of our beloved. Hence we begin to look around among our fellows; we begin to compare ourselves with them, there is emulation, rivalry and jealousy.[6]

The lover wants his love to be reciprocated. She must see him as pre-eminent in virtue and beauty, if he is to succeed. This necessarily activates the human capacity for *amour propre*, for jealousy, rivalry and the desire to gain an invidious esteem. He must strive to be or at least appear to be in her eyes the pre-eminent possessor of the qualities she prizes most. His child's autonomy, were he lucky enough to have achieved it, falls away. It is perilous to human autonomy to need another. But love, were it possible, would more than fully compensate. The lover loses his autonomy in a deeper sense. He must give up a life guided by *amour de soi*, by the pursuit of the natural desires that his heart has and which would realize the potentialities of his personality, and assume the straightjacket of being or appearing to be the man of her heart's desire. So it is with love and so it is in all other human relations in which the affections and esteem of others are courted. They necessarily make rivals of men, force us to give up independent standards of self-esteem for socially imposed standards of our worth. We lose touch with our natural feelings, forfeit the chance for self-actualization. We lose ourselves and present a false self in the lists of social competition. While it does not prevent feelings of affection or continual growth of sympathy for others, it does neutralize or prevent affection and concern for others whenever one's own desire for the affection and esteem of others is active. *Amour propre* haunts and destroys all our attempts to reach out and make genuine contact with others.

With these psychological doctrines as necessary background, let us look at Rousseau's theory of love, at what a benign and happy love would be like and of what love must become in the irremediable circumstances of human social living.

Natural Attraction, the Fusion of Egos

Rousseau emphasizes the affective aspects of love. The goal of love is the fusion of two personalities. For this union to occur there must first be an initial attraction founded in like sensibility. This initial recognition of one's male or female counterpart provides the sentimental basis and the pull which draws us into union. Julie writes to her lover, Saint-Preux,

[5] *Ibid.*, p. 175.
[6] *Ibid.*, p. 176.

Our souls touch, so to speak at all points, and we feel an entire coherence . . . hence forward we shall have only mutual pleasures and pains; and like those magnets of which you were telling me that have, it is said, the same movements at different places, we shall have the same sensations though we were at the two poles of the earth.[7]

Dependency

Love begins with the recognition of a need for another, with the discovery of the radical insufficiency of the self and one's own powers for self-realization. The lover recognizes and feels his lack of or loss of autonomy. Saint-Preux writes to Julie, "I am no longer master of myself, I confess, my estranged soul is wholly absorbed in yours."[8]

Mutuality

Love would be mutual. Saint-Preux wants to possess as well as be possessed by Julie. If love is to be returned both man and woman must regard each other as worthy of love. Rousseau is certainly a male supremacist. He holds male and female nature are essentially different. Woman was made for man. The essence of womanhood is to serve, to please and to nurture man. Yet men value and respect the complementary and alien submissive virtues of women despite the defectiveness of female nature when judged by the standard of male nature. All the intellectual and moral inequalities of the sexes are neutralized by the mutual recognition of the need for love. Men do not respect women as full persons in the male sense. But they respect the terrible power women have to give or withhold the love they need. Men and women are equal in love. They are equally vulnerable and equally powerful.

Idealization

Love begins with the attraction and recognition of a like sensibility which seems to hold out the possibility of fusion of personalities. But love also requires that we see in the other and continue to see features of personality radically different from our own. The lover must find the perfections of the other and alien sex in the beloved, the perfections he or she necessarily lacks. Since love involves choice and standards of compassion between members of a sex, love's choice is for the man or woman pre-eminent of their sex. The standard of perfection will be a mixture of the personal and the public. It will be public insofar as canons of male and female beauty and virtue are cultural norms. It will be personal insofar as it involves placing a high value on the possession of certain qualities which may be found in either sex and which the lover finds in both himself and the beloved. These make possible the natural affinity of particular men and women for each other.

[7] *La Nouvelle Héloïse*, Pennsylvania State University Press, 1968, p. 47.
[8] *Ibid.*, p. 83.

Exclusivity

If one man or woman is found perfect and finding perfection is a requirement for loving, there must be exclusive, complete fusion with and absorption
in another. A multiplicity of love relations is precluded.

Rousseau holds that the achievement of love is illusional or delusional.
To see why we must look at one more feature of love.

The Logic of Dependence

The lover is dependent, entirely, terribly dependent on his beloved for
something he needs, the reciprocity of his love. Therefore loving falls under
the domain of *amour propre,* not *amour de soi.* The lover cannot achieve love's
desire, reciprocity, by the exercise of his own powers. He will only be loved if
she finds him pre-eminent. He must present himself in the guise in which she
would see her beloved. This leads to a false presentation of the self and the
chronic fear of exposure and loss of love. Along the way the lover loses himself
and necessarily the opportunity to gain love for this lost self.

But what of the fortunate possibility that a pair of lovers actually possess
the very virtues that they seek and find in each other? Might not fortunate
couples each rich in personal merit not escape the predicament of self-falsification
and self-loss in love? The answer, I think, must be no. Love operates in the
domain of *amour propre,* not *amour de soi.* The reciprocity of need and dependence cannot prevent the disastrous working out of the effects of dependence
in the human personality. To be happy we must be autonomous. But we are
not autonomous in love. Therefore we cannot be happy in love. Love operates
in the domain of *amour propre.* Human beings can only act in a fashion not
self and mutually destructive when they are motivated by desires whose satisfaction is within their own powers. If we need another, the terrible possibility
remains that their gratification of our need will be withdrawn. Even if love
has been met with complete responsiveness, there is the future to dread. It is
not within our power to secure the future love of our beloved against surfeit,
disillusionment, or a rival found more worthy. Therefore, the lover is in a
position of weakness, of impotence. Impotence forces him to employ tyrannical
or servile means in futile attempts to secure what cannot be secured. The lover
becomes a tyrant or a slave because of his impotence. In so doing he must
both become and reveal a personality lacking in the perfections the lover sought
and that he or she had found. In his weakness he confirms or creates the very
doubts about his worthiness he feared his beloved was entertaining. Even if the
doubts and fears that consume lovers and the jealous and craven responses they
make do not result in the withdrawal of love, these feelings themselves, together with the sense of impotence they spring from, make the lover miserable.
Such is certainly the case with Saint-Preux, who is given to depressive fits of
jealous rage against his friend and protector, Lord Edward. Love is an illusion
or a delusion. Or if you prefer, love is a genuine enough human experience, but
a miserable one. Lovers may possess each other and consume each other, but
they lose themselves.

I believe that Rousseau's two great fictional accounts of love, the story of Emile and Sophie and of Saint-Preux and Julie, support my interpretation of Rousseau's theory of love if properly read. Despite the undeniable aspects of the sentimental celebration of romantic love characteristic of these works and which largely account for their tremendous popular success, love is portrayed as a tragic disappointment in both. Rousseau had what has been called a bourgeois conception of love.[9] The ideal is married love. In one of his two great love stories the hero marries the girl and loses her. In the other he simply loses her. Both losses propel the male lovers, whose side of the story Rousseau identifies with and treats more fully, into massive depressions and send them off on years-long travels to try to forget and heal their wounds. Both Emile and Saint-Preux are depicted as men of unusual pasts and merits. Emile is unusual in that he has been carefully educated for the attainment of happiness and virtue despite, and in the midst of, what Rousseau regarded as a deplorable social environment. Saint-Preux is portrayed as a man of unusual talents and qualities. Both, as a result of loving, succeed in doing nothing of any note in the world, more significant in Saint-Preux's case, and feeling nothing but intense misery, more significant in Emile's case.

Julie writes to her lover, Saint-Preux:

Love is accompanied by a continual uneasiness over jealousy or privation, little suited to marriage, which is a state of enjoyment and peace. People do not marry in order to think exclusively of each other, but in order to fulfill the duties of civil society jointly, to govern the house prudently, to rear their children well. Lovers never see anyone but themselves, they incessantly attend only to themselves, and the only thing they are able to do is love each other.[10]

Despite his bourgeois ideal of love, it seems to be Rousseau's opinion that even the slight requirements for the fulfillment of women's social role are incompatible with love, while potentially great and virtuous men have their capacity to act in the world as well as their happiness destroyed by love. In the little read and as far as I know untranslated sequel to *Emile*, *Emile et Sophie*, the tragic dissolution of Emile's marriage is portrayed. Emile's marriage falters because that paragon of virtue is distracted by Parisian pleasures and neglects his wife. It seems that when a social evil is not introduced as an obstacle to love's desire (Saint-Preux's low birth prevents his marriage to Julie), and even when the best of men and women have the best of chances for success, love fails. His desire realized, Emile loses interest in his wife until her unfaithfulness revives the fires and torments of love.

THE FUTURE OF LOVE: SEXUAL LOVE AND SOCIAL PSYCHOLOGY

. . .

There is a paradox at the heart of Rousseau's account of social relations. To be humanly happy we need others. But if we need others we are lost.

---

[9] Denis de Rougemont, *Love in the Western World*, New York, 1956.
[10] *La Nouvelle Héloïse*, pp. 261–262.

Rousseau wanted to repudiate the kind of psychological egoism which regarded human beings as wholly selfish and as having purely instrumental interactions with each other. Interactions whose goal was the satisfaction of the self, a self which was only in peripheral ways affected by or a product of its society and culture. But he was too deeply mired in individualism to make more than a very partial break with its social and psychological theory. He was able to project the essential effects of social living on the individual's personality structure only as threats to the integrity and happiness of the self. The result is a theory which posits the insufficiency of the human individual to achieve his or her self-realization in society. But what is really wanted is a theoretical critique of the insufficiency of individualism. This is a very large and a very difficult theoretical task which it goes without saying I cannot undertake here. But a few remarks will show the relevance of this critical task to the rehabilitation of love.

If autonomy from the need for others is posited as a necessary condition for human happiness, all dependency relations are necessarily pernicious. Add that they are unavoidable and you have the plight of Rousseauvian love. But suppose that the just fear of dependency of men on women and women on men that now obtains is the product of dysfunctional economic and social relations not just between the sexes but throughout social life, not the product of some deficiency in human nature. Suppose that the fear of dependency is a variable feature of human personality attributable to social conditions which drive them into invidious competition for the social status and esteem which could be accorded everyone in a society where cooperative institutions supported fruitful and healthy interdependency. Suppose that the thesis is false, that love, respect, and esteem are only given to him who is so pre-eminent in the eyes of others as to scarcely seem to require the further perfection of being loved by others. Suppose we could grant our love on some basis other than the supposed absolute pre-eminence of the beloved. Under conditions in which lovers did not seek pre-eminence according to social norms of attainment in those whom they loved, dependency would not have the terrible aspect of courting almost certain exposure and failure. Love's eye could still seek and find the special qualities that lead to preferment, draw affection and nourish the growth of personality in lovers. Human differences and variety in sensibility and qualities would still guide and motivate love-choices. Such encounters would still be fraught with the perils of rejection and failure but not hopelessly and inevitably so. What I propose is a socialist theory of social psychology, of which we have now only the barest sketch. Love may be rehabilitated if the just fear of dependency relations we learn from love as we know it turns out to be grounded not in fear of ourselves but the pathological distortions of human personality produced by an unjust, destructive and successfully alterable social order.

Radical feminists have forced an admission on the part of many socialists that traditional socialist programs are insufficient for achieving women's liberation. The insufficiency of a feminist program alone to give love a future shows that this most personal of political problems requires more than sexual equality for its solution.

ᨠ9 *Mary Wollstonecraft*

Mary Wollstonecraft was born in London in 1759. Her father, Edward John Wollstonecraft, was employed as a weaver until, upon the receipt of a small inheritance, he left London to begin a series of unsuccessful attempts to establish himself as a gentleman farmer. All that he managed to establish, however, was a reputation for drinking heavily and tyrannizing his family. At one point in his nomadic existence he settled for a time in Hoxton, a village near London, where his eldest daughter, Mary, met Fanny Blood. Fanny's family background was similar to Mary's and the two became close friends. Mr. Blood, too, was domineering and ineffectual as the head of a family. Consequently both Fanny and the three Wollstonecraft daughters were forced to rely on their own resources to earn their living, a relatively rare situation for eighteenth-century Englishwomen. They managed to rent a house and open a school, which flourished briefly and then went bankrupt. After an interval as a governess, Mary repaired to London, where, as a member of the small circle of intellectuals that gathered around Joseph Johnson, the publisher, she dedicated herself to a literary career.

In England during the eighteenth century, a woman was seldom faced with the necessity of having to support herself. Normally she spent her entire life under the guardianship of a man—first her father, then her husband. But in the circumstances of the Wollstonecraft family, in those of the Bloods, and in those of her own sister, who had contracted a brief and unhappy marriage, Mary Wollstonecraft was witness to situations that belied the popular thesis of female inferiority, for in each of these cases the guardian was incompetent and brutal, and his ward was competent and victimized. This observation had a profound effect on young Mary Wollstonecraft.

Understandably enough, she developed a strong aversion to marriage; yet she let herself drift into romantic attachments that were scarcely happier than those of her mother, her sister, or Mrs. Blood. Her platonic friendship with artist Henry Fuseli ended abruptly when his wife rejected Mary's proposal of a ménage à trois. An affair with an American, Gilbert Imlay, led to an illegitimate daughter and two attempts at suicide. A later involvement with William Godwin, which resulted in another pregnancy, softened Wollstonecraft's views on marriage, and on March 29, 1797, she and Godwin were quietly wed. On September 10, 1797, less than two weeks after giving birth to a second daughter, Mary Wollstonecraft Godwin died of postnatal complications.

By the end of the eighteenth century the spirit of freedom, which had led to revolutions in the New World and across the channel, had spread to England, where it infected not only men, but women as well. Most educated Englishwomen were conservative, to be sure, but a few of them saw in the literature of liberty that was pouring from the presses a hope for their own sex. Mary Wollstonecraft was chief among them. Her works cry out for women to be given enough education and to be permitted to develop enough strength to enable them to become financially independent. Her most famous book, A Vindication of the Rights of Woman, is dedicated to Talleyrand, who had pointedly ignored women in his proposal for a new system of education for France. Women as well as men need to be educated, Wollstonecraft argues, for virtue is not innate; it is a product of reason and knowledge, and it requires careful cultivation.

In the Vindication Wollstonecraft answered, point by point, virtually all the allegations concerning her sex that Rousseau had made in Book V of Emile. First, she charged that Rousseau, like all other writers on the subject, tended to exaggerate female weakness and artificiality and to depict women as even more useless to society than they actually were at that time. Not only is Rousseau's picture of woman inaccurate; he erred in the opposite direction concerning his own sex, depicting men as far more mature than they often are. Thus Wollstonecraft observed far less difference between the sexes than Rousseau had detected—an ironic conclusion when one considers that Rousseau had conceded to her sex superior powers of observation. Wollstonecraft insisted that the two sexes are identical in both knowledge and virtue; that women, like men, are both rational and moral; and that women should therefore seek to acquire virtue by the same means as men.

Many of those differences that do exist between the sexes are in Wollstonecraft's eyes not natural but acquired, a view challenged by Rousseau in the earlier work. The fondness for dolls and dress that Rousseau considered a natural feminine trait she attributed to adaptation to environment: any little girl, given half a chance, would elect to be a tomboy. Deprived of the opportunity to play outdoors, girls prefer play with dolls to no play at all.

Wollstonecraft held that the superior physical strength with which men are endowed was exaggerated by Rousseau. A man is stronger than a woman, to be sure, but nothing other than custom and tradition prevents a woman from cultivating the strength to earn her living and the resolution to develop her mind—the only things really necessary for her independence.

That docility and good temper are essentially feminine traits Wollstonecraft flatly denied. As a matter of fact, the tempers of most men are more even than those of most women, she said, but again only because of the different situations with which the two sexes are usually confronted. Men are more likely to be engaged in jobs that develop the mind and therefore involve less frustration than the typical female activity. Reason, not nature, controls temper, and circumstances conspire to see to it that man's reason is better developed than woman's.

Wollstonecraft challenged not only Rousseau's specific ideas but his general laissez-faire attitude as well. As far as the status of women in society was concerned, Rousseau believed that whatever is, is right. Although he questioned the foundations of the French monarchy and argued with educators who believed that children are inherently evil, he had no doubts concerning the position of woman in society. He devoted his attention to enabling her to fill ever more adequately that position to which she had been relegated. But, although Wollstonecraft agreed that to God in his omniscience whatever is, is right, her concern was with the finite human being, to whom things *not infrequently appear to be very wrong indeed. Whenever this is the case, she believed, there is a moral obligation to change what is.*

Wollstonecraft's most pervasive criticism of Rousseau seems to be that he celebrated the feminine virtue of obedience even at the expense of truth and fortitude. Truth and fortitude are virtues common to men and women alike. They are human virtues and therefore are superior to unquestioning obedience. Rousseau's aim was to render woman pleasing to man. Weak as he believed her to be, he adjudged her incapable of achieving her goals directly. Therefore he urged her to pursue them indirectly, by discovering the means to motivate men to desire them also, to "rule in obedience." But to do so, woman must sacrifice truth and sincerity at the altar of utility—and utility as seen by men, at that. The price is far too great, according to Wollstonecraft. She rejected Rousseau's distinction between male and female duties. All human duties, she thought, are founded on the same principles and should be pursued by the same means.

From *A Vindication of the Rights of Woman*

CHAPTER 1

The Rights and Involved Duties of Mankind Considered

In the present state of society it appears necessary to go back to first principles in search of the most simple truths, and to dispute with some prevailing prejudice every inch of ground. To clear my way, I must be allowed to ask some plain questions, and the answers will probably appear as unequivocal as the axioms on which reasoning is built; though, when entangled with various motives of action, they are formally contradicted, either by the words or conduct of men.

In what does man's pre-eminence over the brute creation consist? The answer is as clear as that a half is less than the whole; in Reason.

What acquirement exalts one being above another? Virtue; we spontaneously reply.

For what purpose were the passions implanted? That man by struggling with them might attain a degree of knowledge denied to the brutes; whispers Experience.

Consequently the perfection of our nature and capability of happiness, must be estimated by the degree of reason, virtue, and knowledge, that distinguish the individual, and direct the laws which bind society: and that from the exercise of reason, knowledge and virtue naturally flow, is equally undeniable, if mankind be viewed collectively.

. . .

CHAPTER 2

The Prevailing Opinion of a Sexual Character Discussed

To account for, and excuse the tyranny of man, many ingenious arguments have been brought forward to prove, that the two sexes, in the acquirement of virtue, ought to aim at attaining a very different character; or, to speak explicitly, women are not allowed to have sufficient strength of mind to acquire what really deserves the name of virtue. Yet it should seem, allowing them to have souls, that there is but one way appointed by Providence to lead *mankind* to either virtue or happiness.

If then women are not a swarm of ephemeron triflers, why should they be kept in ignorance under the specious name of innocence? Men complain, and with reason, of the follies and caprices of our sex, when they do not keenly satirise our headstrong passions and grovelling vices. Behold, I should answer, the natural effect of ignorance! The mind will ever be unstable that has only prejudices to rest on, and the current will run with destructive fury when there are no barriers to break its force. Women are told from their infancy, and taught by the example of their mothers, that a little knowledge of human weakness, justly termed cunning, softness of temper, *outward* obedience, and a scrupulous attention to a puerile kind of propriety, will obtain for them the protection of man; and should they be beautiful, everything else is needless, for at least twenty years of their lives.

. . .

How grossly do they insult us who thus advise us only to render ourselves gentle, domestic brutes! For instance, the winning softness so warmly and frequently recommended, that governs by obeying. What childish expressions, and how insignificant is the being—can it be an immortal one?—who will condescend to govern by such sinister methods? . . .

Children, I grant, should be innocent; but when the epithet is applied to men, or women, it is but a civil term for weakness. For if it be allowed that women were destined by Providence to acquire human virtues, and, by the exercise of their understandings, that stability of character which is the firmest ground to rest our future hopes upon, they must be permitted to turn to the fountain of light, and not forced to shape their course by the twinkling of a mere satellite.

. . .

In treating therefore of the manners of women, let us, disregarding sensual arguments, trace what we should endeavour to make them in order to co-operate, if the expression be not too bold, with the Supreme Being.

. . .

. . . [T]he most perfect education, in my opinion, is such an exercise of the understanding as is best calculated to strengthen the body and form the heart. Or, in other words, to enable the individual to attain such habits of virtue as will render it independent. In fact, it is a farce to call any being virtuous whose virtues do not result from the exercise of its own reason. This was Rousseau's opinion respecting men; I extend it to women, and confidently assert that they have been drawn out of their sphere by false refinement, and not by an endeavour to acquire masculine qualities. Still the regal homage which they receive is so intoxicating, that until the manners of the times are changed, and formed on more reasonable principles, it may be impossible to convince them that the illegitimate power which they obtain by degrading themselves is a curse, and that they must return to nature and equality if they wish to secure the placid satisfaction that unsophisticated affections impart. But for this epoch we must wait—wait perhaps till kings and nobles, enlightened by reason, and, preferring the real dignity of man to childish state, throw off their gaudy hereditary trappings; and if then women do not resign the arbitrary power of beauty—they will prove that they have *less* mind than man.

. . .

. . . [T]o reason on Rousseau's ground, if man did attain a degree of perfection of mind when his body arrived at maturity, it might be proper, in order to make a man and his wife *one,* that she should rely entirely on his understanding; and the graceful ivy, clasping the oak that supported it, would form a whole in which strength and beauty would be equally conspicuous. But, alas! husbands, as well as their helpmates, are often only overgrown children,—nay, thanks to early debauchery, scarcely men in their outward form,—and if the blind lead the blind, one need not come from heaven to tell us the consequence.

Many are the causes that, in the present corrupt state of society, contribute to enslave women by cramping their understandings and sharpening their senses. One, perhaps, that silently does more mischief than all the rest, is their disregard of order.

To do everything in an orderly manner is a most important precept, which women, who, generally speaking, receive only a disorderly kind of education, seldom attend to with that degree of exactness that men, who from their infancy are broken into method, observe. This negligent kind of guesswork—for what other epithet can be used to point out the random exertions of a sort of instinctive common-sense never brought to the test of reason?—prevents their generalising matters of fact; so they do to-day what they did yesterday, merely because they did it yesterday.

This contempt of the understanding in early life has more baneful consequences than is commonly supposed; for the little knowledge which women of strong minds attain is, from various circumstances, of a more desultory kind than the knowledge of men, and it is acquired more by sheer observations on real life than from comparing what has been individually observed with the results of experience generalized by speculation. Led by their dependent situation and domestic employments more into society, what they learn is rather by snatches; and as learning is with them in general only a secondary thing, they do not pursue any one branch with that persevering ardour necessary to give vigour to the faculties and clearness to the judgment. In the present state of society a little learning is required to support the character of a gentleman, and boys are obliged to submit to a few years of discipline. But in the education of women, the cultivation of the understanding is always subordinate to the acquirement of some corporeal accomplishment. Even while enervated by confinement and false notions of modesty, the body is prevented from attaining that grace and beauty which relaxed half-formed limbs never exhibit. Besides, in youth their faculties are not brought forward by emulation; and having no serious scientific study, if they have natural sagacity, it is turned too soon on life and manners. They dwell on effects and modifications, without tracing them back to causes; and complicated rules to adjust behaviour are a weak substitute for simple principles.

As a proof that education gives this appearance of weakness to females, we may instance the example of military men, who are, like them, sent into the world before their minds have been stored with knowledge, or fortified by principles. The consequences are similar; soldiers acquire a little superficial knowledge, snatched from the muddy current of conversation, and from continually mixing with society, they gain what is termed a knowledge of the world; and this acquaintance with manners and customs has frequently been confounded with a knowledge of the human heart. But can the crude fruit of casual observation, never brought to the test of judgment, formed by comparing speculation and experience, deserve such a distinction? Soldiers, as well as women, practise the minor virtues with punctilious politeness. Where is then the sexual difference, when the education has been the same? All the difference that I can discern arises from the superior advantage of liberty which enables the former to see more of life.

.   .   .

The great misfortune is this, that they both acquire manners before morals, and a knowledge of life before they have from reflection any acquaintance with the grand ideal outline of human nature. The consequence is natural. Satisfied with common nature, they become a prey to prejudices, and taking all their opinions on credit, they blindly submit to authority. So that if they have any sense, it is a kind of instinctive glance that catches proportions, and decides with respect to manners, but fails when arguments are to be pursued below the surface, or opinions analysed.

May not the same remark be applied to women? Nay, the argument may be carried still further, for they are both thrown out of a useful station by the unnatural distinctions established in civilised life. Riches and hereditary honours have made cyphers of women to give consequence to the numerical figure; and idleness has produced a mixture of gallantry and despotism into society, which leads the very men who are the slaves of their mistresses to tyrannise over their sisters, wives, and daughters. This is only keeping them in rank and file, it is true. Strengthen the female mind by enlarging it, and there will be an end to blind obedience; but as blind obedience is ever sought for by power, tyrants and sensualists are in the right when they endeavour to keep women in the dark, because the former only want slaves, and the latter a plaything. The sensualist, indeed, has been the most dangerous of tyrants, and women have been duped by their lovers, as princes by their ministers, whilst dreaming that they reigned over them.

.   .   .

Women are therefore to be considered either as moral beings, or so weak that they must be entirely subjected to the superior faculties of men.

Let us examine this question. Rousseau declares that a woman should never for a moment feel herself independent, that she should be governed by fear to exercise her *natural* cunning, and made a coquettish slave in order to render her a more alluring object of desire, a *sweeter* companion to man, whenever he chooses to relax himself. He carries the arguments, which he pretends to draw from the indications of nature, still further, and insinuates that truth and fortitude, the corner-stones of all human virtue, should be cultivated with certain restrictions, because, with respect to the female character, obedience is the grand lesson which ought to be impressed with unrelenting rigour.

What nonsense! When will a great man arise with sufficient strength of mind to puff away the fumes which pride and sensuality have thus spread over the subject? If women are by nature inferior to men, their virtues must be the same in quality, if not in degree, or virtue is a relative idea; consequently, their conduct should be founded on the same principles, and have the same aim.

Connected with man as daughters, wives, and mothers, their moral character may be estimated by their manner of fulfilling those simple duties; but the end, the grand end, of their exertions should be to unfold their own faculties, and acquire the dignity of conscious virtue. They may try to render their road pleasant; but ought never to forget, in common with man, that life yields not the felicity which can satisfy an immortal soul. I do not mean to insinuate that either sex should be so lost in abstract reflections or distant views as to forget the affections and duties that lie before them, and are, in truth, the means appointed to produce the fruit of life; on the contrary, I would warmly recommend them, even while I assert, that they afford most satisfaction when they are considered in their true sober light.

   . . .

Let it not be concluded that I wish to invert the order of things. I have already granted that, from the constitution of their bodies, men seemed to be designed by Providence to attain a greater degree of virtue. I speak collectively of the whole sex; but I see not the shadow of a reason to conclude that their virtues should differ in respect to their nature. In fact, how can they, if virtue has only one eternal standard? I must therefore, if I reason consequentially, as strenuously maintain that they have the same simple direction as that there is a God.

It follows then that cunning should not be opposed to wisdom, little cares to great exertions, or insipid softness, varnished over with the name of gentleness, to that fortitude which grand views alone can inspire.

   . . .

Women ought to endeavour to purify their heart; but can they do so when their uncultivated understandings make them entirely dependent on their senses for employment and amusement, when no noble pursuit sets them above the little vanities of the day, or enables them to curb the wild emotions that agitate a reed, over which every passing breeze has power? To gain the affections of a virtuous man, is affection necessary? Nature has given woman a weaker frame than man; but, to ensure her husband's affections, must a wife, who, by the exercise of her mind and body whilst she was discharging the duties of a daughter, wife, and mother, has allowed her constitution to retain its natural strength, and her nerves a healthy tone,—is she, I say, to condescend to use art, and feign a sickly delicacy, in order to secure her husband's affection? Weakness may excite tenderness, and gratify the arrogant pride of man; but the lordly caresses of a protector will not gratify a noble mind that pants for and deserves to be respected. Fondness is a poor substitute for friendship!

. . . [T]he woman who strengthens her body and exercises her mind will, by managing her family and practising various virtues, become the friend, and not the humble dependent of her husband; and if she, by possessing such substantial qualities, merit his regard, she will not find it necessary to conceal her affection, nor to pretend to an unnatural coldness of constitution to excite her husband's passions. In fact, if we revert to history, we shall find that the women who have distinguished themselves have neither been the most beautiful nor the most gentle of their sex.

To recommend gentleness, indeed, on a broad basis is strictly philosophical. A frail being should labour to be gentle. But when forbearance confounds right and wrong, it ceases to be a virtue; and, however convenient it may be found in a companion—that companion will ever be considered as an inferior, and only inspire a vapid tenderness, which easily degenerates into contempt. Still, if advice could really make a being gentle, whose natural disposition admitted not of such a fine polish, something towards the advancement of order would be attained; but if, as might quickly be demonstrated, only affection be produced by this indiscriminate counsel, which throws a stumbling-block in the way of gradual improvement, and true melioration of temper, the sex is not much benefited by sacrificing solid virtues to the attainment of superficial graces, though for a few years they may procure the individuals regal sway.

As a philosopher, I read with indignation the plausible epithets which men use to soften their insults; and, as a moralist, I ask what is meant by such heterogeneous associations, as fair defects, amiable weaknesses, etc.? If there be but one criterion of morals, but one archetype for man, women appear to be suspended by destiny, according to the vulgar tale of Mahomet's coffin; they have neither the unerring instinct of brutes, nor are allowed to fix the eye of reason on a perfect model. They were made to be loved, and must not aim at respect, lest they should be hunted out of society as masculine.

But to view the subject in another point of view. Do passive indolent women make the best wives? Confining our discussion to the present moment of existence, let us see how such weak creatures perform their part? Do the women who, by the attainment of a few superficial accomplishments, have strengthened the prevailing prejudice, merely contributed to the happiness of their husbands? Do they display their charms merely to amuse them? And have women who have early imbibed notions of passive obedience, sufficient character to manage a family or educate children? So far from it, that, after surveying the history of woman, I cannot help agreeing with the severest satirist, considering the sex as the weakest as well as the most oppressed half of the species. What does history disclose but marks of inferiority, and how few women have emancipated themselves from the galling yoke of sovereign man?

So few that the exceptions remind me of an ingenious conjecture respecting Newton—that he was probably a being of superior order accidentally caged in a human body. Following the same train of thinking, I have been led to imagine that the few extraordinary women who have rushed in eccentrical directions out of the orbit prescribed to their sex, were *male* spirits, confined by mistake in female frames. But if it be not philosophical to think of sex when the soul is mentioned, the inferiority must depend on the organs; or the heavenly fire, which is to ferment the clay, is not given in equal portions.

But avoiding, as I have hitherto done, any direct comparison of the two sexes collectively, or frankly acknowledging the inferiority of woman, according to the present appearance of things, I shall only insist that men have increased that inferiority till women are almost sunk below the standard of rational creatures. Let their faculties have room to unfold, and their virtues to gain strength, and then determine where the whole sex must stand in the intellectual scale. Yet let it be remembered, that for a small number of distinguished women I do not ask a place.

It is difficult for us purblind mortals to say to what height human discoveries and improvements may arrive when the gloom of despotism subsides, which makes us stumble at every step; but when morality shall be settled on a more solid basis, then, without being gifted with a prophetic spirit, I will venture to predict that woman will be either the friend or slave of man. We shall not, as at present, doubt whether she is a moral agent, or the link which unites man with brutes. But should it then appear that like the brutes they were principally created for the use of man, he will let them patiently bite the bridle, and not mock them with empty praise; or, should their rationality be proved, he will not impede their improvement merely to gratify his sensual appetites. He will not, with all the graces of rhetoric, advise them to submit implicitly their understanding to the guidance of man. He will not, when he treats of the education of women, assert that they ought never to have the free use of reason, nor would he recommend cunning and dissimulation to beings who are acquiring, in like manner as himself, the virtues of humanity.

Surely there can be but one rule of right, if morality has an eternal foundation, and whoever sacrifices virtue, strictly so called, to present convenience, or whose *duty* it is to act in such a manner, lives only for the passing day, and cannot be an accountable creature.

．　．　．

These may be termed Utopian dreams. Thanks to that Being who impressed them on my soul, and gave me sufficient strength of mind to dare to exert my own reason, till, becoming dependent only on Him for the support of my virtue, I view with indignation, the mistaken notions that enslave my sex.

I love man as my fellow; but his sceptre, real or usurped, extends not to me, unless the reason of an individual demands my homage; and even then the submission is to reason, and not to man. In fact, the conduct of an accountable being must be regulated by the operations of its own reason; or on what foundation rests the throne of God?

It appears to me necessary to dwell on these obvious truths, because females have been insulated, as it were; and while they have been stripped of the virtues that should clothe humanity, they have been decked with artificial graces that enable them to exercise a short-lived tyranny. Love, in their bosoms, taking place of every nobler passion, their sole ambition is to be fair, to raise emotion instead of inspiring respect; and this ignoble desire, like the servility in absolute monarchies, destroys all strength of character. Liberty is the mother of virtue, and if women be, by their very constitution, slaves, and not allowed to breathe the sharp invigorating air of freedom, they must ever languish like exotics, and be reckoned beautiful flaws in nature.

As to the argument respecting the subjection in which the sex has ever been held, it retorts on man. The many have always been enthralled by the few; and monsters, who scarcely have shown any discernment of human excellence, have tyrannised over thousands of their fellow-creatures. Why have men of superior endowments submitted to such degradation? For, is it not universally acknowledged that kings, viewed collectively, have ever been inferior, in abilities and virtue, to the same number of men taken from the common mass of mankind—yet have they not, and are they not still treated with a degree of reverence that is an insult to reason? China is not the only country where a living man has been made a God. *Men* have submitted to superior strength to enjoy with impunity the pleasure of the moment; *women* have only done the same, and therefore till it is proved that the courtier, who servilely resigns the birthright of a man, is not a moral agent, it cannot be demonstrated that woman is essentially inferior to man because she has always been subjugated.

Brutal force has hitherto governed the world, and that the science of politics is in its infancy, is evident from philosophers scrupling to give the knowledge most useful to man that determinate distinction.

I shall not pursue this argument any further than to establish an obvious inference, that as sound politics diffuse liberty, mankind, including woman, will become more wise and virtuous.

❧ *Carolyn W. Korsmeyer*

Carolyn Korsmeyer is an associate professor of philosophy at the State University of New York at Buffalo. Her interests range from feminism to aesthetics, and she has contributed papers to a number of journals, among them the Journal of the History of Ideas and The Journal of Aesthetics and Art Criticism. In the following selection, taken from The Philosophical Forum, she suggests that the eighteenth century is not the only one in which women have been dissuaded from fully developing their rational abilities. Even today, she points out, women are not infrequently held to be inferior to men in the ability to reason.

Reason and Morals in the Early Feminist Movement: Mary Wollstonecraft

It is difficult to generalize about the theories at work in a social movement as broadly based and diversified as the women's rights movement of the nineteenth century, for its presuppositions, demands, even its goals changed and evolved during the century or so before women obtained the vote. Then, as now, the politics of the women's rights movement proceeded less from a systematic political theory than from a recognition of personal oppression and injustice. Naturally, as women became conscious of and actively dissatisfied with their place in the social order, their oppression as they perceived it was explained in the context of the prevailing ideas of the time, and, accordingly, prescription for change mirrored much contemporary political philosophy as well.

One such "perceived oppression" was founded in the moral philosophy prevalent in England and America at that time. The connection between reason and morals which lies at the root of Locke's political philosophy and which enjoyed popular acceptance as well, was for women both a means of their oppression and a rallying point for the assertion of political equality. Denied education and inculcated with the idea that they were frivolous, irrational creatures, the early feminists saw that the establishment of woman as a fully rational human being was one of the first steps towards political, legal, and social equality.

In this paper I shall explore some of the issues and arguments relevant to the subject of women, reason, and moral responsibility. I see this issue as one of the first theoretical questions to appear in feminist thinking of the early nineteenth century, though, needless to say, it represents only one aspect of the whole social movement. I have limited this study to the period between 1792 and 1848, dates which mark respectively the publication of Mary Wollstonecraft's *A Vindication of the Rights of Woman* and the Declaration of Sentiments and Resolutions presented at Seneca Falls, New York, a document which is commonly regarded as signifying the beginning of the organized women's rights movement in the United States.

Although Wollstonecraft was not herself a part of the women's rights movement (she died in 1797), her work was widely read and served as a reference for a number of active feminists in both England and America. Additionally, in her work we find the questions of morals and reason treated with a depth of analysis less frequent in the later feminist writings. Accordingly, I have relied largely on her *Vindication* for the source of philosophical arguments advanced in behalf of feminism.

Wollstonecraft's general line of argument can be separated into three parts: (1) First and foremost, she argues that reason is essential for the development of moral character, whether that of a man or of a woman. (2) Then she presents a refutation of what I call the "separation of virtues" doctrine, then a popular belief that there is a difference between "male" and "female" virtues. (3) In explanation of the position of women in society, she offers an argument based on the theory of associated ideas for "nurture" over "nature" as the cause of any deficiency found in the reasoning powers of females of the time. Wollstonecraft also points out an important inconsistency contained in the current theories about women and their moral character. . . .

In the eighteenth and nineteenth centuries, when the seeds of the women's rights movement first began to grow in England and America, it was the popular conception that men and women enjoyed different "spheres" of activity, and that their virtues—the character qualities and abilities they should strive to attain—were specifically tailored to these spheres. Considered too weak physically to venture into the world outside the home and too deficient in reason to make important decisions, the woman was relegated to the domestic sphere where, under the guidance and direction of her rationally superior husband, she tended house, raised children, and gave her family comfort and pleasure. Correspondingly, her "virtues" were an outgrowth of her sensitive, yielding nature: kindness, humility, gentleness, protectiveness, and so on.

Female nature and feminine virtues were often touted as the complement of male nature and masculine virtues, the two together making a perfect whole of human behavior. For example, Rousseau states in *Emile,*

A perfect man and a perfect woman should no more be alike in mind than in face, and perfection admits of neither less nor more.

In the union of the sexes, each alike contributes to the common end, but in different ways.[1]

However, this notion of sexually distinct "spheres of activity" can in no way be construed as a doctrine of "separate but equal." Rousseau goes on to say,

From this diversity springs the first difference which may be observed between man and woman in their moral relations. The man should be strong and active; the woman should be weak and passive; the one must have both the power and the will; it is enough that the other should offer little resistance.

When this principle is admitted, it follows that woman is specially made for man's pleasure.[2]

Furthermore, as Aileen Kraditor has noted, the whole notion of proper activity being delineated by a "sphere," a term which implies limitation and confinement, really applies only to the woman, not to the man. "Strictly speaking, men have never had a 'proper sphere,' since their sphere has been the world and all its activities."[3] Woman's sphere and the female virtues are to be considered more accurately as a glorification of a genuinely inferior social status, one which had to be attacked before even the first steps towards political and legal equality could be taken.

[1] J. J. Rousseau, *Emile,* trans. Barbara Foxley (New York: Everyman's Library), p. 322.

[2] *Ibid.*

[3] Aileen Kraditor, ed., *Up from the Pedestal* (Chicago: Quadrangle Books, 1968), p. 9. (The first section of Kraditor's collection deals with the subject of "spheres" of activity.)

This time-honored notion of woman's place had significant political effects, for the acceptance of the existence of such a thing as a female sphere, so conceived, precluded any possibility of admitting women into full citizenship. Under the powerful influence of Locke and the political theorists who followed him, almost anyone interested in theories of citizenship and rights of the governed would also accept as a first principle the notion that a person derives natural and political rights through the possession of *reason*, that faculty which distinguishes human beings from the animals. Women, as a sex, were considered deficient in reasoning ability. It is reason, according to Locke, which enables one to discover the laws of nature—God's moral order—thus qualifying one as a participating member of society. So long as woman's reason was under suspicion, the early advocates of feminism could not make use of Locke's premise that "equals must have equal measure"[4] in order to lay claim to their natural rights, hitherto enjoyed only by a certain class of men. It was precisely with regard to reason, which defined the fully functioning citizen, that women were considered *un*equal. Lacking full use of reason, they could be unstable, capricious, wily, cunning, sensitive, and sentimental, and, it was thought, they had to be kept in the home for their own protection as well as for the good of society at large.

Mary Wollstonecraft attacked the notion of there being separate female virtues—a lesser feminine measure for virtue, adequate for women but not to be compared with the rationally-founded male virtue—as the first stage in her argument for the rationality and therefore the social equality of women.

Her attack on the notion of spheres of activity and female virtues focuses on what she regards as a logical fault in the very notion of there being two different standards for virtue. This fault is discoverable through analysis of the separation of virtues doctrine, which reveals it to be in fact a disguised form of relativism, a position as unacceptable to proponents of that doctrine as it is to Wollstonecraft herself.

Virtue and the exercise of virtuous conduct, Wollstonecraft holds with Locke, are to be attained only through the use of reason. Reason is what she calls the 'primary human characteristic,' and virtue is its best achievement. Experience should combine with reasoning ability to produce the stable foundation of knowledge which is necessary for good moral judgment.[5] From these principles it follows that there can be only one kind of virtue, and that which passes as the female counterpart, based on sensitivity rather than on reason, is a sham and a contradiction.

. . . the perfection of our nature and capability of happiness, must be estimated by the degree of reason, virtue, and knowledge, that distinguish the individual, and direct the laws which bind society: and that from the exercise of reason, knowledge and virtue naturally flow, is equally undeniable, if mankind be viewed collectively.[6]

[4] John Locke, *Second Treatise on Civil Government*, chapter 2, #5. (Locke is quoting Hooker.)

[5] Mary Wollstonecraft, *A Vindication of the Rights of Woman* (1792), ed. Charles W. Hagelman, Jr. (New York: W. W. Norton and Co., 1967), p. 39.

[6] *Ibid.*

Since real virtue is only discoverable by reason, she argues, it is inconsistent to maintain that there is a different type of virtue for females which demands sensitivity, intuition, and obedience rather than reason and self-discipline. Not only is this type of "virtue" counterfeit, but also any attempt to set up a double-standard undermines the whole concept of virtue itself, making proper conduct and moral laws merely a relative matter. Taking the double-standard a step further, Wollstonecraft sees a danger that "virtue for women" and "virtue for men" will give way to "virtue for some people is not the same as for others," an unacceptably relativistic conclusion.[7] "If any class of mankind be so created that it must necessarily be educated by rules not strictly deducible from truth," she states, then "virtue is an affair of convention."[8] Only by means of a developed reasoning ability can one discover moral truths, thereby perceiving what virtue is and how to pursue it. One must conclude that there is only one measuring stick for both sexes: ". . . It is a farce to call any being virtuous whose virtues do not result from the exercise of its own reason."[9]

Having established that there is but one moral standard and it is based on reason, that the so-called female virtues founded on special sensitivity are not virtues at all, Wollstonecraft clears the way for approaching the question—Are women, then, in fact rational? Are they morally responsible human beings? In short, there are only two options:

Women are . . . to be considered either as moral beings, or so weak that they must be entirely subjected to the superior faculties of men.[10]

Needless to say, Wollstonecraft and the early feminists claimed the potential of full rationality and complete moral responsibility for women. But at the same time, they were sorely conscious of the damaging effects produced by the social forces acting on women. Surveying their general circumstances (especially those of the women in the middle and upper classes), feminists were quick to observe that centuries of conditioning had in fact often produced a debased creature who conformed to the stereotype of misogynists. But that this condition in women was the effect of female nature was clearly false; by being excluded from positions which demanded the use of reason and moral responsibility, by being denied adequate education and experience, the frivolous "lady" of the nineteenth century was a product of definite, distinguishable social forces.

Accordingly, the feminists demanded not only political and legal rights for freedom from the confinement of the domestic sphere; they also demanded to be accorded moral responsibility and the education and experience deemed necessary to carry out that responsibility. The catalog of commentary on this score is significant, for in being deprived of the development of their reason and thereby of their moral character, as they thought, the women of the late eighteenth and

[7] Wollstonecraft, pp. 58–59.
[8] Wollstonecraft, p. 138.
[9] Wollstonecraft, p. 52.
[10] Wollstonecraft, p. 58.

early nineteenth centuries felt they were being deprived of a defining part of their humanity.

In 1838 Sarah Grimké, American abolitionist and feminist, wrote that ". . . the noble faculties of our minds are crushed, and our reasoning powers are almost totally uncultivated."[11] Furthermore, man "has done all he could to debase and enslave her [woman's] mind; and now he looks triumphantly on the ruin he has wrought and says, the being he has thus deeply injured is his inferior."[12]

Perhaps the most systematic documentation of the abridgement of the rights of women which infringes on their ability to perform as morally responsible, fully human adults occurs in the Declaration of Sentiments and Resolutions proclaimed at Seneca Falls, New York, in 1848. Modeled on the Declaration of Independence, the document lists fifteen grievances and twelve resolutions, and fully seven of the total mention matters pertinent to morals, responsibility, and the exercise of both. Phrased as an accusation by womankind against her oppressor, mankind, the document declares that

He has made her, morally, an irresponsible being, as she can commit many crimes with impunity, provided they be done in the presence of her husband.[13]

(This grievance makes reference to the fact that for years women were denied legal recognition to such an extent that without legal identity separate from her husband's, a woman was not held responsible for crimes she committed in his presence or with his consent.) The most critical aspect about the legal status of women, in the minds of the framers of the Seneca Falls Declaration, was the lack of responsible behavior expected of women. With no responsibility expected of them, they surmised, women would often fail to develop into mature adults. The picture of woman as delicate, sensitive, and innocent was a way of viewing her as a perpetual child, and, as Wollstonecraft remarked, "Children, I grant, should be innocent, but when the epithet is applied to men, or women, it is but a civil term for weakness."[14]

Harriet Taylor Mill, Lucretia Mott, Emma Willard, and many others allude time and again to the position of women in society as an enforced lack of moral responsibility, caused by "man-made restrictions [which] enervated the minds and powers of women."[15] Harriet Martineau, a visitor to America, observed in 1837 that

The morals of women are crushed. If there be any human power and business and privilege which is absolutely universal, it is the discovery and adoption of the

[11] Sarah Grimké, in Kraditor, pp. 86–87.

[12] Sarah Grimké, quoted in W. L. O'Neill, *Everyone Was Brave* (Chicago: Quadrangle Books, 1969), p. 12.

[13] Declaration of Sentiments and Resolutions, in Miriam Schneir, ed., *Feminism: The Essential Historical Writings* (New York: Vintage Books, 1972), p. 79.

[14] Wollstonecraft, p. 50.

[15] Lucretia Mott, quoted in Alice Felt Tyler, *Freedom's Ferment* (New York: Harper and Row, 1962, first published, 1944), p. 455.

principle and laws of duty. As every individual, whether man or woman, has a reason and a conscience, this is a work which each is thereby authorized to do for him or herself. But it is not only virtually prohibited to beings who, like the American woman, have scarcely any objects in life proposed to them; but the whole apparatus of opinion is brought to bear offensively upon individuals among women who exercise freedom of mind in deciding upon what duty is, and the methods by which it is to be pursued.[16]

It is not the case, then, that women are by nature less rational than men; rather, with their sex, reason has been "crushed" because of upbringing and education.

Wollstonecraft argued from the then-popular theory of *associated ideas* to explain how women's upbringing discouraged the development of powers of reason. By this theory, the ideas which are temporally linked in childhood and adolescent experiences greatly shape the character, the moral stature, and the aesthetic proclivities of the adult. Wollstonecraft notes that early education is crucial to adult abilities, for it is then that the ideas are implanted which will serve as future guides in the powerful form of habits and propensities.

When the ideas and matters of fact are once taken in, they lie by for use till some fortuitous circumstance makes the information dart into the mind with illustrative force that has been received at very different periods of our lives . . . Over these instantaneous associations we have little power, for when the mind is once enlarged by excursive flights or profound reflection, the raw materials will in some degree arrange themselves . . .

So ductile is the understanding, and yet so stubborn, that the associations which depend on adventitious circumstances, during the period that the body takes to arrive at maturity, can seldom be disentangled by reason.[17]

Since girls are not encouraged to develop the reflective powers of reason which could override and counteract the power of associated ideas, they are particularly vulnerable to them. Added to this is the kind of associations which their education permits:

Everything they see or hear serves to fix impressions, call forth emotions, and associate ideas that give a sexual character to the mind.[18]

If Wollstonecraft's appeal to associationism is now obsolete, the general thrust of her remarks—that education can explain thoroughly the significant social differences between men and women—is still quite alive. Perhaps this is most true of her observations concerning the behavior the female learns to exhibit towards the male (an aspect of that "sexual character of mind" mentioned above). Being dominated on account of their sex, and also being valued primarily as sexual beings, women are quick to see that it is only by exploiting their sexuality that they can effectively influence any particular decision. Little girls learn, observes Wollstonecraft, that reasoned, open actions are less effective

[16] Harriet Martineau, *Society in America* (1837), Vol. 1 (New York: AMS Press, Inc., 1966), pp. 229–230.

[17] Wollstonecraft, pp. 177–179.

[18] Wollstonecraft, p. 179.

than covert, flirtatious actions. Therefore from their earliest life to adulthood they are encouraged and molded into a position which is morally debasing.

This cruel association of ideas which everything conspires to twist into all their habits of thinking . . . receives new force when they begin to act a little for themselves; for they then perceive that it is only through their address to excite emotions in men, that pleasure and power are to be obtained.[19]

Given the strong and damaging force of the education of women, it is scarcely surprising that by adulthood they do not always have the same abilities as men. Complicating this fact, notes Wollstonecraft, women are generally economically dependent upon men, and must live off them by *charm*, a further incentive to remain the frivolous coquette, at least as long as beauty lasts. In fact, the more astonishing thing is that women ever escape the effects of their upbringing at all:

Educated in worse than Egyptian bondage, it is unreasonable, as well as cruel, to upbraid them with faults that can scarcely be avoided, unless a degree of native vigour be supposed that falls to the lot of very few amongst mankind.[20]

The conclusion is clear: it is society and men in society who perpetuate the customs which keep women in "worse than Egyptian bondage." Full moral responsibility must be granted to women, and to insure that responsibility, women must be allowed the kind of education that develops the use of their reason. Indeed, a change of this sort would not only benefit women, but society as well, for ". . . that society is formed in the wisest manner, whose constitution is founded on the nature of man . . ."[21] Since at present, society does not give a chance to half of humanity to develop fully, we can conclude that ". . . the most salutary effects tending to improve mankind might be expected from a REVOLUTION in female manners . . ."[22]

So far, in examining the idea that women were considered deficient in their reasoning powers and therefore in their moral judgment, I have been emphasizing only one aspect of the theories concerning female morals that were important during the early years of the feminist movement. In fact, the theories affecting women were more complex than this, and taken as a whole, can be seen to contain an important inconsistency. Since women were viewed as creatures whose moral nature could not depend for its foundation on rationality, sometimes they were regarded as totally amoral beings, if not actually evil. But most who adopted the notion of there being a female sphere of activity also maintained that women did have a moral nature, and sometimes even a spiritual superiority over men. Their virtue, however, was founded not in reason but in sensitivity and intuition. Wollstonecraft refuted this combination of beliefs as inconsistent, but inconsistent or not, this "double-standard" of virtue had a profound social effect on those who lived under its aegis.

[19] *Ibid.*
[20] *Ibid.*
[21] Wollstonecraft, p. 40.
[22] Wollstonecraft, p. 284.

This confusing duality which pervaded the concepts of woman's character is in fact manifested in the Seneca Falls Declaration itself, giving that document the initial appearance of internal inconsistency. While for the most part it accuses men and society for making women beings who lack moral responsibility, as in the passages quoted earlier, later it makes reference to the current notion that indeed in some ways women were actually accorded moral *superiority* over men. ("That inasmuch as man, while claiming for himself intellectual superiority, does accord to woman moral superiority. . . .")[23]

This inconsistency is not a logical slip on the part of Stanton and Mott, framers of the document. It is a reflection of the paradoxical expectations operating on women at that time. As guardians of the domestic sphere, to women fell the task of rearing their children in the laws of God and decency. Woman's superior intuition and sensibility were supposed to grant her a moral and spiritual excellence; yet *at the same time* her deficient reason and poor cognitive ability were supposed to preclude the possibility of stable moral character! The mystified natural sentiments of woman, presumably, were supposed to take the place, as she attained wife and motherhood, of the reasoning abilities and self-discipline denied her in her education.

Claiming that moral responsibility was only possible through the development of good judgment and reason, and the self-discipline necessary to exercise both, Mary Wollstonecraft focused on this paradoxical view of women as a major cause of their misery. Gentlewomen are brought up to be flirtatious, lively, pleasing, and unassertive, yet in marriage and motherhood they are expected to become suddenly the guides of morality and virtue, to manifest their 'natural sensitivity' and 'spiritual nature.' (Even though, with the same breath, those who exhort them to do so remind them that they must obey the superior reason of their husbands.) Wollstonecraft notes resentfully the unfairness of these expectations: ". . . How could Rousseau expect them to be virtuous and constant when reason is neither allowed to be the foundation of their virtue, nor truth the object of their inquiries?"[24] She also observes how this theoretical inconsistency has its practical consequences:

And why is the life of a modest woman a perpetual conflict? I should answer, that this system of education makes it so. Modesty, temperance, and self-denial, are the sober offspring of reason; but when sensibility is nurtured at the expense of the understanding, such weak beings must be restrained by arbitrary means, and subjected to continual conflicts.[25]

This confusion in moral theory which, as Wollstonecraft argues, lies at the heart of the misguided separation of virtues into male and female, must have taken its toll on the women who lived under its contradictory credo. At least one historian, Carol Smith Rosenberg, has argued that the prevalence of hysteria, a broadly-conceived ailment that was not unusual among middle and upper class women in America in the nineteenth century, can be explained as the result of

[23] Seneca Falls Declaration, in Schneir, p. 81.

[24] Wollstonecraft, p. 145.

[25] Wollstonecraft, p. 138.

the conflicting demands made of women at that time—specifically, the conflict between an upbringing which taught women to be frivolous and dependent young ladies, and the subsequent expectation that, if necessary, they would bear heavy responsibility upon becoming wives and mothers.[26] It would seem that Wollstonecraft was right, and that the reliance on natural sensitivity for the female virtues was an inadequate substitute for an education which prepared one for the realities of adult life.

The analysis of woman's distorting upbringing and its consequences, both social and personal, clearly was an important feature of the early feminist movement. In addition, the claim that women are innately as rational as men and the demand that they be treated as such formed the foundation for their revolutionary appeal, based, like the demands of the liberal democratic social movements of the times, on the popular notion of "natural rights." "Equals must have equal measure," quoted Locke from Hooker. And all who are created equal are endowed with certain inalienable rights, continued Jefferson. With the assertion and the demonstration of their equal rationality and their equal responsibility, the feminists, appealing to their long-denied natural rights, demanded equal citizenship along with men. It is safe to assume that the inconsistency of application of the principles of the American Declaration of Independence had occurred to women frequently in the early years of the nineteenth century, even before the Seneca Falls Declaration made those inconsistencies explicit. Harriet Martineau noted this anomaly in 1837:

The democratic principle condemns all this as wrong; and requires the equal political representation of all rational beings . . . but it is interesting to inquire how so obvious a decision has been so evaded as to leave women no political rights whatever.[27]

Clearly, one way this 'decision was so evaded' was through the denial that women were in fact rational beings.

Gradually, the conditions of women began to improve under law. After a series of state Married Women's Property Acts, they began to have a separate legal identity. Active women began institutions of higher learning for women, opening the doors for that 'exercise of reason' so long awaited. Eventually, of course, the crusade for women's rights simultaneously culminated and sputtered out with the extension of the suffrage to women.

That the "first" feminist movement did not achieve all its goals, that the vote was not enough, has been realized and analyzed now for some years. But it is perhaps not repetitive to direct our hindsight to an evaluation of this particular feature of the early years of the movement: to the preoccupation with moral responsibility and reason.

Clearly, this problem was perceived as an acute contributor to woman's oppression. But we should also ask the question: to what extent did the image of woman as irrational and irresponsible reach the heart of the oppression of *all*

[26] Carol Smith Rosenberg, from a lecture given at the State University of New York at Buffalo, Fall, 1972.
[27] Martineau, p. 200.

women? Mary Wollstonecraft stated at one point that indeed it was the main problem, for in her introduction she asserts her ". . . profound conviction that the neglected education of my fellow-creatures is the grand source of the misery I deplore."[28] However, by her own description, she is really writing for and about a certain class of women—of women of leisure who, for example, ". . . make up their faces for the day—five hours, and who could do it in less— do many spend in dressing, including preparation for bed, washing with Milk of roses, etc., etc."[29]

That she ignored the problems of laboring women is perhaps not surprising, even though in certain of her other writings she indicated an awareness of the trouble of those born to poverty and misfortune. Most of her experience gave her the opportunity for close observation of women belonging to the middle and upper classes. Additionally, we should bear in mind that for some time after the advent of liberal democratic thought, not only the women but also the men of the laboring classes were considered to be lacking in rationality and therefore not candidates for full citizenship.

It goes without saying that not all women were oppressed by a belief that they were weak and delicate, demanding the guidance and protection of men. The women working in factories, the women who tended farms, the female slaves laboring in the fields all suffered more from other causes than from the problems presented by reason, moral responsibility, and the image of woman as irrational and frivolous.

However, although the problems surrounding reason and morals may have been acute only for women of the more leisure classes, the struggles which they engendered attacked the degrading *stereotype* of woman at its root. If we can charge that political reform movements sometimes ignore the working classes, it is still more the case that popular sex stereotype does so as well. The image of woman which the early feminists fought, the social concepts of womanhood which kept them in a narrow and sometimes maddeningly unproductive sphere, were the product of the popular notion of a "lady," and not of a farmer's, a fisherman's, a miller's wife, nor of a female slave in the South.

Juliet Mitchell has stated that revolutionary ideas usually begin within or in relation to dominant ideology, and that it is the expected course of development for oppression to be articulated first by members of the middle or upper classes.[30] The arguments against spheres of activity, against the doctrine of the separation of virtues, and for the rational nature of woman and her natural rights as a citizen, perhaps are viewed most productively in this way.

Many new theories have developed within the contemporary woman's movement which, in some respects, supplant the old ones (such as the substitution of analyses drawn from historical materialism for the earlier claims that men themselves were the sole source of oppression). In many ways, the subject we have been discussing is no longer a significant political issue. How-

---

[28] Wollstonecraft, Introduction, p. 31.

[29] From a letter from Mary to her sister, 1787, quoted in Flexner, p. 76.

[30] Juliet Mitchell, *Woman's Estate* (Baltimore: Penguin Books, 1971), pp. 21–22.

ever, it would be inaccurate to claim that this early question has been entirely laid to rest. Although they speak in considerably diluted tones, there are still those who would claim that women's reason is less reliable than men's, or that it occurs in a different—perhaps even in an intuitive—manner. Unfortunately, Mary Wollstonecraft's arguments, dated though they should be, have more than historical importance, for her particular battle has not altogether been won.

part four: THE IMPACT OF IDEALISM

. . . there lie chiefly in the character of mind of this sex peculiar strokes, which clearly distinguish it from ours, and which principally tend to make it known by the criterion, fair.
  —Immanuel Kant

. . . if we turn to Kant's Observations on the Feeling of the Beautiful and the Sublime *. . . , we find that women lack . . . humanly essential characteristics and most clearly they lack the sort of moral agency which is characteristic of human nature . . .*
  —Carol C. Gould

Since the community gets itself subsistence only by breaking in upon family happiness, . . . it creates its enemy for itself within its own gates, creates it in what it suppresses, and what is at the same time essential to it—womankind in general.
  —Georg Wilhelm Friedrich Hegel

I would argue that the family . . . is pervaded throughout by bourgeois or civil society, and that the characterization of the family as a domain of love, privacy, and immediacy is largely a mystification, masking the intricate and intimate relations in which the family stands to capital and to production.
  —Carol C. Gould

I wish Woman to live first for God's sake. Then she will not make an imperfect man her god, and thus sink to idolatry.
  —Margaret Fuller

. . . we have been accustomed to place Margaret Fuller at the head of the ameliorating movement for woman; and though others may have done much, we consider her its greatest representative.
  —Elizabeth Dorcas Livermore

Neither reason nor experience, according to Immanuel Kant, is capable of yielding complete truth. To be sure, the two may combine to reveal the truth about things *as they appear*, but the nature of things themselves, things as they are, is impenetrable. It is to woman as she appears that Kant confines his attention. And to him she appears beautiful, beautiful in mind or spirit as well as in body—a decidedly one-dimensional view, in the estimation of Carol C. Gould. In attributing to the male sex nobility rather than beauty, Kant seems to be looking beyond appearance and making an attempt to penetrate reality. Nevertheless, in *The Philosophy of Law* he delineates a reciprocal relationship between the sexes in his consideration of marriage—a relationship on which Hegel expands in his *Philosophy of Right*. But as Carol Gould points out, the family as depicted by Hegel is outside the realm of right, and the relationships within it are not reciprocal but patriarchal.

Margaret Fuller writes mystically of man as a composite of masculine and feminine. She considers the sexes not only equal but equally necessary to the balance of the pantheistic whole. And Fuller is thought by her contemporary Elizabeth Dorcas Livermore to be living proof of her own thesis.

≈§≈10 *Immanuel Kant*

Immanuel Kant was born in Königsberg in 1724, the son of a saddler of Scottish descent, Johann Georg Kant (or Cant), and his wife, Anna Regina Reuter, who was the daughter of a fellow craftsman. His childhood was materially impoverished but spiritually rich: according to their famous son's later testimony, neither mother nor father was ever seen to commit an improper act or heard to utter an angry word. The mother, a devout Pietist who took delight in educating Immanuel in the beauties of nature, died in 1737. Upon the death of Johann Georg Kant nine years later, the three daughters (an older one, who never married, and two younger ones, who eventually made humble matches) went into service. Immanuel, who had been studying at the University of Königsberg, was forced to abandon his studies and accept a series of tutorships. But eventually, in 1755, he became lecturer at the university and, in 1770, full professor.

Although his extreme poverty in his youth would have prevented any thought of marriage at the usual age, Kant appears to have seriously entertained the notion at least twice during his later years. On one occasion he was allegedly in the process of assessing his financial situation to determine whether it would be feasible to propose to a young widow when her marriage to another man put an end to his calculations. The object of his later interest, the companion of a Westphalian visitor to Königsberg, left town with her employer before Kant could make up his mind. Thus he was confirmed in his bachelorhood.

In daily life Kant adhered to an inflexible schedule. He would arise at five, lecture from seven until nine, resume his studies until twelve-forty-five, entertain luncheon guests (from three to nine men, never any women), walk for an hour, work again from six until nine, and retire at ten. He died in 1804, after having attained international renown for his three Critiques. At the time of his death he was suffering from senile dementia.

In typifying woman as the fair sex, Immanuel Kant was in large measure mirroring eighteenth-century German society, where fashions were imported from France and women deliberately cultivated the art of "femininity" through careful study. Lavish costume and coiffure complemented affected manners. Such practices as swooning and melting into tears were deemed indicative of sensitivity and refinement, and were part of every woman's repertoire. Kant's later comments on the "reciprocity" between husband and wife reflect another aspect of German custom: the inflexible social convention of marrying within one's class. The nobility, the clergy, the army, the professions, the merchant class, and the peasantry formed discrete units, and marriage outside the ranks was indeed almost unthinkable.

Many of the views expressed in Rousseau's chapter on Sophia appear in the third chapter of Kant's Observations on the Feeling of the Beautiful and Sublime. *They are developed as specific applications of an aesthetic theory sketched earlier in the work. Unlike Wollstonecraft, Kant agreed with*

153

Rousseau on the basic and pervasive difference between the sexes. The fair sex is aptly named, he thought, not only because woman is more comely than man in figure and feature but also because her entire character is an embodiment of beauty, just as man's nature is essentially noble or sublime. Thus, while women have neither more nor less understanding than men, their understanding is different—it is a beautiful or facile understanding as opposed to the deep understanding that is men's. Woman senses; man meditates. And woman's virtue is beautiful as opposed to the noble virtue of the male. Even her faults are beautiful: tearfulness, vanity, coquetry, and the like.

All the education and instruction given a woman, then, should serve to enhance the beauty within her. Rigorous disciplines, such as geometry, geography, philosophy, astronomy, physics, are not for her. She should devote herself to developing her feeling for the beautiful, which in most cases is best self-taught. Woman tends to be impatient with restraint, incapable of principles, and motivated by pleasure. Thus virtue is best instilled in her when it is equated with beauty and vice with ugliness.

Like Rousseau, Kant thought woman a vital influence on man, particularly in matters involving feeling, but rather than dubbing her a helpmate, he referred to husband and wife as a single moral person, guided by the understanding of the husband, the taste of the wife.

From *Observations on the Feeling of the Beautiful and Sublime*

SECTION 3

Of the Difference of the Sublime and of the Beautiful in the Counterrelation of Both Sexes

He, who first comprehended the women under the name of the *fair sex,* wished perhaps to say something flattering: but he has hit it better, than he himself may have imagined. For, without taking into consideration, that their form is in general finer, their features softer and more delicate, their mien in the expression of friendliness, of joking, of kindness and humanity more significant and engaging, than that of the male sex, not forgetting, however, that which must be deducted for the secret magic power, whereby they render our passion favourable to the most advantageous judgment of them, there lie chiefly in the character of mind of this sex peculiar strokes, which clearly distinguish it from ours, and which principally tend to make it known by the criterion, *fair.* We, on the other hand, lay claim to the denomination of the *noble sex,* were it not required of a noble disposition of mind, to decline names of honour and rather to bestow than to receive them. By this is not to be understood, that women want noble properties, or that the male sex must totally dispense with the beauties: it is rather expected, that each sex shall unite both, yet so, that all other excellencies of a woman shall unite themselves but in order to elevate the character of the *beautiful*, which is the proper point of reference; whereas among the male properties the *sublime*, as the criterion of his sex, must be the most eximious. To this must refer all judgments of these two sexes, as well the commendable, as the blameable. This must all education and instruction, and all endeavours to forward the moral perfection of both, have in view; unless the charming distinction, which nature intended to make between two human sexes, shall be rendered indiscernible. For it is here not enough to represent men to one's self, it must at the same time be noticed that these men are not of the same nature.

Women have an innate strong feeling for all that is beautiful, ornamented and embellished. Already in youth they are willingly dressed and take a pleasure in being set off. They are cleanly and very delicate with regard to every thing that occasions disgust. They love jesting, and can be entertained with trifles, if they are but sprightly and agreeable. They acquire very early a modest behaviour, know to assume a polite carriage or manner, and possess themselves; and this at an age, when our wellbred male youth is yet untoward, awkward and embarrassed. They have many sympathetic feelings, much goodheartedness and compassion, prefer the beautiful to the useful, and willingly turn the superfluity of maintenance into parsimony, in order to support the expence of glitter and dress. They are very sensible of the smallest offence, and in general acute in observing the smallest want of attention and reverence for them. In fine, they contain the chief ground of the contrast of the beautiful properties with the noble in human nature, and even refine the male sex.

I hope I may be excused from the enumeration of the male properties, so far as they run parallel with those, as it may suffice to contemplate both in the comparison. The female sex have understanding, as well as the male, yet is it but a *fine understanding*; our understanding must be a *profound* one, which is an expression of the same signification with a sublime.

To the beauty of all actions it belongs, chiefly, that they show an easiness in themselves and seem to be accomplished without a painful exertion; whereas efforts and surmounted difficulties excite admiration and belong to the sublime. Deep reflection and a long continued contemplation are noble, but difficult, and are not suitable to a person, in whom ought to appear charms without constraint and a beautiful nature. Laborious study, or painful investigation, though a woman should succeed in it, destroys the excellencies peculiar to her sex, and may because of the singularity render her an object of cold admiration; but it at the same time weakens the charms, by which she exercises her great power over the other sex. Women, who have their heads stuffed with Greek, like Mrs. Dacier, or carry on profound disputes about mechanics, like the marchioness of Chastelet, might have a beard to boot; for this would perhaps express more remarkably the air of penetration, to which they aspire. The fine understanding choses for its objects all that is nearly connected with the fine feeling, and leaves abstract speculations and knowledge, which are useful but dry, to the diligent, solid and profound understanding. Ladies consequently do not study geometry; they know but as much of the position of sufficient reason, or of monades, as is necessary, in order to perceive the salt in the satires of the shallow fancymongers of our sex. The fair may let Cartesius' vortices continue to revolve, without giving themselves any trouble on that account, even should the agreeable Fontenelle bear them company among the planets, and the attraction of their charms loses nothing of its power, though they should know nothing of all that Algarotti endeavoured to point out, for their use, of the powers of attraction of coarse matter according to Newton. They should fill their heads neither with battles from history, nor with forts from geography; for it becomes them as little to smell of gunpowder, as men of musk.

It seems to be a wicked artifice of men to have wished to mislead the fair sex to this perverted taste. For, well aware of their weakness with regard to its natural charm, and that a single waggish look throws them into more confusion, than the most difficult question of the schools, they find themselves, as soon as the sex gives into this taste, decidedly superior, and in the advantage, which they otherwise would scarcely have, assist the weaknesses of its vanity with a generous indulgence. The subject of the great science of women is rather a husband, and of men, man. The philosophy of women is not to reason, but to feel. In the opportunity that is afforded them to cultivate their beautiful nature, this relation must always be had in view. One must endeavour to enlarge their whole moral feeling, but not their memory, and that not by universal rules, but by some judgments on the conduct which they see around them. The examples that are borrowed from other times in order to perspect the influence that the fair sex have had in the affairs of the world, the various relations, in which they stood towards the male sex in other ages, as well as in foreign countries; the character of both, so far as it may be hereby illustrated, and the variable taste of pleasures, constitute their whole history and geography. It is proper, that the view of a map, which represents either the whole globe, or the chief parts of the world, should be rendered agreeable to women. This may be done by presenting it but for the purpose of describing the various characters of nations that inhabit them, the differences of their taste and moral feeling, especially with regard to the effect which these have on the relations of the sexes; with a few easy dilucidations from the difference of climates, of their liberty or slavery. It is of little moment, whether or not they know the particular divisions of these countries, their commerce, potency and rulers. In like manner it will not be useful for them to know more of the fabric of the world, than is necessary to render moving to them the aspect of the heavens in a beautiful evening, if they have in some measure comprehended, that there are to be met with still more worlds and in them other beautiful creatures. Feeling for expressive descriptions, and for music, not so far as it shows art, but sentiment, all this forms and refines the taste of this sex, and has always some connection with moral emotions. Never a cold and speculative instruction, always sentiments or feelings, which remain as near as possible to their relation of sex. This instruction is so rare, because it requires talents, experience and a feeling heart, and women may do without every other, as even without these they commonly cultivate or improve themselves very well.

The virtue of the female sex is a *beautiful virtue*. That of the male must be a *noble one.* Those avoid the bad, not because it is wrong, but because it is ugly, and virtuous actions signify, with them, such as are morally beautiful. Nothing of *ought,* nothing of *must,* nothing of *due.* All orders and all surly compulsion are to women insupportable. They do something but because they are pleased so to do, and the art consists but in making that which is good pleasing to them. I hardly believe that the fair sex are capable of principles, and in this I hope I do not offend, for these are very rare with men. Instead of which, however, Providence hath implanted in their breasts humane and benevolent sentiments, a fine feeling for becomingness, and a complaisant soul. Let not sacrifices and magnanimous self-compulsion be required. A man must never tell his wife, when he risks a part of his fortune on account of a friend. Why should he fetter her sprightly affability by burdening her mind with a weighty secret, the keeping of which is incumbent on him only? Even many of their weaknesses are, so to speak, *beautiful faults.* Injury or misfortune moves their delicate souls to sorrow. A man must never shed but generous tears. Those which he sheds in pain or for circumstances of fortune render him contemptible. The *vanity,* with which the fair sex is so often upbraided, if it be a fault in them, it is but a beautiful one. For not to mention, that men, who so willingly flatter the fair, would be in a sad case, were these not inclined to take it well; they really animate thereby their charms. This inclination is an incitement, to show agreeableness and good grace, to give play to their sprightly wit, as also to glitter by the variable sensations occasioned by dress, and to heighten their beauty. In this now there is nothing so offensive to others, but rather, when it is done with good taste, something so comely and elegant, that it is very unmannerly to inveigh severely against it. A woman, who flirts and dazzles too much with this, is named a *fool;* which term, however, has no such harsh meaning, as when applied to a man, insomuch that, when persons understand one another, it may sometimes denote even a familiar flattery. If vanity is a fault which in a woman well merits excuse; to be puffed up with pride is not only blameable in them, as in men in general, but totally disfigures the character of their sex. For this property is stupid, ugly, and totally opposite to the engaging, insinuating, modest charm. Then such a person is in a slippery situation. She must be content to be judged severely and without the smallest indulgence; for whoever boasts of meriting esteem, invites all around her to censure. Each discovery of even the smallest fault affords a real joy to every body, and the word fool here loses its softened signification. Vanity and haughtiness must always be distinguished. The former seeks applause and in some measure honours those, on whose account it gives itself this trouble; the latter believes itself already in its full possession, and as it does not endeavour to acquire it, it gains none. A few ingredients of vanity by no means disfigure a woman in the eyes of the male sex; yet they serve, the more evident they are, the more to disunite the fair sex among one another. They then judge one another very sharply, because the one seems to eclipse the charms of the other, and those who have great pretension to conquest, are seldom friends in the true sense.

To the beautiful there is nothing so opposite as the disgustful, and nothing sinks more beneath the sublime than the ridiculous. Hence no abuse can be more cutting to a man, than to name him a fool, and to a woman, than that she is disgusting. The spectator takes it, that no reproach can be more mortifying to a man, than to be held a liar, and to a woman none bitterer, than that she is unchaste. I shall let this, so far as it is judged according to strict morality, remain valid. But here the question is not, what in itself merits the greatest blame, but what is actually the most severely felt. And I put the question to the reader, whether, when he has reflected on this case, he does not coincide with my opinion. Miss Ninon Lenclos laid not the smallest claim to the honour of chastity, and yet she would have been irreconcilably offended, had one of her lovers transgressed so much in his judgment: and we all know the cruel fate of Monaldeschi, on account of an insulting expression of this nature, from a princess, who did not even wish to represent a Lucretia. It is insupportable, that one should not even be able to do bad, though he had a mind to it, as the forbearance from it is never but a very ambiguous virtue.

In order to avoid this disgustfulness as much as possible, *cleanliness* is necessary, which indeed becomes every person, but in the fair sex is among the virtues of the first rank, and by them cannot easily be carried too far; men, however, sometimes carry it to excess and it is then named trifling.

Modesty is a secret of nature, to set bounds to an inclination which is very ungovernable, and, as it has the call of nature for it, always seems, though it rambles, to agree with good moral properties. It, therefore, as a supplement to principles, is highly necessary; for there is no case where the inclination becomes so easily a sophist, to invent agreeable principles, as here. But modesty serves at the same time to throw a mysterious veil even over the fittest and most necessary ends of nature, in order that the too intimate acquaintance with them may not occasion disgust, or at least indifference, with regard to the final designs of an instinct, upon which are grafted the finest and most lively inclinations of human nature. This property is chiefly peculiar to the fair sex, and very beseeming to them. It is coarse and contemptible ill-breeding to occasion embarrassment or indignation to this delicate pudicity by that sort of vulgar joking named obscenity. As, however, let the mystery be ever so much preserved, the inclination to sex ultimately forms the basis of all other charms, and a woman, as a woman, is always the agreeable subject of a good-mannered conversation; so it may perhaps be thence explained, why men, otherwise polite, sometimes take the liberty of insinuating through their wanton jokes a few fine allusions, which occasion them to be denominated *loose* or *waggish*, and who, as they neither offend by prying looks, nor intend to violate the due reverence, believe to be entitled to name the person, who takes it with a reserved or an indignant mien, a *female pedant of honour*. I mention this but because it is commonly considered as a somewhat bold stroke of fine intercourse, and indeed much wit has hitherto been lavished on it: but as to the judgment according to moral strictness, it belongs not to this disquisition, as I have to observe and to explain but the phenomena in the feeling of the beautiful.

The noble properties of this sex, which, however, as we have already noticed, must never render indiscernible the feeling of the beautiful, announce themselves by nothing more distinctly or more surely, than by *discretion*, a species of noble simplicity and *naiveté* accompanying great excellencies. From which proceed a calm benevolence and reverence for others, at the same time combined with a certain *noble confidence* in one's self and a just self-estimation, which are always to be met with in a sublime temper of mind. As this fine mixture engages at the same time by charms and touches by reverence; it puts all the other glittering properties in safety against the petulance of censure and the rage of derision. Persons of this frame of mind have also a heart for friendship which, as it is so very rare in a woman and at the same time must be so highly charming, never can be sufficiently valued.

.   .   .

At last however age, the great destroyer of beauty, threatens all these charms, and, if the natural order is to be followed, the sublime and noble properties must gradually occupy the place of the beautiful, in order to render a person, as she ceases to be lovely, always worthy of a greater reverence. In my opinion the whole perfection of the fair sex ought in the bloom of years to consist in the beautiful simplicity, elevated by a refined feeling in all that is charming and noble. As the pretensions to charms remit, the reading of books and the enlarging of knowledge might insensibly supply the vacant place of the Graces by the Muses, and the husband ought to be the first instructor. However, when old age, an epoch so terrible to all women, advances, they even then still belong to the fair sex and they disfigure themselves, when, in a sort of despair to maintain this character longer, they give themselves up to a morose and waspish humour.

A woman advanced in years, who graces a society with her modest and friendly behaviour, is affable in a cheerful and rational manner, favours with decency the pleasure of youth, in which she herself has no share, and, while she takes care of every thing, betrays contentment and complacency in the joy she sees around her, is still a finer person, than a man of the same age, and perhaps more amiable than a young woman, though in another sense. Indeed the platonic love, which an ancient philosopher pretended, when he said of the object of his inclination, *the Graces reside in her wrinkles, and my very soul seems to hover on my lips, when I kiss her withered mouth,* may be somewhat too mystical; but such claims must then be relinquished. An old man in love is a gawk, and similar pretensions of the other sex are disgustful. It is never the fault of nature if we appear not with a good grace, but of our endeavouring to pervert nature.

In order not to lose sight of my text, I shall yet make a few observations on the influence which the one sex may have on the other, either to embellish or to ennoble its feeling. Women have chiefly a feeling for the *beautiful*, so far as it belongs to themselves; but for the *noble,* so far as it is to be met with in the male sex. Man on the other hand has a decided feeling for the *noble* that pertains to his properties; but for the *beautiful,* so far as it is to be met with in the women. Hence must follow, that the ends of nature tend still more to *ennoble* the man by the inclination to sex and still more to *embellish* the woman by the very same inclination. A woman is at no loss, because she does not possess certain deep introspections, because she is timid and not fit for weighty affairs, etc., etc.; she is beautiful, she is engaging, and that is enough. Whereas, she requires all these properties in a man and the sublimity of her soul discovers itself but by her knowing to value these noble properties, so far as they are to be met with in him. How would it otherwise be possible, that so many male apish faces, though they may have merit, could get so handsome and fine wives? Man, on the other side, is much more delicate with regard to the beautiful charms of the women. He is by their fine figure, their sprightly *naiveté* and their charming friendliness, sufficiently indemnified for the want of book-learning and for other wants, which he must supply by his own talents. Vanity and modes may easily give a false direction to these natural impulses and of many a man make a *beau,* but of many a woman a *pedant* or an *amazon*; but nature always endeavours to return to her own order. From this may be judged, what potent influence the inclination to sex would have chiefly on the male sex, in order to ennoble them, if, instead of much dry instruction, the moral sentiment of the women were early developed, in order to feel sufficiently what belongs to the dignity and the sublime properties of the other sex, and they were thereby prepared to consider the trifling fops with contempt, and to be attached to no other property than merit. It is beyond a doubt that the power of their charms would thereby gain in general; for it is obvious, that their magic for the most part acts but on noble souls, others are not fine enough to feel it. As the poet Simonides, when he was advised to let the Thessaliens hear his fine cantatas, said, These fellows are too stupid to be deceived by such a man as I am. It has always been considered as an effect of the intercourse with the fair sex, that the manners of the men are grown softer, their behaviour more agreeable and more polite; and their address more elegant; however this is but a secondary matter.[1] The greatest consequence is, that the man as a man grow more perfect and the woman as a woman, that is, that the springs of the inclination to sex act conformably to the hint of nature, to ennoble the one still more and to embellish the properties of the other. When things come to the extreme, the man may boldly say of his merit, Though you do not love me, I will compel you to esteem me, and the women, sure of the might of their charms, answer, Though you do not esteem us profoundly, we will compel you to love us. For want of such principles men may be seen to adopt effeminacies, in order to please, and women sometimes (though much seldomer) to affect a masculine air, in order to inspire esteem; but what is done contrary to the course of nature is always very badly done.

In the connubial life the united pair must in a manner constitute one single moral person, who is animated and governed by the understanding of the man and by the taste of the woman. For not only that more insight grounded

---

[1] Even this advantage is very much diminished by the observation, which one pretends to have made, that those men, who have too early and too often frequented such societies, in which women give the *ton,* commonly grow somewhat trifling, and in the commerce with men are either tiresome or contemptible, because they have lost the taste for a conversation, which must be sprightly, it is true, but of intrinsic value, facetious, or useful by serious discourse.

upon experience may be attributed to him, and to her more freedom and justness of feeling, but a disposition of mind, the more sublime it is, is the more inclined to place the greatest design of the exertions in the contentment of a beloved object, and on the other hand the more beautiful it is, the more it endeavours to retaliate this exertion. In such a relation therefore a contest for preference is trifling and, where it happens, the surest criterion either of a coarse, or of an unequally matched taste. When it comes to that pass, that the question is concerning the right to command, the matter is already highly spoiled; for, where the whole union is founded but upon inclination, it is, as soon as *shall* begins to be heard, immediately dissolved. The pretension of the woman in this harsh tone is extremely ugly, and of the man in the highest degree ignoble and contemptible. The wise order of things, however, will have it, that all these finenesses and delicacies of feeling shall have their whole strength in the beginning only, but afterwards by commerce and domestic affairs grow insensibly blunter, and then degenerate into familiar love, where at last the great art consists in preserving sufficient rests of those, in order that indifference and disgust may not destroy the whole value of the pleasure, by which only is requited the entering into such a conjunction.

From *The Philosophy of Law*

THE RIGHTS OF THE FAMILY AS A DOMESTIC SOCIETY

The Natural Basis of Marriage

The domestic Relations are founded on Marriage, and Marriage is founded upon the natural Reciprocity or intercommunity (*commercium*) of the Sexes.[1] This natural union of the sexes proceeds either according to the mere animal Nature (*vaga libido, venus vulgivaga, fornicatio*), or according to Law. The latter is MARRIAGE (*matrimonium*), which is the Union of two Persons of different sex for life-long reciprocal possession of their sexual faculties.—The End of producing and educating children may be regarded as always the End of Nature in implanting mutual desire and inclination in the sexes; but it is not necessary for the rightfulness of marriage that those who marry should set this before themselves as the End of their Union, otherwise the Marriage would be dissolved of itself when the production of children ceased.

And even assuming that enjoyment in the reciprocal use of the sexual endowments is an end of marriage, yet the Contract of Marriage is not on that account a matter of arbitrary will, but is a Contract necessary in its nature by the

---

[1] *Commercium sexuale est usus membrorum et facultatum sexualium alterius.* This *'usus'* is either natural, by which human beings may reproduce their own kind, or unnatural, which, again, refers either to a person of the same sex or to an animal of another species than man. These transgressions of all Law, as *'crimina carnis contra naturam,'* are even 'not to be named;' and as wrongs against all Humanity in the Person they cannot be saved, by any limitation or exception whatever, from entire reprobation.

Law of Humanity. In other words, if a man and a woman have the will to enter on reciprocal enjoyment in accordance with their sexual nature, they *must* necessarily marry each other; and this necessity is in accordance with the juridical Laws of Pure Reason.

The Rational Right of Marriage

For, this natural *'Commercium'*—as a *'usus membrorum sexualium alterius'*—is an enjoyment for which the one person is given up to the other. In this relation the human individual makes himself a *'res,'* which is contrary to the Right of Humanity in his own Person. This, however, is only possible under the one condition, that as the one Person is acquired by the other as a *res,* that same Person also equally acquires the other reciprocally, and thus regains and re-establishes the rational Personality. The Acquisition of a part of the human organism being, on account of its unity, at the same time the acquisition of the whole Person, it follows that the surrender and acceptation of, or by, one sex in relation to the other, is not only *permissible* under the condition of Marriage, but is further *only* really possible under that condition. But the Personal Right thus acquired is at the same time, *real in kind*; and this characteristic of it is established by the fact that if one of the married Persons run away or enter into the possession of another, the other is entitled, at any time, and incontestably, to bring such a one back to the former relation, as if that Person were a Thing.

Monogamy and Equality in Marriage

For the same reasons, the relation of the Married Persons to each other is a relation of EQUALITY as regards the mutual possession of their Persons, as well as of their Goods. Consequently Marriage is only truly realized in MONOGAMY; for in the relation of Polygamy the Person who is given away on the one side, gains only a part of the one to whom that Person is given up, and therefore becomes a mere *res*. But in respect of their Goods, they have severally the Right to renounce the use of any part of them, although only by a special Contract.

From the Principle thus stated, it also follows that Concubinage is as little capable of being brought under a Contract of Right, as the hiring of a person on any one occasion, in the way of a *pactum fornicationis*. For, as regards such a Contract as this latter relation would imply, it must be admitted by all that any one who might enter into it could not be legally held to the fulfillment of their promise if they wished to resile from it. And as regards the former, a Contract of Concubinage would also fall as a *pactum turpe;* because as a Contract of the *hire* (*locatio, conductio*), of a part for the use of another, on account of the inseparable unity of the members of a Person, any one entering into such a Contract would be actually surrendering as a *res* to the arbitrary Will of another. Hence any party may annul a Contract like this if entered into with any other, at any time and at pleasure; and that other would have no ground, in the circumstances, to complain of a lesion of his Right. The same holds likewise of a morganatic or 'left-hand' Marriage contracted in order to turn the inequality in the social status of the two parties to advantage in the way of establishing the social supremacy of the one over the other; for, in fact, such a relation is not really different from Concubinage, according to the principles of Natural Right, and therefore does not constitute a real Marriage. Hence the question may be raised as to whether it is not contrary to the Equality of married Persons when the Law says in any way of the Husband in relation to the Wife, 'he shall be thy master,' so that he is represented as the one who commands, and she as the one who obeys. This, however, cannot be regarded as contrary to the natural Equality of a human pair, if such legal Supremacy is based only upon the natural superiority of the faculties of the Husband compared with the Wife, in the effectuation of the common interest of the household; and if the Right to command, is based merely upon this fact. For this Right may thus be deduced from the very duty of Unity and Equality in relation to the *End* involved.

Fulfilment of the Contract of Marriage

The Contract of Marriage is completed only by conjugal cohabitation. A Contract of two Persons of different sex, with the secret understanding either to abstain from conjugal cohabitation or with the consciousness on either side of incapacity for it, is a *simulated Contract;* it does not constitute a marriage, and it may be dissolved by either of the parties at will. But if the incapacity only arises after marriage, the Right of the Contract is not annulled or diminished by a contingency that cannot be legally blamed.

The Acquisition of a Spouse either as a Husband or as a Wife, is therefore not constituted *facto*—that is, by Cohabitation—without a preceding Contract; nor even *pacto*—by a mere Contract of Marriage, without subsequent Cohabitation; but only *lege,* that is, as a juridical consequence of the obligation that is formed by two Persons entering into a sexual Union solely on the basis of a reciprocal *Possession* of each other, which Possession at the same time is only effected in reality by the reciprocal 'usus facultatum sexualium alterius.'

⇜ *Carol C. Gould*

Carol C. Gould is an assistant professor in the Department of Philosophy at Swarthmore College. She has written articles on philosophy and feminism and has co-edited, with Marx W. Wartofsky, a volume entitled Women and Philosophy, *based on a recent issue of* The Philosophical Forum. *In the following excerpt, taken from an article in that work, Professor Gould attacks Kant on the grounds of what she calls "abstract universality." Women as Kant sees them, she contends, lack qualities that in his ethical works are said to characterize the human species. This fact, in her estimation, indicates either that there is a fundamental contradiction in Kant's philosophy or that he has consciously or unconsciously engaged in ideological distortion. In either case, she suggests, Kant needs a new criterion of universality whereby he can take into account actual individual differences.*

From "The Woman Question: The Philosophy of Liberation and the Liberation of Philosophy"

A CRITIQUE OF ABSTRACT UNIVERSALITY IN PRACTICE: HUMAN NATURE—UNIVERSAL OR MALE?

. . .

In the . . . cases to be examined, the connection between human nature and male nature is either explicitly made or implied, with women characterized quite differently. The case of Kant is perhaps paradigmatic here. According to Kant in the *Fundamental Principles of the Metaphysics of Morals,*

That is practically *good,* however, which determines the will by means of the conceptions of reason . . . on principles which are valid for every rational being as such. It is distinguished from the *pleasant* as that which influences the will only by means of sensation from merely subjective causes, valid only for the sense of this or that one and not as a principle of reason which holds for everyone.[1]

Now I say: man and generally any rational being exists as an end in himself.[2]

But if we turn to Kant's *Observations on the Feeling of the Beautiful and the Sublime* (admittedly an early work), we find that women lack these humanly essential characteristics and most clearly they lack the sort of moral agency which is characteristic of human nature (*qua* rational). Thus Kant writes,

Women will avoid the wicked not because it is unright, but only because it is ugly. . . . Nothing of duty, nothing of compulsion, nothing of obligation! . . . They do something only because it pleases them. . . . I hardly believe that the fair sex is capable of principles.[3]

Rather, "Her philosophy is not to reason, but to sense."[4] Furthermore,

All the other merits of a woman should unite solely to enhance the character of the beautiful which is the proper reference point; . . . all education and instruction must have [this] before its eyes. . . . Deep meditation and long-sustained reflection are noble but difficult, and do not well befit a person in whom unconstrained charms should show nothing else than a beautiful nature. A woman who has a head full of

---

[1] Kant, *Fundamental Principles of the Metaphysics of Morals* (Indianapolis, Bobbs-Merrill, 1949), p. 30.

[2] *Ibid.,* p. 45.

[3] Kant, *Observations on the Feeling of the Beautiful and the Sublime,* trans. by John Goldthwait (Berkeley, Univ. of Calif., 1960), p. 81.

[4] *Ibid.,* p. 79.

Greek, like Mme. Dacier, or carries on fundamental controversies about mechanics, might as well have a beard.[5]

A similar prejudice is revealed by Fichte who, when speaking of "our race" in *The Vocation of Man,* writes:

I must be free; for that which constitutes our true worth is not the mere mechanical act, but the free determination of free will, for the sake of duty . . .[6]

but who, when speaking of woman in *The Science of Rights* claims that

[she] is subjected through her own necessary wish—a wish which is the condition of her morality—to be so subjected . . .[7]

Furthermore,

The woman who thus surrenders her personality, and yet retains her full dignity in so doing, necessarily gives up to her lover all that she has. For, if she retained the least of her own self, she would thereby confess that it had a higher value for her than her own person; and this undoubtedly would be a lowering of that person. . . . The least consequence is, that she should renounce to him all her property and all her rights. Henceforth . . . her life has become a part of the life of her lover. (This is aptly characterized by her assuming his name.)[8]

Or, compare Rousseau in *The Social Contract:*

To renounce one's liberty is to renounce one's quality as a man, the rights and also the duties of humanity.[9]

with the suggestion on the education of women in the *Emile:*

They must be trained to bear the yoke from the first, so that they may not feel it, to master their own caprices and to submit themselves to the will of others.[10]

For Schopenhauer also, in his essay 'On Women' (though not in *The World as Will and Representation*), it is quite clear that women lack essential human properties. He writes that woman

is in every respect backward, lacking in reason and reflection . . . a kind of middle step between the child and the man, who is the true human being. . . . In the last resort, women exist solely for the propagation of the race.[11]

---

[5] *Ibid.,* pp. 76–78.

[6] Fichte, *The Vocation of Man* (Indianapolis, Bobbs-Merrill, 1956), p. 117.

[7] Fichte, *The Science of Rights* (Philadelphia, Lippincott & Co., 1869), First Appendix, sec. 3, Part III, p. 441; cf. also sec. 1, Part II–Part VII, pp. 396–403.

[8] *Ibid.,* section 1, Part VI, pp. 401–402. Cited by Eva Figes, *Patriarchal Attitudes* (New York, Fawcett Books, 1971), p. 124.

[9] Rousseau, *The Social Contract,* Book I, Chap. 4.

[10] Rousseau, *Emile,* Book V. Cited by E. Figes, pp. 98–99.

[11] Schopenhauer, "On Women," in *Selected Essays,* ed. by E. B. Bax (London, George Bell, 1900), pp. 338–346. But when talking of the hereditary nature of qualities, Schopenhauer presents a contradictory account, arguing that the faculty of reason and intelligence, and thus the capacity for reflection and deliberation are inherited from the mother, whereas the moral nature, character and heart and will are inherited from the father. (*The World as Will and Representation,* New York, Dover, 1958, Vol. II, pp. 517–520.) See also E. Figes' discussion, *op. cit.,* pp. 121–123.

These quotations suggest that human nature or essence, whether it be construed as freedom or reason or in some other way, is a sex-linked characteristic, since it is found only or truly in men and not women; or at the very least, that this nature is actualized only by men.[12] (Fichte's position is ambiguous because the continuous wishing to be subjected which he requires of women would seem to necessitate that they possess the human property of freedom in order to wish not to possess it.)[13] In all these cases, however, the philosophers' prejudices about women seem clearly at odds with their systematic philosophy which doesn't discriminate between the sexes. Is it the case then, that all we have here is a plain expression of the cultural prejudices of the time, in even so rational a group of philosophers? That they, like most people, are often inconsistent in their beliefs; and that they therefore simply fail to meet the very criterion of universality which they propose? Such an explanation, though common-sensical and plausible, can be shown to be too simple. Instead, let me propose another interpretation of the discrepancy.

These quotations show two things: (a) that these philosophers' views regarding universal human nature are simply contradicted by their views of concrete individuality in the case of women and that therefore their philosophical universalism is no protection against the crassest prejudices and (b) that their statements regarding women are ideological, in the sense of both reflecting and supporting the oppression of women, and that this ideological position is masked by the abstract universality which is proclaimed in their principles. (What I mean here by ideology will be discussed shortly.)

Either interpretation lends support to the critique of abstract universality. (a) The first possibility suggests that because of the abstractness of the universal principle, because it has no bridge to the concrete, the conceptions of concrete individuality of the philosophers in question remain accidental and uncriticized. Thus despite its claims to normative status, the abstract universal principle lacks critical force.

However, it would appear that this sort of discrepancy between the abstract universal principle and concrete prejudices can be overcome within Essentialism, by simply insisting on greater consistency in the interpretation of the universal principle (supposing that the practitioners were cleansed of their male-dominating tendencies), and by requiring bridge laws to the concrete. While greater attention to consistency is desirable, in that it may force the Essentialist to reject those of his statements which contradict his principles, still he has no way of bringing to bear any critical reflections on the genesis or sources of his prejudice. His consistency becomes at best a formal matter of correcting a mistake of reasoning, but does not constitute a recognition of the substance of the error, nor of its cause. He remains open to the intrusion of further prejudices. As to bridge laws to the concrete: unless the Essentialist can take the concrete

[12] In treating these authors together, I do not mean to compare their systematic philosophies, nor to suggest that they are Essentialists in [any] rigorous sense . . .

[13] It should be noted that Fichte himself at a few points seems to be aware of this contradiction. See *Science of Rights, op. cit.,* First Appendix, sec. 1, Part IV, p. 400 and sec. 2, Part VII, p. 418. Cf. related point in E. Figes, *op. cit.,* p. 125.

present or actual circumstances into account philosophically, i.e., systematically, such bridge laws are anchored only at one end and do not extend beyond what is systematically philosophical. But the Essentialist cannot take such concrete circumstances into account without violating his own premises (i.e., that such considerations are philosophically irrelevant because accidental). He cannot be self-critical with regard to his prejudices, because it is precisely the concrete present or the contemporary social context which generates these prejudices, and this context lies beyond him *qua* philosopher. Therefore, his philosophy is critically defenseless against the intrusion of such prejudices.

(b) The second possibility suggests that the discrepancy between universal and female nature is an ideological distortion. I will use the term ideological to denote a case in which a particular or partial aspect of social reality is taken to be the universal and essential characterization of that reality on the basis of particular interests. The form of such ideological distortion is to take (or mistake), unreflectively and therefore uncritically, the part for the whole, the particular for the universal and essential, or the present for the eternal. There are two sorts of distortion possible here on ideological grounds: first, the deliberate use of ideological distortion as an instrument for domination; second— and more significant because more pervasive—the unconscious ideological distortions which come from the uncritical acceptance of whatever partial view is expedient or current. Accordingly, in the instances examined here, we may distinguish ideological distortions in a strong and a weak sense. The strong sense takes them to be instrumentalities in the subordination of women. This interpretation is suggested, e.g., in Kant's and Rousseau's recommendations for educating women or in Fichte's fervent argument that for a woman to do less than submit and lose herself entirely (including all her property and rights) would undoubtedly be a lowering of her person.

On the other hand, it might be more appropriate to interpret the remarks as ideological in the weaker sense—in the sense of passively reflecting the subordination of women in a male-dominated society, but not actively encouraging such subordination. On this hypothesis, we might interpret Kant's view— that rationality is the dominant and essential human characteristic and male, while beauty or aesthetic sensibility is a subordinate characteristic and female—in the following way: At a given historical stage—namely that of the development of civil society and the state—the trait of rationality (and a similar argument could be made for the traits of contracting, and of freedom, and of productive labor) became the dominant one required for social life and for political rule and therefore it was raised to the level of *the* essential human characteristic. On this view, by an inversion of Plato's approach, the state is not "man writ large," but rather what is essentially human or "man" is the state writ small. As the priorities of changing forms of society themselves change, what are taken to be "essentially human characteristics" change with them. In the case at hand, we may hypothesize that since in historical fact (1) rationality played the dominant role in social life and political rule in the transition to civil society and the political state, and (2) since males were dominant in that social and political life of that society, therefore rationality became identified not only as the essential human trait, but by association as a male trait. Thus it is not because male nature is rational that men become rulers, but it is because men rule that rationality is assigned as a male trait.

What's lacking, therefore, in this alleged essential characterization of human nature are those traits which were historically and contingently subordinate in civil society and in the political state, and which were associated with women, e.g., aesthetic sensitivity, intuition, caring, etc.,[14] which were historically characterized by Kant, for example, as non-rational (if not irrational), or as part of the life of sentiment or of the affections, by contrast to the life of reason or intellect. Therefore, though the abstract universalist does not deny that these allegedly subordinate and female traits are human, he gives them a subordinate status and doesn't see them as essential. Here, we may further hypothesize that the historically contingent fact that women played a subordinate role in social and political life therefore led to the identification of such traits as aesthetic sensitivity and intuition as feminine characteristics. Thus it is not (1) because women are intuitive and aesthetically sensitive and (2) because these traits are of secondary importance to society, that women are assigned a subordinate role, but rather (1) because women are subordinate and (2) because these traits are of secondary importance, that these traits are assigned to women as "feminine" characteristics. On this hypothesis it can be seen that the assignment of "male" and "female" characteristics as respectively dominant or subordinate, or essential and accidental, is a product of contingent priorities at a given historical stage of social and political development.

Now this is not to deny that rationality is a universal and necessary human property. However, my argument suggests that the subordination of other essential properties to this one, the rank order of properties, so to speak, is not given by an *a priori* intuition, but rather by the relative roles and priorities which these properties had in a given social system.

. . .

---

[14] Indeed, sensitivity to human differences, such as I argue for in this paper, has been characteristic especially of women. By contrast, what has had priority in the state and civil society—external contracting between self-interested individuals—has been characteristic especially of men.

❦ 11 *Georg Wilhelm Friedrich Hegel*

Although Georg Wilhelm Friedrich Hegel's views on marriage and the family constitute an integral part of his philosophical system—indeed, the very crux of it, according to translator J. B. Baillie—they were not of solely academic concern to him, for Hegel was not altogether devoid of personal experience in the matter. Born in Stuttgart on August 27, 1770, he began his formal education at the age of five and proved to be a model pupil. Upon entering the University of Tübingen, however, he earned the reputation of being a mediocre student (in theology) and offended the local women by his slovenly appearance. During several years as a private tutor, he apparently improved on both scores. In 1801 he began an academic career at the University of Jena, where by 1805 he had become an associate professor of philosophy; and on February 5, 1807, his landlord's wife, Christiana Charlotte Burkhardt, bore him an illegitimate son, Ludwig. Shortly afterward, upon the death of Herr Burkhardt, Hegel allegedly promised to marry Christiana, but this promise was never kept. In the wake of the Battle of Jena, in the same month in which the baby was born, Hegel assumed the editorship of a newspaper in Bamberg, where The Phenomenology of Mind was published. In 1808 he proceeded to Nuremberg as headmaster of a preparatory school, in 1816 he became professor of philosophy at the University of Heidelberg, and in 1818 he went to occupy a similar position at the University of Berlin. It was in Nuremberg in 1811, at the age of forty-one, that Hegel married Marie von Tucher, who was twenty; and it was there that Frau Burkhardt soon appeared, demanding a settlement. The Hegels relieved her of Ludwig, who, it appears, turned out to be a rather difficult child. Two legitimate sons, Karl and Immanuel, were born to what to all appearances was a most happy marriage.

In the early nineteenth century Germany was still a rather loose federation of more or less independent principalities bound together by geographic proximity and by a common language, literature, and art. In the eyes of Hegel's contemporaries, the family assumed greater importance than the state, the church, or the school. The rigidly stratified class system that prevailed in society had its roots in the family, where the wife and mother, dominated by a stern husband and idolized by loving children, occupied a central position. And it was the family, more than the church or the school, that taught moral discipline. The struggle that Hegel depicts between the custodian of the family and that of the community was very real, and it was further intensified by the fact that—except at court, where French morals prevailed—women were almost totally excluded from social life. The conception of the family found in Hegel's dialectical philosophy reflects the prevailing attitudes of his time and place.

In The Phenomenology of Mind, intended as an introduction to his philosophical system, Hegel gave an account of the experience of consciousness *in its progressive development from bare awareness of sense objects through various stages to a culmination in absolute knowledge. Consciousness of the external object, he asserted, leads to consciousness of self and objects not as individuals but as universals. This awareness comes about through reason, which relates the individual self to things; through spirit, which relates it to other selves; and through religion, which relates it to God.*

The self is related to other selves most simply and naturally in the family, which is the product of some kind of divine law that places it in the custody of women. Woman, like everything else, is best viewed not "abstractly," alone, but "concretely," by a consideration of her relationships with all other things. Woman figures prominently in three relationships constituting family life: parent–child, brother–sister, and husband–wife. In the first of these relationships, woman is most universalized, for only through the death of her parents can she become an individual in her own right and free of the natural ties that bind her to them. In her relationship with her brother she is most individualized, recognizing herself in him, identifying with him, but independently and asexually, so that the fraternal relationship is distinct from both the filial and the marital. In marriage and the establishment of her own family, a woman arrives at a synthesis of the universal and the individual; as she sees in her own husband and children, husband and children in general, she achieves an awareness of the universal that a man can never achieve. According to Hegel, man's family ties are less strong by nature than those of woman, for man leaves both wife and child to go out into the community. Woman's relationship to the community is therefore hostile, as she sees in it the enemy that has broken up her family. It in turn oppresses her, although she is among its constituents. She retaliates by mocking mature wisdom, celebrating youth at the expense of age, for the son she bears will become eventually her lord and master; her brother, her contemporary, is the only one with whom she can identify; and it is a youth who will confer wifehood, and thus a measure of independence, upon her daughter.

From *The Phenomenology of Mind*

THE ETHICAL WORLD

The divine law which holds sway in the family has also on its side distinctions within itself, the relations among which make up the living process of its realisation. Amongst the three relationships, however, of husband and wife, parents and children, brothers and sisters, the relationship of husband and wife is to begin with the primary and immediate form in which one consciousness recognises itself in another, and in which each finds reciprocal recognition. Being natural self-knowledge, knowledge of self on the basis of nature, and not on that of ethical life, it merely represents and typifies in a figure the life of spirit, and is not spirit itself actually realised. This figurative representation, however, gets its realisation in an other than it is. This relationship, therefore, finds itself realised not in itself as such, but in the child— an other, in whose coming into being that relationship consists, and with which it passes away. And this change from one generation onwards to another is permanent in and as the life of a nation.

The reverent devotion of husband and wife towards one another is thus mixed up with a natural relation and with feeling, and their relationship is not inherently self-complete; similarly, too, the second relationship, the reverent devotion of parents and children to one another. The devotion of parents towards their children is affected and disturbed just by its being consciously realised in what is external to themselves (viz. the children), and by seeing them become something on their own account without this returning to the parents: independent existence on the part of the children remains a foreign reality, a reality all their own. The devotion of children, again, towards their parents is conversely affected by their coming into being from, or having their essential nature in, what is external to themselves (viz. the parents) and passes away; and by their attaining independent existence and a self-consciousness of their own solely through separation from the source whence they came—a separation in which the spring gets exhausted.

Both these relationships are constituted by and hold within the transience and the dissimilarity of the two sides, which are assigned to them.

An unmixed intransitive form of relationship, however, holds between brother and sister. They are the same blood, which, however, in them has entered into a condition of stable equilibrium. They therefore stand in no such natural relation as husband and wife, they do not desire one another; nor have they given to one another, nor received from one another, this independence of individual being; they are free individualities with respect to each other. The feminine element, therefore, in the form of the sister, premonishes and foreshadows most completely the nature of ethical life. She does not become conscious of it, and does not actualise it, because the law of the family is her inherent implicit inward nature, which does not lie open to the daylight of consciousness, but remains inner feeling and the divine element exempt from actuality. The feminine life is attached to these household divinities; and sees in them both her universal substance, and her particular individuality, yet so views them that this relation of her particular being to them is at the same time not the natural one of pleasure.

As a daughter, the woman must now see her parents pass away with natural emotion and yet with ethical resignation, for it is only at the cost of this condition that she can come to that individual existence of which she is capable. She thus cannot see her independent existence positively attained in her relation to her parents. The relationships of mother and wife, however, are individualised partly in the form of something natural, which brings pleasure; partly in the form of something negative, which finds simply its own evanescence in those relationships; partly again the individualisation is just on that account something contingent, which can be replaced by another particular individuality. In a household of the ethical kind, a woman's relationships are not based on a reference to this particular husband, this particular child, but to *a* husband, to children *in general*,—not to feeling, but to the universal. The distinction between her ethical life (while it determines her particular existence and brings her pleasure) and that of her husband consists just in this, that it has always a directly universal significance for her, and is quite alien to the impulsive condition of mere particular desire. On the other hand, in the husband these two aspects get separated; and since he possesses, as a citizen, the self-conscious power belonging to the universal life, the life of the social whole, he acquires thereby the rights of desire, and keeps himself at the same time in detachment from it. So far, then, as particularity is implicated in this relationship in the case of the wife, her ethical life is not purely ethical; so far, however, as it is ethical, the particularity is a matter of indifference, and the wife is without the moment of knowing herself as *this* particular self in and through an other.

The brother, however, is in the eyes of the sister a being whose nature is unperturbed by desire and is ethically like her own; her recognition in him is pure and unmixed with any sexual relation. The indifference characteristic of particular existence, and the ethical contingency thence arising, are, therefore, not present in this relationship; instead, the moment of individual selfhood, recognising and being recognised, can here assert its right, because it is bound up with the balance and equilibrium resulting from their being of the same blood, and from their being related in a way that involves no mutual desire. The loss of a brother is thus irreparable to the sister, and her duty towards him is the highest.[1]

This relationship at the same time is the limit, at which the circumscribed life of the family is broken up, and passes beyond itself. The brother is the member of the family in whom its spirit becomes individualised, and enabled thereby to turn towards another sphere, towards what is other than and external to itself, and pass over into consciousness of universality. The brother leaves this immediate, rudimentary, and therefore, strictly speaking, negative ethical life of the family, in order to acquire and produce the concrete ethical order which is conscious of itself.

He passes from the divine law, within whose realm he lived, over to the human law. The sister, however, becomes, or the wife remains, director of the home and the preserver of the divine law. In this way both the sexes overcome their merely natural being, and become ethically significant, as diverse forms dividing between them the different aspects which the ethical substance possesses. Both these universal factors of the ethical world have their specific individuality in naturally distinct self-consciousnesses, for the reason that the spirit at work in the ethical order is the immediate unity of the substance [of ethical life] with self-consciousness—an immediacy which thus appears as the existence of a natural difference, at once as regards its aspect of reality and of difference. It is . . . the specific opposition of the two sexes, whose natural character acquires at the same time the significance of their respective ethical determinations.

The distinction of the sexes and of their ethical content remains all the same within the unity of the ethical substance, and its operation is just the constant process of that substance. The husband is sent forth by the spirit of

[1] Cp. *Antigone,* l. 910.

the family into the life of the community, and finds there his self-conscious reality. Just as the family thereby finds in the community its universal substance and subsistence, conversely the community finds in the family the formal element of its own realisation, and in the divine law its power and confirmation. Neither of the two is alone self-complete. Human law as a living and active principle proceeds from the divine, the law holding on earth from that of the nether world, the conscious from the unconscious, mediation from immediacy; and returns to whence it came. The power of the nether world, on the other hand, finds its realisation upon earth; it comes through consciousness to have existence and efficacy.

.   .   .

The ethical realm remains in this way permanently a world without blot or stain, a world untainted by any internal dissension. So, too, its process is an untroubled transition from one of its powers to the other, in such a way that each preserves and produces the other. We see it no doubt divided into two ultimate elements and their realisation: but their opposition is rather the confirming and substantiation of one through the other; and where they directly come in contact and affect each other as actual factors, their mediating common element straightway permeates and suffuses the one with the other. The one extreme, universal spirit conscious of itself, becomes, through the individuality of man, linked together with its other extreme, its force and its element, with *unconscious* spirit. On the other hand, divine law is individualised, the unconscious spirit of the particular individual finds its existence in woman, through the mediation of whom the spirit of the individual comes out of its unrealisedness into actuality, out of the state of unknowing and unknown, and rises into the conscious realm of universal spirit. The union of man with woman constitutes the operative mediating agency for the whole, and constitutes the element which, while separated into the extremes of divine and human law, is, at the same time, their immediate union. This union, again, turns both those first mediate connections into one and the same synthesis, and unites into one process the twofold movement in opposite directions,—one from reality to unreality, the downward movement of human law, organised into independent members, to the danger and trial of death,—the other, from unreality to reality, the upward movement of the law of the nether world to the daylight of conscious existence. Of these movements the former falls to man, the latter to woman.

GUILT AND DESTINY

Human law . . . in its universal mode of existence is the community, in its efficient operation in general is the manhood of the community, in its actual efficient operation is government. It has its being, its process, and its subsistence by consuming and absorbing into itself the separatist action of the household gods, the individualisation into insular independent families which are under the management of womankind, and by keeping them dissolved in the fluent continuum of its own nature. The family at the same time, however, is in general its element, the individual consciousness its universal operative basis. Since the community gets itself subsistence only by breaking in upon family happiness, and dissolving [individual] self-consciousness into the universal, it creates its enemy for itself within its own gates, creates it in what it suppresses, and what is at the same time essential to it—womankind in general. Womankind—the everlasting irony in the life of the community—changes by intrigue the universal purpose of government into a private end, transforms its universal activity into a work of this or that specific individual, and perverts the universal property of the state into a possession and ornament for the family. Woman in this way turns to ridicule the grave wisdom of maturity, which, being dead to all particular aims, to private pleasure, personal satisfaction, and actual activity as well, thinks of, and is concerned for, merely what is universal; she makes this wisdom the laughing-stock of raw and wanton youth, an object of derision and scorn, unworthy of their enthusiasm. She asserts that it is everywhere the force of youth that really counts; she upholds this as of primary significance; extols a son as one who is the lord and master of the mother who has borne him; a brother as one in whom the sister finds man on a level with herself; a youth as one through whom the daughter, deprived of her dependence (on the family unity), acquires the satisfaction and the dignity of wifehood.

. . .

ᴖᵇᵉᴖ Carol C. Gould

Carol C. Gould challenges Hegel's notion of the opposition between family and community. The family is fundamentally an economic unit, she contends, not a haven of love. The wife, far from struggling with the community over the allegiance of her husband, serves it by playing the role of housekeeper, cook, and laundress for the purpose of preparing him to fulfill his duties there. In a similar way she prepares her children to assume comparable duties. And as a shopper and consumer she herself participates directly in community life as well.

From "The Woman Question: The Philosophy of Liberation and the Liberation of Philosophy"

THE WOMAN QUESTION AND THE FAMILY: DEMYSTIFICATION IN THEORY AND PRACTICE

To exemplify what I mean by a critical analysis of the concrete situation of women, as well as the metacritique of philosophy, I shall now consider a leading example of philosophical theorizing on the family: Hegel's discussion in the *Philosophy of Right*.[1] My aim is to criticize Hegel's understanding of the modern family, which is still to a surprising extent a prevailing interpretation of it. The critique will lead to an alternative analysis. Moreover, since I take the role of woman in the contemporary family to provide the central focus for a theoretical understanding and critique of the present situation, this case study may also serve as the beginning for a theory of women's special oppression, especially as her oppression in the family is related to her oppression in other spheres. In focusing on Hegel's understanding of the family, I do not mean to suggest that the actual form of the family has persisted unchanged since his time. Rather, it is the mystifications[2] present in Hegel's theory—e.g., the privacy of the family—which persist in contemporary interpretations and which obscure its present actuality as well. . . .

In the Greek *polis*, as Aristotle described it, the household was the center of the economy. By contrast, for Hegel, in his reflections upon the modern state, the family no longer serves this function; instead, the economic realm is removed to and develops in civil society. Consequently, instead of the Greek division of institutions into the family and the *polis*, there is for Hegel a three-fold distinction into family, civil society and the state.

Accordingly, for Hegel in the *Philosophy of Right*, the family is not defined in terms of its economic functions. Rather it is understood as the domain of love and immediacy, as fundamentally private, whose main function is that of the socialization of children. The family is based on the sentiment of love. The state also for Hegel is based on sentiment, in this case that of patriotism. Both of these sentimental realms are contrasted by Hegel with civil society which is based on need and labor, rather than on sentiment. Now Karl Marx—in *On the Jewish Question* and in *The Critique of Hegel's Philosophy of Right*—criticized Hegel's notion of the state by showing that Hegel's understanding of it as autonomous and as a realm of (patriotic) sentiment was only an appearance. In reality, the state could only be rightly understood as dominated by its relation to civil society, i.e., the sphere of economic needs and interests.[3]

[1] Hegel, *Philosophy of Right*, trans. by T. M. Knox (Oxford University Press), pp. 106–122.

[2] "Mystification," used sparsely as a term in this section, needs demystifying. The term is borrowed from the Hegelian and Marxist mode of discussion. To be mystified is to be dominated by an illusion, by a particular appearance or image of a thing. A mystification functions to mask the reality from view, by taking its (usually distorted) reflection or its symbolic surrogate in place of it. Thus, Marx talks of the relationship of exchange of commodities, which is portrayed by classical political economy as an exchange of equivalent values, as such a "mystification," in that it masks what he considers to be the real relations of exploitation, i.e., of unequal exchange of values. It is in this sense that I am speaking of Hegel's theory of the family as a "mystification."

[3] Thus Marx writes in *On The Jewish Question*: "The political state, in relation to civil society, is just as spiritual as is heaven in relation to earth. It stands in the same opposition to civil society, and overcomes it in the same manner as religion overcomes the narrowness of the profane world; i.e., it has always to acknowledge it again, re-establish it, and allow itself to be dominated by it." (In Robert Tucker, ed., *The Marx-Engels Reader*, New York, Norton, 1972, p. 32.) My claim in this paper is that this remark could just as well apply to the family.

However, Marx never carried out a similar critique of Hegel's notion of the family, and I think he ought to have.[4]

I would argue that the family, like the state, is pervaded throughout by bourgeois or civil society, and that the characterization of the family as a domain of love, privacy, and immediacy is largely a *mystification,* masking the intricate and intimate relations in which the family stands to capital and to production. As such, the ascription of sentiment—i.e., of love—as the tie that binds serves to conceal the concrete nature of the family as a social and political institution under capitalism.

Let's begin with Hegel's account. Since the husband and wife were tied by bonds of love, Hegel did not regard marriage as a contract. The family was outside the domain of right. But this view serves to remove the first right conferred on women, which also brought them into civil society—namely, contractual marriage, with its attendant rights (for the woman, to be supported, and for the man, the right to consummate the marriage, among many others) and obligations (to love, honor and obey). Indeed, marriage is so clearly a contract that society recognizes *only* a contract, as marriage. That it is a contract, an agreement of both parties to conditions explicitly stated, is evidenced by the words "I do"; and that this contract has the status of law is evident from the extensive body of marital law of religious and civil authority. Hegel's romantic claim here—that the family is outside the domain of right—can only be understood as reflecting the patriarchal character of the German family. In this view, the so-called immediacy of the family reduces to the claim that Papa was boss. That it is not in the civil realm amounts to saying that nobody has any business telling the man not to rule his wife. The grimness of this situation is then ameliorated by saying that the family is an ethical and spiritual realm. If we understand the economic and political realms to be realms where you agree by contract to do something, then on this view the ethical realm becomes one where you have to do what someone tells you to do because it is right to do it, and the spiritual realm is one where you undertake to do what someone wants you to do without his even having to tell you.

Love and privacy, then, are the *religion* of the family, its "fantastic" or illusory reality, "its moral sanction, its solemn complement, its general basis of consolation and justification, . . . its spiritual aroma."[5] These notions continue to mystify the present functions of the family as well. Peggy Morton[6] and

---

[4] This claim needs qualification. My point is that although Marx makes some suggestive remarks about women and the family, he offers no systematic critique of the family comparable to that which he provides for the state. Engels' discussion in *Origin of the Family* is of a different sort, focusing on an anthropological account of the origin of the family and only briefly on its modern form.

[5] "Contribution to a Critique of Hegel's Philosophy of Right: Introduction" in Tucker, *op. cit.,* p. 12.

[6] Peggy Morton, "A Woman's Work Is Never Done" in Altbach, ed., *From Feminism to Liberation* (Cambridge, Schenkman, 1971), pp. 211–227.

Mariarosa Dalla Costa[7] among others have argued that the family serves the central economic function of producing and reproducing labor-power or workers; that the central task of the wife in the family, through which she becomes essential to capital, is to ready the worker for work each day by shopping, cleaning, cooking, etc.; insofar as she does this she contributes to the profits of the capitalist by reducing his costs. As such, part of her work is also unpaid. Because of this, the wage which the husband gets buys the labor of two, and insofar as he in his person incorporates (literally) her work, part of which is unpaid, she also is exploited by the capitalist through him.[8]

The wife also reproduces labor power by raising the children, by "socializing them." But this socialization is closely related to the needs of capital, for as we know, the children as future workers must learn the requisite qualities of possessiveness, obedience to authority, and the treatment of people as commodities and understood in terms of money. Indeed, as Firestone,[9] R. D. Laing[10] and others have pointed out, "love" in the family is made a tool in the production of these characteristics. It is used as a device to manipulate children.

Furthermore, the family as the consuming unit is a major market for capital and the woman is especially significant here for she does the shopping. Consequently, all her qualities and characteristics as well as her domestic labor are understood as commodities. By an inversion of the "fetishism of commodities"—the case in which human relations (of exploitation) in the political economic sphere are masked or appear only in their economically abstracted form as relations among commodities—here, in the family, the commodity or production relations are masked or appear only as "sentimental" relations, i.e., in the form of love, care for children, etc. The "fetishism of love" plays an analogous role, in the bourgeois ideology of the family, to that which the fetishism of commodities plays in the sphere of political economy.

But in all of these ways, the woman is no longer a person but an instrument of production.[11] The family is fundamentally economic and in this sense

[7] Mariarosa Dalla Costa, "The Power of Women and the Subversion of the Community," Bristol, Falling Wall Press, 1972.

[8] In this section, I describe the particular form which the family takes in capitalist society. Many of the functions of the capitalist family appear also in present socialist societies. But I shall not here attempt a discussion of the socialist family. We may, however, raise some questions concerning the family under socialism: first, is Engels' description of the family as "the productive unit of society" no longer applicable? If so, what are the functions of the family under socialism? Further, if these are economic functions, why have they been incompletely socialized, contrary to Engels' prediction? Moreover, although in socialist countries many women work, the larger part of the task of reproducing workers still falls to women and not to men; we may wonder why this is, and whether it can be explained adequately as being simply a residue of earlier modes of social organization.

[9] Firestone, *The Dialectic of Sex: The Case for Feminist Revolution* (New York, Bantam Books, 1970), chapter 4.

[10] R. D. Laing, *The Politics of Experience* (New York, Ballantine Books, 1967), chapter 3.

[11] Cf. Marx and Engels, *Manifesto of the Communist Party*, Tucker, *op. cit.*, p. 350.

public.[12] Instead of being a haven of love protecting the worker from the ravages of bourgeois society, the family is thoroughly in the service of capital. It is not merely being used by capital, but in its present form it is necessary to capital, for its functions of reproducing labor power are essential economic functions. As performing these functions, the relations between family members are hardly "immediate," but are rather mediated through and through by their relation to capital. Correlatively, the family itself and the housewife at its center mediate the functioning of the economy. However, it should be clear that I do not mean to imply that human relations within the family are impossible; in fact, love and care for children may take place even within the constraints of social and economic roles. But the family, as a unit of social reality, serves a different purpose.

Insofar as the woman in the family is exploited (by performing unpaid labor) and oppressed (by having to take the money from her husband, by being commodified and manipulated by advertisements and the media, by being coerced to raise the children by herself and in "appropriate" ways), the political emancipation of the woman, as well as the assurance of equal opportunity for her, reveals itself to be inadequate. Minimally we might say that concrete emancipation requires the overcoming of the dependence of the family on capital. Much more needs to be said of the nature of her specific exploitation, and I have only presented some preliminary considerations.

The exploitation and oppression of women in the family, and of all women insofar as all women are understood as potentially housewives,[13] is thus fully social and historical; all of women's relations take on a form specific to capital; women's function is the reproduction of labor power. However, this social and cultural character of woman's work is mystified and hidden from us and this mystification takes two fundamental forms.

The first mystification—present already in Hegel—is the glorification and spiritualization of love, marriage, child-raising and housekeeping. Woman here is understood as super-human; she is a heavenly or mysterious creature— love goddess, madonna or earth mother. Woman's relation to nature and her body take on a spiritual form. This spiritualization of woman, including the spiritualization of her body, here obscures the social and economic functioning of women in the family. It keeps her unaware of her exploitation and also

[12] In the text, I follow the now common usage of having "public" refer to the political-economic realm as a whole, reserving the word "private" for the domestic sphere, i.e., the allegedly purely personal and extraeconomic functioning of individuals in the family. It is in this sense that I have argued that the family in its actual functions is not a private domain, but rather public. Furthermore, my argument suggests that, except as a conceptual or terminological distinction, a sharp distinction between the public and private realms is, at least in present actuality, a myth. There is another use of "public" and "private" however, in which the state is understood as the public sphere, as distinct from civil society as the private sphere.

[13] The expectation that the woman should function as a housewife affects professional women also. It shows itself in the lower salary scale of women professionals and in the supportive roles which women professionals are sometimes expected to play. The understanding of woman as housewife is found also in the jobs in which women tend to be employed—as secretaries, salegirls, school teachers and garment workers—jobs which parallel women's functions in the home.

provides a compensatory fantasy (as well as an atonement) for her repressed humanity. This spiritualization also serves to justify to woman her non-effectuality in the running of things; it hides her instrumentality in a process of production which is not of her own making and not under her control. It also fills up the isolation of existence in the family with a fantasy world of social participation manufactured in the image of true romances. Indeed, this mystification of woman's exploitation is itself exploited in turn. Woman as love goddess gives rise to the romance industry, and attractiveness becomes a matter of commodity production; thus fashions and cosmetics, dietetic foods and exercise equipment are represented by the media as necessary and indispensable if one is to be thin, young and beautiful and thus loved.

The first mystification of woman as love goddess and madonna—in which even her natural functioning is spiritualized and glorified—is complemented by a second, equally pervasive mystification. Here the social and historical exploitation of women is hidden under the guise of its being her natural biological inheritance to bear and raise children, to be a housewife. This mystification seeks to keep woman in her place by making it her lot; it seeks to make her role acceptable by making it inevitable. Woman is regarded as by nature a child-breeder. In this way, woman is kept out of the public sphere, she is restrained from relating to other women and from becoming a public force, because she is understood as a creature not of discourse but of intercourse. This mystification treats woman as closer to animal than human nature. Like the slave, she is regarded as having no will of her own. That she is a natural rather than human being, and that she is a creature without a will serves to rationalize using the woman as an instrument of production, as instrumental to the process of producing and reproducing the worker's life and that of future workers. Thus the myth of woman's naturalness, like that of her spirituality, serves to conceal the social and historical character of her real life, which although founded on a natural basis, nonetheless transcends it. And just as the myth of the spiritual love goddess and madonna was itself exploited by being commodified, so here too the myth of the woman as natural and as animal is put to economic use in sexploitation and in prostitution.

Demystification, therefore, means a return from the "heaven" of spiritualized feminity, and the "hell" (or "jungle") of sheer animality, to a changed social reality, in which the very basis for these mystifications is eliminated. If we ask *why* the woman has come to be regarded either as madonna or as whore, we then begin to raise a problem concerning the concrete social reality itself which requires these mystifications—i.e., we begin to do *critical* philosophy. The negative aspect of philosophy as critique is the elimination of illusions and specifically of those illusions which bind us all to exploitation. But philosophy as critique also has a positive dimension. As for human liberation in general, to be liberated from such illusions now makes women free to discover and to *choose* what they want to become. It is the first step in such a choice—the ground-clearing for making what was previously regarded as "natural," or what was previously imposed on women in the form of social exploitation, a matter for their own determination.

~§~12 Margaret Fuller

Sarah Margaret Fuller, born on May 23, 1810, in Cambridge, Massachusetts, was provided with an extremely rigorous education at the knee of her domineering father. Timothy Fuller, disappointed that his first child was a girl, had determined to prepare her, despite her sex, for an intellectual life. The result was an extremely knowledgeable and self-assured woman, said to have remarked to Ralph Waldo Emerson on one occasion, "I know all the people worth knowing in America, and I find no intellect comparable to my own." Eager to render other women equally capable and independent, in 1838 she inaugurated a series of "conversations" for intellectual Bostonians, addressing herself to sundry topics: classical mythology, the fine arts, ethics, education. Fuller's relations with these women were not dominated solely by intellect. "Woman is born for love," she once wrote, "and it is impossible to turn her from seeking it." And a now lost journal entry begins, "It is so true that a woman may be in love with another woman, and a man with a man . . . it is the same which angels feel."

Whatever the angels may have felt, in 1844 Margaret Fuller left the group of New England transcendentalists with whom she had been associating around Boston and moved to New York. There she became America's first professional newspaperwoman, and there she met and fell deeply in love with James Nathan, a German immigrant of Jewish extraction. The romance was cut short when he returned to Europe. Shortly afterward, in 1847, Fuller commenced her own European travels, armed with letters of introduction to the most illustrious people in England and on the continent: Thomas Carlyle, Walter Savage Landor, Robert and Elizabeth Barrett Browning, Hugues Félicité Robert de Lamennais, George Sand. But it was Italy that Margaret Fuller loved most. She espoused Mazzini's revolutionary movement, and again she fell in love, this time with the Marchese Giovanni Angelo Ossoli, ten years her junior, and her inferior in both intellect and education. They were married probably during the following April, and young Angelo was born to the couple on September 5. All three died in a shipwreck off Fire Island on the way to America almost two years later.

The American transcendentalists were rebels: Bronson Alcott in his educational theories, Henry David Thoreau in his doctrine of and practice of civil disobedience, Margaret Fuller in her feminism. Her major work, Woman in the Nineteenth Century, has been called the first "considered statement" of feminism to appear in America. Fanny Wright, Lucretia Mott, and the Grimké sisters had already spoken out on the subject, to be sure, but primarily from the lecture platform and originally in connection with the abolition movement. Fuller herself had addressed the subject in her Boston "conversations." But in Woman in the Nineteenth Century she not only discussed such problems as employment and the franchise, she examined such taboo topics as sexual equality, marriage, passion, even prostitution.

180

Margaret Fuller was the woman who announced to Thomas Carlyle in a famous exchange, "I accept the universe." Carlyle, ignoring whatever philosophical implications may have been intended by that assertion, is said to have replied, "By Gad, madam, you'd better." But Fuller did not accept those aspects of the universe in which woman was relegated to a position of subservience to man. Her most fervent wish was to strengthen awareness that humankind was made up of women as well as men and that optimal development of the one sex could not be effected without optimal development of the other. Fuller bristled at the suggestion that the impact of women on society must be indirect, that their education must be male-oriented, and that the highest compliment that could be paid to them was to describe them as "manly," or "above their sex." As evidence of woman's fitness to assume positions of leadership, she offered such historical figures as Elizabeth I of England and Isabella of Castile; and that women can wield the pen, she noted, had been proved by Mary Wollstonecraft, Lady Mary Wortley Montagu, Mary Somerville, Germaine de Staël, and George Sand.

To be sure, Margaret Fuller observed a distinction between the sexes. Women she thought to be more intuitive, more spiritual, more "electrical" than men. Men tend to exhibit more energy than harmony, more power than beauty, and more intellect than love, while the opposite could be said of women. The two sets of qualities are "perpetually passing into one another." Man partakes of the feminine and woman of the masculine. Fuller spoke pantheistically of Man (by which she meant, she explained, both men and women), who has but one soul and one body, formed equally of male and female. This whole cannot be perfect, Fuller thought, while imperfection remains in any of its parts. While the development of man antedated that of woman, who was therefore under his aegis for a time, his abuse of the power he held operated to the detriment of the whole. The time had come, Fuller thought, for women to help one another attain the liberty for which they were now ready. Men needed only to remove the arbitrary barriers that separated women from any occupations they might choose—even, to take her much-noted example, that of sea captain. Women must rely on themselves and on each other, and no longer on men.

From *Woman in the Nineteenth Century*

. . .

Man is a being of two-fold relations, to nature beneath, and intelligences above him. The earth is his school, if not his birth-place; God his object; life and thought his means of interpreting nature, and aspiring to God.

Only a fraction of this purpose is accomplished in the life of any one man. Its entire accomplishment is to be hoped only from the sum of the lives of men, or Man considered as a whole.

As this whole has one soul and one body, any injury or obstruction to a part, or to the meanest member, affects the whole. Man can never be perfectly happy or virtuous, till all men are so.

To address Man wisely, you must not forget that his life is partly animal, subject to the same laws with Nature.

But you cannot address him wisely unless you consider him still more as soul, and appreciate the conditions and destiny of soul.

The growth of Man is two-fold, masculine and feminine.

So far as these two methods can be distinguished, they are so as

Energy and Harmony;
Power and Beauty;
Intellect and Love;

or by some such rude classification; for we have not language primitive and pure enough to express such ideas with precision.

These two sides are supposed to be expressed in Man and Woman, that is, as the more and the less, for the faculties have not been given pure to either, but only in preponderance. There are also exceptions in great number, such as men of far more beauty than power, and the reverse. But, as a general rule, it seems to have been the intention to give a preponderance on the one side, that is called masculine, and on the other, one that is called feminine.

There cannot be a doubt that, if these two developments were in perfect harmony, they would correspond to and fulfill one another, like hemispheres, or the tenor and bass in music.

But there is no perfect harmony in human nature; and the two parts answer one another only now and then; or, if there be a persistent consonance, it can only be traced at long intervals, instead of discoursing an obvious melody.

What is the cause of this?

Man, in the order of time, was developed first; as energy comes before harmony; power before beauty.

Woman was therefore under his care as an elder. He might have been her guardian and teacher.

But, as human nature goes not straight forward, but by excessive action and then reaction in an undulated course, he misunderstood and abused his advantages, and became her temporal master instead of her spiritual sire.

On himself came the punishment. He educated Woman more as a servant than a daughter, and found himself a king without a queen.

The children of this unequal union showed unequal natures, and, more and more, men seemed sons of the handmaid, rather than princess.

At last, there were so many Ishmaelites that the rest grew frightened and indignant. They laid the blame on Hagar, and drove her forth into the wilderness.

But there were none the fewer Ishmaelites for that.

At last men became a little wiser, and saw that the infant Moses was, in every case, saved by the pure instincts of Woman's breast. For, as too much adversity is better for the moral nature than too much prosperity, Woman, in this respect, dwindled less than Man, though in other respects still a child in leading-strings.

So Man did her more and more justice, and grew more and more kind.

But yet—his habits and his will corrupted by the past—he did not clearly see that Woman was half himself; that her interests were identical with his; and that, by the law of their common being, he could never reach his true proportions while she remained in any wise shorn of hers.

And so it has gone on to our day; both ideas developing, but more slowly than they would under a clearer recognition of truth and justice, which would have permitted the sexes their due influence on one another, and mutual improvement from more dignified relations.

Wherever there was pure love, the natural influences were, for the time, restored.

Wherever the poet or artist gave free course to his genius, he saw the truth, and expressed it in worthy forms, for these men especially share and need the feminine principle. The divine birds need to be brooded into life and song by mothers.

Wherever religion (I mean the thirst for truth and good, not the love of sect and dogma) had its course, the original design was apprehended in its simplicity, and the dove presaged sweetly from Dodona's oak.

I have aimed to show that no age was left entirely without a witness of the equality of the sexes in function, duty and hope.

Also that, when there was unwillingness or ignorance, which prevented this being acted upon, women had not the less power for their want of light and noble freedom. But it was power which hurt alike them and those against whom they made use of the arms of the servile,—cunning, blandishment, and unreasonable emotion.

That now the time has come when a clearer vision and better action are possible—when Man and Woman may regard one another as brother and sister, the pillars of one porch, the priests of one worship.

I have believed and intimated that this hope would receive an ampler fruition, than ever before, in our own land.

And it will do so if this land carry out the principles from which sprang our national life.

I believe that, at present, women are the best helpers of one another.

Let them think; let them act; till they know what they need.

We only ask of men to remove arbitrary barriers. Some would like to do more. But I believe it needs that Woman show herself in her native dignity, to teach them how to aid her; their minds are so encumbered by tradition.

. . .

You ask, what use will she make of liberty, when she has so long been sustained and restrained?

I answer; in the first place, this will not be suddenly given. I read yesterday a debate of this year on the subject of enlarging women's rights over property. It was a leaf from the class-book that is preparing for the needed instruction. The men learned visibly as they spoke. The champions of Women saw the fallacy of arguments on the opposite side, and were startled by their own convictions. With their wives at home, and the readers of the paper; it was the same. And so the stream flows on, thought urging action, and action leading to the evolution of still better thought.

But, were this freedom to come suddenly, I have no fear of the consequences. Individuals might commit excesses, but there is not only in the sex a reverence for decorums and limits inherited and enhanced from generation to generation, which many years of other life could not efface, but a native love, in Woman as Woman, of proportion, of "the simple art of not too much,"—a Greek moderation, which would create immediately a restraining party, the natural legislators and instructors of the rest, and would gradually establish such rules as are needed to guard, without impeding, life.

.   .   .

But if you ask me what offices they may fill, I reply—any. I do not care what case you put; let them be sea-captains, if you will. I do not doubt there are women well fitted for such an office, and, if so, I should be . . . glad to see them in it . . .

I think women need, especially at this juncture, a much greater range of occupation than they have, to rouse their latent powers. A party of travellers lately visited a lonely hut on a mountain. There they found an old woman, who told them she and her husband had lived there forty years. "Why," they said, "did you choose so barren a spot?" She "did not know; *it was the man's notion.*"

And, during forty years, she had been content to act, without knowing why, upon "the man's notion." I would not have it so.

In families that I know, some little girls like to saw wood, others to use carpenters' tools. Where these tastes are indulged, cheerfulness and good-humor are promoted. Where they are forbidden, because "such things are not proper for girls," they grow sullen and mischievous.

Fourier had observed these wants of women, as no one can fail to do who watches the desires of little girls, or knows the ennui that haunts grown women, except where they make to themselves a serene little world by art of some kind. He, therefore, in proposing a great variety of employments, in manufactures or the care of plants and animals, allows for one third of women as likely to have a taste for masculine pursuits, one third of men for feminine.

Who does not observe the immediate glow and serenity that is diffused over the life of women, before restless or fretful, by engaging in gardening, building, or the lowest department of art? Here is something that is not routine, something that draws forth life towards the infinite.

I have no doubt, however, that a large proportion of women would give themselves to the same employments as now, because there are circumstances that must lead them. Mothers will delight to make the nest soft and warm. Nature would take care of that; no need to clip the wings of any bird that wants to soar and sing, or finds in itself the strength of pinion for a migratory flight unusual to its kind. The difference would be that *all* need not be constrained to employments for which *some* are unfit.

I have urged upon the sex self-subsistence in its two forms of self-reliance and self-impulse, because I believe them to be the needed means of the present juncture.

I have urged on Woman independence of Man, not that I do not think the sexes mutually needed by one another, but because in Woman this fact has led to an excessive devotion, which has cooled love, degraded marriage, and prevented either sex from being what it should be to itself or the other.

I wish Woman to live, *first* for God's sake. Then she will not make an imperfect man her god, and thus sink to idolatry. Then she will not take what is not fit for her from a sense of weakness and poverty. Then, if she finds what she needs in Man embodied, she will know how to love, and be worthy of being loved.

By being more a soul, she will not be less Woman, for nature is perfected through spirit.

Now there is no woman, only an overgrown child.

. . .

A profound thinker has said, "No married woman can represent the female world, for she belongs to her husband. The idea of Woman must be represented by a virgin."

But that is the very fault of marriage, and of the present relation between the sexes, that the woman *does* belong to the man, instead of forming a whole with him. Were it otherwise, there would be no such limitation to the thought.

Woman, self-centered, would never be absorbed by any relation; it would be only an experience to her as to man. It is a vulgar error that love, *a* love, to Woman is her whole existence; she also is born for Truth and Love in their universal energy. Would she but assume her inheritance, Mary would not be the only virgin mother. Not Manzoni alone would celebrate in his wife the virgin mind with the maternal wisdom and conjugal affections. The soul is ever young, ever virgin.

And will not she soon appear?—the woman who shall vindicate their birthright for all women; who shall teach them what to claim, and how to use what they obtain? Shall not her name be for her era Victoria, for her country and life Virginia? Yet predictions are rash; she herself must teach us to give her the fitting name.

An idea not unknown to ancient times has of late been revived, that, in the metamorphoses of life, the soul assumes the form, first of Man, then of Woman, and takes the chances, and reaps the benefits of either lot. Why then, say some, lay such emphasis on the rights or needs of Woman? What she wins not as Woman will come to her as Man.

That makes no difference. It is not Woman, but the law of right, the law of growth, that speaks in us, and demands the perfection of each being in its kind—apple as apple, Woman as Woman. Without adopting your theory, I know that I, a daughter, live through the life of Man; but what concerns me now is, that my life be a beautiful, powerful, in a word, a complete life in its kind. Had I but one more moment to live I must wish the same.

Suppose, at the end of your cycle, your great world-year, all will be completed, whether I exert myself or not (and the supposition is *false*,—but suppose it true), am I to be indifferent about it? Not so! I must beat my own pulse true in the heart of the world; for *that* is virtue, excellence, health.

. . .

I stand in the sunny noon of life. Objects no longer glitter in the dews of morning, neither are yet softened by the shadows of evening. Every spot is seen, every chasm revealed. Climbing the dusty hill, some fair effigies that once stood for symbols of human destiny have been broken; those I still have with me show defects in this broad light. Yet enough is left, even by experience, to point distinctly to the glories of that destiny; faint, but not to be mistaken streaks of the future day. I can say with the bard,

"Though many have suffered shipwreck, still beat noble hearts."

Always the soul says to us all, Cherish your best hopes as a faith, and abide by them in action. Such shall be the effectual fervent means to their fulfilment;

> For the Power to whom we bow
> Has given its pledge that, if not now,
> They of pure and steadfast mind,
> By faith exalted, truth refined,
> *Shall* hear all music loud and clear,
> Whose first notes they ventured here.
> Then fear not thou to wind the horn,
> Though elf and gnome thy courage scorn;
> Ask for the castle's King and Queen;
> Though rabble rout may rush between,
> Beat thee senseless to the ground,
> In the dark beset thee round;
> Persist to ask, and it will come;
> Seek not for rest in humbler home;
> So shalt thou see, what few have seen,
> The palace home of King and Queen.

⋙ *Elizabeth Dorcas Livermore*

Elizabeth Dorcas Livermore was a contemporary of Margaret Fuller and author of the following article, which appeared in the New York Christian Inquirer shortly after Fuller's death. Livermore refers to her subject as a "representative woman," apparently borrowing a concept from a work published in the year of Margaret Fuller's death: Ralph Waldo Emerson's Representative Men. "Every man is a cause," Emerson had written," . . . and all history resolves itself very easily into the biography of a few stout and earnest persons." The persons included in Emerson's volume were Plato, Swedenborg, Montaigne, Shakespeare, Napoleon, and Goethe. Livermore, it would seem, was proposing a seventh name for the list: that of Margaret Fuller, whose cause was the plight of her own sex in a male-dominated world.

Margaret Fuller Ossoli, A Representative Woman

We have but lately received the Memoirs and Works of Margaret Fuller Ossoli; and we have only waited to reperuse thoughts which have always been full of suggestion to us, before we give our latest impressions of one who, for want of a better term, we denominate a *representative woman*.

In doing this, we will endeavor to express what we mean by it, as applied to one who, by her native talent and acquired culture, and through authorship, stands prominent before the American public. If we mistake not, she was the first who raised a clear note, so as to command attention, in behalf of a *higher culture, greater privilege*, and a *rightful sphere of activity* for the women of her country.

It is curious to note the result, through an overruling Providence, of the intention of her father to give her what is called a masculine education (though he evidently meant only to properly unfold her uncommon powers), by which she rose to the point of most thoroughly appreciating what is peculiarly feminine in woman, and by her advocacy of its worth, to open a way for its needed influence.

That she did not create the desire for a better culture, privilege, and sphere of activity, is manifest by the almost simultaneous rising of persons in different localities in favor of the same, which has resulted in what is called the "Woman's Rights Movement." She but expressed in strong and definite terms the promptings of her own full nature, and therefore stands as the representative of a general want.

It is not necessary to suppose that she suffered peculiar disabilities in any form of her outward lot; on the contrary, she was unusually favored with affection, respect, and opportunities of mental acquisition. But she was one of the disinterested few, who, through warm sympathy and a keen sensibility, gather into themselves the woes of their race, suffering their evils, and lacking their needed good.

For this large-hearted, this magnetic and electrifying life, even more than for her uncommon attainments, do we place her foremost of all who have plead for their sex, and we cannot but regard the full publication of her writings as an important era in the movement, and as giving a fit opportunity to say a few words upon the same.

To the unobservant and unthinking, it must seem revolutionary for a class who from nature and custom seem to love and to rest in dependence, to ask and even demand the enjoyment of rights and the performance of duties which in the past have been confined to the masculine minds of the community.

But we must consider the different position woman at once assumed in the emancipation of our country from British rule. The commencement of our hostilities with England, which gave her a share of the responsibilities and dangers of that struggle, was the true date of her resistance to the established order of things, and essentially instituted her equal freedom by its success. Ever since that time her way of life has been one specially suited to develop her energies and increase her self-respect. In pioneering, planting, and building, she has had her full share of incidental privations and toils; while, in her desire to aid the common cause, she has seldom paused to think whether her helping hand stopped short or went beyond the employments usually assigned her. Added to this, since education has become the ruling passion of our people, her brain has been stimulated to incessant activity, while the very air she breathes, filled as it is with the life of unprecedented action, compels her, as a matter of course, to new uses of her powers. As the pressure of business keeps the head of the family much from home, and its weight of care returns him to it wearied and oppressed, longing for rest and recreation rather than to enter it as a scene of discipline and correction, the government of its younger members devolves much upon herself, which, when added to the experimental character which our republican principles give to our whole domestic *menage,* no less than to our social life, taxes her faculties to an uncommon degree. So when, as often occurs, he whose protection she would gladly shelter herself under, falters through manifold worldly temptations, and falls by the way-side helpless and burdensome, or worse still, comes home to heap upon her abuse, and those to whom she has given life return, it may be, from its snares, marred and spoiled, to mock her best endeavors in their nurture, it is but a natural and slightly forward step for her to seek to bring more within her own power the hoarded means of the family, by calling for a change of law to aid her, and to ask to share in devising social and public restraints to save her own from moral and physical ruin. Or, if this is impossible, that the prohibitions of society, or the selfish rivalry of the more fortunate, may not prevent her seeking in some sphere a little aside from the common one that support denied her by her appointed guardian. This, in simple terms, is what we understand by the plea for woman's rights. It is for this that Margaret Fuller entreated; and when she said, "Let her be a sea-captain if she will," she but expressed in strong and somewhat exaggerated terms her wish for them to be allowed to prepare for any emergency. Singularly enough, this duty has since devolved upon a lady through pressing necessity, and was performed, as is well known, with such success as to win unmingled approbation.[1]

That there has been heat and passion in the discussion, is but the necessary accompaniment of the introduction of a new subject for public attention. It seems as if it were necessary that the human mind should thrust itself beyond the boundaries of reason and thorough judgment, that it may obtain a vantage ground from which to overlook a subject, before it settles down into that medium position safe alike from the degradation of servitude and the dangers of license.

It is for the restrained tone of feeling with which she advocates her cause, for its mingled womanly earnestness and lady-like reserve, that we turn to

---

[1] Mrs. Patten.

Margaret Fuller's pages with satisfaction and hope. Through her own example and precepts she shows that an increase of benefit is to come to us chiefly by the culture of a higher tone of thought, a truer life, and a more faithful employment of time and talent. For this end she was ever ready to help and encourage both the older and the younger. To her inspiration as a teacher many must date the upward tendencies of their lives. Her keen discernment of their qualities of mind, her ready perception of character, and her generous sympathy, must have had an untold force upon those whom she taught, and made her their truest benefactor.

The rapid and intense working of her mind, connected with its uncommon grasp, caused her to include within the moderate term of her one life the thoughts, feelings, and experiences of many, while the necessity there was for busy action gave it a practical and wise direction. This told, also, upon her natural temper, being one to seek the original right and reason of things, rather than to walk unreflectingly in the beaten way, which, in itself, creating for her a loneliness of spirit, might, but for industry, have degenerated into morbidness and misanthropy.

Though at times, through her thoughtful far-sightedness, her native idealism, and inherent energy, she becomes impatient of the slow unfolding of events, and forgetful of life's limitations,—feels herself, as it were, withheld by fate,—yet she never abates her labors, or loses her faith in the final triumph of good.

For her wonderful combination of natural talent for study, genius for colloquial expression, ability to use her varied gifts for her wide-spread philanthropy and domestic virtues and especially for her power of moral inspiration, we might challenge the world to produce her equal. As critic, narrator, essayist, journalist, and historian, this woman of a century, who never wrote a sentence which her own conscience did not sanction, and which was not the fruit of rigid self-culture, may well stand for us as a symbol of woman's capabilities.

Her poems, as she says, were but the attempt to vary for herself her mode of expression, and do not reveal her full power. Had she stopped to muse until the fire burned in that direction, she might have become a lyrist of no mean stamp. Her "Farewell to Summer" shows a thirst for harmony, and a sense of melody which, when worked and waited for patiently, flows out into verse. But then she might not have been our representative woman. As it was, her poetic feeling heightened for her the value of life and its opportunities; it exalted her conceptions of duty, opened her eyes to the worth of humanity, and made her eloquent in behalf of the suffering. It cleared from her vision the false illusions which often surround the most applauded, and ennobled for her the least virtues of the lowly. It made her country's interests her own, and induced her to share in the sufferings of Italy, and rejoice in its every gleam of success. It nerved her to moral courage when painful truths were to be uttered, and gave to her presence a dignity from which the selfish coxcomb retired, thanking her for a rebuke, and melted to tears the murderous brigands who, with a strong arm, at the risk of her life, she divided from their strife. It drew to her the young maiden in loving and wholesome confidence; it sent from her the young man with the dawn of new and better purposes in his breast, and softened the prejudices of the older and more cautious who had been slow to approach her.

It is for this unfaltering poetic spirit, an essentially religious one as it is, which ever points to higher and more refined excellence, and infuses itself through every page of her works, for which more than anything else we cordially hope they may find a place in every woman's library. It is not that she is faultless, a model woman, a pattern for all,—far from it. She had quick impulses and a spirit of sarcasm which she found hard to train, prejudices which were with difficulty corrected, the imperiousness of a strong mind, which knows its power, and is determined to use it for her own good and others' welfare, and which is slow to mellow into that just and graceful influence which in the end is most effective. There was in her the visible self-consciousness of a nature continually pressing upon itself from its abundant fulness, and at times an abandonment to self-laudation, which were absurd did we not see in it a recognition of the value of our common humanity; and an assertion of her influence over other minds simply amusing were it not in spirit so true. But with all her idealism, her love of progress, and intensity of interior life, she was yet eminently conservative, and self-denying for herself and others in the application of means to ends. While she demands privilege for her sex, she inculcates the idea, and sets herself to work to secure their proportionate culture. While she asks for them a healthful sphere of activity, and aspires after a wider range for her own faculties, she is yet chary of attempting what she fears not to achieve, and in advocating the cause of woman she never forgets the self-restraint appropriate to the lady.

For this mingling of reserve and frankness in writing of woman's disabilities and needs, for her energy of character and general grasp of mind, we have been accustomed to place Margaret Fuller at the head of the ameliorating movement for woman; and though others may have done much, we consider her its greatest representative.

And as we turn from the mists and mazes of transcendentalism and rationalism to the clear teachings of Dr. CHANNING, in which he points to the pure theism of the Scriptures, and to the value of our common nature, as is shown in the Gospels, so do we turn with equal satisfaction from the extravagances of womanly conventions to the books before us, and give our assent to her definition of what is peculiar to woman, in words somewhat enigmatical, it is true, in which she speaks of their quickness of perception, their promptness in action, and their religious desires. Add to these the patience which, through much pondering, becomes, so to speak, an *intellectual* virtue, and the tact which, through a never-sleeping sense of responsibility, becomes a *moral* one, and the circle of traits which enable her to act most beneficently may be considered complete.

If it should be said that our notice of Margaret Fuller bears a tone of exaggerated praise, it is from no personal friendship for her. We knew her not, and were but seldom in the way of hearing of her. Once only we took a glance at her as she walked with stately step through the hall of the White Mountain

Hotel (in familiar conversation with a friend), where for an hour our ways chanced to meet. We have but taken these books, read and re-read them, and what we have written of her is the spirit of their teaching, and the summary of our study of her character and life.

It was in Italy, now so present to our interests and hopes, that she found a second home, and the companion of her life. Shipwrecked in their worldly fortunes by the disasters of his country, she sought in her own a support for her beloved ones, and the sympathies of her friends. There were hearts waiting to claim her again as their own, minds whose opening genius mothers desired to consign to her direction, and eyes to see how the muse and the authoress would act the part of the mother and the wife. But the waves closed over her and she was no more. But not so; for a soul so living can never die; and that among the many mansions where her spirit has found a home, must ever be a beneficient element in creation. Peace to her *memory* we cannot say to what will be more and more a *presence* among us, but rather joy to her re-awakening; henceforth go on rejoicing!

In conclusion we must be allowed to thank the devoted brother who, through years of patient labor, has gathered up these literary remains of a sister so revered, and given them to the public in so readable and worthy a form. Wherever Margaret Fuller Ossoli is known, he will be named with her as one who appreciated her genius, venerated her worth, and did what he could to make them known to the world.

part
five:

MANIFESTA-TIONS OF THE WILL

Woman is more in dread than man.
   —Søren Kierkegaard

. . . it would be impossible to say in the case of this or that particular woman that she is more in dread than a particular man.
   —Howard P. Kainz, Jr.

Women form the sexus sequior—the second sex, inferior in every respect to the first . . .
   —Arthur Schopenhauer

Women have been conditioned to believe that they are inferior to men, and they have assumed that what everyone believes is a fact of nature . . .
   —Ashley Montagu

Woman has so much cause for shame; in women there is so much pedantry, superficiality, schoolmasterliness, petty presumption, unbridledness, and indiscretion concealed . . .
   —Friedrich Nietzsche

. . . despite his remarks, Nietzsche was no simple misogynist. His distaste for women was a distaste for the slavish character shown by nineteenth-century woman.
   —Kathryn Pyne Parsons

Unlike the idealist, who sets great store by reason and understanding, the voluntarist celebrates will. It is not what one understands that is important to Kierkegaard, but what one wills. The choice of a way of life is therefore not the conclusion of a logical argument but an act of the will. And if man's will leads him from indulgence in the senses to absorption with the spirit, he leaves woman behind him as he ascends to ever higher stages upon life's way. Yet the characteristics that Kierkegaard ascribes to woman herself will inevitably vary from individual to individual, Howard P. Kainz, Jr., seems to suggest.

Schopenhauer's voluntarism is more earthbound than Kierkegaard's; he writes of a cosmic will, a will to live, which in woman takes the form of a desire, conscious or unconscious, to procreate. It is to this end that her every act is directed, for it is through her that nature preserves the human species. But whereas Schopenhauer seems to view this preoccupation as a mark of woman's inferiority, Ashley Montagu is convinced that women are biologically and psychologically superior to men.

Nietzsche's voluntarism, in contrast to Schopenhauer's, centers around a will not to life but to power. In woman Nietzsche finds not power but weakness. But despite Nietzsche's apparent misogynism, Kathryn Pyne Parsons finds that his philosophy lends itself to applications he himself declined to make. She uses his thesis to elucidate certain principles of the women's revolution.

⚘ 13 Søren Kierkegaard

Søren Aabye Kierkegaard was born in Copenhagen on May 5, 1813, the youngest child of a moody and religious father who, retired from business, had an abundance of time to lavish on his son's education and upbringing. Upon his matriculation at the University of Copenhagen, Søren, in rebellion, turned from religion to a life of pleasure—dining, drinking, and dressing in a highly extravagant fashion. But on his twenty-fifth birthday he became reconciled with his father, just three months before the octogenarian's death. And at about the same time he experienced the "indescribable joy" of a religious conversion.

Earlier, in 1837, Kierkegaard had met and resolved to offer himself to a fourteen-year-old girl, Regine Olsen. He proposed marriage to her on September 8, 1840, and she accepted his proposal on September 10. But by the following morning Kierkegaard had had second thoughts, and eventually the engagement was broken. There was no apparent reason for his change of heart. A number of explanations are hinted at in his journals, none of them completely adequate: He was subject to a melancholia that he feared might make a vivacious girl unhappy; there were dim memories of unconfessed events that took place during a drunken debauch in a brothel during his student days; born to a forty-five-year-old mother and a fifty-seven-year-old father, he was not physically robust and feared impotence; he had a Socratic daemon that warned him repeatedly against the impending nuptials; marriage might hinder his life's work. Whatever the reason, the breaking of the engagement seems to have obsessed Kierkegaard for many years, and he tells the tale over and over again in his works: in Either/Or, in Repetition, in Stages on Life's Way.

Until the time of the Industrial Revolution, Danish society had been basically feudal and thoroughly patriarchal. Women lived completely within the confines of the family. Their work was hard, and, although on occasion they were able to wield influence and command respect, their social status was completely dependent on that of the man who headed the family. When Europe began to industrialize, Danish women—and children as well—were pressed into service in factories, generally working long hours for low wages. Only gradually did these women return to housework. But the rise of a strong middle class soon liberated the bourgeois woman from this task as well, and she assumed the role of the lady, who, refined and protected, amused herself with such pursuits as embroidery and entertaining.

Kierkegaard appears unable to comprehend such a life: "How strange it must seem to be a young girl," he comments in Stages on Life's Way, "to live one's life offhandishly." Again, "Would that for a half a year I might be transformed into a woman in order to understand her nature." And in a longer passage he speaks as follows:

To be a woman is something so strange, so mixed, so complex that no predicate can express it, and the many predicates one might use contradict one another so sharply that only a woman can endure it, and, still worse, enjoy it. The fact that she actually has less significance than man is not what constitutes her misfortune, even if she were to come to know it, for after all this is something which can be endured. No, the misfortune is that owing to the romantic way in which she is regarded, her life has become meaningless, so that one moment she has the utmost significance and the next moment none whatever, without ever coming to know what her significance really is—yet this is not the whole of her misfortune, for the worst of it is that she can never come to know it because she is a woman.

Although Kierkegaard seems to suggest that the heavy reliance of woman on man might restrict the number of ways in which she can develop, it is by no means her chief limitation. Kierkegaard spoke of woman in many voices. Various characters in his works express various concepts of woman. At times she is depicted in the context of the family, at times apart from it, but always woman is viewed from the vantage point of Kierkegaard's existentialist philosophy.

Kierkegaard was profoundly impressed by what may be called the existential human situation. What the human being actually is, he thought, is a far cry from the essential human nature. The gulf between the two has come about as man, a finite creature, has grown aware of his finitude, felt disturbed by it, and become ever more deeply involved in attempts to overcome it. Attempts inevitably fail, and so his awareness and his sense of trouble deepen into anxiety, guilt, and despair. But man may in some sense recapture his essential self by conscious effort, by making choices, decisions, commitments. On the lowest level of existence, the aesthetic, man lives by his emotions and instincts. Here life is unsatisfying, for sensuousness is cultivated at the expense of spirit. The gap between the aesthetic self and the essential self yawns wide. But man may decide to bridge this gap by resolving to leave the aesthetic stage for the ethical life, governed by rules of conduct based on reason. Here too, however, life is less than satisfying, for man soon discovers that his violation of moral law is deliberate. This discovery leads to despair or dread, both of which culminate in guilt, the realization that one is responsible for one's own sick and sinful condition. Thereupon one may choose to leap—by faith—to the religious life.

Naturally man's view of woman changes as he progresses from stage to stage along life's way. On the aesthetic level she is considered a sex object pure and simple. On the ethical level, although she may be deemed "quite as good as a man," her existence is defined in terms of the man whom she is quite as good as, but nevertheless submissive to. On the religious level, woman is regarded negatively. Woman is capable of awakening ideality in man, but she may do so only by rejecting him, by dying, by causing him to reject her. Man becomes a genius, a hero, a poet, or a saint through the woman he does not get; through the woman he marries he becomes only a privy councillor or a general or a father.

But what about woman's own progress along life's way? Woman, according to Kierkegaard, is capable of existence on the aesthetic and religious levels, *but not on the ethical. On the aesthetic level woman is thoroughly vain, and she becomes comic in her demands to be taken seriously. It is love that elevates her from the aesthetic to the religious level, as her love for man is transformed into love of God. But the ethical stage that man goes through is completely absent from woman's development, apparently because of her intellectual deficiency. Ethical development requires understanding, and, according to Kierkegaard, "a woman in understanding is not a man in understanding." She lacks "the sort of reflection a man has" and "rarely possesses much dialectic."*

And woman is inferior to man in another and more important way. Although she is more sensuous than he and therefore more in dread than he, she is not responsible for her own actions: her husband is responsible for them. Thus she has no capacity for guilt, and without guilt she is incapable of the kind of awareness of her existential situation that would motivate her to strive to recapture her essential self. Indeed, she has no essential self.

From *The Concept of Dread*

SUBJECTIVE DREAD

. . .

By sin sensuousness became sinfulness. This proposition has a double significance: by sin sensuousness became sinfulness; and by Adam sin came into the world. These definitions must constantly balance one another, for otherwise something untrue is said. The fact that once upon a time sensuousness became sinfulness is the history of generation; but that sensuousness continues to become this is due to the qualitative leap of the individual.

. . . [T]he creation of Eve already prefigured symbolically the consequence of generation. In a way she represented the derived individual. The derived is never as perfect as the original.[1] In this case, however, the difference is only quantitative. The later individual is essentially as original as the first. The difference common to all later individuals is derivation; but for the particular individual derivation may again signify more or less.

This derivation of woman explains also in what sense she is weaker than man, a fact which has been assumed in all times, whether it is a pasha who speaks or a romantic knight. The difference, however, does not mean that man and woman are not essentially alike in spite of the difference. The expression for the difference is that dread is more reflected in Eve than in Adam. This is due to the fact that woman is more sensuous than man. Here of course it is not a question of an empirical condition or of an average but of a difference in the synthesis. If in one part of the synthesis there is a "more," the consequence will be that when the spirit posits itself the cleft in the division will be more

---

[1] Of course this holds true only of the human race, because the individual is characterized as spirit. On the other hand, in animal species every later example is just as good as the first, or, to put it better, to be the first has no significance whatsoever.

profound, and dread will find in the possibility of freedom more ample scope. In the account in Genesis it is Eve who seduces Adam. From this it does not by any means follow that her guilt is greater than Adam's, and still less that dread is an imperfection, since on the contrary the greatness of it is prophetically a measure of the perfection.

Here already the investigation sees that sensuousness corresponds proportionally with dread. As soon as generation is posited what was said about Eve is merely a hint of what is characteristic of the relation of every later individual to Adam, that when sensuousness is increased by the fact of generation dread also is increased. The consequence of generation signifies a "more," in such a way that no individual escapes from that "more" characteristic of all individuals in comparison with Adam, but never does it amount to such a "more" that he becomes essentially different from Adam.

But before we go on to speak of this I would illustrate a little more fully the proposition that woman is more sensuous than man and has more dread.

The fact that woman is more sensuous than man is shown at once by her bodily organism. To follow this out more in detail is not my affair but is a theme for physiology. I shall prove my thesis, however, in a different way, by introducing her aesthetically in her ideal aspect, which is beauty, noting that the fact that this *is* her ideal aspect is precisely the proof that she is more sensuous than man. Next I shall introduce her ethically in her ideal aspect, noting that the fact that this is her ideal aspect is precisely the proof that she is more sensuous than man.

Where beauty claims the right to rule it brings about a synthesis from which spirit is excluded. This is the secret of the whole Hellenic culture. Owing to this there is a sense of security, a quiet solemnity, which characterizes all Greek beauty; but precisely for this cause there was also a sense of dread, which the Greek likely did not notice, although his plastic beauty trembles with it. There is a carefreeness in the Greek beauty because the spirit is excluded, but therefore there is also a profound sorrow unexplained. Therefore sensuousness is not sinfulness but an unexplained riddle which causes dread; therefore this naïveté is accompanied by an inexplicable nothing which is that of dread.

It is true that the Greek beauty conceives man and woman essentially in the same way, without consideration of spirit; but nevertheless it makes a distinction within this likeness. The spiritual finds expression in the countenance. But in manly beauty the face and its expression are more essential than in feminine beauty, even though the eternal youth of the plastic art constantly prevents the deeper spiritual meaning from showing itself. To follow this out further is not my affair, but I will indicate this difference by a single suggestion. Essentially Venus remains equally beautiful whether she is represented sleeping or waking— indeed, she is perhaps most beautiful sleeping, and yet the sleeping state is precisely the expression for the absence of spirit. Hence it comes that the more spiritual and developed an individuality is, the less beautiful is such a person in sleep, whereas the child is most beautiful in sleep. Venus emerges from the sea and is represented in an attitude of repose, or in an attitude which reduces the expression of the face to the unessential. On the other hand, if Apollo is to be represented, it would not do to let him sleep, any more than in a Jupiter this would be appropriate. This would detract from the beauty of Apollo, and it would make Jupiter ridiculous. An exception could be made for Bacchus, but in Greek art he represents the point of indifference between manly and womanly beauty, and hence the lines of his figure are feminine. In the case of a Ganymede, on the other hand, the expression of his face is more essential.

When the conception of beauty became different, Romanticism again made the distinction within the essential likeness. Whereas the history of spirit (and it is precisely the secret of spirit that it always has history) dares to stamp itself upon the countenance of man, so that all is forgotten if only its writing is clear and noble, woman will make her effect in another way, as a totality, even though the face has acquired a greater importance than it had in classical art. The impression now must be of a totality which has no history. Therefore silence is not only woman's highest wisdom, but also her highest beauty.

Ethically regarded, woman culminates in procreation. Therefore the Scripture says that her desire shall be to her husband. It is true also that the husband's desire is to her, but his life does not culminate in this desire, unless it is either a sorry sort of life or a lost life. But the fact that in this woman reaches her culmination shows that she is more sensuous.

Woman is more in dread than man. This is not implied in the fact that she has less physical strength, etc., for here there is no question about that sort of dread; but it is implied in the fact that she is more sensuous and yet essentially, like man, is qualified by spirit. What is so frequently said, that she is the weaker sex, leaves me completely indifferent, for notwithstanding this she might very well have less dread. Dread is constantly to be understood as oriented towards freedom. So when the story in Genesis, running directly counter to all analogies, represents woman as seducing man, this upon closer inspection appears nevertheless perfectly natural, for this seduction is precisely a feminine seduction, since in fact it was only through Eve that Adam was seduced by the serpent. In other instances of seduction, language, speaking of deluding, talking around, etc., ascribes superiority to man.

That which can be assumed as the result of all experience I shall show merely by an experimental observation. If I picture to myself a young and innocent girl and then let a man fasten upon her a look of desire, she experiences dread. Besides that she may be indignant, etc., but first she feels dread. If on the other hand I imagine that a woman fixes a desirous glance upon an innocent young man, his feeling will not be dread, but at the most a sense of abhorrence mingled with shame, precisely because he is more characterized by spirit.

By Adam's sin came sinfulness into the world, and sexuality, which came to signify for him sinfulness. The sexual was posited. There has been much twaddle in the world, both written and oral, about naïveté. However, only innocence is naïve, but it is also ignorant. As soon as the sexual is brought to consciousness, it is thoughtlessness, affectation, and sometimes worse, namely, a cover for lust, to want to talk about naïveté. But because man is no longer naïve it does not follow by any means that he sins. It is only that vapid coquettishness which allures men, precisely by drawing attention away from the true, the moral.

.   .   .

Let us now return to the subject with which we were dealing above, the consequence for the individual of the fact of generation, which is the common "more" which every individual has in contrast with Adam. At the instant of conception the spirit is far away, and therefore the dread is greatest. In this dread the new individual comes into existence. At the instant of birth dread culminates a second time in woman, and at this instant the new individual comes into the world. That a woman in childbirth has dread is well known. Physiology has its explanation, psychology must also have its own. In childbirth woman is again at the utmost point of one extreme of the synthesis, hence the spirit trembles, for at this instant, when there is nothing for it to do, it is as it were suspended. Dread, however, is an expression for the perfection of human nature, and it is therefore only among the lesser kinds one finds analogies to the easy delivery of the beasts.

But the more dread, the more sensuousness. The procreated individual is more sensual than the original, and this "more" is the usual "more" which the fact of generation entails for every later individual in relation to Adam.

But the more of dread and sensuousness which every later individual has in comparison with Adam may of course in the particular individual signify a more or a less. This is the ground of the differences which in truth are so terrible that surely no one ventures to think of them in a deeper sense, that is, with genuine human sympathy, unless with a firmness which nothing can shake he is convinced that never is there found in this world, nor ever shall be found, such a "more" that by a simple transition it transforms the quantitative into the qualitative. What the Scripture teaches, that God visits the sins of the fathers upon the children unto the third and fourth generation, life itself proclaims in a loud enough voice. To want to chatter oneself away from this terrible fact by the explanation that this saying is a Jewish doctrine is of no avail. Christianity has never subscribed to the notion that every particular individual is in an outward sense privileged to begin from scratch. Every individual begins in a historical nexus, and the consequences of natural law are still as valid as ever. The difference now consists only in this, that Christianity teaches us to lift ourselves above that "more," and condemns him who does not do so as not willing to do so.

Precisely because sensuousness is here defined as a "more," the dread of the spirit in assuming responsibility for this "more" becomes a greater dread. There is implied here as a maximum the terrible fact that *dread of sin produces sin*. If one represents that evil desires, concupiscence, etc., are innate in the individual, one does not get the ambiguity in which the individual becomes both guilty and innocent. In the impotence of dread the individual succumbs, but precisely for this reason he is both guilty and innocent.

I will not adduce detailed examples of this infinitely fluctuating more and less. If such examples are to have any significance, they demand a vast aesthetic-psychological treatment.

. . .

∗§∗ *Howard P. Kainz, Jr.*

Howard P. Kainz, Jr., associate professor of philosophy at Marquette University, is best known for his work on German philosophy, particularly for two books on Hegel. In the article presented here, first published in The Modern Schoolman, he turns his attention to the Danish philosopher Søren Kierkegaard, who describes woman with a wealth of predicates that appear to contradict one another. Professor Kainz analyzes three of the statements Kierkegaard makes in The Concept of Dread in an attempt to find in them more consistency than meets the eye.

The Relationship of Dread to Spirit in Man and Woman, According to Kierkegaard

Kierkegaard was dedicated to the principle that "only the truth that edifies is the truth for me and for thee." Thus he seems to strive in his writings to keep definitions and distinctions down to the minimum, in order to avoid enticing his reader into the game of logic and speculation, into thought for thought's sake. He was interested in having an effect on the personal life of his reader—and a paradox is often as likely to do this as a clear-cut logical demonstration. Thus, for example, he tells us that man is a synthesis of the finite and the infinite, without telling us much more about how this takes place than that Christ tells us just exactly how a man can "save his life" by losing it. But still, for us to understand the truth behind the stunning and persuasive paradox, the synthesis behind the apparent contradiction—it behooves us to examine words and their concepts, to distinguish the sense in which they are used in one place, from the sense in which they are used in another.

One such apparent contradiction confronts the reader in Kierkegaard's *The Concept of Dread*, where he describes the relationship of dread to spirit in man and woman, respectively. The apparent contradiction can be presented summarily as follows:

1) Kierkegaard definitely indicates that dread is in some way directly proportional to spirit:

The less spirit, the less dread. . . .[1] The greatness of dread is prophetically a measure of human perfection.[2]

[1] *The Concept of Dread* (Princeton: Princeton Univ. Press, 1957), p. 38.
[2] *Ibid.*, p. 57.

And yet, 2) he seems to contradict this view when he concludes further that a) there is *more spirit* in man than in woman, but b) there is *less dread* in man than in woman:

a) He [man] is more characterized by spirit.[3]
b) Woman is more in dread than man. . . .[4]

Using these summary statements as a starting point, we will strive here to elucidate Kierkegaard's doctrine on dread, spirit, man, and woman by solving the paradox or contradiction which the statements present:

1) "THE LESS SPIRIT, THE LESS DREAD"

If we would understand this statement, we must first understand the general way in which Kierkegaard uses the word, "spirit"; and the particular way in which Kierkegaard is using the word, "dread," here in this statement.

"Spirit" is a word used quite often in *The Concept of Dread,* but not really defined or clarified in any satisfactory way for the benefit of the reader who is not quite sure of the signification which Kierkegaard is lending to the word. If we want a more exact formulation of Kierkegaard's understanding of "spirit," we must look elsewhere. A more exact formulation of this type may be found in *The Sickness unto Death,* by the same author:

What is spirit? Spirit is the self. But what is the self? The self is a relation which relates itself to its own self. . . . Man is a synthesis of the infinite and the finite . . . a synthesis is a relation between two factors. . . . If . . . the relation relates itself to its own self, the relation is then the positive third term, and this is the self.[5]

First of all, we should note that the notion of "spirit" here is coterminous with the notion of "man"; that is, it is not attributable to inorganic or even organic existences below man, neither is it univocally attributable to God or angel. He is concentrating, perhaps also as Hegel did, on the ultimate phenomenal spirit comprehensible to the human mind. The only difference is that Hegel saw this spirit primarily as a universal through mankind; while Kierkegaard sees it as eminently individual in man. Secondly, we should note that spirit, according to the above statement, is not just the relation between the infinite and finite poles of man's existence. If it were this, it would be just a dead, negative, quasi-spatial mutual reference between the two opposite poles. It is more than this. It is the positive *relating* of the relationship between the two contradictory but reconcilable poles. This positive dynamic relating to each other of the two opposed constituents which a man has in himself comprises his self, that is, his spirit. The two opposed constituents which spirit synthesizes can also be variously expressed—on the side of the infinite—as soul, freedom, the eternal; and—on the side of the finite—as body, necessity, the temporal. Spirit, then, is

[3] *Ibid.*, p. 60.
[4] *Ibid.*, p. 59.
[5] *Sickness unto Death* (New York: Doubleday, 1964), p. 147.

the means through which soul, for instance, is not just found to be related to body in an abstract way, but is positively fused with body, in a very real sense, and likewise, soul can only be understood through body; necessity is made into freedom, freedom is oriented to necessity; the eternal engulfs the temporal, the temporal opens up into the eternal—in short, the finite and infinite mutually seek out each other. All this in man. But only through spirit. But in different ways. For instance, the reflection of the infinite in the body will be more remarkable in one individuality; the overshadowing of the body by the soul will be more remarkable in another. And thus we have, in general, the distinction between women and men. Again, in one individuality (either male or female) the finite and infinite may positively seek each other out more, instead of being more passively related. And thus we have the phenomenon of *genius*, which indeed only reveals itself by the historical course of an individual's life, but in itself must be an "omnipotent *Ansich*,"[6] an extraordinary primal natural concentration of spirit, that is, an unusually restless seeking-out of the finite by the infinite, or *vice versa*. And it is here with the phenomenon of genius that we have an archetype for judging about the "more" and the "less" of spirit. The genius seems to have received a greater natural endowment with regard to the natural distribution of spirit. This greater natural endowment may be expressed in the way of a man, or in the way of a woman. But, in general, the case of the genius "evinces clearly what in less original men exists in such a way that it cannot easily be reduced to categories"[7]—fundamentally the fact of a greater or lesser concentration of natural spiritual endowment in human beings (we shall examine how this is related to dread in what follows). Spirit, then, is a restlessness in opposition conditioned by natural personal endowments, and varies quantitatively according to the degree of restlessness, or positive seeking-out, which obtains between the opposed elements or poles. It may be expressed variously in this man and that man, in male and female. Finally, it is to be distinguished from spirit in the *religious* sense, which finds its archetypal example in the "*religious* genius," and does not seem to be related to natural spiritual endowment, but primarily to acquired purity or sincerity of will (which is related to natural "gifts" or talents only as an "x" factor).[8]

"Dread" as used in the text given above does not mean 1) the dread of evil, nor 2) the dread of the good, nor 3) the dread by which one is overcome, nor even 4) that dread which is a "sweet feeling of apprehension"[9] and which leads the subject of dread to "maintain a sly intercourse with" his object.[10] It cannot be 1), because the dread of the evil only exists in the state of the "bondage of sin,"[11] and no such bondage is here presupposed. For a similar reason, it cannot be 2), since the dread of the good is always concomitant to the

[6] *The Concept of Dread*, p. 88.
[7] *Ibid.*, p. 93.
[8] *Ibid.*, p. 102.
[9] *Ibid.*, p. 38.
[10] *Ibid.*, p. 92.
[11] *Ibid.*, p. 106.

state of "the demoniacal."[12] It is not 3), since sin, that is, the "succumbing of freedom," does not necessarily arise from dread.[13] Finally, it could not even be 4), which is the state of dread in the paramount Kierkegaardian sense, since it is entirely possible that even a person with "more" spirit could be in the state of lively faith, or could have achieved victory of spirit over erotic sexuality: and the former contingency would amount to the continual renunciation of dread, while the latter contingency brings about the final expulsion of dread. But in the statement quoted above, Kierkegaard is obviously making a general assessment of the relation of dread to spirit in *all* of the contingent states which may obtain in the human spirit.

We can perhaps best understand the nature of that dread which is related in a most abstract and generic way to the presence of spirit in man, by returning to the original definition which Kierkegaard gives of dread: as "freedom's reality as possibility for possibility." This definition would be a meaningless tautology if we understood "possibility" as meaning the same thing in both of its instances here. The meaning seems to be—if we would paraphrase the definition—that dread is the actual positive relating of self to itself of a free human spirit, in so far as the relating contains in its very nature the intrinsic *capacity* for the *possibility* of operations. "Possibility" thus in its first instance would signify an intrinsic dynamic *capacity* of freedom itself; in its second instance would signify the infinity of external *possibilities* which by the nothingness of their very infinity would pose a threat to the freedom residing in a necessarily finite being. Dread would thus be analogous to "temptation," which we might call "the actuality of passion as possibility for possibility," that is, as an inner tendency to irrational movements externally elicited. But temptation can disappear for a person who has no passion, or who has subdued passion through virtue. Then temptation is only left as something purely external to that person, that is, as the objects to which his passion might be directed in a disorderly way, *if* the inner tendency were still there. So all that is left of the possibility of temptation is the external possibility in the form of the object. So also with dread, it would seem. In the infant in whom spirit is completely dormant, there is only an external possibility of dread—that is, the objective nothingness surrounding it unaware. In the man who has reached salvation by consciously and painstakingly opening up to himself the full infinity of possibility, and then, having confronted the most fearful object and having nothing else to fear, takes refuge in providence and faith—in this man the intrinsic "possibility," or capacity, has been put behind. He abandons this possibility which is deceptive in itself, and now reposes in faith. In this case, all that is left is the extrinsic possibility of an infinity of *finite* free operations, which no longer pose a *proximate* threat to his freedom, since such an individual has already struggled with, and overcome, the *infinity* of possibilities in dread itself. Thus all that is left is the *remote* possibility of purely finite operations opposed to his present state of faith.

[12] *Ibid.*
[13] *Ibid.*, p. 19.

Thus when Kierkegaard says, "the less spirit, the less dread," he seems to mean that a greater or lesser natural endowment of spirit, that is, a greater or lesser "primitiveness" of spirit, is related in a negative, that is, in a static, merely ontological way, to a correspondingly greater or lesser nothingness of the infinity of its own possibility. *If* the individuality positively relates itself to such possibility, then there results the intrinsic possibility of freedom, and proximate possible dread; *if* the individuality succumbs before dread, then there is sin, and dread is actual.

2A) "MAN IS MORE CHARACTERIZED BY SPIRIT"

As we have seen, the human spirit in its most generic notion is the ultimate, primitive *Ansichsein* by which the human being is enabled to relate himself to his self with more or less force in a positive, that is, free, manner. This primitive degree of spirit may be expressed or not expressed; if expressed, it may be expressed in this way or that. But the primitive *Ansichsein*, though it conditions the expression, is something distinguishable from its expression. For instance, an infant genius would have greater primitiveness of spirit than, say, some adult man of slow conceptual intelligence. But the latter would be *expressing* spirit more than the former. The rational bungling of a Dagwood is more an expression of spirit than the crying and gurgling of the infant-Einstein.

So also, the man differs from the woman in the expression he gives to spirit. This is to say nothing of the primal innate greatness of spirit. It is only to say that man and woman are not just physically differentiated, but also psychologically and metaphysically. But in order to understand the precise way in which Kierkegaard understands the psychological and metaphysical characteristics predominating in man, and, in general, differentiating him from woman, we must turn our attention to the corresponding differences in woman— since it is of the latter that Kierkegaard speaks more at length.

According to Kierkegaard, woman differs from a man *a*) (psychologically) in that her spirit is more oriented to expressing the psychic in a corporeal way; and *b*) (metaphysically) in that she epitomizes devotion and external existential reference, being-for-another.

As a result of her psychological constitution, the spirit of a woman, however great its primordial *Ansichsein* may be, must express itself, in general, as the reflection of the infinite, which is to be found on the side of soul, within the compass of the corporeal. It is in this way that spirit makes its synthesis in woman. And thus it is that woman is characterized more than man by *beauty*— that is, the immediately apprehensible presence of soul in the body and the body's activity; by *sensuousness*—that is, the termination in the body and bodily responses of all the syntheses which spirit makes or fails to make; and by *delicate sensitivity*—that is, the ability to enhance even the smallest details of that which she is dealing with, with a spiritual beauty.

As a result of her metaphysical "category," she receives an existential orientation, the state of being "for another," which appears under various aspects in the development of her personality. It shows itself as *self-less devotion,* woman's connatural ability to find herself and the perfection of her personality in seemingly giving herself away by submission to another; as *intuitive perception,* a gift which nature has given her, in order that she may be able to judge, without the necessity for reflection, by her "fineness of feeling," about "where it is she is to admire," about "what it is she ought to devote herself to";[14] as *love,* which awakens in her when she finds out that she corresponds to the dream of a man, or wants to correspond to his dream.

By contrasting man with woman, we can now come to appreciate the peculiar expression which is given to spirit in man: in the psychological sphere, when spirit does not accent the corporeal in the synthesis that it makes, it must accent the psychic. Thus, psychologically speaking, man is, in general, a being in whom body is overshadowed by soul. Thus man is not beautiful, strictly speaking; his sensuousness does not exist in himself, but is elicited from without; delicate sensitivity is something he, for the most part, is incapable of, and would not want to be capable of. Rather, in him, the body and the body's activities pale before the rational control and spiritual dominance which is accentuated in them. In one way or another, the man expresses spirit as *psychic strength,* and more so than the woman.

Again, in the metaphysical sphere, since both man and woman are "in themselves" spirit, and since woman is the human spirit "for another"; we would logically expect that in man we would complete the dialectical movement, and find the being "present to himself" or "*for himself.*" And nature, at least in this case, does seem to conform to the laws of dialectic, for the power of reflection, of discursive thought, of conceptual mediation—in short, the power of existing "for himself" through consciousness—does predominate as a natural attribute more in man than in woman. And as a sign of this, Kierkegaard notes, we have the evident fact that the "beauty" of a man in art consists primarily in his being represented with the reflection of spirit on his countenance, with the expression of spirit in the activities depicted, never as a "sleeping beauty."

Man, therefore, differs from woman in the psychological sphere, in that he more generally expresses psychic strength, while she expresses sensuous soulishness; and in the metaphysical sphere, in that he expresses conscious reflectiveness, "existence for oneself," while woman expresses love and devotion, "existence for another."

But man, in so far as he gives expression to strength of spirit, and to that which is the ultimate manifestation of the phenomenal spirit apprehensible by man—namely, mediated reflection on self—can thus be said to be "more characterized by spirit." Both man and woman are essentially spirit, but only men are capable, on the whole, of giving explicit expression to spirit in the activities and products of mediation, that is, to spirit *qua* spirit. But woman, just as the infant genius requires the medium of time in order to express the latent spirit which he possesses, requires, on her part, the medium with which nature

[14] *Sickness unto Death,* p. 183.

has endowed her—that is, her psychic and ontological make-up—in order to express the spirit that is in her, the spirit that she is.

2B) "WOMAN IS MORE IN DREAD THAN MAN . . ."

Granted that dread, as a remote infinity of possibility corresponding to the actual freedom possessed, is proportional to the initial primitiveness of spirit in man or woman—it is not too hard to see why, all other things being equal, a woman is more in dread than a man.

Let us take the archetypal case: that of Adam and Eve, before sin. By considering this case, we remove all the contingent factors which might render it extremely difficult to understand the problem: for example, actual sins committed, the presence or non-presence of faith, the cumulative effect of objective dread from the world of nature on the subjective dread of the individuality, and so forth. For it does not always happen that a woman is more in dread than a man, but only when all other factors are equal.

If we further grant, then, that Adam and Eve had a similar primitive natural endowment—which is likely—we are in a position to raise the question: why would Eve, under such conditions, be more in dread than Adam?

First of all, we should note that dread (as the remote possibility which presents itself as a natural correlate to the actuality of freedom) would be equal in Adam and Eve if they had the same primitiveness of spirit. For, considered in regard to spirit, man and woman are essentially alike. If there is the same initial magnitude of spirit, there will always be the same amount of corresponding nothingness of the infinity of finite possibility, just as much as two subtracted from seventy-two always leaves seventy. But this is an abstraction from reality. *De facto,* when spirit comes to be related in a less and less remote, and a more and more positive, way to its possibilities—that is, when the first almost imperceptible movements of freedom begin to make their appearance in the human spirit—then spirit has to express itself as man or as woman, and as this man or this woman. And here, where dread begins to be a more proximate possibility positively encountered by the intrinsic possibility in freedom itself, it becomes, in general, a "more" for woman and a "less" for man.

In order to understand this, we must reflect that dread as a proximate possibility is occasioned by two factors: 1) that the human spirit is a "nothing," that is, is, so to speak, arrested in its existence by the fact that it is not yet in movement reconciling the opposites within it, and does not yet rest in the infinity of innermost movement to be found in freedom posited as freedom; and 2) that such a spirit projects its own nothingness as its self, and sees its self from the vantage point of this nothingness. This is seen in a paramount way in the primaeval innocence of the protoparents in which spirit was essentially in a dreaming state, and in which there is no objective social culture which might take away the "sting" of one's own nothingness, that is, no "objective" dread which could transform the utter ambiguity of dread's nothingness into at least an encompassing relief of shadow and light.

Thus in the case of Adam and Eve, as in the case of the *later* individual who is in actual sin, there is no distinction between objective and subjective dread. Such a distinction only comes when we have a "later individual" who in his qualitative innocence and greater reflectiveness encounters the purely quantitative determinants of sin and dread in his milieu, as a contrast which makes him psychologically dizzy. But in the case of the innocent individual encompassed by the complete nothingness of possibility, and in the case of the guilty individual faced with the objective determinants of his own guilt, the objective dread is nothing but the reflex of possibility in the subjectivity, and the subjective dread is nothing but the possibility of freedom "manifesting itself," that is, becoming objective.

But, if, in the case of Adam and Eve, we pass by the moment in which the subjective reflex in its initial restlessness coincides with the expression of the possibilities of one's freedom, and indeed *is* that objective expression, and if we concentrate on the next moment, where freedom actually begins to manifest itself—here we can see why Eve must be in more dread than Adam.

For Eve must express her freedom, posit her spirit, as a woman. But as she begins to do this, she finds herself surrounded by a twofold nothingness which is a "more" than in the case of Adam. 1) She is oriented by her psychological synthesis to a bodily, to a sensuous, expression of spiritual reality. But such psychological immediacy puts her into closest possible contact with the world of otherness where she must express spirit. Thus, while Adam is one step removed from the dangers of such impinging nothingness, and is somewhat securely situated in the vantage point of soul, Eve is right in the thick of the battle, so to speak. The surrounding nothingness is psychologically closer to her; is a "more" for her. Thus her very sensuousness renders her more in dread than Adam. 2) She was—in some way—derived from Adam. But the derived being is never as perfect as the original. Thus the human nature, which existed in its pristine integrity in Adam, was in some way partitioned and shared with Eve; but in such a way that she would have a one-sided perfection and lack of the perfections of Adam. Thus she was weaker than Adam, in respect to those perfections which were not passed on in their integrity. Thus in dealing with the remote possibilities of dread, and coming to positively express her freedom, she had less natural integral perfection to rely on. The dread was proportionally stronger, in relation to her constitutional weakness. Thus from this point of view also, the nothingness of dread becomes a "more" to her.

But still there is no sin. Eve's sensuousness and constitutional weakness through derivation render it more difficult to find salvation in inwardness and to will her own religious transcendence. But sin comes only if she succumbs before the difficulties which dread insinuates to her dreaming consciousness. If she does thus succumb, then there is freedom, but posited illegitimately; then there is sin. Then objective dread becomes a "less," in so far as it is more determinate, less ambiguous, finding its concrete expression in the form of positively differentiated sexuality; then also subjective dread becomes a "more," in so far as the spirit is more awake, more reflective, and now begins to assimilate the possibilities of its dread in this new, reflective manner. Then it happens that subjectively reflected sensuousness undergoes a purely quantitative increment, proportional to the non-ambiguous, concrete, purely quantitative progression of sensuousness and sexuality as objective dread in its archetypal form—so that we have a new formula: "the more [objective] dread, the more [subjectively reflected] sensuousness."[15] Then, finally, it happens in the case of the human being after sin has been posited, that, though he is not guilty of the sin, the quantitative determinants of dread which he *de facto* encounters may be reproduced quantitatively in his own reflective subjectivity, to the point where he is induced to make the "qualitative" leap into guilt, in order to escape the ambiguity of guilt accruing to the reflective assimilation of the quantitative determinants of his own sensuousness.

But because of the quantitative progression of objective dread, and because of the other factors mentioned above, it would be impossible to say in the case of *this or that particular woman* that she is more in dread than a particular man. All we can say is that, as has been shown in the archetypal example of Eve, other factors being assumed equal, the proximate possibilities of dread to which a woman positively relates herself in expressing freedom, are greater than in man's case.

Thus although the relationship of dread to spirit in man and woman is beyond the sphere of mathematics, it might be aptly represented through the analogy of a mathematical proportionality, as follows.

Dread as a remote infinity of ambiguous possibilities is directly proportional to the primitive implicit concentration of spirit, considered in abstraction from the positive relating of freedom to its possibilities. Dread as a proximate possibility becomes more menacing to the freedom of a woman, because of her sensuous exposure to the surrounding "other," and because of the relative weakness accruing to her "derived" existence. Dread, however, is inversely proportional to the greater explicit manifestation of spirit to be found in man in contrast with woman—provided other factors are equal. Dread, finally, is non-proportional to the perfect positing of spirit as spirit which takes place through "salvation."

15 *The Concept of Dread*, p. 65.

~~❧~~ 14 *Arthur Schopenhauer*

Arthur Schopenhauer was born in Danzig in 1788, the son of a German trader of partly Dutch descent. Educated for two years in France and for three in a private school in Hamburg, the boy developed a strong interest in literature, which he was inclined to pursue. His father was determined that the young man should follow a commercial career, however, and the bribe of a two-year tour of France and England accomplished his purpose. Three months after apprenticing his son to a business concern, however, Heinrich Floris Schopenhauer died. Young Arthur, out of respect for the wishes of the deceased, remained in the business world for two more years, until his mother released him from the promise he had made.

The death of her husband freed Johanna Schopenhauer to leave Hamburg, where the family had resided for a decade; to open a salon in Weimar; and to begin writing what proved to be fairly popular romantic novels. Her extravagant new life, however, complete with romantic attachments, shocked and disgusted her son. Eventually they quarreled—never to be reconciled.

After abandoning the business world, Schopenhauer turned first to medicine, then to philosophy. Although his major work, The World as Will and Idea, was written before he was thirty, fame was late in coming to him. His irritation over that fact was matched only by his enjoyment of it when it did arrive.

Throughout most of his life Schopenhauer was a lonely and bitter man. Although in his youth his liaisons with women had been numerous and intense, none of them was lasting—a response, it would seem, to the strong sexual desire that he found to be at the crux of the evil, insatiable cosmic will to live, as it is manifest in human beings. He was relieved when age dispelled these longings. Although he identified love and sympathy as the two emotions capable of negating the will, he himself was decidedly more egoistic than altruistic. His biography abounds with incidents in which regard for self is coupled with disregard for others. Perhaps the most notorious example is his altercation with Caroline Luise Marguet, a middle-aged seamstress whom he threw down the stairs of his boardinghouse because her chatter with friends on the landing had disturbed him. In 1860 Schopenhauer died of a heart attack in Frankfurt-am-Main, where he had spent his last twenty-seven years living a highly regulated life as a confirmed bachelor.

In the decades immediately preceding the publication of Parerga and Paralipomena, the volume containing Schopenhauer's essay "On Women," a number of the Young German writers, under the influence of George Sand, had been publishing Frauenromane, novels describing the plight of woman—especially the sexually liberated woman—in the contemporary world. These works, although generally sympathetic to the women's movement, had probably given the liberated woman a bad image, and in 1839 Toinette Homberg, a veteran of twenty years' teaching in a girls' school, criticized *her erring contemporaries for focusing on woman's physical freedom and urged her intellectual liberation instead. Schopenhauer, more or less ignoring his contemporaries, echoes the view of Joachim Heinrich Campe, who, late in the preceding century, had argued that the physical weakness of women rendered them unfit for mental exertion. Although Campe had been rather effectively answered by a woman, Esther Bernhard, Schopenhauer persists in the same non sequitur. Perhaps his own strength of will, often verging on obstinacy, was sufficient to cause him to exaggerate the weakness of women's will and to move him to extend his observations on their physical frailty to the mental sphere. At any rate, he applauds both ancient and Eastern cultures for keeping such inferior creatures in their place.*

Schopenhauer's views on woman are in many ways an extension of his metaphysical system. He believed the universe to be permeated everywhere by a vital force that is constantly struggling against itself. Everything and everyone may be explained as a manifestation of this cosmic will: plants climb on one another, choking each other in an effort to reach the sun so that they may survive; animals in the jungle are "red in tooth and claw" as they prey on one another in an attempt to stay alive; even inanimate objects are constituted of this will, in an unconscious and therefore relatively unstriving form. The human being certainly constitutes no exception to the will's omnipresence. The human will is conscious and is accompanied by reason, which serves not to mitigate unhappiness, as one might expect, but rather to foster social injustice. Reason merely enables its possessor to devise ever more diabolical ways of asserting the individual will by combatting the will of others. And unhappiness is inevitable, for the will is never satisfied. It reveals to a person an object of desire. An individual who is thwarted in an attempt to attain that object is miserable, but an individual who succeeds is even more miserable, for that person is soon discontented with it and desires something else instead. Furthermore, unlike a plant or an animal, the human being is endowed with anticipation and memory, and thus not only suffers today's misery but recalls yesterday's and expects tomorrow's.

In the human being the will manifests itself most intensely in the sexual drive. It is in terms of this drive that Schopenhauer explains every aspect of the relationship between man and woman. These explanations are somewhat less than consistent, however. Early in the essay Schopenhauer voices the opinion that nature acts with typical economy in endowing woman with beauty just long enough to effect the propagation of the species. A few paragraphs later he describes woman's physical characteristics in pejorative terms, declaring that it "is only the man whose intellect is clouded by his sexual impulses that could give the name of the fair sex to that undersized, narrow-shouldered, broad-hipped, and short-legged race." He suggests that the "unaesthetic sex" would be a more appropriate designation.

But attractive or not, woman's build, Schopenhauer maintains, is sufficient evidence that she is not intended for extremely strenuous physical or mental activity. The transition from body to mind he leaves unexplained. But having made it, he is highly consistent in his evaluation of woman's reason as de- cidedly inferior to man's. This deficiency in reason accounts for her cheer- fulness, inasmuch as she is unable to look ahead and is unconcerned with anything else as long as the present is reasonably tolerable. To the same characteristic may be traced her sympathy and philanthropy, for, being incapable of formulating abstract principles as a man does, she is guided by mercy rather than justice, which, along with honor and conscientiousness, Schopenhauer believed to be completely foreign to her nature. In their place she has cunning, subtlety, and dissimulation. She is false, unfaithful, treacherous, and ungrateful. These characteristics she employs effectively to ensnare man and procreate, for it is to her, not her mate, that nature has entrusted the survival of the species.

From *Parerga and Paralipomena*

ON WOMEN

Schiller's poem in honour of women, *Würde der Frauen*, is the result of much careful thought, and it appeals to the reader by its antithetic style and its use of contrast; but as an expression of the true praise which should be accorded to them, it is, I think, inferior to these few words of Jouy's: *Without women the beginning of our life would be helpless; the middle, devoid of pleasure; and the end, of consolation.* The same thing is more feelingly expressed by Byron in *Sardanapalus:*—

> *The very first*
> *Of human life must spring from woman's breast,*
> *Your first small words are taught you from her lips,*
> *Your first tears quench'd by her, and your last sighs*
> *Too often breathed out in a woman's hearing,*
> *When men have shrunk from the ignoble care*
> *Of watching the last hour of him who led them.*
> (Act I. Scene 2.)

These two passages indicate the right standpoint for the appreciation of women.

You need only look at the way in which she is formed to see that woman is not meant to undergo great labour, whether of the mind or of the body. She pays the debt of life not by what she does but by what she suffers; by the pains of childbearing and care for the child, and by submission to her husband, to whom she should be a patient and cheering companion. The keenest sorrows and joys are not for her, nor is she called upon to display a great deal of strength. The current of her life should be more gentle, peaceful and trivial than man's, without being essentially happier or unhappier.

Women are directly fitted for acting as the nurses and teachers of our early childhood by the fact that they are themselves childish, frivolous and short-sighted; in a word, they are big children all their life long—a kind of intermediate stage between the child and the full-grown man, who is man in the strict sense of the word. See how a girl will fondle a child for days together, dance with it and sing to it; and then think what a man, with the best will in the world, could do if he were put in her place.

With young girls Nature seems to have had in view what, in the language of the drama, is called *a coup de théâtre*. For a few years she dowers them with a wealth of beauty and is lavish in her gift of charm, at the expense of the rest of their life, in order that during those years they may capture the fantasy of some man to such a degree that he is hurried into undertaking the honourable care of them, in some form or other, as long as they live—a step for which there would not appear to be any sufficient warranty if reason only directed his thoughts. Accordingly Nature has equipped woman, as she does all her creatures, with the weapons and implements requisite for the safe-guarding of her existence, and for just as long as it is necessary for her to have them. Here, as elsewhere, Nature proceeds with her usual economy; for just as the female ant, after fecundation, loses her wings, which are then superfluous, nay, actually a danger to the business of breeding; so, after giving birth to one or two children, a woman generally loses her beauty; probably, indeed, for similar reasons.

And so we find that young girls, in their hearts, look upon domestic affairs or work of any kind as of secondary importance, if not actually as a mere jest. The only business that really claims their earnest attention is love, making conquests, and everything connected with this—dress, dancing, and so on.

The nobler and more perfect a thing is, the later and slower it is in arriving at maturity. A man reaches the maturity of his reasoning powers and mental faculties hardly before the age of twenty-eight; a woman, at eighteen. And then, too, in the case of woman, it is only reason of a sort—very niggard in its dimensions. That is why women remain children their whole life long; never seeing anything but what is quite close to them, cleaving to the present moment, taking appearance for reality, and preferring trifles to matters of the first importance. For it is by virtue of his reasoning faculty that man does not live in the present only, like the brute, but looks about him and considers the past and the future; and this is the origin of prudence, as well as of that care and anxiety which so many people exhibit. Both the advantages and the dis-advantages which this involves, are shared in by the woman to a smaller extent because of her weaker power of reasoning. She may, in fact, be described as intellectually shortsighted, because, while she has an intuitive understanding of what lies quite close to her, her field of vision is narrow and does not reach to what is remote: so that things which are absent or past or to come have much less effect upon women than upon men. This is the reason why women are more often inclined to be extravagant, and sometimes carry their inclination to a length that borders upon madness. In their hearts women think that it is men's business to earn money and theirs to spend it—if possible during their husband's life, but, at any rate, after his death. The very fact that their husband hands them over his earnings for purposes of housekeeping strengthens them in this belief.

However many disadvantages all this may involve, there is at least this to be said in its favour: that the woman lives more in the present than the man, and that, if the present is at all tolerable, she enjoys it more eagerly. This is the source of that cheerfulness which is peculiar to woman, fitting her to amuse man in his hours of recreation, and, in case of need, to console him when he is borne down by the weight of his cares.

It is by no means a bad plan to consult women in matters of difficulty, as the Germans used to do in ancient times; for their way of looking at things is quite different from ours, chiefly in the fact that they like to take the shortest way to their goal, and, in general, manage to fix their eyes upon what lies before them; while we, as a rule, see far beyond it, just because it is in front of our noses. In cases like this, we need to be brought back to the right standpoint, so as to recover the near and simple view.

Then, again, women are decidedly more sober in their judgment than we are, so that they do not see more in things than is really there; whilst, if our passions are aroused, we are apt to see things in an exaggerated way, or imagine what does not exist.

The weakness of their reasoning faculty also explains why it is that women show more sympathy for the unfortunate than men do, and so treat them with more kindness and interest; and why it is that, on the contrary, they are inferior to men in point of justice, and less honourable and conscientious. For it is just because their reasoning power is weak that present circumstances have such a hold over them, and those concrete things which lie directly before their eyes exercise a power which is seldom counteracted to any extent by abstract principles of thought, by fixed rules of conduct, firm resolution, or, in general, by consideration for the past and the future, or regard for what is absent and remote. Accordingly, they possess the first and main elements that go to make a virtuous character, but they are deficient in those secondary qualities which are often a necessary instrument in the formation of it.[1]

Hence it will be found that the fundamental fault of the female character is that it has *no sense of justice.* This is mainly due to the fact, already mentioned, that women are defective in the powers of reasoning and deliberation; but it is also traceable to the position which Nature has assigned to them as the weaker sex. They are dependent, not upon strength, but upon craft; and hence their instinctive capacity for cunning, and their ineradicable tendency to say what is not true. For as lions are provided with claws and teeth, and elephants and boars with tusks, bulls with horns, and the cuttle fish with its cloud of inky fluid, so Nature has equipped woman, for her defence and protection, with the arts of dissimulation; and all the power which Nature has conferred upon man in the shape of physical strength and reason has been bestowed upon women in this form. Hence dissimulation is innate in woman, and almost as much a quality of the stupid as of the clever. It is as natural for them to make use of it on every occasion as it is for those animals to employ their means of defence when they are attacked; they have a feeling that in doing so they are only within their rights. Therefore a woman who is perfectly truthful and not given to dissimulation is perhaps an impossibility, and for this very reason they are so quick at seeing through dissimulation in others that it is not a wise thing to attempt it with them. But this fundamental defect which I have stated, with all that it entails, gives rise to falsity, faithlessness, treachery,

---

[1] In this respect they may be compared to an animal organism which contains a liver but no gall-bladder. . . .

ingratitude, and so on. Perjury in a court of justice is more often committed by women than by men. It may, indeed, be generally questioned whether women ought to be sworn at all. From time to time one finds repeated cases everywhere of ladies, who want for nothing, taking things from shop-counters when no one is looking and making off with them.

Nature has appointed that the propagation of the species shall be the business of men who are young, strong and handsome; so that the race may not degenerate. This is the firm will and purpose of Nature in regard to the species, and it finds its expression in the passions of women. There is no law that is older or more powerful than this. Woe, then, to the man who sets up claims and interests that will conflict with it; whatever he may say and do, they will be unmercifully crushed at the first serious encounter. For the innate rule that governs women's conduct, though it is secret and unformulated, nay, unconscious in its working, is this: *We are justified in deceiving those who think they have acquired rights over the species by paying little attention to the individual, that is, to us. The constitution and, therefore, the welfare of the species have been placed in our hands and committed to our care, through the control we obtain over the next generation, which proceeds from us; let us discharge our duties conscientiously.* But women have no abstract knowledge of this leading principle; they are conscious of it only as a concrete fact; and they have no other method of giving expression to it than the way in which they act when the opportunity arrives. And then their conscience does not trouble them so much as we fancy; for in the darkest recesses of their heart they are aware that in committing a breach of their duty towards the individual, they have all the better fulfilled their duty towards the species, which is infinitely greater.

And since women exist in the main solely for the propagation of the species, and are not destined for anything else, they live, as a rule, more for the species than for the individual, and in their hearts take the affairs of the species more seriously than those of the individual. This gives their whole life and being a certain levity; the general bent of their character is in a direction fundamentally different from that of man; and it is this which produces that discord in married life which is so frequent, and almost the normal state.

The natural feeling between men is mere indifference, but between women it is actual enmity. The reason of this is that trade-jealousy—*odium figulinum*—which, in the case of men, does not go beyond the confines of their own particular pursuit but with women embraces the whole sex; since they have only one kind of business. Even when they meet in the street women look at one another like Guelphs and Ghibellines. And it is a patent fact that when two women make first acquaintance with each other they behave with more constraint and dissimulation than two men would show in a like case; and hence it is that an exchange of compliments between two women is a much more ridiculous proceeding than between two men. Further, whilst a man will, as a general rule, always preserve a certain amount of consideration and humanity in speaking to others, even to those who are in a very inferior position, it is intolerable to see how proudly and disdainfully a fine lady will generally behave towards one who is in a lower social rank (I do not mean a woman who is in her service), whenever she speaks to her. The reason of this may be that, with women, differences of rank are much more precarious than with us; because, while a hundred considerations carry weight in our case, in theirs there is only one, namely, with which man they have found favour; as also that they stand in much nearer relations with one another than men do, in consequence of the one-sided nature of their calling. This makes them endeavour to lay stress upon differences of rank.

It is only the man whose intellect is clouded by his sexual impulses that could give the name of *the fair sex* to that undersized, narrow-shouldered, broad-hipped, and short-legged race: for the whole beauty of the sex is bound up with this impulse. Instead of calling them beautiful, there would be more warrant for describing women as the unæsthetic sex. Neither for music, nor for poetry, nor for fine art, have they really and truly any sense or susceptibility; it is a mere mockery if they make a pretence of it in order to assist their endeavour to please. Hence, as a result of this, they are incapable of taking a *purely objective interest* in anything; and the reason of it seems to me to be as follows. A man tries to acquire *direct* mastery over things, either by understanding them or by forcing them to do his will. But a woman is always and everywhere reduced to obtaining this mastery *indirectly*, namely through a man; and whatever direct mastery she may have is entirely confined to him. And so it lies in woman's nature to look upon everything only as a means for conquering man; and if she takes an interest in anything else it is simulated—a mere roundabout way of gaining her ends by coquetry and feigning what she does not feel. Hence even Rousseau declared: *Women have, in general, no love of any art; they have no proper knowledge of any; and they have no genius.*[2]

No one who sees at all below the surface can have failed to remark the same thing. You need only observe the kind of attention women bestow upon a concert, an opera, or a play—the childish simplicity, for example, with which they keep on chattering during the finest passages in the greatest masterpieces. If it is true that the Greeks excluded women from their theatres, they were quite right in what they did; at any rate you would have been able to hear what was said upon the stage. In our day, besides, or in lieu of saying, *Let a woman keep silence in the church*, it would be much to the point to say, *Let a woman keep silence in the theatre*. This might, perhaps, be put up in big letters on the curtain.

And you cannot expect anything else of women if you consider that the most distinguished intellects among the whole sex have never managed to produce a single achievement in the fine arts that is really great, genuine, and original; or given to the world any work of permanent value in any sphere. This is most strikingly shown in regard to painting, where mastery of technique is at least as much within their power as within ours—and hence they are diligent in cultivating it; but still, they have not a single great painting to boast of, just because they are deficient in that objectivity of mind which is so directly

[2] Lettre à d'Alembert. Note xx.

indispensable in painting. They never get beyond a subjective point of view. It is quite in keeping with this that ordinary women have no real susceptibility for art at all; for Nature proceeds in strict sequence—*non facit saltum*. And Huarte[3] in his *Examen de ingenios para las scienzias*—a book which has been famous for three hundred years—denies women the possession of all the higher faculties. The case is not altered by particular and partial exceptions; taken as a whole, women are, and remain, thorough-going philistines, and quite incurable. Hence, with that absurd arrangement which allows them to share the rank and title of their husbands, they are a constant stimulus to his ignoble ambitions. And, further, it is just because they are philistines that modern society, where they take the lead and set the tone, is in such a bad way. Napoleon's saying— that *women have no rank*—should be adopted as the right standpoint in determining their position in society; and as regards their other qualities Chamfort makes the very true remark: *They are made to trade with our own weaknesses and our follies, but not with our reason. The sympathies that exist between them and men are skin-deep only, and do not touch the mind or the feelings or the character.* They form the *sexus sequior*—the second sex, inferior in every respect to the first; their infirmities should be treated with consideration; but to show them great reverence is extremely ridiculous, and lowers us in their eyes. When Nature made two divisions of the human race, she did not draw the line exactly through the middle. These divisions are polar and opposed to each other, it is true; but the difference between them is not qualitative merely, it is also quantitative.

This is just the view which the ancients took of woman, and the view which people in the East take now; and their judgment as to her proper position is much more correct than ours, with our old French notions of gallantry and our preposterous system of reverence—that highest product of Teutonico-Christian stupidity. These notions have served only to make women more arrogant and overbearing; so that one is occasionally reminded of the holy apes in Benares, who in the consciousness of their sanctity and inviolable position think they can do exactly as they please.

But in the West the woman, and especially the *lady*, finds herself in a false position; for woman, rightly called by the ancients *sexus sequior*, is by no means fit to be the object of our honour and veneration, or to hold her head higher than man and be on equal terms with him. The consequences of this false position are sufficiently obvious. Accordingly it would be a very desirable thing if this Number Two of the human race were in Europe also relegated to her natural place, and an end put to that lady-nuisance, which not only moves all Asia to laughter but would have been ridiculed by Greece and Rome as well. It is impossible to calculate the good effects which such a change would bring about in our social, civil and political arrangements. There would be no necessity

[3] *Translator's Note.* Juan Huarte (1520?–1590) practised as a physician at Madrid. The work cited by Schopenhauer is well known, and has been translated into many languages.

for the Salic law: it would be a superfluous truism. In Europe the *lady*, strictly so-called, is a being who should not exist at all; she should be either a house-wife or a girl who hopes to become one; and she should be brought up, not to be arrogant, but to be thrifty and submissive. It is just because there are such people as *ladies* in Europe that the women of the lower classes, that is to say, the great majority of the sex, are much more unhappy than they are in the East. And even Lord Byron says: *Thought of the state of women under the ancient Greeks—convenient enough. Present state, a remnant of the barbarism of the chivalric and the feudal ages—artificial and unnatural. They ought to mind home—and be well fed and clothed—but not mixed in society. Well educated, too, in religion—but to read neither poetry nor politics—nothing but books of piety and cookery. Music—drawing—dancing—also a little gardening and ploughing now and then. I have seen them mending the roads in Epirus with good success. Why not, as well as hay-making and milking?*

The laws of marriage prevailing in Europe consider the woman as the equivalent of the man—start, that is to say, from a wrong position. In our part of the world where monogamy is the rule, to marry means to halve one's rights and double one's duties. Now when the laws gave women equal rights with man, they ought to have also endowed her with a masculine intellect. But the fact is that, just in proportion as the honours and privileges which the laws accord to women exceed the amount which Nature gives, there is a diminution in the number of women who really participate in these privileges; and all the remainder are deprived of their natural rights by just so much as is given to the others over and above their share. For the institution of monogamy, and the laws of marriage which it entails, bestow upon the woman an unnatural position of privilege, by considering her throughout as the full equivalent of the man, which is by no means the case; and seeing this men who are shrewd and prudent very often scruple to make so great a sacrifice and to acquiesce in so unfair an arrangement.

Consequently, whilst among polygamous nations every woman is provided for, where monogamy prevails the number of married women is limited; and there remains over a large number of women without stay or support, who, in the upper classes, vegetate as useless old maids, and in the lower succumb to hard work for which they are not suited; or else become *filles de joie*, whose life is as destitute of joy as it is of honour. But under the circumstances they become a necessity; and their position is openly recognised as serving the special end of warding off temptation from those women favoured by fate, who have found, or may hope to find, husbands. In London alone there are 80,000 prostitutes. What are they but the women, who, under the institution of mono-gamy, have come off worst? Theirs is a dreadful fate: they are human sacrifices offered up on the altar of monogamy. The women whose wretched position is here described are the inevitable set-off to the European lady with her arrogance and pretension. Polygamy is therefore a real benefit to the female sex if it is taken as a whole. And, from another point of view, there is no true reason why a man whose wife suffers from chronic illness, or remains barren, or has gradually become too old for him, should not take a second. The motives which induce so many people to become converts to Mormonism appear to be just those which militate against the unnatural institution of monogamy.

Moreover, the bestowal of unnatural rights upon women has imposed upon them unnatural duties, and nevertheless a breach of these duties makes them unhappy. Let me explain. A man may often think that his social or financial position will suffer if he marries, unless he makes some brilliant alliance. His desire will then be to win a woman of his own choice under conditions other than those of marriage, such as will secure her position and that of the children. However fair, reasonable, fit and proper these conditions may be, if the woman consents by forgoing that undue amount of privilege which marriage alone can bestow, she to some extent loses her honour, because marriage is the basis of civic society; and she will lead an unhappy life, since human nature is so constituted that we pay an attention to the opinion of other people which is out of all proportion to its value. On the other hand, if she does not consent, she runs the risk either of having to be given in marriage to a man whom she does not like, or of being landed high and dry as an old maid; for the period during which she has a chance of being settled for life is very short. And in view of this aspect of the institution of monogamy, Thomasius' profoundly learned treatise *de Concubinatu* is well worth reading; for it shows that, amongst all nations and in all ages, down to the Lutheran Reformation, concubinage was permitted; nay, that it was an institution which was to a certain extent actually recognized by law, and attended with no dishonour. It was only the Lutheran Reformation that degraded it from this position. It was seen to be a further justification for the marriage of the clergy; and then, after that, the Catholic Church did not dare to remain behindhand in the matter.

There is no use arguing about polygamy; it must be taken as *de facto* existing everywhere, and the only question is as to how it shall be regulated. Where are there, then, any real monogamists? We all live, at any rate, for a time, and most of us, always, in polygamy. And so, since every man needs many women, there is nothing fairer than to allow him, nay, to make it incumbent upon him, to provide for many women. This will reduce woman to her true and natural position as a subordinate being; and the *lady*—that monster of European civilisation and Teutonico-Christian stupidity—will disappear from the world, leaving only *women*, but no more *unhappy women*, of whom Europe is now full.

In India no woman is ever independent, but in accordance with the law of Manu, she stands under the control of her father, her husband, her brother or her son. It is, to be sure, a revolting thing that a widow should immolate herself upon her husband's funeral pyre; but it is also revolting that she should spend her husband's money with her paramours—the money for which he toiled his whole life long, in the consoling belief that he was providing for his children. Happy are those who have kept the middle course—*medium tenuere beati*.

The first love of a mother for her child is, with the lower animals as with men, of a purely *instinctive* character, and so it ceases when the child is no longer in a physically helpless condition. After that, the first love should give way to one that is based on habit and reason; but this often fails to make its appearance, especially where the mother did not love the father. The love of a father for his child is of a different order, and more likely to last; because it has its foundation in the fact that in the child he recognises his own inner self; that is to say, his love for it is metaphysical in its origin.

In almost all nations, whether of the ancient or the modern world, even amongst the Hottentots, property is inherited by the male descendants alone; it is only in Europe that a departure has taken place; but not amongst the nobility, however. That the property which has cost men long years of toil and effort, and been won with so much difficulty, should afterwards come into the hands of women, who then, in their lack of reason, squander it in a short time, or otherwise fool it away, is a grievance and a wrong, as serious as it is common, which should be prevented by limiting the right of women to inherit. In my opinion the best arrangement would be that by which women, whether widows or daughters, should never receive anything beyond the interest for life on property secured by mortgage, and in no case the property itself, or the capital, except where all male descendants fail. The people who make money are men, not women; and it follows from this that women are neither justified in having unconditional possession of it, nor fit persons to be entrusted with its administration. When wealth, in any true sense of the word, that is to say, funds, houses or land, is to go to them as an inheritance, they should never be allowed the free disposition of it. In their case a guardian should always be appointed; and hence they should never be given the free control of their own children, wherever it can be avoided. The vanity of women, even though it should not prove to be greater than that of men, has this much danger in it that it takes an entirely material direction. They are vain, I mean, of their personal beauty, and then of finery, show and magnificence. That is just why they are so much in their element in society. It is this, too, which makes them so inclined to be extravagant, all the more as their reasoning power is low. Accordingly we find an ancient writer describing woman as in general of an extravagant nature—Γυνὴ τὸ σύνολον ἔστι δαπανηρὸν φύσει.[4] But with men vanity often takes the direction of non-material advantages, such as intellect, learning, courage.

In the *Politics*[5] Aristotle explains the great disadvantage which accrued to the Spartans from the fact that they conceded too much to their women, by giving them the right of inheritance and dower, and a great amount of independence; and he shows how much this contributed to Sparta's fall. May it not be the case in France that the influence of women, which went on increasing steadily from the time of Louis XIII, was to blame for that gradual corruption of the Court and the Government, which brought about the Revolution of 1789, of which all subsequent disturbances have been the fruit? However that may be, the false position which women occupy, demonstrated as it is, in the most glaring way, by the institution of the *lady*, is a fundamental defect in our social scheme, and this defect, proceeding from the very heart of it, must spread its baneful influence in all directions.

That woman is by nature meant to obey may be seen by the fact that every

[4] Brunck's *Gnomici poetae graeci*, v. 115.
[5] Bk. I., ch. 9.

woman who is placed in the unnatural position of complete independence, immediately attaches herself to some man, by whom she allows herself to be guided and ruled. It is because she needs a lord and master. If she is young, it will be a lover; if she is old, a priest.

✥ *Ashley Montagu*

Ashley Montagu, a distinguished anthropologist, is a prolific writer whose works cover a wide range of interest, from the dolphin to the human being, from life before birth to life after death. Among his books are several on woman and the relationship between the sexes: The Natural Superiority of Women (an expansion of the following Saturday Review article), The Practice of Love, The Reproductive Development of the Female, and Sex, Man, and Society. In the following article he follows an old and honorable tradition, dating from Cornelius Agrippa, in adducing evidence that woman is neither man's inferior nor his equal, but in many ways his superior.

The Natural Superiority of Women

Oh, no!, I can hear it said, *not* superior. Equal, partners, complementary, different, but *not* superior. I can even foresee that men will mostly smile, while women, alarmed, will rise to the defense of men—women always have, and always will. I hope that what I shall have to say in this article will make them even more willing to do so, for men need their help more than they as yet, mostly, consciously realize.

Women superior to men? This is a new idea. There have been people who have cogently, but apparently not convincingly, argued that women were as good as men, but I do not recall anyone who has publicly provided the evidence or even argued that women were better than or superior to men. How, indeed, could one argue such a case in the face of all the evidence to the contrary? Is it not a fact that by far the largest number of geniuses, great painters, poets, philosophers, scientists, etc., etc., have been men, and that women have made, by comparison, a very poor showing? Clearly the superiority is with men? Where are the Leonardos, the Michelangelos, the Shakespeares, the Donnes, the Galileos, the Whiteheads, the Kants, the Bachs, *et al.*, of the feminine sex? In fields in which women have excelled, in poetry and the novel, how many poets and novelists of the really first rank have there been? Haven't well-bred young women been educated for centuries in music? And how many among them have been great composers or instrumentalists? Composers—none of the first rank. Instrumentalists—well, in the recent period there have been such accomplished artists as Myra Hess and Wanda Landowska. Possibly there is a clue here to the answer to the question asked. May it not be that women are just about to emerge from the period of subjection during which they were the "niggers" of the masculine world?

The Royal Society of London has at last opened its doors and admitted women to the highest honor which it is in the power of the English scientific world to bestow—the Fellowship of the Royal Society. I well remember that when I was a youth—less than a quarter of a century ago—it was considered inconceivable that any woman would ever have brains enough to attain great distinction in science. Mme. Curie was an exception. But the half dozen women Fellows of the Royal Society in England are not. Nor is Lise Meitner. And Mme. Curie no longer remains the only woman to share in the Nobel Prize award for science. There is Marie Curie's daughter, Irène Joliot-Curie, and there is Gerty Cory (1947) for physiology and medicine. Nobel prizes in literature have gone to Selma Lagerlöf, Grazia Deledda, Sigrid Undset, Pearl Buck, and Gabriela Mistral. As an artist Mary Cassatt (1845–1926) was every bit as good as her great French friends Degas and Manet considered her to be, but it has taken the rest of the world another fifty years grudgingly to admit it. Among contemporaries Georgia O'Keeffe can hold her own with the best.

It is not, however, going to be any part of this article to show that women are about to emerge as superior scientists, musicians, painters, or the like. I believe that in these fields they may emerge as equally good, and possibly not in as large numbers as men, largely because the motivations and aspirations of most women will continue to be directed elsewhere. But what must be pointed out is that women are, in fact, just beginning to emerge from the period of subjection when they were treated in a manner not unlike that which is still meted out to the Negro in the Western world. The women of the nineteenth century were the "niggers" of the male-dominated world. All the traits that are mythically attributed to the Negro at the present time were for many generations saddled upon women. Women had smaller brains than men and less intelligence, they were more emotional and unstable, in a crisis you could always rely upon them to swoon or become otherwise helpless, they were weak and sickly creatures, they had little judgment and less sense, could not be relied upon to handle money, and as for the world outside, there they could be employed only at the most menial and routine tasks.

The biggest dent in this series of myths was made by World War I, when women were for the first time called upon to replace men in occupations which were formerly the exclusive preserve of men. They became bus drivers, conductors, factory workers, farm workers, laborers, supervisors, executive officers, and a great many other things at which many had believed they could never work. At first it was said that they didn't do as well as men, then it was grudgingly admitted that they weren't so bad, and by the time the war was over many employers were reluctant to exchange their women employees for men! But the truth was out—women could do as well as men in most of the fields which had been considered forever closed to them because of their alleged natural incapacities, and in many fields, particularly where delicate precision work was involved, they had proved themselves superior to men. From 1918 to 1939 the period for women was one essentially of consolidation of gains, so that by the time that World War II broke out there was no hesitation on the part of anyone in calling upon women to serve in the civilian roles of men and in many cases also in the armed services.

But women have a long way to go before they reach full emancipation—emancipation from the myths from which they themselves suffer. It is, of course, untrue that women have smaller brains than men. The fact is that in proportion to body weight they have larger brains than men; but this fact is in itself of no importance because within the limits of normal variation of brain size and weight there exists no relation between these factors and intelligence. Women have been conditioned to believe that they are inferior to men, and they have assumed that what everyone believes is a fact of nature; and as men occupy the superior positions in almost all societies, this superiority is taken to be a natural one. "Woman's place is in the home" and man's place is in the counting house and on the board of directors. "Women should not meddle in men's affairs." And yet the world does move. Some women have become Members of Parliament and even attained Cabinet rank. In the United States they have even gotten as far as the Senate. They have participated in peace conferences, but it is still inconceivable to most persons that there should ever be a woman Prime Minister or President. And yet that day, too, will come. *Eppure si muove!*

Woman has successfully passed through the abolition period, the abolition of her thraldom to man; she has now to pass successfully through the period of emancipation, the freeing of herself from the myth of inferiority, and the realization of her potentialities to the fullest.

And now for the evidence which proves the superiority of woman to man. But first, one word in explanation of the use of the word "superiority." The word is used in its common sense as being of better quality than, or of higher nature or character. Let us begin at the very beginning. What about the structure of the sexes? Does one show any superiority over the other? The answer is a resounding "Yes!" And I should like this "Yes" to resound all over the world, for no one has made anything of this key fact which lies at the base of all the differences between the sexes and the superiority of the female to the male. I refer to the chromosomal structure of the sexes. The chromosomes, those small cellular bodies which contain the hereditary particles, the genes, which so substantially influence one's development and fate as an organism, provide us with our basic facts.

In the sex cells there are twenty-four chromosomes, but only one of these is a sex chromosome. There are two kinds of sex chromosomes, X and Y. Half the sperm cells carry X and half carry Y chromosomes. All the female ova are made up of X-chromosomes. When an X-bearing sperm fertilizes an ovum the offspring is always female. When a Y-bearing chromosome fertilizes an ovum the offspring is always male. And this is what makes the difference between the sexes. So what? Well, the sad fact is that the Y-chromosome is but an iota, the merest bit, of a remnant of an X-chromosome; it is a crippled X-chromosome. The X-chromosomes are fully developed structures; the Y-chromosome is the merest comma. It is as if in the evolution of sex a particle one day broke away from an X-chromosome, and thereafter in relation to X-chromosomes could produce only an incomplete female—the creature we now call the male! It is to this original chromosomal deficiency that all the various troubles to which the male falls heir can be traced.

In the first place the chromosomal deficiency of the male determines his incapacity to have babies. This has always been a sore point with men, though consciously they would be the last to admit it, although in some primitive societies, as among the Australian aborigines, it is the male who conceives a child by dreaming it, and then telling his wife. In this way a child is eventually born to them, the wife being merely the incubator who hatches the egg placed there through the grace of her husband.

The fact that men cannot have babies and suckle them nor remain in association with their children as closely as the wife has an enormous effect upon their subsequent psychological development. Omitting altogether from consideration the psychologic influences exercised by the differences in the hormonal secretions of the sexes, one can safely say that the mother–child relationship confers enormous benefits upon the mother which are not nearly so substantively operative in the necessary absence of such a relationship between father and child. The maternalizing influences of being a mother in addition to the fact of being a woman has from the very beginning of the human species—about a million years ago—made the female the more humane of the sexes. The love of a mother for her child is the basic patent and the model for *all* human relationships. Indeed, to the extent to which men approximate in their relationships with their fellow men to the love of the mother for her child, to that extent do they move more closely to the attainment of perfect human relations. The mother–child relationship is a dependent-interdependent one. The interstimulation between mother and child is something which the father misses, and to that extent suffers from the want of. In short, the female in the mother–child relationship has the advantage of having to be more considerate, more self-sacrificing, more cooperative, and more altruistic than usually falls to the lot of the male.

The female thus acquires, in addition to whatever natural biological advantages she starts with, a competence in social understanding which is usually denied the male. This, I take it, is one of the reasons why women are usually so much more able to perceive the nuances and pick up the subliminal signs in human behavior which almost invariably pass men by. It was, I believe, George Jean Nathan who called woman's intuition merely man's transparency. With all due deference to Mr. Nathan and sympathy for his lot as a mere male, I would suggest that man's opacity would be nearer the mark. It is because women have had to be so unselfish and forbearing and self-sacrificing and maternal that they possess a deeper understanding than men of what it is to be human. What is so frequently termed feminine indecision, the inability of women to make up their minds, is in fact an inverse reflection of the trigger-thinking of men. Every salesgirl prefers the male customer because women take time to think about what they are buying, and the male usually hasn't the sense enough to do so. Women don't think in terms of "Yes" or "No." Life isn't as simple as all that—except to males. Men tend to think in terms of the all-or-none principle, in terms of black and white. Women are more ready to make adjustments, to consider the alternative possibilities, and see the other colors and gradations in the range between black and white.

By comparison with the deep involvement of women in living, men appear to be only superficially so. Compare the love of a male for a female with the love of the female for the male. It is the difference between a rivulet and a great deep ocean. Women love the human race; men are, on the whole, hostile to it. Men act as if they haven't been adequately loved, as if they had been frustrated and rendered hostile, and becoming aggressive they say that aggressiveness is natural and women are inferior in this respect because they tend to be gentle and unaggressive! But it is precisely in this capacity to love and unaggressiveness that the superiority of women to men is demonstrated, for whether it be natural to be loving and cooperative or not, so far as the human species is concerned, its evolutionary destiny, its very survival is more closely tied to this capacity for love and cooperation than with any other. So that unless men learn from women how to be more loving and cooperative they will go on making the kind of mess of the world which they have so effectively achieved thus far.

And this is, of course, where women can realize their power for good in the world, and make their greatest gains. *It is the function of women to teach men how to be human.* Women must not permit themselves to be deviated from this function by those who tell them that their place is in the home in subservient relation to man. It is, indeed, in the home that the foundations of the kind of world in which we live are laid, and in this sense it will always remain true that the hand that rocks the cradle is the hand that rules the world. And it is in this sense that women must assume the job of making men who will know how to make a world fit for human beings to live in. The greatest single step forward in this direction will be made when women consciously assume this task—the task of teaching their children to be like themselves, loving and cooperative.

As for geniuses, I think that almost everyone will agree that there have been more geniuses for being human among women than there have been among men. This, after all, is the true genius of women, and it is because we have not valued the qualities for being human anywhere nearly as highly as we have valued those for accomplishment in the arts and sciences that we have out-of-focusedly almost forgotten them. Surely, the most valuable quality in any human being is his capacity for being loving and cooperative. We have been placing our emphases on the wrong values—it is time we recognized what every man and every woman at the very least subconsciously knows—the value of being loving, and the value of those who can teach this better than anyone else.

Physically and psychically women are by far the superiors of men. The old chestnut about women being more emotional than men has been forever destroyed by the facts of two great wars. Women under blockade, heavy bombardment, concentration camp confinement, and similar rigors withstand them vastly more successfully than men. The psychiatric casualties of civilian populations under such conditions are mostly masculine, and there are more men in our mental hospitals than there are women. The steady hand at the helm is the hand that has had the practice at rocking the cradle. Because of their greater size and weight men are physically more powerful than women—which is not the same thing as saying that they are stronger. A man of the same size and weight as a woman of comparable background and occupational status would probably not be any more powerful than a woman. As far as constitutional strength is concerned women are stronger than men. Many diseases from which men suffer can be shown to be largely influenced by their relation to the male Y-chromosome. From fertilization on more males die than females. Deaths from almost all causes are more frequent in males at all ages. Though women are more frequently ill than men, they recover from illness more easily and more frequently than men.

Women, in short, are fundamentally more resistant than men. With the exception of the organ systems subserving the functions of reproduction women suffer much less frequently than men from the serious disorders which affect mankind. With the exception of India women everywhere live longer than men. For example, the expectation of life of the female child of white parentage in the United States at the present time is over seventy-one years, whereas for the male it is only sixty-five and a half years. Women are both biologically stronger and emotionally better shock absorbers than men. The myth of masculine superiority once played such havoc with the facts that in the nineteenth century it was frequently denied by psychiatrists that the superior male could ever suffer from hysteria. Today it is fairly well known that males suffer from hysteria and hysteriform conditions with a preponderance over the female of seven to one! Epilepsy is much more frequent in males, and stuttering has an incidence of eight males to one female.

At least four disorders are now definitely known to be due to genes carried in the Y-chromosomes, and hence are disorders which can appear only in males. These are barklike skin (ichthyosis hystrix gravior), dense hairy growth on the ears (hypertrichosis), nonpainful hard lesions of the hands and feet (keratoma dissipatum), and a form of webbing of the toes. It is, however, probable that the disadvantages accruing to the male are not so much due to what is in the Y-chromosome as to what is wanting in it. This is well shown in such serious disorders as hemophilia or bleeder's disease. Hemophilia is inherited as a single sex-linked recessive gene. The gene, or hereditary particle, determining hemophilia is linked to the X-chromosome. When, then, an X-chromosome which carries the hemophilia gene is transmitted to a female it is highly improbable that it will encounter another X-chromosome carrying such a gene; hence, while not impossible, hemophilia has never been described in a female. Females are the most usual transmitters of the hemophilia gene; but it is only the males who are affected, and they are affected because they don't have any properties in their Y-chromosome capable of suppressing the action of the hemophilia gene. The mechanism of and the explanation for (red-green) color blindness is the same. About 8 percent of all white males are color blind, but only half of one percent of females are so affected.

Need one go on? Here, in fact, we have the explanation of the greater constitutional strength of the female as compared with the male, namely, in the possession of two complete sex chromosomes by the female and only one by the male. This may not be, and probably is not, the complete explanation of the physical inferiorities of the male as compared with the female, but it is certainly physiologically the most demonstrable and least questionable one. To the unbiased student of the facts there can no longer remain any doubt of the constitutional superiority of the female. I hope that I have removed any remaining doubts about her psychological superiority where psychological superiority most counts, namely, in a human being's capacity for loving other human beings.

I think we have overemphasized the value of intellectual qualities and grossly underemphasized the value of the qualities of humanity which women possess to such a high degree. I hope I shall not be taken for an anti-intellectual when I say that intellect without humanity is not good enough, and that what the world is suffering from at the present time is not so much an overabundance of intellect as an insufficiency of humanity. Consider men like Lenin, Stalin, and Hitler. These are the extreme cases. What these men lacked was the capacity to love. What they possessed in so eminent a degree was the capacity to hate. It is not for nothing that the Bolsheviks attempted to abolish the family and masculinize women, while the Nazis made informers of children against their parents and put the state so much before the family that it became a behemoth which has well-nigh destroyed everyone who was victimized by it.

What the world stands so much in need of at the present time, and what it will continue to need if it is to endure and increase in happiness, is more of the maternal spirit and less of the masculine. We need more persons who will love and less who will hate, and we need to understand how we can produce them; for if we don't try to understand how we may do so we shall continue to flounder in the morass of misunderstanding which frustrated love creates. For frustrated love, the frustration of the tendencies to love with which the infant is born, constitutes hostility. Hatred is love frustrated. This is what too many men suffer from and an insufficient number of women recognize, or at least too many women behave as if they didn't recognize it. What most women have learned to recognize is that the much-bruited superiority of the male isn't all that it's cracked up to be. The male doesn't seem to be as wise and as steady as they were taught to believe. But there appears to be a conspiracy of silence on this subject. Perhaps women feel that men ought to be maintained in the illusion of their superiority because it might not be good for them or the world to learn the truth. In this sense this article, perhaps, should have been entitled "What Every Woman Knows." But I'm not sure that every woman knows it. What I am sure of is that many women don't appear to know it, and that there are even many women who are horrified at the thought that anyone can entertain the idea that women are anything but inferior to men. This sort of childishness does no one any good. The world is in a mess. Men, without any assistance from women, have created it, and they have created it not because they have been failed by women, but because men have never really given women a chance to serve them as they are best equipped to do—by teaching men how to love their fellow men.

Women must cease supporting men for the wrong reasons in the wrong sort of way, and thus cease causing men to marry them for the wrong reasons, too. "That's what a man wants in a wife, mostly," says Mrs. Poyser (in *Adam Bede*), "he wants to make sure o' one fool as 'ull tell him he's wise." Well, it's time that men learned the truth, and perhaps they are likely to take it more gracefully from another male than from their unacknowledged betters. It is equally important that women learn the truth, too, for it is to them that the most important part, the more fundamental part, of the task of remaking the world will fall, for the world will be remade only by remaking, or rather helping, human beings to realize themselves more fully in terms of what their mothers have to give them. Without adequate mothers life becomes inadequate, nasty, and unsatisfactory, and Mother Earth becomes a battlefield on which fathers slay their young and are themselves slain.

Men have had a long run for their money in running the affairs of the world. It is time that women realized that men will continue to run the world for some time yet, and that they can best assist them to run it more humanely by teaching them, when young, what humanity means. Men will thus not feel that they are being demoted, but rather that their potentialities for good are so much more increased, and what is more important, instead of feeling hostile towards women they will for the first time learn to appreciate them at their proper worth. There is an old Spanish proverb which has it that a good wife is the workmanship of a good husband. Maybe. But of one thing we can be certain: a good husband is the workmanship of a good mother. The best of all ways in which men can help themselves is to help women realize themselves. This way both sexes will come for the first time fully into their own, and the world of mankind may then look forward to a happier history than it has thus far enjoyed.

ᨸᨲ᨞᨞15 *Friedrich Nietzsche*

Friedrich Wilhelm Nietzsche was born in 1844 in the village of Röcken in Saxony, then a province of Prussia. Five years later, when first his father and then his infant brother died, he became the only male member of a household composed of his mother, his sister, a grandmother, and two unmarried aunts. In 1850 the family moved to Naumburg, and in 1858 young Nietzsche was sent to the famous boarding school at nearby Pforta. He entered the University of Bonn in 1864 and transferred to the University of Leipzig the following year. In 1869, his university education complete, he was appointed to a chair of classical letters at the University of Basel, where, except for a few months' service in the Franco-Prussian War, he remained until 1876, when poor health forced him to take a leave of absence. Nietzsche never returned to the university and he submitted his resignation in 1879.

Nietzsche had begun writing the year he went to Basel; after his resignation from the university he was able to devote to it all the energy his poor health left him. His life, so far as can be ascertained, was ascetic. He idolized Cosima Wagner, wife of the composer, but never confessed his love to her. He made two proposals of marriage: one, in 1876, to a young Dutch woman whom he had met at a spa on Lake Geneva; the other, in 1882, to Lou Salomé, who came as close as anyone ever did to being the disciple Nietzsche had always longed for. Both times he was rejected. And he paid one visit to a brothel, to which he was taken by a porter at a railway station, allegedly by mistake. But according to Paul Deussen, his friend and biographer, Nietzsche, terrified at the sight of so many half-clad bodies, struck a single chord upon the piano in the parlor and fled. Although sexually ascetic throughout most of his life, Nietzsche apparently contracted syphilis during his university days or shortly afterward and as a result lapsed into insanity in 1889. He died in Weimar in 1900.

By the latter half of the nineteenth century the women's movement in Germany had gained impetus. Although he numbered among his close friends one of its leading exponents, Malwida von Meysenbug, Nietzsche remained unaffected by her views. Feminism, in his estimation, like Christianity, like democracy, stems from the wrong set of values and leads to political philosophies that are even worse: socialism and anarchy. An attempt to liberate woman amounts to the enslavement of man. Furthermore, women themselves lose prestige and power in their attempt to gain freedom. Nietzsche reëchoes the maxims of Schopenhauer: woman is weak, woman is stupid, woman is designed solely to bear children.

In the Preface to Beyond Good and Evil Nietzsche drew an analogy between seeking the truth and courting a woman. The dogmatic philosopher, he

229

suggested, is far too clumsy in his approach to win the lady in question. Nietzsche's own philosophical method was that of the iconoclast, not the dogmatist. Only by examining critically the so-called truths of the past, only by reëvaluating traditional values, turning them upside down, substituting new ones, he thought, can the philosopher even approach the ever elusive truth. He considered nineteenth-century European society degenerate, sick, asleep, having listened too long to the lullaby of Judeo-Christian tradition, which he termed "a continual suicide of reason." Society, he said, must exempt from traditional morality a few gifted individuals (Übermenschen, supermen) so that they may set things right. One might expect Nietzsche, then, to reevaluate society's views on woman along with everything else, even to allow for the possibility of superwomen, for Übermensch means literally "superperson," not "supermale."

His failure to break away from traditional attitudes concerning women is well known. A number of Nietzsche scholars dismiss his views on women as vituperation, philosophically irrelevant prejudices picked up from Schopenhauer, and simply exclude them from consideration as part of Nietzsche's serious philosophical thought. In Beyond Good and Evil Nietzsche himself appeared to exclude from the province of philosophy the entire "problem of 'man and woman,'" as he termed it. But by the same token he should have excluded every other "cardinal problem," for he claimed that with regard to all these basic matters one can learn nothing more nor less than what is in oneself. The solutions one may think one has found to such problems, then, are in the last analysis self-knowledge. And so all philosophy, since it is constituted of these very cardinal problems, is, as Socrates held, knowledge of oneself.

In this respect Nietzsche's views on woman were no different from his views on anything else. But in most other respects they were very different. For when it came to sex, he did not discard old values and seek out new ones. He offered the reader the same old clichés: "In woman," he complained in Beyond Good and Evil, "there is so much pedantry, superficiality, schoolmasterliness, petty presumption, unbridledness, and indiscretion . . ." Nietzsche considered woman boring, stupid, deficient in taste, and insensitive to the truth. And if these "truths" are indeed his truths, as Nietzsche himself attested, and if this knowledge is only self-knowledge, one might do well to probe biographies rather than philosophical treatises for explanations of them.

But perhaps these views on women are not so at variance with his other philosophical views as might first appear. Here he has not transvalued value, true. But in The Genealogy of Morals, in casting aside traditional concepts of good and evil, Nietzsche expressed a preference for a dichotomy between good and worthless (schlecht) instead. Those things that enhance life, notable among them strength, should be considered of value; weakness, of course, is worthless. The characteristics that Nietzsche despised in women—weakness, fear, submissiveness, and the like—are the very traits he despised in the slaves of bygone eras: those things that do not enhance life, but frustrate it. And yet he did not call upon women to assume other values. He called upon men to impose values upon them.

From *Beyond Good and Evil*

OUR VIRTUES

. . .

231

Learning alters us, it does what all nourishment does that does not merely "conserve"—as the physiologist knows. But at the bottom of our souls, quite "down below," there is certainly something unteachable, a granite of spiritual fate, of predetermined decision and answer to predetermined, chosen questions. In each cardinal problem there speaks an unchangeable "I am this"; a thinker cannot learn anew about man and woman, for instance, but can only learn fully—he can only follow to the end what is "fixed" about them in himself. Occasionally we find certain solutions of problems which make strong beliefs for *us;* perhaps they are henceforth called "convictions." Later on—one sees in them only footsteps to self-knowledge, guide-posts to the problem which we ourselves *are*—or more correctly to the great stupidity which we embody, our spiritual fate, the *unteachable* in us, quite "down below."—In view of this liberal compliment which I have just paid myself, permission will perhaps be more readily allowed me to utter some truths about "woman as she is," provided that it is known at the outset how literally they are merely—*my* truths.

232

Woman wishes to be independent, and therefore she begins to enlighten men about "woman as she is"—*this* is one of the worst developments of the general *uglifying* of Europe. For what must these clumsy attempts of feminine scientificality and self-exposure bring to light! Woman has so much cause for shame; in woman there is so much pedantry, superficiality, schoolmasterliness, petty presumption, unbridledness, and indiscretion concealed—study only woman's behaviour towards children!—which has really been best restrained and dominated hitherto by the *fear* of man. Alas, if ever the "eternally tedious in woman"—she has plenty of it!—is allowed to venture forth! if she begins radically and on principle to unlearn her wisdom and art—of charming, of playing, of frightening-away-sorrow, of alleviating and taking-easily; if she forgets her delicate aptitude for agreeable desires! Female voices are already raised, which, by Saint Aristophanes! make one afraid:—with medical explicitness it is stated in a threatening manner what woman first and last *requires* from man. Is it not in the very worst taste that woman thus sets herself up to be scientific? Enlightenment hitherto has fortunately been men's affair, men's gift—we remained therewith "among ourselves"; and in the end, in view of all that women write about "woman," we may well have considerable doubt as to whether woman really *desires* enlightenment about herself—and *can* desire it. If woman does not thereby seek a new *ornament* for herself—I believe ornamentation belongs to the eternally feminine?—why, then, she wishes to make herself feared: perhaps she thereby wishes to get the mastery. But she does not *want* truth—what does woman care for truth! From the very first nothing is more foreign, more repugnant, or more hostile to woman than truth—her great art is falsehood, her chief concern is appearance and beauty. . . .

233

It betrays corruption of the instincts—apart from the fact that it betrays bad taste—when a woman refers to Madame Roland, or Madame de Staël, or Monsieur George Sand, as though something were proved thereby in *favour* of "woman as she is." Among men, these are the three *comical* women as they are—nothing more!—and just the best involuntary *counter-arguments* against feminine emancipation and autonomy.

234

Stupidity in the kitchen; woman as cook; the terrible thoughtlessness with which the feeding of the family and the master of the house is managed! Woman does not understand what food *means*, and she insists on being cook! If woman had been a thinking creature, she should certainly, as cook for thousands of years, have discovered the most important physiological facts, and should likewise have got possession of the healing art! Through bad female cooks—through the entire lack of reason in the kitchen—the development of mankind has been longest retarded and most interfered with; even to-day matters are very little better.—A word to High School girls.

. . .

238

To be mistaken in the fundamental problem of "man and woman," to deny here the profoundest antagonism and the necessity for an eternally hostile tension, to dream here perhaps of equal rights, equal training, equal claims and obligations: that is a *typical* sign of shallow-mindedness; and a thinker who has proved himself shallow at this dangerous spot—shallow in instinct!—may generally be regarded as suspicious, nay more, as betrayed, as discovered; he will probably prove too "short" for all fundamental questions of life, future as well as present, and will be unable to descend into *any* of the depths. On the other hand, a man who has depth of spirit as well as of desires, and has also the depth of benevolence which is capable of severity and harshness, and easily confounded with them, can only think of woman as *Orientals* do: he must conceive of her as a possession, as confinable property, as a being predestined for service and accomplishing her mission therein—he must take his stand in this matter upon the immense rationality of Asia, upon the superiority of the instinct of Asia, as the Greeks did formerly; those best heirs and scholars of Asia—who, as is well known, with their *increasing* culture and amplitude of power, from Homer to the time of Pericles, became gradually *stricter* towards woman, in short, more oriental. *How* necessary, *how* logical, even *how* humanely desirable this was, let us consider for ourselves!

239

The weaker sex has in no previous age been treated with so much respect by men as at present—this belongs to the tendency and fundamental taste of democracy, in the same way as disrespectfulness to old age—what wonder is it that abuse should be immediately made of this respect? They want more, they learn to make claims, the tribute of respect is at last felt to be well-nigh galling; rivalry for rights, indeed actual strife itself, would be preferred: in a word, woman is losing modesty. And let us immediately add that she is also losing taste. She is unlearning to *fear* man: but the woman who "unlearns to fear" sacrifices her most womanly instincts. That woman should venture forward when the fear-inspiring quality in man—or more definitely, the *man* in man— is no longer either desired or fully developed, is reasonable enough and also intelligible enough; what is more difficult to understand is that precisely thereby—woman deteriorates. This is what is happening nowadays: let us not deceive ourselves about it! Wherever the industrial spirit has triumphed over the military and aristocratic spirit, woman strives for the economic and legal independence of a clerk: "woman as clerkess" is inscribed on the portal of the modern society which is in course of formation. While she thus appropriates new rights, aspires to be "master," and inscribes "progress" of woman on her flags and banners, the very opposite realises itself with terrible obviousness: *woman retrogrades.* Since the French Revolution the influence of woman in Europe has *declined* in proportion as she has increased her rights and claims; and the "emancipation of woman," in so far as it is desired and demanded by women themselves (and not only by masculine shallow-pates), thus proves to be a remarkable symptom of the increased weakening and deadening of the most womanly instincts. There is *stupidity* in this movement, an almost mascu- line stupidity, of which a well-reared woman—who is always a sensible woman— might be heartily ashamed. To lose the intuition as to the ground upon which she can most surely achieve victory; to neglect exercise in the use of her proper weapons; to let-herself-go before man, perhaps even "to the book," where formerly she kept herself in control and in refined, artful humility; to neutralise with her virtuous audacity man's faith in a *veiled,* fundamentally different ideal in woman, something eternally, necessarily feminine; to emphatically and loquaciously dissuade man from the idea that woman must be preserved, cared for, protected, and indulged, like some delicate, strangely wild, and often pleasant domestic animal; the clumsy and indignant collection of everything of the nature of servitude and bondage which the position of woman in the hitherto existing order of society has entailed and still entails (as though slavery were a counter-argument, and not rather a condition of every higher culture, of every elevation of culture):—what does all this betoken, if not a disintegration of womanly instincts, a de-feminising? Certainly, there are enough of idiotic friends and corrupters of woman amongst the learned asses of the masculine sex, who advise woman to de-feminise herself in this manner, and to imitate all the stupidities from which "man" in Europe, European "manliness," suffers,— who would like to lower woman to "general culture," indeed even to newspaper reading and meddling with politics. Here and there they wish even to make women into free spirits and literary workers: as though a woman without piety would not be something perfectly obnoxious or ludicrous to a profound and godless man;—almost everywhere her nerves are being ruined by the most morbid and dangerous kind of music (our latest German music), and she is daily being made more hysterical and more incapable of fulfilling her first and last function, that of bearing robust children. They wish to "cultivate" her in general still more, and intend, as they say, to make the "weaker sex" *strong* by culture: as if history did not teach in the most emphatic manner that the "cultivating" of mankind and his weakening—that is to say, the weakening, dissipating, and languishing of his *force of will*—have always kept pace with one another, and that the most powerful and influential women in the world (and lastly, the mother of Napoleon) had just to thank their force of will—and not their schoolmasters!—for their power and ascendency over men. That which inspires respect in woman, and often enough fear also, is her *nature*, which is more "natural" than that of man, her genuine, carnivora-like, cunning flexibility, her tiger-claws beneath the glove, her *naïveté* in egoism, her untrainableness and innate wildness, the incomprehensibleness, extent, and deviation of her desires and virtues. . . . That which, in spite of fear, excites one's sympathy for the dangerous and beautiful cat, "woman," is that she seems more afflicted, more vulnerable, more necessitous of love and more condemned to disillusionment than any other creature. Fear and sympathy: it is with these feelings that man has hitherto stood in presence of woman, always with one foot already in tragedy, which rends while it delights.—What? And all that is now to be at an end? And the *disenchantment* of woman is in progress? The tediousness of woman is slowly evolving? Oh Europe! Europe! We know the horned animal which was always most attractive to thee, from which danger is ever again threatening thee! Thy old fable might once more become "history"—an immense stupidity might once again overmaster thee and carry thee away! And no God concealed beneath it—no! only an "idea," a "modern idea"! . . . .

◄ﾞﾞ►*Kathryn Pyne Parsons*

Kathryn Pyne Parsons, professor of philosophy at Smith College, is particularly interested in ethical theory and the philosophy of science. She is the author of a number of articles that have appeared in Nous *and the* Philosophical Review, *as well as of the following selection, which first appeared in* Nietzsche, *edited by Robert Solomon, and was later reprinted in* Feminist Studies. *Despite Nietzsche's views on women and their emancipation, Professor Parsons finds in the nineteenth-century women's revolution an ideal illustration of the German thinker's fundamental precepts concerning moral change.*

Nietzsche and Moral Change

What is moral change? An answer to this question is necessary if we are to answer the question, "What is essential to morality?" But among moral philosophers, Nietzsche stands almost alone in trying to examine the full structure of moral change.

There is a reason for this. The main body of tradition in ethics has occupied itself with the notions of obligation, moral principle, justification of acts under principle, justification of principle by argument. When moral change was considered at all, it was seen as change to bring our activities into conformity with our principles, as change to dispel injustice, as change to alleviate suffering. In short, moral change was seen as moral reform, with no other sort of moral change acknowledged or even imagined.

But moral reform is not the only sort of moral change. There is also moral revolution. Moral revolution has not to do with making our principles consistent, not to do with greater application of what we *now* conceive as justice. That is the task of moral reform, because its aim is the preservation of values. But the aim of moral revolution is the creation of values.

The traditional view in ethics has been unable to see this because moral creativity cannot be understood when the theory of morality is exhausted by the notions of obligation, principle, and justification. Nor can certain types of morality be understood, those which don't concern themselves (or those which concern themselves very little) with the notions of obligation, rightness of act, justification of principle.

By paying attention to moral revolution, Nietzsche was able to understand some of these things. I'd like to work with his insights and develop some of the points I think he was trying to make. This means that I shall not be doing "Nietzsche scholarship" but rather trying to apply some of his insights to theoretical and practical problems which face us. Given his views on the interpretation of literature, I don't believe this is against the Nietzschean spirit.

I shall argue that the narrow focus of traditional ethics makes it impossible to account for the behavior of the moral revolutionary *as* moral behavior. In seeing this, we shall see that the traditional view misrepresents the structure of morality, and why a Nietzschean typology of morals offers us new moral notions which are more adequate. In the end, we shall be able to distinguish moral revolution from moral reform on the basis of his typology and have greater insight into moral phenomena.

. . .

I shall argue from a particular case of moral revolution—the women's revolution of the nineteenth century. This is one of the clearest examples of a moral revolution, and it offers ideal illustrations of some of the moral phenomena Nietzsche discusses.

In using this example, I shall go beyond Nietzsche—and perhaps in a direc-

The numerical references in my paper refer to entries in the bibliography.—K.P.P.

tion he would not endorse. This is not because it is a *women's* revolution. Despite its name, it was a human revolution, affecting men, women, and children. And despite his remarks, Nietzsche was no simple misogynist. His distaste for women was a distaste for the slavish character shown by nineteenth-century women. It was this slave morality in women which the women's revolution hoped to overthrow.

But the women's revolution was a revolution of the people, and Nietzsche looked sourly upon such things. His highest moral categories are aimed at capturing moral revolution in the *individual.* However, I think that these categories can be used to understand the individual moral revolutionary and, through him, moral revolution itself. In the end, I think such a use of Nietzsche's categories reveals the phenomena of morality in a way he himself was unable to reveal it.

. . . Part II [below] takes up some central arguments given by conservatives and revolutionaries in the nineteenth century to show that the traditional views in ethics cannot account for the behavior of the moral revolutionary as moral, while Part III suggests a new understanding of the women's revolution in light of . . . Nietzschean explanations.

Part IV considers a typology of morals based on certain Nietzschean distinctions. With the aid of the typology, a separation is made between moral revolution and moral reform in Part V, and it is suggested that Nietzsche is correct in taking the essential parts of morality to consist in creation and self-overcoming.

.   .   .

II

[Morality] works against our acquiring new experiences and correcting morality accordingly, which means that morality works against a better, newer morality.[1]

The traditional philosopher of science explains the structure of science in terms of theories, scientific principles, observations, and, in addition, all the scientific methods of justification which he is at pains to explicate. The traditional moral philosopher explains the structure of morality in terms of moral principles, as well as all the moral methods of justification which he is at pains to explicate. In both cases, change is said to take place by reform.

According to the traditional view, it is through moral principles that situations are categorized as morally relevant or not. For example, the principle "One ought to tell the truth" picks out situations in which I am reporting facts to others as morally relevant but leaves situations in which I am not (situations in which I am alone and eating supper, for example) as morally neutral. This means that moral principles enter into our activities in two ways. They enter *internally*, in that I categorize the world of my possible actions in their terms and act in accord with them or not. They enter *externally* in that others see and judge my acts in their terms, and I justify my own acts to others in part by

[1] The remark is from *The Dawn*, 19. It is quoted on p. 138 of (2).

their means. It is a fundamental assumption here that morally proper behavior must be morally *justifiable* behavior.

Moral principles themselves must be justified. Sometimes this is done in terms of higher-level moral principles. But there are *very* high-level moral principles ("One ought to act so as to bring about the greatest happiness . . .") which require metaphysical or philosophical justification.

It is important to look at moral justifications which are actually given to see how all of these elements enter. I shall do this in some detail, to show that the conservative fares well and the revolutionary fares very ill indeed under this traditional view of morality.

During the nineteenth century in the United States, there was an attempt to bring about a moral revolution—an attempt which was in part successful. The main attack was on those values which operated to keep women in a morally, culturally, and socially subordinate position, as well as a legally subordinate one. That is, the thrust was against the *humanly* subordinate position of women, against a double standard of humanity, one which adversely affected the moral being of *both* men and women. The organized part of this moral revolution deteriorated into a movement toward mere reform as the twentieth century began, with the increased emphasis on woman suffrage. So its earlier phases are the ones of interest to us. But these earlier phases constitute one of the clearest examples of moral revolution there is, and they offer admirable illustrations of some of the moral phenomena which Nietzsche emphasized but which philosophers in ethics generally overlook.

There was an argument presented by Senator Frelinghuysen of New Jersey shortly after the Civil War which captures the essence of the conservative position against the women's revolution.

It seems to me as if the God of our race has stamped upon [the women of America] a milder, gentler nature, which not only makes them shrink from, but disqualifies them for the turmoil and battle of public life. They have a higher and holier mission. It is in retiracy to make the character of coming men. Their mission is at home, by their blandishments and their love to assuage the passions of men as they come in from the battle of life, and not themselves by joining in the contest to add fuel to the very flames. It will be a sorry day for this country when those vestal fires of love and piety are put out ([4] p. 149).

Eleanor Flexner, an historian of the women's rights struggle, says that emotional arguments like this characterized all debates down to 1919, and that no rational argument was able to make a dent in them ([4] p. 150). But she is mistaken in dubbing this a mere emotional argument. It is a perfectly rational justification of the moral claim that one ought to oppose the attempts of the women's rights workers, and there are reasons that the moral revolutionaries couldn't make a dent in it. Let's look more carefully at the argument.

(1) Senator Frelinghuysen's justification uses the scientific claim that women differ by nature from men. We might call this the "Aristotelian claim," after an early espouser of it. It is supported on the one hand by a vague, "Aristotelian" scientific theory (still held in the nineteenth century) about the natures of individuals and the relations of these to their natural capacities. One's

nature attaches to him as a member of a kind. For example, all women have the same nature in this sense.

The claim that women differ by nature from men is overwhelmingly supported by differences in their behavior. In ancient Greece, nineteenth-century America, and even twentieth-century America, women did not show the abilities to command or the abilities to reason which men showed. They were in fact timid and dependent, better followers than leaders. Of contributions to human development deemed worthy of report in the history books, virtually all were made by men. What great women statesmen, scientists, musicians, painters, religious leaders, or philosophers does history show? Such data not only support the claim that there is a difference between men and women, they show what the difference is.

In addition, the claim for the difference was supported on religious grounds, for example, on the basis of standard interpretations of Genesis. Woman's place, and her tasks, were taken to have been intended by "the God of our race."

(2) Senator Frelinghuysen's justification presupposes the moral claim that *one ought to act according to his or her nature.* This claim is essential, since some women showed better abilities to lead and reason than the senator did.

This moral principle was a central one, and it was considered generally impeccable down to our own time. It has been used, for example, to justify condemnation of sexual "deviates" and to justify monstrous treatment of homosexuals on grounds of "unnaturalness" even in our own day.

The principle can be given religious support—we ought to act as God intended. But even in the nineteenth century, it was given other support. It is *harmful* to the person to act against his nature. As a worthy group of Massachusetts ministers said in attacking the Grimké sisters' efforts toward women's liberation,

We invite your attention to the dangers which at present seem to threaten the FEMALE CHARACTER with widespread and permanent injury ([5] p. 39).

This indicates that Senator Frelinghuysen's case rests ultimately on the high-level moral principle that one should act so as to promote the highest moral character in oneself and in others.

Through the senator's argument itself, we see that the traditional view would classify his activity as morally relevant, and it appears that he has justified his behavior. But what of the moral revolutionary? We need to look at her behavior through the glasses of the traditional moral philosopher. I'd like to take Sarah Grimké as protagonist here and consider some of the moral reasoning and argument she uses in 1837, in her *Letters on the Equality of the Sexes and the Condition of Women.* Like Senator Frelinghuysen's arguments, hers involve claims that were put forward throughout the nineteenth century—for example, we find their echo in Mill's later and better-known paper "The Subjection of Women."

In brief, Grimké argued that what appear to be natural differences between men and women are due to differences in education, training, and expectation. She claimed that "women are educated from childhood to regard themselves as inferior" ([5] p. 44), and that "our powers of mind have been crushed, as far as man could do it, our sense of morality has been impaired by his interpretation of our duties" ([5] p. 42). She argued directly against the interpretation of the Bible used to support the "natural difference" view, saying that Genesis actually shows that God created men and women equal.

There is also an egalitarian principle underlying the arguments in her *Letters,* one which is clearly present in her argument in favor of equal pay for equal work ([5] pp. 45–46). We might make it explicit in Mill's terms:

The principle of the modern movement in morals and politics, is that conduct, and conduct alone, entitles to respect . . . that, above all, merit and not birth, is the only rightful claim to power and authority ([8] p. 177).

Now these remarks seem directly aimed at conservative arguments against the women's movement. Living in the 1970s, most of us would accept them. But that fact is not at all to the point, for the question is whether they constituted arguments which could serve as a justification for Grimké's behavior in 1837, and whether they could serve as a basis for counting her behavior as moral behavior—much less morally *proper* behavior. I shall argue that they could not so serve, that they are at best calls for a new paradigm.

(1) Grimké's claim that nurture, not nature, determines the difference in behavior and ability in men and women is meant to undermine the claim that the Aristotelian theory is data-supported. The form of the argument here is exactly correct: to undermine the empirical support for the Aristotelian theory, the data must be reinterpreted, explained by a different scientific theory. Unfortunately, Grimké was ahead of her time in her scientific as well as her moral views. There *was* no scientific theory to support her interpretation of the data. This point is important, but perhaps difficult to grasp in this case because we now accept a scientific view properly interpreting her hypothesis. But merely putting a scientific hypothesis into *words* does not constitute giving a justification.

If the hypothesis is understood against the background of the conservative paradigm, then "education" and "nature" will be understood as interpreted under that paradigm, and evidence for the hypothesis will be construed as it is construed under that paradigm. What Grimké needs is an alternate theory on nature and education and their effects on human capacity and behavior. Her argument at best *suggests* that a scientific justification for her position can be developed. It is not itself a justification but rather a call for a new scientific paradigm.

One might object here that the Aristotelian sort of theory is subject to a direct test which does not require development of an alternative theory. Grimké herself suggests such a test:

All I ask of our brethren is that they will take their feet from off our necks and permit us to stand upright on that ground which God designed us to occupy. If he has not given us the rights which have, as I conceive, been wrested from us, we shall soon give evidence of our inferiority . . . ([5] p. 38).

Such a "direct test" would no more falsify the Aristotelian theory than it did the more recent Freudian one. Freudian theory postulated a difference in nature

for men and women too, a difference which was strikingly similar to that postulated under the Aristotelian theory. Behavior of women which might falsify
the theory was accommodated by altering the theory slightly, to admit that
some few women had "masculine natures" (and were thus natural anomalies).
But the vast majority of women were supposed to have natural feminine natures.
Aggressiveness and "unwomanly" behavior among these are explained by saying
that they are driven by penis envy into a neurotic emulation of men. Such
emulation was judged to be an illness requiring treatment to bring the woman
to accept her nature. To change the educational process so as to develop these
unnatural characteristics in all women would be, in Freudian eyes as well as the
eyes of the Massachusetts ministers, "to threaten the FEMALE CHARACTER with
widespread and permanent injury" ([5] p. 39).

But of course in asking that "our brethren . . . take their feet from off our
necks," Grimké is not merely suggesting a test for the conservative theory. She
is making a call for the moral revolution.

(2) The claim that merit, not birth, is the only rightful claim to power and
authority is aimed at overthrowing the moral principle that one ought to act
according to his nature as it limits the participation of women in society. However, rather than relying on that principle as it is understood under the conservative moral paradigm, Mill is suggesting a *reinterpretation* of it. For that
principle was understood to mean that birth into a particular social *class* should
not disqualify an adult male. The principle cannot support Mill's position because it presupposes his position on women. Again, we have merely a call to
bring about the revolution, and an example of how a particular moral principle
would be reinterpreted under the new paradigm.

In the case of legal principles, we have a formal structure (the court system)
to take care of interpretation of their meaning. An examination of the changes
in interpretation of the Bill of Rights, for example, shows how paradigm-
dependent our legal and governmental principles are for their interpretation.
My claim here is that an analogous situation exists with regard to scientific and
moral principles, even so-called "trans-societal" principles. It may be less
well noticed only because we lack a formal structure to take care of their
interpretation.

There is, however, one principle which does not seem quite so paradigm-
dependent for its understanding, and that is the hedonistic act utilitarian principle. The principle might be stated roughly in this way: One ought to choose
that act which produces a greater surplus of happiness over unhappiness than
any alternative act. What *makes* people happy before and after the revolution
will be different. But a utilitarian would hope for psychological tests of happiness which are independent of the *moral* paradigm at least.

There are general difficulties in applying this principle, since a comparison
of possible acts and their possible consequences is necessary. This is particularly
difficult in the case of moral revolution, since calculating the consequences of
the revolutionary's acts requires knowing what *would* make people happy after
the revolution as well as calculating their degrees of happiness.

These difficulties are not the major ones. It is more important that there is scarcely a person who would hold the unmodified hedonistic act utilitarian principle. This is because the resultant *quantity* of happiness is at best only one element we're concerned with. Fairness in the distribution of happiness is also important. The methods used to bring about the happiness are important. To be acceptable, this utilitarian principle needs to be "restricted" by other principles, particularly a principle of justice. But other principles, *particularly* the principle of justice, are heavily dependent on the paradigm for their interpretation.

If a revolutionary wishes, he may give some justification to his actions by using the hedonistic act utilitarian principle. If he cannot himself accept that principle unsupplemented—and I am sure that there is scarcely one who will accept it—then there seems to be no way for him to give a justification.

The revolutionary must, then, proceed without proper justification. But this is not all. Most philosophers holding a traditional view don't feel that moral principles merely enter after the fact, merely enter in giving a justification. One doesn't merely act willy-nilly, then fish about for some principle which will justify the act. One assesses the situation morally before acting. But even to assess the situation as moral requires the use of moral categories, thus principles of one sort or another (or so it seems, on the traditional view).

The moral revolutionary cannot do this. If he is to be seen as acting under principles at all, they must be principles interpreted under the new paradigm. Principles as understood under the old paradigm will not properly characterize the moral features of the current situation. But the new paradigm is not yet in existence. So even if the revolutionary cites principles, even if he himself says the words to himself, he has only a limited understanding of those words. Let me support this by a quotation from Paul Feyerabend:

One often takes it for granted that a clear and distinct understanding of new ideas precedes and should precede any formulation and any institutional expression of them . . . [but] we must expect, for example, that the idea of liberty could be made clear only by means of the very same actions which were supposed to create liberty. Creation of a thing, and creation plus full understanding of a correct idea of the thing, are very often parts of one and the same indivisible process and they cannot be separated without bringing the process to a standstill ([3a] p. 24).

The arguments of the moral revolutionary constitute a call for change, not a justification. But even as a call, they are not statements of principles interpreted fully under the new paradigm but a *hint* at a direction in which to go in the creative process.

III

That the value of the world lies in our interpretation . . . ; that previous interpretations have been perspective valuations by virtue of which we can survive in life, i.e., in the will to power for the growth of power . . . ([9e] 616).

Some traditional philosophers will not be surprised that the moral revolutionary cannot justify himself and, if he is seen as acting morally at all, he is seen as being *evil*. A contemporary Hobbesian might grant that revolution is sometimes necessary (though he would see any such revolution as political). But since the only way to judge rightness and wrongness and obligation is under the laws and rules of the existing system, the revolutionary must be a traitor or subversive. It is only after the revolution that he can justify what he has done—if the revolution is a success, that is. Here, as with Nietzsche's morality of custom (*Sitte*), change is immoral (*unsittlich*) ([9b] 18).

But this is unsatisfactory so far as moral theory goes, and it is certainly unsatisfactory if we try to apply moral theory to practice. It allows no adequate explanation of the structure of moral revolution *as moral*. And it sacrifices whatever light may be shed on normal morality, and the traditional view itself by the phenomenon of moral revolution. . . .

Seen in a Nietzschean light, moral revolution contains what is essential to morality in a way that morality in stasis does not. In focusing on morality in stasis, and especially on morality as it concerns justification and principle, the traditional philosopher is "human, all too human." He offers the rationalization that is necessary to the herd, the rationalization which operates *against* creation and change. This will become more evident in Part IV. Here, we might look again at the women's revolution to put traditional ethics in perspective.

I mentioned in Part II that the data that supported Senator Frelinghuysen's conservative view on women were *facts*. Women understood themselves and their lives in terms of the way they were characterized under this view. Grimké saw this when she said that women are "educated from earliest childhood, to regard themselves as inferior creatures . . ." ([5] p. 46).

This picture of women was not one which was imposed from outside by a sexist science. . . . [T]he adequate characterization of the situation is given far better by Nietzsche. . . . For it was Nietzsche's insight that our science does not operate independently of our morality. Science and morality work together not only in giving us a picture of the world but also in creating that world and the human beings in it. I think that this is evident from the discussions in Part II. But those discussions were concerned with principle and argument, and there is more to the matter than that.

Throughout written history, the structure of the family has been closely integrated with the structure of the society, the one supporting the other. Revolutionaries and conservatives in the nineteenth century used two radically different analogies in describing the family and the relationship of husband and wife within it. Revolutionaries see the family structure on analogy with a tyrant-slave or master-servant relationship ("The Subjection of Women"). Conservatives see it roughly on analogy with a parent-child relationship. The husband protects the weaker wife. There is a biological basis for the parent-child relationship, and they see one in the relationship of husband to wife.

The family was seen by conservatives as a unit made up of individuals with specialized functions—the social closely following the biological. Each individual must fulfill his or her function, for that is necessary for the survival of the unit. And survival of the family unit is necessary for the survival of the society. Conservatives argued that the whole theory of government and society presupposed this view of the family, in terms of this division of functions.

Women were different from men in their capacities and personalities because it was *necessary* for them to be different from men. The survival of the family and state depended on it. This offers a striking confirmation of Nietzsche's claim that what is necessary for our survival we see as truth. Of course, to take something as truth doesn't make it true. But Nietzsche remarks on this,

No matter how strongly a thing may be believed, strength of belief is no criterion of truth. But what is truth? Perhaps a kind of belief that has become a condition of life? ([9e] 532).

Without departing from Nietzsche, we might say that what is necessary for our survival *becomes truth.* Theory follows fact, and human facts of this sort follow need. The traditional view has stood the matter on its head.

The *way* in which our principles are embedded in fact makes it clear that a moral revolution cannot be one based on principle, with its major struggle one to make act conform with principle. That is at best the task of moral reform. The women's revolution had to proceed by making the facts different. The revolutionaries had to proceed by bringing a new paradigm into being. Principles followed. They followed as they always have, as a rationalization of what is and what is necessary. Traditionalists overlook this because they focus on "normal morality," morality in stasis. Of that, Nietzsche says, "Whatever lives long is gradually so saturated with reason that its irrational origins become improbable" ([9b] 1). But what seems improbable may nonetheless not be.

A moral, social, and scientific paradigm (the paradigm of a conceptual scheme) is not merely something through which we see the world. It is something which shapes the facts of the human world. The traditional view deals with only a certain sort of *post hoc* rationalization, taking this rationalization as what is essential to morality. Accepting it as the whole story, we cannot understand the moral revolutionary and we cannot understand normal morality either.

To understand these things, and to understand how morality might be liberated from necessity, we need to look at *other* views on morality, or rather, other *moralities* alternative to those picked out by the traditional view. In Nietzsche's writings, we find alternatives.

IV

The beautiful exists just as little as does *the* good, or *the* true. In every case it is a question of the conditions of preservation of a certain type of man ... ([9e] 804).

Nietzsche's interest in psychological and developmental aspects of morality, his emphasis on transvaluation of values and on self-overcoming make him one of the few philosophers who have put "normal morality" in perspective. But in understanding this, it's important to put aside the dogmatism of the traditional view. Otherwise, the transvaluation is seen merely as the replacement of one set of values by another (all encapsulated in principles), and self-overcoming is seen merely as self-discipline of the usual moral sort.

If we look at a (somewhat) Nietzschean categorization of different varieties of morality, I think it's possible to understand the varieties of moral revolution and of normal morality more fully. In doing this, I'd like to consider "slave morality," "morality of the person of conscience," and what I shall call "noble morality" as varieties. Using these notions to pick out varieties of morality requires leaving aside negative or positive connotations of "slave" or "noble."

What might slave morality be? A slave's life, *qua* slave, is full of duties. Freedom is essential to any moral agent, but the slave's freedom consists in his freedom to obey or disobey. Because there are sanctions which follow upon disobedience of a rule, the slave must be able to *justify* what he does. Sometimes the sanctions are external. If the slave cannot give an acceptable justification, he may be punished by the law courts (a political sanction) or by the ill opinion and acts of his compatriots (a moral sanction). But sometimes the sanctions are internalized, and conscience and feelings of guilt are the instruments ensuring obedience. In fact, the primary value in slave morality is obedience, and it's axiomatic that the moral person is the obedient person: obedient to the moral rule.

It should be evident that what Nietzsche calls "slave morality" comes very close, as a *type* of morality, to what I've been calling "morality on the traditional view."

Nietzsche felt that a fairly widespread sort of morality which grew out of the Christian tradition was a slave morality—a morality of the weak, with their fear of strength and their resentment. Women constituted slaves *par excellence* in this sense, and that fact may explain some of Nietzsche's diatribes against them. It was *this* sort of slave morality which the women's rights workers had to root out of themselves. But for our typology, it is better to abstract from these characteristics and see slave morality as one involving principle, rule, and justification, with acts taken as the basic moral units and with obedience to rule the cardinal virtue.

What I shall call "noble morality" differs essentially from slave morality, not in being a morality of the strong, but in being a different *type* of morality. It happens that strength of one sort or another is required in this morality, and that the weak find protection under slave morality, and this is morally and psychologically important. But more important to us is the difference in their structures.

Within noble morality, there is no concern with rules, obedience, and justification. The person, not the act, is the basic moral unit. Nietzsche says, "It is obvious that moral designations were everywhere applied to *human beings* and only later, derivatively, to actions" ([9a] 260). But this shouldn't be taken to mean that in noble morality it is the *person* who is judged, justified, etc., instead of the act. Rather, "The noble type of man experiences *itself* as determining values; it does not need approval" ([9a] 260). The noble person apprehends himself as worthy, and he *confers* values in his acts.

I have called this sort of morality "noble morality" rather than "master morality" because, in Nietzsche's discussions, master morality is sometimes not clearly distinct from what I shall call "the morality of the person of conscience." It is not clearly a type which Nietzsche himself set out, although some readers of Nietzsche seem to interpret his master morality in this way.

In discussing the noble distinction "good–bad" (which contrasts with the slave distinction "good–evil"), Nietzsche explicitly mentions the very ancient Greeks (9[c] 15). These "noble ones" do not have a noble morality in my sense because they have not attained the necessary, partial "self-overcoming" (see their behavior in [9c] I 11). But we might take a later development of this morality, as exemplified by some ideals in classical Greece, to represent noble morality.

Here, the noble person sees himself as worthy (see Aristotle's "great-souled person"). He confers value in his acts. He has overcome himself in the sense Kaufmann stresses: He has triumphed over his impulses ([6] chs. 7, 8). He is disciplined, so much so that his triumph and discipline flow from his nature. He is not a slave to a moral code. In fact, on a somewhat Aristotelian analysis, his valuations are the *foundation* of values for the society. A just act is one which the just person would do, and to act justly is to do such an act as the just person would do it.

There is a third type of morality, the morality of the person of conscience (following Nietzsche, [9c] II 2). This individual is "master of a free will." He is free *not* to obey or disobey, as the slave is free. Like the noble person, he is free from the slavery to the moral codes and opinions of his society. But in addition, he is free to create.

The person of conscience creates values, but only by creating himself. Here, I think self-overcoming has a different import from that which it has under noble morality. Noble morality involves only a partial self-overcoming. Self-overcoming in the person of conscience requires a self-disciplining, it is true. But it cannot properly be described as reason overcoming impulse, as Kaufmann describes self-overcoming ([6] p. 235). Rather, an overcoming of the *entire* old self is involved, of the old ways of perceiving oneself and the world, of the old ways of *being*. It is an overcoming which is *necessarily* a creation of oneself. It involves, in part, a phenomenon analogous to what is currently called "consciousness raising." One overcomes the old self which is structured within the old paradigm and becomes "the sovereign individual, like only to himself" ([9c] II 2). In this self-overcoming, one creates himself anew, and creates values.

Given these unfortunately sketchy remarks on types of morality, we might use them to look at moral phenomena.

First, we might see (as Nietzsche did) that different societies emphasize one sort of morality over others. Greek society emphasized noble morality. Nineteenth-century Anglo-American society emphasized slave or rule morality. It is only a myopia induced by the traditional view on morality that would bring us to see these differences as a mere difference in *moral code*.

Second, we might use the typology to investigate different sorts of moral phenomena which occur within a single society. Nietzsche himself suggests that master and slave morality "at times . . . occur directly alongside each other—even in the same human being, within a *single* soul" ([9a] 260). Our own society seems to be a mixed one.

Finally, we might use the typology to look at moral change. The first thing we would learn is that a moral revolution need not result in replacement of one set of principles by another, or in the reinterpretation of principles held under the old paradigm. It might result in a *morality of a new type*. This parallels the way a political revolution might result not in the replacement of one form of government by another, but in an anarchistic society.

The second thing we would learn is that the moral revolutionary *is* behaving morally, but under a different type of morality from that which the traditional view recognizes. I mentioned in Part II that the women's revolution workers had had to *change the way they were as women* in bringing about their revolution. I don't want to claim that all—or even that any—of these women became "persons of conscience." But it is *that* sort of morality which best captures the moral behavior of each of them, as revolutionaries.

Each of the serious workers in this revolution had to overcome herself in the sense of morality disciplining herself. But she also had to create herself as an individual like only to herself. That she later met others like her is irrelevant. The southern aristocrat who was Sarah Grimké, the overworked farm girl who was Lucy Stone, the slave mother of thirteen who became Sojourner Truth, all had to be overcome. Each woman had to create herself anew, in a process of self-overcoming which took no models (there were none to take) and which continued as long as she was a revolutionary. Today we have example after example of black young people who have gone through this self-overcoming, and many others of us have gone through it in a more modest way.

Nietzsche's morality of the person of conscience captures the morality of individual revolutionaries far better than the traditional view does. It offers a beginning for understanding how moral revolutions take place. As we saw in Part III, it is necessary to change the world, to create new facts and a new paradigm, in bringing about the revolution. The process of self-overcoming explains some of this, and it indicates that the creation of values begins with the creation of the individual revolutionary as a new sort of human being.

But this is individual morality. It is not the aim of the moral revolutionary to become the "sovereign individual" when this brings with it the *isolation* of uniqueness. And given Nietzsche's attitude toward revolutions of the people, we would not expect his favorite moral type to fit revolutionaries too well.

The revolutionary cannot create himself in isolation as a sovereign individual. Rather, he must begin to create himself as the "first of his kind." This creation, this self-overcoming, continues throughout the revolutionary process. But it is part of his task as a revolutionary of the people to help *them* to overcome themselves, to help each create himself as a new kind of individual. In the course of this process, the new paradigm comes into being—that is, the new values are created.

V

... art is *worth more* than truth ([9e] 853).

Given all of this, we can begin to see the difference between the moral revolutionary and the moral reformer. Both activities involve a struggle against the conservative forces in power. But the moral revolutionary is like the scientific revolutionary in struggling to overthrow some part of the present structure. In doing this, he must overcome himself in the process of the revolution. He must work to help his people overcome themselves. And this is a necessary process to the end that a new kind of human being may be brought into being, and thus a new paradigm and new values as well. For a moral revolution essentially involves creation of a new human being. It was one of Nietzsche's insights that moralities determine *kinds* of persons.

The reformer, on the other hand, is doing "normal morality." Like the scientist doing normal science, he operates within the present paradigm. He finds contradictions in held principles, or contradictions between principle and application of principle; he acts to eliminate suffering or injustice (as justice is understood under the prevailing paradigm). He makes those demands which the minority group he represents wants *now*. And this is necessary so that the principles of his paradigm are consistent and so that practice follows principle. Reform essentially involves the *preservation* of values.

The behavior of the moral reformer *seems* to be explicable under the traditional view on morality—after all, he is doing "normal morality." But because the behavior of the moral revolutionary is not explicable under the traditional view, all moral change is seen as reform. This may explain why so many contemporary Anglo-American philosophers find virtue in the reformer but not in the revolutionary.

Of course, the moral revolutionary may sometimes *feel* he wants to relieve suffering and injustice. But it is creation, and not the relief of suffering and injustice, which must serve as his foundation. And there are reasons for this.

Workers in the women's revolution might have *felt* that injustice was being done, but according to the notion of justice within their paradigm, it was not. They may have *felt* that women were suffering under a sexist society, but the vast majority of nineteenth-century women *did not feel* they were suffering from sexism. It's difficult to make a case that one is struggling to relieve suffering when the "sufferers" themselves deny the suffering.

It is of the reformer that we might say,

Either his reforms will be acceptable to the people, or they will not; if they are acceptable the people have in principle the power to implement them, and it will be a question not of overthrowing the system but of making it function; if they are not, he has no business to impose them ([1] p. 98).

The revolutionary will not (generally, cannot) impose his demands. But he ceases to be a revolutionary if he makes only those demands which are acceptable to the people at the time. *That* is not a way to creation of values, to creation of a new human being.

I have spoken of "normal morality" and "moral revolution." But the condition which is normal to human life is not a state of stasis but a state of revolution. Stasis is less painful, more easy to rationalize, more *sure*, more safe. It encourages us to believe we can rest, because we have the truth. But if we think in terms of Nietzschean epistemology, . . . we see that in science and morality, it is a continued state of revolution which expresses our humanity best. Nietzsche says, in *Zarathustra,*

And life itself confided this secret to me: "Behold," it said, "I am *that which must always overcome itself*. Indeed, you call it a will to procreate or a drive to an end, to something higher, farther, more manifold; but all this is one. . . . whatever I create and however much I love it—soon I must oppose it and my love . . ." ([9d] II 12).

BIBLIOGRAPHY

1. Peter Caws, "Reform and Revolution," in *Philosophy and Political Action,* V. Held, K. Nielsen, and C. Parsons, eds., Oxford University Press (1972).
2. Arthur C. Danto, *Nietzsche as Philosopher,* The Macmillan Co., New York (1965).
3. Paul Feyerabend
   a. "Against Method," in *Minnesota Studies in the Philosophy of Science,* Vol. IV. M. Radner and S. Winokur, eds., University of Minnesota Press, Minneapolis (1970).
   b. "Explanation, Reduction, and Empiricism," in *Minnesota Studies in the Philosophy of Science,* Vol. III. H. Feigl and G. Maxwell, eds., University of Minnesota Press, Minneapolis (1962).
4. Eleanor Flexner, *Century of Struggle,* Atheneum, New York (1971).
5. Sarah M. Grimké, *Letters on the Equality of the Sexes and the Condition of Women.* Selections quoted are in (12).
6. Walter Kaufmann, *Nietzsche: Philosopher, Psychologist, Antichrist,* Vintage Books, New York (1968).
7. Thomas S. Kuhn, *The Structure of Scientific Revolutions,* University of Chicago Press, Chicago (1970).
8. John Stuart Mill, "The Subjection of Women," in (12).
9. Friedrich Nietzsche
   a. *Beyond Good and Evil,* W. Kaufmann, transl., Vintage Books, New York (1966).
   b. *The Dawn,* selections appearing in (9c), pp. 186–90.
   c. *On the Genealogy of Morals,* W. Kaufmann, ed., Vintage Books, New York (1969).
   d. *Thus Spoke Zarathustra,* in *The Portable Nietzsche,* W. Kaufmann, ed., The Viking Press, New York (1968).
   e. *The Will to Power,* W. Kaufmann, ed., Vintage Books, New York (1968).
10. Kathryn Pyne Parsons
    a. "On Criteria of Meaning Change," *Brit. J. Phil. Sci. 22* (1971).
    b. "Law Cluster Concepts."
    c. "Empiricism Without the Dogmas."
11. Israel Scheffler, *Science and Subjectivity,* Bobbs-Merrill Company, Indianapolis (1967).
12. Miriam Schneir, ed., *Feminism: The Essential Historical Writings,* Vintage Books, New York (1972).
13. Simmie Freeman Turner, "Nietzsche on Truth," unpublished essay.
14. Michael Walzer, "The Obligations of Oppressed Minorities," *Commentary,* May 1970.

part six: CRIES FOR REFORM

. . . women, especially . . . women without instruction . . . alone can fully understand the preponderance that ought to be given to the habitual cultivation of the heart . . .
—Auguste Comte

. . . few women have yet managed to extricate themselves from the Compassion Trap—that pervasive social philosophy that believes that woman's primary social function is to provide tenderness and compassion.
—Margaret Adams

. . . every restraint on the freedom of conduct of any . . . human fellow creatures dries up pro tanto the principal fountain of human happiness, and leaves the species less rich, to an inappreciable degree, in all that makes life valuable to the individual human being.
—John Stuart Mill

. . . to the women of the twentieth century . . . The Subjection of Women *continues to serve as a resounding affirmation of their human right to full equality and a sophisticated analysis of the obstacles that bar their way to it.*
—Alice S. Rossi

. . . the necessity and the manner of accomplishing the real social equality of {man and woman} will appear only . . . when both of them will enjoy complete legal equality.
—Friedrich Engels

. . . it is crucial to the organization of women for their liberation to understand that it is the monogamous family as an economic unit, at the heart of class society, that is basic to their subjugation.
—Eleanor Burke Leacock

It is plain that no man can call himself truly a democrat if he is in favour of excluding half the nation from all participation in public affairs.
    —Bertrand Russell

{Woman} can give suffrage or the ballot no new quality, nor can she receive anything from it that will enhance her own quality. Her development, her freedom, her independence, must come from and through herself.
    —Emma Goldman

The nineteenth century was an age of reform: economic, political, intellectual, religious. Some of the century's would-be reformers—notably Auguste Comte, John Stuart Mill, Friedrich Engels, and Bertrand Russell—included women in their proposals. Comte's proposals, liberal as they may first appear, in the last analysis involved little change: men were to engage in virtually all the physical and intellectual activity society might provide, leaving women free to devote themselves entirely to their "holy function," motherhood. He celebrated women for their altruism—a trait that leads, Margaret Adams is convinced, not to the salvation of society, as Comte suggested, but to the exploitation of those who possess it.

John Stuart Mill proposed real change, familial as well as societal. He urged not only that women be given the vote and enabled to enter the job market but that they be treated as equals at home as well. And while the contemporary women's movement may have broader goals, Alice Rossi finds them much closer to Mill's ideals than to goals of many social movements of his own day.

Friedrich Engels saw freedom for women as but one of the many changes that would result from the abolition of private property, and with it monogamous marriage—a view shared by Eleanor Burke Leacock.

While Bertrand Russell wished not only to secure the vote for women but to effect their sexual emancipation as well, Emma Goldman confined her efforts to securing the latter goal. An anarchist, she believed that the franchise would not emancipate women in the least. Their freedom, she was convinced, must come from within.

ᴁᴂ16 *Auguste Comte*

Isidore Auguste Marie François Xavier Comte, eldest son of a French revenue clerk, was born in Montpellier in 1798. His mother, twelve years older than her husband, was overpossessive; his father enjoyed ill health; his sister showed symptoms of hysteria. Perhaps by way of reaction against this Catholic and royalist family, Auguste seems to have become an atheist and a republican by the time he was in his teens, and he was expelled from the École Polytechnique in Paris for his cockiness. Consequently Comte was forced to educate himself if he was to be educated at all. He fell under the influence of Claude-Henri de Rouvroy, Comte de Saint-Simon, whom he served as secretary for seven years, until their relationship ended in a stormy rupture.

Subsequently Comte attempted to support himself with tutoring and journalism. He entered into a liaison with Caroline Massin, which eventually, at the insistence of his mother, was formalized into marriage. The marriage was unhappy. Comte suffered an acute nervous breakdown, which in 1827 led him to attempt suicide. His wife, after nursing him back to health, sought to add to the family income by prostitution—a sacrifice Comte declined to accept. The union was finally dissolved in 1842.

In 1844 Comte met and became deeply enamored of Clothilde de Vaux, the author of a novelette and a few poems and the wife of an embezzler who had fled Paris to escape arrest. Mme de Vaux returned Comte's love with a friendship that lasted until she died of consumption in 1846. Subsequently Comte communed with her spirit in morning and evening "prayers" and made weekly visits to her tomb. It was apparently her memory that inspired Comte to cap his positivism with a "religion of humanity," a sort of secularized version of Catholicism that replaced service to God with service to humanity and substituted for the Virgin Mary the woman who had meant most in the life of the worshiper—in Comte's case, of course, Clothilde de Vaux. Comte died in 1857.

During the days of the French Revolution, woman had enjoyed almost unprecedented liberty. The Napoleonic Code, however, shackled her anew. Again she became totally dependent on her husband, who chose her residence, controlled her property, and had authority over her children. Were she caught in adultery, he could consign her to solitary imprisonment, divorce her, even kill her with impunity. Only if he brought a concubine into her home could she seek redress.

Partly by way of protest against the Napoleonic Code, many French reformers envisioned ideal societies in which such inequities did not exist. Chief among these utopians was Saint-Simon, who conceived a Platonic regime in which the slavery of women was abolished. Comte, however, while insisting on the regenerating powers of women, envisioned a society in which their situation was little if at all improved. Convinced that in women the affective portion of the brain prevailed over the active and the speculative, and that within the affective sector altruistic instincts dominated egoistic ones, Comte assigned to women a "holy function" in society—motherhood. And while he conceded that they were entitled to education, he would have had them educated specifically to fill their peculiar role. Furthermore, adopting William Harvey's theory that the male serves merely as a stimulus in the process of conception, Comte foresaw a time when that stimulus might be dispensed with. And so the virgin mother becomes an actual goal of the society he envisioned, not an impossible ideal.

Comte was dedicated to a single absolute principle: that there is no absolute principle. He interpreted the universe relativistically. The progress of human thought he explained historically, according to his law of the three stages. The first stage in human philosophical development, Comte proposed, was theological. The universe was viewed empathically; that is, human feelings were ascribed to things, which were then believed to be moved supernaturally. The first phase of this stage, fetishism, soon gave way to polytheism and ultimately to monotheism. The theological stage was then replaced by a metaphysical stage, in which the belief in God was rejected but the search for absolutes in other forms—causes, purposes, essences—was retained. The final, positivistic stage was dedicated to fact and characterized by precision, certitude, coherence, and a relativistic and utilitarian orientation.

As society passed from stage to stage, various sciences were developed: first mathematics, then astronomy, physics, chemistry, biology, and finally sociology, the science that Comte himself formulated. The development of the sciences reflected a logical as well as a historical order, for they were evolved in order of increasing complexity and decreasing universality, exactness, and dependence on deduction as a scientific method.

Eventually Comte added a seventh science, morality (or social psychology), which he regarded as the culmination of his philosophy. Here he set forth his views on woman. Of the three main parts of the human brain postulated in Comte's theory—the affective, the active, and the speculative—only the affective portion of woman's brain is superior to that of man. And of the affective part of the brain, the altruistic component is superior in woman, while in man the egoistic component is dominant. Altruism Comte deemed necessary for the salvation of society. Only through the charms of women and the numbers of the proletariat was there any hope of abating the selfishness of the leaders of capitalistic society.

From *The Catechism of Positive Religion*

PREFACE

.   .   .

The adoption of this method for the new religious instruction shows that it addresses by preference the sex in which affection predominates. This preference, quite in accordance with the true spirit of the final regime, is in an especial manner adapted to the last transition, in which every influence recognised by the normal state must always work with greater strength, if with less regularity. The better proletaries are likely, it seems to me, ere long to welcome heartily this short but decisive work; yet it is more suited to women, especially to women without instruction. They alone can fully understand the preponderance that ought to be given to the habitual cultivation of the heart, so borne down by the coarse activity, both in speculation and action, which prevails in the modern Western world. It is solely in this sanctuary that, at the present day, we can find the noble submissiveness of spirit required for a systematic regeneration. During the last four years, the reason of the people has suffered profoundly from the unfortunate exercise of universal suffrage; it had previously been preserved from the constitutional sophisms and Parliamentary intrigues of which the rich and the literary class had had the monopoly. Developing a blind pride, our proletaries have thought themselves able to settle the highest social questions without submitting to any serious study. Though this deterioration is much less in the southern populations of the West, the resistance of Catholicism sheltering them against the metaphysics of Protestantism or Deism, the reading of negative books is beginning to spread it too much even there. I see none anywhere but women, who, as a consequence of their wholesome exclusion from political action, can give me the support required to secure the free ascendency of the principles which shall in the end qualify the proletaries to place their confidence aright on points of theory as well as on points of practice.

Besides, the deep-seated mental anarchy justifies this special appeal of the Positive religion to the affective sex, as it renders more necessary than ever the predominance of feeling, the sole existing preservative of Western society from a complete and irreparable dissolution. Since the close of the Middle Ages, the influence of women has been the sole though unacknowledged check on the moral evils attaching to the mental alienation towards which the West more and more tended, especially its centre—France. This chronic unreason being henceforth at its height, since there is no social maxim but succumbs to a corrosive discussion, feeling alone maintains order in the West. But feeling even is seriously weakened already by the reaction of the sophisms of the intellect, these being always favourable to the personal instincts which are, moreover, the more energetic.

Of the three sympathetic instincts which belong to our true cerebral constitution, the first and last are much weakened, and the intermediate nearly extinct, in the majority of the men who take an active part at present in Western agitation. Penetrate to the interior of existing families, and you find how little strength attachment has left, in the intercourse which should foster it most. As for the general kindness, so much vaunted at present, it is more an indication of hatred of the rich than of love of the poor. For modern philanthropy too often expresses its pretended benevolence in forms appropriate to anger or envy. But the social instinct of most constant use, as affording the only immediate basis of all true discipline of man, has suffered even more than the two others. The deterioration in this respect, most traceable in the rich and educated, spreads even among proletaries, unless a wise indifference divert them from the political movement.

Still, veneration can continue to exist in the midst of the wildest revolutionary aberrations; it is indeed their best natural corrective. I learnt this formerly by personal experience during the profoundly negative phase which necessarily preceded my systematic development. At that time enthusiasm alone preserved me from a sophistical demoralisation, though it laid me peculiarly open for a time to the seductions of a shallow and depraved juggler. Veneration, at the present day, is the decisive mark which distinguishes the revolutionists susceptible of a real regeneration, however behind they may be in point of intelligence, especially among the Communists who are without instruction.

But, though in the immense majority of those who are negative we may still discern this valuable symptom, in the majority of their chiefs it is certainly not found, the existing anarchy giving everywhere a temporary predominance to bad natures. These men, absolutely insusceptible of discipline, despite their small number wield a vast influence, which infects with the ferment of subversive ideas the heads of all who are without firmly-rooted convictions. There is no general remedy at present for this plague of the West except the contempt of the people or the severity of the governments. But the doctrine which alone will secure the regular action of these two safeguards can at the outset find no commanding support but in the feeling of women, soon to be aided by the reason of the proletariate.

Without the due intervention of women, the discipline of Positivism would not succeed in driving back to the last ranks these pretended thinkers who speak with decision on sociological questions though ignorant of arithmetic. For the people, still sharing in many respects their worst faults, is incapable as yet of supporting the new priesthood against these dangerous talkers. At least, I can, for the moment, hope for no collective assistance except from the proletaries who, standing aloof hitherto from our political discussions, are not the less instinctively attached, as women are, to the social aim of the great revolution. These two classes form the milieu prepared for this Catechism.

Over and above the general reasons which should in this place direct my attention chiefly to women, I was long ago led to look principally to them for the triumphant advent of the solution of the Western problem indicated by the whole Past.

In the first place, it would be absurd to propose to end without them the most thorough of all human revolutions, whilst in all previous revolutions they took a very large share. Were their instinctive repugnance to the modern movement really invincible, that would be enough to ensure its failure. It is the true source of the strange and fatal anomaly which forces retrograde chiefs on progressive populations, as though idiocy and hypocrisy were to supply the official securities for Western order. Till Positive religion has sufficiently overcome this resistance of women it will not be able, in its treatment of the leading partisans of the different belated systems, to give free scope to its decided and just reprobation of their mental and moral inferiority.

Those who at the present day deny the innate existence of the disinterested affections lay themselves open to the just suspicion of rejecting on this point the demonstrations of modern science only because of the radical imperfection of their own feelings. As they pursue no good, however trifling, but from the lure of an infinite reward or from the fear of an eternal punishment, they prove their heart to be as degraded as their intellect evidently is, considering the absurdity of their beliefs. And yet, by the tacit adhesion of women, the direction of the West is still intrusted to those whom such characteristics will exclude, and wisely, from all the higher functions, when Positivism shall have duly systematised the reason of mankind.

But the Religion of Humanity will soon strip the retrograde party of this august support, which it retains solely from a just horror of anarchy. For in spite of adverse conceptions resting on previous associations, women are well disposed to value aright the only doctrine which in the present day can thoroughly combine order with progress. Above all, they will recognise the fact that this final synthesis, while it comprehends every phase of our existence, better secures the supremacy of feeling than did the provisional synthesis which sacrificed to it the intellect and the activity. Our philosophy comes into perfect agreement with the tendencies of women by ending the encyclopedic scale with morals, which, as science and as art, are necessarily the most important and the most difficult study, condensing and controlling all the others. Giving at length full scope to the feelings of chivalry, which in earlier times were compressed by the conflicts with theology, Positive worship makes the affective sex the moral providence of our species. In that worship every true woman supplies us in daily life with the best representative of the true Great Being. The Positive regime constituting, on systematic principles, the family as the normal basis of society, ensures the due prevalence therein of the influence of women, at length become the supreme private authority on the common education. On all these grounds, the true religion will be fully appreciated by women, as soon as they grasp adequately its leading characteristics. Even those who at first should regret the loss of chimerical hopes will not be slow to feel the moral superiority of our subjective immortality, so thoroughly altruistic in its nature, as compared with the old objective immortality, which could never be other than radically egoistic. The law of eternal widowhood, the distinctive feature of Positivist marriage, would be enough to form, on this point, a decisive contrast.

The better to incorporate women into the Western revolution, its last phase must be looked on as having naturally for them a deep and special interest, in direct relation with their own peculiar destiny.

The four great classes which substantially constitute modern society, were destined to experience in succession the radical convulsion required at first for its final regeneration. It began, in the last century, with the intellectual element, which rose in successful insurrection against the whole system based on theology and war. The political explosion which was its natural result took its rise soon after in the middle classes, who had long been growing more eager to take the place of the nobility. But the resistance of the nobility throughout Europe could only be overcome by calling in the French proletariate to the aid of its new temporal chiefs. Thus introduced into the great political struggle, the proletariate of the West put forward irresistible claims to its just incorporation into the modern order, as soon as peace allowed it to make its own wishes sufficiently clear. Still this revolutionary chain does not yet include the most fundamental element of the true human order. The revolution in regard to women must now complete the revolution which concerned the proletariate, just as this last consolidated the revolution of the middle classes, sprung originally from the philosophical revolution.

Then only will the modern convulsion have really prepared all the essential bases of the final regeneration. Till it takes in women, it can only result in prolonging our lamentable oscillations between retrogression and anarchy. But this final complement is a more natural outcome of the whole of the antecedent phases than any one of them is of its predecessor. It connects most closely with the popular phase, as the social incorporation of the proletariate is evidently bound up with and dependent on, the due enfranchisement of women from all labour away from home. Without this universal emancipation, the indispensable complement of the abolition of serfage, the proletary family cannot be in a true sense constituted, since in it women remain habitually exposed to the horrible alternative of want or prostitution.

The best practical summary of the whole modern programme will soon be this indisputable principle—*Man ought to maintain woman*, in order that she may be able to discharge properly her holy function. This Catechism will, I hope, make sensible the intimate connection of such a condition with the whole of the great renovation, not merely moral, but also mental, and even material. Influenced by the holy reaction of this revolution in the position of women, the revolution of the proletariate will by itself clear itself of the subversive tendencies which as yet neutralise it. Woman's object being everywhere to secure the legitimate supremacy of moral force, she visits with especial reprobation all collective violence: she is less tolerant of the yoke of numbers than of that of wealth. But her latent social influence will soon introduce into the Western revolution, under its two other aspects, modifications less directly traceable to it, but not less valuable. It will facilitate the advent to political power of the industrial patriciate and of the Positive priesthood, by leading both to dissociate themselves once and for all from the heterogeneous and ephemeral classes which directed the transition in its negative phase. So completed, and so purified, the revolution of the West will proceed firmly and systematically towards its peaceful termination, under the general direction of the true servants of Humanity. Their organic and progressive guidance will completely set aside the retrograde and anarchical parties, all persistence in the theological or metaphysical state being treated as a weakness of brain incapacitating for government.

Such are the essential conditions which represent the composition of this Catechism as fully adapted to its most important office, in the present or for the future. When the Positive religion shall have gained sufficient acceptance, it will be the best summary for constant use. For the present it must serve, as a general view, to prepare the way for its free acceptance, by a successful propagation, for which hitherto there was no systematic guidance available.

Taken as a whole, this episodic construction expresses, even by its form and conduct, all the great intellectual and moral attributes of the new faith. There will be felt in it throughout a worthy subordination of the reason of man to the feeling of woman, in order that the heart may bring all the powers of the intellect to the most difficult and important teaching. Its ultimate reaction should then secure respect for, and even the extension to others of, my own private worship of the incomparable angel from whom I derive at once the chief inspirations and their best exposition. Such services will soon render my sainted interlocutress dear to all truly regenerated spirits. Henceforward inseparable from mine, her glorification will constitute my most precious reward. Irrevocably incorporated into the true Supreme Being, her tender image supplies me, in the eyes of all, with its best impersonation. In each of my three daily prayers, the adoration of the two condenses all my wishes for inward perfection in the admirable form in which the sublimest of Mystics foreshadowed in his own way the moral motto of Positivism— (*Live for others*) :—

May I love Thee more than myself, nor love myself save for Thee.

> *Amem te plus quam me, nec me nisi propter te!*
> —*Imitatio Christ*, iii. 5, 82, 83—(ed. Hirsche.)

✥ *Margaret Adams*

Margaret Adams has attained eminence in the field of social work primarily as author of books on mental retardation and subnormality. More recently, however, she has turned her attention to another area with such publications as Single Blessedness: Observations on the Single Status in Married Society *and the following essay, which appeared in* Woman in Sexist Society, *edited by Vivian Gornick and Barbara K. Moran. Far from finding in women's altruism a remedy for social evils, Adams regards their compassion as a snare in which they are entrapped and thereby prevented from making any meaningful contribution to society. They are encouraged to develop their sympathetic instincts, she asserts, to the extent that other facets of the psyche atrophy, and the apparent good that they do in philanthropic professions is merely illusory.*

The Compassion Trap

Despite growing acceptance of the women's-liberation philosophy, few women have yet managed to extricate themselves from the Compassion Trap— that pervasive social philosophy that believes that woman's primary social function is to provide tenderness and compassion.

Through the exercise of these traits, the belief runs, women have set themselves up as the exclusive model for protecting and nurturing others. Fundamental to this model is the synthesizing of fragmented elements into a viable whole—a basic ingredient of any society's survival and one that informs the activities of every woman, whether in one-to-one relationships, or in keeping the family united, or in maintaining a home that eases the day-to-day living of those it shelters.

This arbitrary definition of woman's prime function has encouraged hypertrophy in a circumscribed part of the feminine psyche, while other qualities have yielded to gradual but persistent attrition. This manipulation of women's psychological resources is exploitation as blatant as the economic version that keeps them out of higher-salaried jobs and pays them less than men at all levels. Furthermore, it has much in common with the more gross exploitative view of women as purely sexual objects.

The Compassion Trap, with its underpinning philosophy and social systems, subverts and distorts both the individual identities and the social roles of women. This anachronistic perception of their innate characteristics and social capacities leads to a great deal of confused thinking and frustrated and ineffectual activity. The resultant misplacement of vital energies has equally negative effects upon women, who are caught in these self-defeating trivialities, and upon society, which is deprived of the many significant contributions women might make.

The framework within which this model has developed and flourished is the family, a social organism that originated from the biological imperative to assure the successful reproduction of the species and the survival of the offspring into independent maturity. This domestic paradigm, the primary device for keeping women in both practical and emotional bondage, also has a potent influence on women's activities outside the home. The single woman and the married woman who have made a partial escape into a professional role frequently find themselves in the same bind that the housewife and mother are in, confronting similar demands and reacting with similar responses.

Educated women tend to cluster in the so-called helping professions. Although it is commonly said that this work is most appropriate for, or congenial to, women's nature, the more significant and prosaic explanation is that only these professions have been open to women in any large numbers until very recent times. The most familiar of the women-dominated professions are secretarial work, nursing, teaching, social work, psychology, and occupational, physical and speech therapy. Their position in the hierarchy of social values, the small degree of direct executive power they carry compared with that wielded by professions that have more prestige and the functions they involve all help to explain why they have been ceded graciously to women and informally defined as the legitimate province of women.

The emergence of the helping professions on a significant scale from the middle of the 19th century was the *psychosocial* counterpart of the general *economic* trend that shifted industrial activity out of the small personal setting of individual homes into larger impersonal centers, usually factories. This shift made it easier to institute the division of labor that was a prerequisite for extracting maximum profit from industrial enterprise. It provided an opening for technological specialization and the eventual breakdown of complex productive processes into numberless minute, repetitive activities.

In the same way, the proliferation of the helping professions into a complex array of welfare services took many of the more highly specialized aspects of the nurturing and protective functions out of the home. This development was necessary partly to keep pace with the social problems that were an inevitable by-product of technological specialization in industry. In addition, when one or both parents were out of the home for a substantial part of the day, they had to delegate their acculturating functions. Thus the synthesizing role traditionally discharged by women in the home was translated to a wider sphere and spread its influence through a broader range of activities. Instead of (or in addition to) keeping the family intact and maximally functional, women became involved in housekeeping tasks on behalf of society at large and assumed responsibility for keeping its operation viable.

In discharging this mandate, working women were subject to demands and standards of responsibility almost identical to those experienced in the home. Both family and professional commitments incorporate the insidious notion that the needs of others should be woman's major, if not exclusive, concern. Implicit in the role that derives from this notion is the virtue of subordinating individual needs to the welfare of others and the personal value and supposed reward of vicarious satisfaction from this exercise. This *indirect* expression of talents and skills and these secondhand rewards are probably the chief features that distinguish women from men in their professional lives. Obviously, woman's shift away from domesticity did not involve a psychological emancipation from the pervasive concept of protection and nurturing. Even worse, women have seen their supposed social strengths gradually turned to their disadvantage, blunt their protest, and bar their escape from the confining role. They have been restrained from taking action on their own behalf for fear of negative repercussions on others toward whom they stand in a protective role. Mothers have kept unsatisfactory marriages going for the sake of their children. Unattached women have sacrificed career opportunities because of other claims on their emotional resources, such as aging or sick relatives. Employed women have weakened their claims for equal treatment and professional equity by their reluctance to apply the final sanction of walking out, for fear of the adverse effects on clients.

Women find it extremely difficult to accept the short-term expediency of permitting (or even failing to prevent) harm to others, even when the long-term results may be highly beneficial.

Nevertheless, professionals in the helping areas have started to resist this sort of emotional blackmail by deliberately participating in boycotts, strikes and walkouts. New York City's social workers and public-school teachers both have demonstrated rigorously the necessity and value of forcibly protesting conditions that are inimical to employees (conditions that therefore in the long run must also have an adverse effect upon the clients and children for whom the women have a protective responsibility).

It is imperative that women feel justified in taking this stand when it is necessary. To insure that they are not constantly lured into the wrong sort of behavior for fear of doing harm, they need to examine their role in today's society, and particularly the psychological contribution they make to the collusive pattern that so easily perverts their judgment. Before they can put an end to this unsatisfactory situation, they must look into the reasons that it persists even in the face of such frustrating consequences.

One cogent explanation that is not immediately obvious has to do with the characteristics of society and the pressures put on women in their state of social transition.

Today's fragmented world makes it essential for every individual and group of individuals to have an easily defined and socially reinforced role that will preserve a sense of identity and counteract the futility and the relentless assault of status-conscious, competitive individualism.

Because of their ambiguous status, women are especially prone to these socially alienating influences. They find it tempting to be designated as the person or group that has special understanding and that remains the willing repository for everyone else's unsolved problems. This overriding need to feel useful in a social system that in other respects accords little opportunity for significant participation makes most women leap at an offer of involvement, even when it means stifling their underlying frustration and disappointment at the soothing rationalization that personal ambition and success are corrupting. The other side of the coin is that women's personal acculturation to the ideal of constant helpfulness, and their early habit of thought that constrains them to this emotional indenture, produce a high level of susceptibility to this very argument, particularly when extricating themselves from its premises takes so much intellectual effort and emotional fortitude.

A lot is said and written about the exploitation of women as sexual objects to further the psychological needs of the male and the consumer needs of an over-producing economy. What I am talking about is a process in which psychological attributes are subject to similar prostitution and misuse. This applies to the invaluable secretary, the personal assistant at the executive level, the woman physician in a rigidly structured medical hierarchy, the social worker, the nurse, the teacher, and many others in feminine jobs who feed their skills into a social program that they have rarely designed and that with few exceptions is geared to the maintenance of society's status quo in all its destructive aspects. Emotional manipulation of this sort distorts women's vision and creates the illusion that they are making a valuable contribution to society's well-being.

On examination, this illusion is impossible to maintain on several counts:

1) Today's society is primarily committed to destruction, both obvious and subtle. Even benign social institutions such as peace movements or progressive political groups are riven by divisiveness and hostilities.

2) Almost every human relationship found between human beings operates from a baseline of exploitation and self-interest rather than from one of mutual trust. The profit motive guides the social goals of most individuals and groups. In this context, women face a devastating dilemma: their traditional investment of skill and energy in other people's enterprises must either be dispensed with or turned to the immoral end of advancing the personal ambitions of ruthless individuals (or groups) or shoring up the crumbling efforts of inadequate ones.

3) Women cannot appropriately fulfill their time-honored function of re-

ciprocal assistance because it depends on a social-cohesiveness level that today's social scene does not attain.

. . .

The primary imperative for social workers—and for all women who intend to assume a meaningful and decisive role in today's vortex of social change—is to begin to perceive that *their* identity and personal integrity have as strong a claim for preservation as those of any *other* individual or group. To achieve this attitude, women must develop an explicit sense of the value of their own concerns and at times insist that they take precedence. They also must abandon the role of the compassionate sibyl who is at everyone's beck and call, because being permanently available to help other people keeps women from pursuing their chosen avocations with the concentration that is essential for their successful completion.

This new situation raises the fundamental question of who will assume the caretaking and healing tasks, which will always be with us. Although the prospect of women absent from their accustomed place is daunting, it may lead to a reshuffling of roles and tasks based on individual preferences—what Ruth Benedict called "congenial responses"—rather than arbitrary division based on biological endowment.

An important task of the women's movement is to free women's congenial responses from the restrictive cultural regime and present them in a new and more functional shape. This demands a great deal of thought about how women can project a living image to replace the lifeless stereotype that society dictates. The urgent—some might say strident—voice of the women's-liberation movement is a long-overdue attempt to redefine women in a fresh set of terms that reflects their congenial and widely varying characteristics.

Implicit in the intellectual effort is the importance of defining the characteristics of women in a culture-free way, so far as that is possible, and ensuring that we keep in mind a very wide range of both emotional and intellectual options.

Women must not delineate themselves solely in terms of revolutionary protest; though it has crucial relevance to their current situation, it cannot serve as a lasting definition. Further, though the plight of all women needs drastic overhaul, not everyone will want the same style of improvement nor espouse the same methods of bringing it about. Women who now speak for their exploited sex must try to understand attitudes and aspirations that are at variance with their own. Otherwise, we will exchange one brand of doctrinaire tyranny for another, alienating a substantial portion of women who are not yet ready for total separation from the symbolic relationship with the dominant male sex.

It is urgently necessary to make an accurate assessment of which of the so-called womanly characteristics have continuing validity and can be used to useful social ends. This may be a rash venture into the controversy about whether differences between the sexes are fundamental and real or artificially contrived by cultural forces.

At the risk of expounding heresy, my feeling is that, if thoughtful analysis is used instead of global stereotyping, we can dispose of many of these questions by pragmatically considering the tasks that need doing and who is best equipped to do them—"best" meaning the individual or group that can discharge them most effectively through the maximum utilization of special skills.

Whether these skills are fundamental and innate or whether they have developed to a high level of proficiency through long-accustomed use is relatively immaterial.

Two attributes particular to women have an increasingly important place in today's society:

1) *flexibility of operation,* and
2) *capacity for intuitive awareness of personal and social phenomena.*

1. Flexibility is a characteristic that most women have had to foster to survive their limiting circumstances without being paralyzed by frustration. Because their skills and creative energies have been expressed mainly through promoting the successful growth and functioning of others, women have developed unusual versatility concerning their own preferences and goals, a heightened ability to grasp opportunity when it occurs, an equal capacity for withstanding disappointment when it is withdrawn, and unlimited competence in making things over—food, clothing, furniture, the home itself, or the total social situation within which they operate. In a period of rapid social change, flexibility in thought and action is an extremely valuable quality: one of the outstanding contributions that the women's-liberation movement can make to the overall revolutionary trend in this country is to set a model for non-doctrinaire policies and flexible goals.

2. The other quality frequently attributed to women is their apparent capacity for picking up subliminal clues that, when they are put together, can produce a diagnostic assessment of individuals or situations with more penetrating insight than more usual processes of conscious thought can achieve. This celebrated characteristic is neither universally nor exclusively feminine, but it is likely to be developed to a higher degree in women.

When women's satisfactions depend on the skillful manipulation of other persons' well-being, it is incumbent upon them to develop a finely calibrated skill for tuning in to the needs and moods of those individuals so that women may be ready with the appropriate response. The group tensions within the structure of the family, the shifting of emphases and the sites of power must all be picked up by the psychic radar equipment of women before they explode into consciousness and disrupt the group's functioning.

This invaluable quality enables women to divine subterranean stresses in larger group systems and alert individuals to the presence of the stresses and to the possible courses they will take if not controlled. Men have not needed to develop this subtle influence to the same extent because their exercise of power has been overt. But in an unstable social setting, men's power tactics tend to be outmoded and to lack the capacity for adroit maneuvering, rather like the Spanish Armada when naval warfare took on a new style.

One further point seems to have equal relevance. Although women have skills that are indispensable to the healthy functioning of society, they have not evolved a systematic method for transmitting their arcane arts. For example, it was left to Dr. Spock—a masculine representative of a male-dominated profession—to write the classic on child rearing, even though this knowledge is possessed sooner or later by most wives and mothers.

Another instance of the same phenomenon is a recent report in a leading social-work journal that men produce the bulk of the literary output in this field. Among its observations, the article mentioned that women favored teaching over writing as a channel for expressing their intellectual concerns in social work, as opposed to their practical concerns. Teaching is one of the most conspicuous helping professions; it strikes me as significant that women social workers fall back on this outlet for their intellectual skills, thus demonstrating, perhaps unconsciously, their continued loyal adherence to the nurturing model. It represents also the persistent attraction of personal involvement as opposed to the more impersonal cerebral activity.

However, the explanation for this preference is not an inborn and immutable tendency so much as the harsh fact that personal, concretely focused activities do not require the same kind of single-minded concentration that writing and other creative ventures require, and they suffer less from the interruption of external activities. In other words, women (and particularly women in social work) are less comfortable dealing with concepts than with concrete problems, *not* because they lack insight and conceptualizing skills but because their self-perception does not permit them to give this item top priority.

In a crisis that demands the full exercise of the compassionate mandate, women are much more ready to push aside a creative enterprise to do so, even though in the long run the latter might represent a social contribution of more lasting value.

. . .

⋘17 *John Stuart Mill*

John Stuart Mill, the eldest son of James Mill, Scottish philosopher, historian, and economist, was born in London in 1806 and almost immediately was placed under the joint tutelage of his father and Jeremy Bentham, both of whom were eager for a subject on whom to test their educational theories. Although the boy was subjected to an unusually rigorous classical discipline (commencing the study of Greek at age three and progressing to Latin five years later), he was given, in his own expressed opinion, little opportunity for emotional development. Until he met Harriet Taylor in 1830, the only members of the female sex he had known well were his beautiful but intellectually limited and unhappily married mother and the wives of two friends. Nevertheless, according to his own testimony, his views on women had already been formulated. They dated, he says in The Subjection of Women, "from the very earliest period when [he] had formed any opinions at all on social or political matters" and were merely strengthened by further thought and experience. Much of that experience was acquired in the company of Harriet Taylor, who became his intimate friend and frequent companion. In 1851, two years after the death of her husband, they were married.

In 1831 or 1832 the two had exchanged essays on the subject of marriage and divorce, and in 1851 there appeared in The Westminster Review an essay entitled "The Enfranchisement of Women," in large measure, Mill tells us, the work of Harriet Taylor herself. The Subjection of Women, written in 1860–1861, two years after her death, seems to have been conceived more or less as a memorial to her. Mill served as a member of Parliament from 1865 to 1868. He died in Avignon in 1873.

Until the 1830s, England, adhering to the principle of "no taxation without representation," had extended the franchise to all taxpayers, women as well as men. But in 1832 the word "male" was inserted before the word "person" in the national election law, and in 1835 a similar change was made with regard to municipal elections. Although women had made little use of their right to vote in the preceding two centuries, a number of them were sensitive to the significance of the rescinding of this privilege. Within a few years women's rights groups began to form. In the mid-1860s the House of Commons, which at the time was considering legislation extending male suffrage by lowering the property requirement, was petitioned to restore the franchise to qualified female voters as well. The petitions were introduced by Mill, who had been elected to the House in 1865. Benjamin Disraeli had already come out strongly in favor of the vote for women: "In a country in which a woman can be ruler, peer, church trustee, owner of estates, and guardian of the poor," he declared, "I do not see in the name of what principle the right to vote can be withheld from her." Nevertheless, Mill's motion to amend the election bill was defeated by a vote of 196 to 73. Although the new law substituted the word "man" for the term "male person," all attempts to have that word interpreted generically met with failure.

In The Subjection of Women *Mill answered the allegations of* Schopenhauer *almost point by point. Mill did not need a catalytic agent. By the time the essay was written he had been an active advocate of women's rights for nearly forty years. At the age of seventeen he had been arrested for distributing tracts on contraception. He became an advocate of all sorts of social and political reforms, proposing, among other things, annual elections, a secret ballot, parliamentary reform, free trade, and removal of a number of restrictions on the franchise. His father had believed that in casting his own ballot, a husband was simultaneously representing his wife's point of view; Mill did not agree. And ultimately he advocated equality between the sexes in educational, professional, and legal matters as well as in the franchise.*

The Subjection of Women *reflects many of Mill's most characteristic beliefs. In* A System of Logic, *his major philosophical work, he proposed the application of the methods of natural science to the social sciences—ethics, politics, economics, history, sociology—with a view to effecting social and political reform. In that work Mill generalized on some of his father's beliefs. James Mill had held that the way to arrive at knowledge concerning human behavior was to study individuals, arrive at a concept of human nature, and then deduce from it general conclusions concerning humankind. John Stuart Mill argued that all reasoning is basically inductive, since the premises of deductive arguments are arrived at inductively, and that in the last analysis people always reason from particular to particular. Theoretically, then, a science of human behavior could be established in much the same way that other sciences have been developed—by analysis of the conduct of individual human beings and by generalization. But because of the highly complex nature of human society, the task would be fraught with enormous if not insuperable difficulties.*

Mill found himself unable to formulate an abstract concept of woman's nature, for instance, because of the impossibility of grounding such a concept in empirical evidence. The human character is malleable, he thought, and it is impossible to say what woman would have been like had she not been subjected to centuries of oppression. Rather than hazard uneducated guesses on the matter, Mill claimed, one must proceed inductively: to open up the competition for all occupations to both sexes and then assess the results. It did seem to him highly unlikely, however, that, given the vast range of individual differences that he had observed, the worst qualified man for every position would invariably be better qualified than the best qualified woman. And so, in the last analysis, Mill did cast educated guesses, his claim to the contrary notwithstanding.

Like Margaret Fuller, Mill pointed to a few outstanding female historical figures as proof of what woman is capable of. While conceding that a generalization based on a few isolated instances could scarcely predict what is likely to occur, he nevertheless argued that such women as Queen Elizabeth, Deborah, Joan of Arc, Queen Victoria, and Margaret of Austria had proved what women could do.

The very fact that queens had demonstrated an ability to govern effectively rendered absurd, Mill thought, any question of the fitness of the female to vote intelligently. Woman's alleged preoccupation with the present moment Mill saw as quite possibly more of an advantage than a disadvantage in politics, for it could easily prove a valuable antidote to the male tendency to overphilosophize. Woman's supposedly excitable nature, her alleged inability to stick to a single topic, could also stand her in good stead, for too much absorption in a single topic can be unhealthy, and the ability to move from topic to topic is invaluable. Mill was forced to admit that women had accomplished little in the fields of philosophy, literature, and art, but he ascribed this lack of achievement to their circumstances, not to their nature.

Mill was influenced by Jeremy Bentham's utilitarianism, an ethical school centered on the belief that the act is right which results in the greatest possible good to the greatest number of people. Although Mill's own version of utilitarianism also advocated the greatest happiness for the greatest number, he by no means overlooked the individual. No one could have been more concerned than John Stuart Mill with the rights of the individual. In his essay "On Liberty" Mill hypothesized, "If all mankind minus one were of one opinion, and only one person were of the contrary opinion, mankind would be no more justified in silencing that one person, than he, if he had the power, would be justified in silencing mankind."

As Mill broadens his concern for the rights of the isolated individual until it embraces the collective rights of half the human race, he by no means neglects the other half, for it was not only for the sake of women that Mill took his stand; it was for men as well. The subjection of women is apt to make tyrants of their husbands, an unenviable role in which to be cast, whereas the liberation of women would promote justice, double the mental resources available to humanity, and serve as an ennobling influence upon it.

From *The Subjection of Women*

CHAPTER 4

There remains a question, not of less importance than those already discussed, and which will be asked the most importunately by those opponents whose conviction is somewhat shaken on the main point. What good are we to expect from the changes proposed in our customs and institutions? Would mankind be at all better off if women were free? If not, why disturb their minds, and attempt to make a social revolution in the name of an abstract right?

It is hardly to be expected that this question will be asked in respect to the change proposed in the condition of women in marriage. The sufferings, immoralities, evils of all sorts, produced in innumerable cases by the subjection of individual women to individual men, are far too terrible to be overlooked. Unthinking or uncandid persons, counting those cases alone which are extreme, or which attain publicity, may say that the evils are exceptional; but no one can be blind to their existence, nor, in many cases, to their intensity. And it is perfectly obvious that the abuse of the power cannot be very much checked while the power remains. It is a power given, or offered, not to good men, or to decently respectable men, but to all men; the most brutal, and the most criminal. There is no check but that of opinion, and such men are in general within the reach of no opinion but that of men like themselves. If such men did not brutally tyrannize over the one human being whom the law compels to bear everything from them, society must already have reached a paradisiacal state. There could be no need any longer of laws to curb men's vicious propensities. Astraea must not only have returned to earth, but the heart of the worst man must have become her temple. The law of servitude in marriage is a monstrous contradiction to all the principles of the modern world, and to all the experience through which those principles have been slowly and painfully worked out. It is the sole case, now that negro slavery has been abolished, in which a human being in the plenitude of every faculty is delivered up to the tender mercies of another human being, in the hope forsooth that this other will use the power solely for the good of the person subjected to it. Marriage is the only actual bondage known to our law. There remain no legal slaves, except the mistress of every house.

It is not, therefore, on this part of the subject, that the question is likely to be asked, *Cui bono?* We may be told that the evil would outweigh the good, but the reality of the good admits of no dispute. In regard, however, to the larger question, the removal of women's disabilities—their recognition as the equals of men in all that belongs to citizenship—the opening to them of all honourable employments, and of the training and education which qualifies for those employments—there are many persons for whom it is not enough that the inequality has no just or legitimate defence; they require to be told what express advantage would be obtained by abolishing it.

To which let me first answer, the advantage of having the most universal and pervading of all human relations regulated by justice instead of injustice. The vast amount of this gain to human nature, it is hardly possible, by any explanation or illustration, to place in a stronger light than it is placed by the bare statement, to any one who attaches a moral meaning to words. All the selfish propensities, the self-worship, the unjust self-preference, which exist among mankind, have their source and root in, and derive their principal nourishment from, the present constitution of the relation between men and women. Think what it is to a boy, to grow up to manhood in the belief that without any merit or any exertion of his own, though he may be the most frivolous and empty or the most ignorant and stolid of mankind, by the mere fact of being born a male he is by right the superior of all and every one of an entire half of the human race: including probably some whose real superiority to himself he has daily or hourly occasion to feel; but even if in his whole conduct he habitually follows a woman's guidance, still, if he is a fool, he thinks that of course she is not, and cannot be, equal in ability and judgment to himself; and if he is not a fool, he does worse—he sees that she is superior to him, and believes that, notwithstanding her superiority, he is entitled to command and she is bound to obey. What must be the effect on his character, of this lesson? And men of the cultivated classes are often not aware how deeply it sinks into the immense majority of male minds. For, among right-feeling and well-bred people, the inequality is kept as much as possible out of sight; above all, out of sight of the children. As much obedience is required from boys to their mother as to their father: they are not permitted to domineer over their sisters, nor are they accustomed to see these postponed to them, but the contrary; the compensations of the chivalrous feeling being made prominent, while the servitude which requires them is kept in the background. Well brought-up youths in the higher classes thus often escape the bad influences of the situation in their early years, and only experience them when, arrived at manhood, they fall under the dominion of facts as they really exist. Such people are little aware, when a boy is differently brought up, how early the notion of his inherent superiority to a girl arises in his mind; how it grows with his growth and strengthens with his strength; how it is inoculated by one schoolboy upon another; how early the youth thinks himself superior to his mother, owing her perhaps forbearance, but no real respect; and how sublime and sultan-like a sense of superiority he feels, above all, over the woman whom he honours by admitting her to a partnership of his life. Is it imagined that all this does not pervert the whole manner of existence of the man, both as an individual and as a social being? It is an exact parallel to the feeling of a hereditary king that he is excellent above others by being born a king, or a noble by being born a noble. The relation between husband and wife is very like that between lord and vassal, except that the wife is held to more unlimited obedience than the vassal was. However the vassal's character may have been affected, for better and for worse, by his subordination, who can help seeing that the lord's was affected greatly for the worse? whether he was led to believe that his vassals were really superior to himself, or to feel that he was placed in command over people as good as himself, for no merits or labours of his own, but merely for having, as Figaro says, taken the trouble to be born. The self-worship of the monarch, or of the feudal superior, is matched by the self-worship of the male. Human beings do not grow up from childhood in the possession of unearned distinctions, without pluming themselves upon them. Those whom privileges not acquired by their merit, and which they feel to be disproportioned to it, inspire with additional humility, are always the few, and the best few. The rest are only inspired with pride, and the worst sort of pride, that which values itself upon accidental advantages, not of its own achieving. Above all, when the feeling of being raised above the whole of the other sex is combined with personal authority over one individual among them; the situation, if a school of conscientious and affectionate forbearance to those whose strongest points of character are conscience and affection, is to men of another quality a regularly constituted Academy or Gymnasium for training them in arrogance and over-bearingness; which vices, if curbed by the certainty of resistance in their intercourse with other men, their equals, break out towards all who are in a position to be obliged to tolerate them, and often revenge themselves upon the unfortunate wife for the involuntary restraint which they are obliged to submit to elsewhere.

The example afforded, and the education given to the sentiments, by laying the foundation of domestic existence upon a relation contradictory to the first principles of social justice, must, from the very nature of man, have a perverting influence of such magnitude, that it is hardly possible with our present experience to raise our imaginations to the conception of so great a change for the better as would be made by its removal. All that education and civilization are doing to efface the influences on character of the law of force, and replace them by those of justice, remains merely on the surface, as long as the citadel of the enemy is not attacked. The principle of the modern movement in morals and politics, is that conduct, and conduct alone, entitles to respect: that not what men are, but what they do, constitutes their claim to deference; that, above all, merit, and not birth, is the only rightful claim to power and authority. If no authority, not in its nature temporary, were allowed to one human being over another, society would not be employed in building up propensities with one hand which it has to curb with the other. The child would really, for the first time in man's existence on earth, be trained in the way he should go, and when he was old there would be a chance that he would not depart from it. But so long as the right of the strong to power over the weak rules in the very heart of society, the attempt to make the equal right of the weak the principle of its outward actions will always be an uphill struggle; for the law of justice, which is also that of Christianity, will never get possession of men's inmost sentiments; they will be working against it, even when bending to it.

The second benefit to be expected from giving to women the free use of their faculties, by leaving them the free choice of their employments, and opening to them the same fields of occupation and the same prizes and encouragements as to other human beings, would be that of doubling the mass of mental faculties available for the higher service of humanity. Where there is now one person qualified to benefit mankind and promote the general improvement, as a public teacher, or an administrator of some branch of public or social affairs, there would then be a chance of two. Mental superiority of any kind is at present everywhere so much below the demand; there is such a deficiency of persons competent to do excellently anything which it requires any considerable amount of ability to do; that the loss to the world, by refusing to make use of one-half of the whole quantity of talent it possesses, is extremely serious. It is true that this amount of mental power is not totally lost. Much of it is employed, and would in any case be employed, in domestic management, and in the few other occupations open to women; and from the remainder indirect benefit is in many individual cases obtained, through the personal influence of individual women over individual men. But these benefits are partial; their range is extremely circumscribed; and if they must be admitted, on the one hand, as a deduction from the amount of fresh social power that would be acquired by giving freedom to one-half of the whole sum of human intellect, there must be added, on the other, the benefit of the stimulus that would be given to the intellect of men by the competition; or (to use a more true expression) by the necessity that would be imposed on them of deserving precedency before they could expect to obtain it.

This great accession to the intellectual power of the species, and to the amount of intellect available for the good management of its affairs, would be obtained, partly, through the better and more complete intellectual education of women, which would then improve *pari passu* with that of men. Women in general would be brought up equally capable of understanding business, public affairs, and the higher matters of speculation, with men in the same class of society; and the select few of the one as well as of the other sex, who were qualified not only to comprehend what is done or thought by others, but to think or do something considerable themselves, would meet with the same facilities for improving and training their capacities in the one sex as in the other. In this way, the widening of the sphere of action for women would operate for good, by raising their education to the level of that of men, and making the one participate in all improvements made in the other. But independently of this, the mere breaking down of the barrier would of itself have an educational virtue of the highest worth. The mere getting rid of the idea that all the wider subjects of thought and action, all the things which are of general and not solely of private interest, are men's business, from which women are to be warned off—positively interdicted from most of it, coldly tolerated in the little which is allowed them—the mere consciousness a woman would then have of being a human being like any other, entitled to choose her pursuits, urged or invited by the same inducements as any one else to interest herself in whatever is interesting to human beings, entitled to exert the share of influence on all human concerns which belongs to an individual opinion, whether she attempted actual participation in them or not—this alone would effect an immense expansion of the faculties of women, as well as enlargement of the range of their moral sentiments.

Besides the addition to the amount of individual talent available for the conduct of human affairs, which certainly are not at present so abundantly provided in that respect that they can afford to dispense with one-half of what nature proffers; the opinion of women would then possess a more beneficial, rather than a greater, influence upon the general mass of human belief and sentiment. I say a more beneficial, rather than a greater influence; for the influence of women over the general tone of opinion has always, or at least from the earliest known period, been very considerable. The influence of mothers on the early character of their sons, and the desire of young men to recommend themselves to young women, have in all recorded times been important agencies in the formation of character, and have determined some of the chief steps in the progress of civilization. Even in the Homeric age, αἰδώς towards the Τρωάδας ἑλκεσιπέπλους is an acknowledged and powerful motive of action in the great Hector. The moral influence of women has had two modes of operation. First, it has been a softening influence. Those who were most liable to be the victims of violence, have naturally tended as much as they could towards limiting its sphere and mitigating its excesses. Those who were not taught to fight, have naturally inclined in favour of any other mode of settling differences rather than that of fighting. In general, those who have been the greatest sufferers by the indulgence of selfish passion, have been the most earnest supporters of any moral law which offered a means of bridling passion. Women were powerfully instrumental in inducing the northern conquerors to adopt the creed of Christianity, a creed so much more favourable to women than any that preceded it. The conversion of the Anglo-Saxons and of the Franks may be said to have been begun by the wives of Ethelbert and Clovis. The other mode in which the effect of women's opinion has been conspicuous, is by giving a powerful stimulus to those qualities in men, which, not being themselves trained in, it was necessary for them that they should find in their protectors. Courage, and the military virtues generally, have at all times been greatly indebted to the desire which men felt of being admired by women: and the stimulus reaches far beyond this one class of eminent qualities, since, by a very natural effect of their position, the best passport to the admiration and favour of women has always been to be thought highly of by men. From the combination of the two kinds of moral influence thus exercised by women, arose the spirit of chivalry: the peculiarity of which is, to aim at combining the highest standard of the warlike qualities with the cultivation of a totally different class of virtues—those of gentleness, generosity, and self-abnegation, towards the non-military and defenceless classes generally, and a special submission and worship directed towards women; who were distinguished from the other defenceless classes by the high rewards which they had it in their power voluntarily to bestow on those who endeavoured to earn their favour, instead of extorting their subjection. Though the practice of chivalry fell even more sadly short of its theoretic standard than practice generally falls below theory, it remains one of the most precious monuments of the moral history of our race; as a remarkable instance of a concerted and organized attempt by a most disorganized and distracted society, to raise up and carry into practice a moral ideal greatly in advance of its social condition and institutions; so much so as to have been completely frustrated in the main object, yet never entirely inefficacious, and which has left a most sensible, and for the most part a highly valuable impress on the ideas and feelings of all subsequent times.

The chivalrous ideal is the acme of the influence of women's sentiments on the moral cultivation of mankind: and if women are to remain in their subordinate situation, it were greatly to be lamented that the chivalrous standard should have passed away, for it is the only one at all capable of mitigating the demoralizing influences of that position. But the changes in the general state of the species rendered inevitable the substitution of a totally different ideal of morality for the chivalrous one. Chivalry was the attempt to infuse moral elements into a state of society in which everything depended for good or evil on individual prowess, under the softening influences of individual delicacy and generosity. In modern societies, all things, even in the military department of affairs, are decided, not by individual effort, but by the combined operations of numbers; while the main occupation of society has changed from fighting to business, from military to industrial life. The exigencies of the new life are no more exclusive of the virtues of generosity than those of the old, but it no longer entirely depends on them. The main foundations of the moral life of modern times must be justice and prudence; the respect of each for the rights of every other, and the ability of each to take care of himself. Chivalry left without legal check all forms of wrong which reigned unpublished throughout society; it only encouraged a few to do right in preference to wrong, by the direction it gave to the instruments of praise and admiration. But the real dependence of morality must always be upon its penal sanctions—its power to deter from evil. The security of society cannot rest on merely rendering honour to right, a motive so comparatively weak in all but a few, and which on very many does not operate at all. Modern society is able to repress wrong through all departments of life, by a fit exertion of the superior strength which civilization has given it, and thus to render the existence of the weaker members of society (no longer defenceless but protected by law) tolerable to them, without reliance on the chivalrous feelings of those who are in a position to tyrannize. The beauties and graces of the chivalrous character are still what they were, but the rights of the weak, and the general comfort of human life, now rest on a far surer and steadier support; or rather, they do so in every relation of life except the conjugal.

At present the moral influence of women is no less real, but it is no longer of so marked and definite a character: it has more nearly merged in the general influence of public opinion. Both through the contagion of sympathy, and through the desire of men to shine in the eyes of women, their feelings have great effect in keeping alive what remains of the chivalrous ideal—in fostering the sentiments and continuing the traditions of spirit and generosity. In these points of character, their standard is higher than that of men; in the quality of justice, somewhat lower. As regards the relations of private life it may be said generally, that their influence is, on the whole, encouraging to the softer virtues, discouraging to the sterner: though the statement must be taken with all the modifications dependent on individual character. In the chief of the greater trials to which virtue is subject in the concerns of life—that conflict between interest and principle—the tendency of women's influence is of a very mixed character. When the principle involved happens to be one of the very few which the course of their religious or moral education has strongly impressed upon themselves, they are potent auxiliaries to virtue: and their husbands and sons are often prompted by them to acts of abnegation which they never would have been capable of without that stimulus. But, with the present education and position of women, the moral principles which have been impressed on them cover but a comparatively small part of the field of virtue, and are, moreover, principally negative; forbidding particular acts, but having little to do with the general direction of the thoughts and purposes. I am afraid it must be said, that disinterestedness in the general conduct of life—the devotion of the energies to purposes which hold out no promise of private advantages to the family—is very seldom encouraged or supported by women's influence. It is small blame to them that they discourage objects of which they have not learnt to see the advantage, and which withdraw their men from them, and from the interests of the family. But the consequence is that women's influence is often anything but favourable to public virtue.

Women have, however, some share of influence in giving the tone to public moralities since their sphere of action has been a little widened, and since a considerable number of them have occupied themselves practically in the promotion of objects reaching beyond their own family and household. The influence of women counts for a great deal in two of the most marked features of modern European life—its aversion to war, and its addiction to philanthropy.

Excellent characteristics both; but unhappily, if the influence of women is valuable in the encouragement it gives to these feelings in general, in the particular applications the direction it gives to them is at least as often mischievous as useful. In the philanthropic department more particularly, the two provinces chiefly cultivated by women are religious proselytism and charity. Religious proselytism at home, is but another word for embittering of religious animosities: abroad, it is usually a blind running at an object, without either knowing or heeding the fatal mischiefs—fatal to the religious object itself as well as to all other desirable objects—which may be produced by the means employed. As for charity, it is a matter in which the immediate effect on the persons directly concerned, and the ultimate consequence to the general good, are apt to be at complete war with one another: while the education given to women—an education of the sentiments rather than of the understanding—and the habit inculcated by their whole life, of looking to immediate effects on persons, and not to remote effects on classes of persons—make them both unable to see, and unwilling to admit, the ultimate evil tendency of any form of charity or philanthropy which commends itself to their sympathetic feelings. The great and continually increasing mass of unenlightened and shortsighted benevolence, which, taking the care of people's lives out of their own hands, and relieving them from the disagreeable consequences of their own acts, saps the very foundations of the self-respect, self-help, and self-control which are the essential conditions both of individual prosperity and of social virtue—this waste of resources and of benevolent feelings in doing harm instead of good, is immensely swelled by women's contributions, and stimulated by their influence. Not that this is a mistake likely to be made by women, where they have actually the practical management of schemes of beneficence. It sometimes happens that women who administer public charities—with that insight into present fact, and especially into the minds and feelings of those with whom they are in immediate contact, in which women generally excel men—recognise in the clearest manner the demoralizing influence of the alms given or the help afforded, and could give lessons on the subject to many a male political economist. But women who only give their money, and are not brought face to face with the effects it produces, how can they be expected to foresee them? A woman born to the present lot of women, and content with it, how should she appreciate the value of self-dependence? She is not self-dependent; she is not taught self-dependence; her destiny is to receive everything from others, and why should what is good enough for her be bad for the poor? Her familiar notions of good are of blessings descending from a superior. She forgets that she is not free, and that the poor are; that if what they need is given to them unearned, they cannot be compelled to earn it: that everybody cannot be taken care of by everybody, but there must be some motive to induce people to take care of themselves; and that to be helped to help themselves, if they are physically capable of it, is the only charity which proves to be charity in the end.

These considerations show how usefully the part which women take in the formation of general opinion, would be modified for the better by that more enlarged instruction, and practical conversancy with the things which their opinions influence, that would necessarily arise from their social and political emancipation. But the improvement it would work through the influence they exercise, each in her own family, would be still more remarkable.

It is often said that in the classes most exposed to temptation, a man's wife and children tend to keep him honest and respectable, both by the wife's direct influence, and by the concern he feels for their future welfare. This may be so, and no doubt often is so, with those who are more weak than wicked; and this beneficial influence would be preserved and strengthened under equal laws; it does not depend on the woman's servitude, but is, on the contrary, diminished by the disrespect which the inferior class of men always at heart feel towards those who are subject to their power. But when we ascend higher in the scale, we come among a totally different set of moving forces. The wife's influence tends, as far as it goes, to prevent the husband from falling below the common standard of approbation of the country. It tends quite as strongly to hinder him from rising above it. The wife is the auxiliary of the common public opinion. A man who is married to a woman his inferior in intelligence, finds her a perpetual dead weight, or, worse than a dead weight, a drag, upon every aspiration of his to be better than public opinion requires him to be. It is hardly possible for one who is in these bonds, to attain exalted virtue. If he differs in his opinion from the mass—if he sees truths which have not yet dawned upon them, or if, feeling in his heart truths which they nominally recognise, he would like to act up to those truths more conscientiously than the generality of mankind—to all such thoughts and desires, marriage is the heaviest of drawbacks, unless he be so fortunate as to have a wife as much above the common level as he himself is.

For, in the first place, there is always some sacrifice of personal interest required; either of social consequence, or of pecuniary means; perhaps the risk of even the means of subsistence. These sacrifices and risks he may be willing to encounter for himself; but he will pause before he imposes them on his family. And his family in this case means his wife and daughters; for he always hopes that his sons will feel as he feels himself, and that what he can do without, they will do without, willingly, in the same cause. But his daughters—their marriage may depend upon it: and his wife, who is unable to enter into or understand the objects for which these sacrifices are made—who, if she thought them worth any sacrifice, would think so on trust, and solely for his sake—who can participate in none of the enthusiasm or the self-approbation he himself may feel, while the things which he is disposed to sacrifice are all in all to her; will not the best and most unselfish man hesitate the longest before bringing on her this consequence? If it be not the comforts of life, but only social consideration, that is at stake, the burthen upon his conscience and feelings is still very severe. Whoever has a wife and children has given hostages to Mrs. Grundy. The approbation of that potentate may be a matter of indifference to him, but it is of great importance to his wife. The man himself may be above opinion, or may find sufficient compensation in the opinion of those of his own way of thinking. But to the women connected with him, he can offer no compensation. The almost invariable tendency of the wife to place her influence in the same scale with social consideration, is sometimes made a reproach to women, and represented as a peculiar trait of feebleness and childishness of character in them: surely with great injustice, Society makes the whole life of a woman, in the easy classes, a continued self-sacrifice; it exacts from her an unremitting restraint of the whole of her natural inclinations, and the sole return it makes to her for what often deserves the name of a martyrdom, is consideration. Her consideration is inseparably connected with that of her husband, and after paying the full price for it, she finds that she is to lose it, for no reason of which she can feel the cogency. She has sacrificed her whole life to it, and her husband will not sacrifice to it a whim, a freak, an eccentricity; something not recognised or allowed for by the world, and which the world will agree with her in thinking a folly, if it thinks no worse! The dilemma is hardest upon that very meritorious class of men, who, without possessing talents which qualify them to make a figure among those with whom they agree in opinion, hold their opinion from conviction, and feel bound in honour and conscience to serve it, by making profession of their belief, and giving their time, labour, and means, to anything undertaken in its behalf. The worst case of all is when such men happen to be of a rank and position which of itself neither gives them, nor excludes them from, what is considered the best society; when their admission to it depends mainly on what is thought of them personally—and however unexceptionable their breeding and habits, their being identified with opinions and public conduct unacceptable to those who give the tone to society would operate as an effectual exclusion. Many a woman flatters herself (nine times out of ten quite erroneously) that nothing prevents her and her husband from moving in the highest society of her neighbourhood—society in which others well known to her, and in the same class of life, mix freely—except that her husband is unfortunately a Dissenter, or has the reputation of mingling in low radical politics. That it is, she thinks, which hinders George from getting a commission or a place, Caroline from making an advantageous match, and prevents her and her husband from obtaining invitations, perhaps honours, which, for aught she sees, they are as well entitled to as some folks. With such an influence in every house, either exerted actively, or operating all the more powerfully for not being asserted, is it any wonder that people in general are kept down in that mediocrity of respectability which is becoming a marked characteristic of modern times?

There is another very injurious aspect in which the effect, not of women's disabilities directly, but of the broad line of difference which those disabilities create between the education and character of a woman and that of a man, requires to be considered. Nothing can be more unfavourable to that union of thoughts and inclinations which is the ideal of married life. Intimate society between people radically dissimilar to one another, is an idle dream. Unlikeness may attract, but it is likeness which retains; and in proportion to the likeness is the suitability of the individuals to give each other a happy life. While women are so unlike men, it is not wonderful that selfish men should feel the need of arbitrary power in their own hands, to arrest *in limine* the life-long conflict of inclinations, by deciding every question on the side of their own preference. When people are extremely unlike, there can be no real identity of interest. Very often there is conscientious difference of opinion between married people, on the highest points of duty. Is there any reality in the marriage union where this takes place? Yet it is not uncommon anywhere, when the woman has any earnestness of character; and it is a very general case indeed in Catholic countries, when she is supported in her dissent by the only other authority to which she is taught to bow, the priest. With the usual bare-facedness of power not accustomed to find itself disputed, the influence of priests over women is attacked by Protestant and Liberal writers, less for being bad in itself, than because it is a rival authority to the husband, and raises up a revolt against his infallibility. In England, similar differences occasionally exist when an Evangelical wife has allied herself with a husband of a different quality; but in general this source at least of dissension is got rid of, by reducing the minds of women to such a nullity, that they have no opinions but those of Mrs. Grundy, or those which the husband tells them to have. When there is no difference of opinion, differences merely of taste may be sufficient to detract greatly from the happiness of married life. And though it may stimulate the amatory propensities of men, it does not conduce to married happiness, to exaggerate by differences of education whatever may be the native differences of the sexes. If the married pair are well-bred and well-behaved people, they tolerate each other's tastes; but is mutual toleration what people look forward to, when they enter into marriage? These differences of inclination will naturally make their wishes different, if not restrained by affection or duty, as to almost all domestic questions which arise. What a difference there must be in the society which the two persons will wish to frequent, or be frequented by! Each will desire associates who share their own tastes: the persons agreeable to one, will be indifferent or positively disagreeable to the other; yet there can be none who are not common to both, for married people do not now live in different parts of the house and have totally different visiting lists, as in the reign of Louis XV. They cannot help having different wishes as to the bringing up of the children: each will wish to see reproduced in them their own tastes and sentiments: and there is either a compromise, and only a half-satisfaction to either, or the wife has to yield—often with bitter suffering; and, with or without intention, her occult influence continues to counterwork the husband's purposes.

It would of course be extreme folly to suppose that these differences of feeling and inclination only exist because women are brought up differently from men, and that there would not be differences of taste under any imaginable circumstances. But there is nothing beyond the mark in saying that the distinction in bringing-up immensely aggravates those differences, and renders them wholly inevitable. While women are brought up as they are, a man and a woman will but rarely find in one another real agreement of tastes and wishes as to daily life. They will generally have to give it up as hopeless, and renounce the attempt to have, in the intimate associate of their daily life, that *idem velle, idem nolle,* which is the recognised bond of any society that is really such: or if the man succeeds in obtaining it, he does so by choosing a woman who is so complete a nullity that she has no *velle* or *nolle* at all, and is as ready to comply with one thing as another if anybody tells her to do so. Even this calculation is apt to fail; dullness and want of spirit are not always a guarantee of the submission which is so confidently expected from them. But if they were, is this the ideal of marriage? What, in this case, does the man obtain by it, except an upper servant, a nurse, or a mistress? On the contrary, when each of two persons, instead of being a nothing, is a something; when they are attached to one another, and are not too much unlike to begin with; the constant partaking in the same things, assisted by their sympathy, draws out the latent capacities of each for being interested in the things which were at first interesting only to the other; and works a gradual assimilation of the tastes and characters to one another, partly by the insensible modification of each, but more by a real enriching of the two natures, each acquiring the tastes and capacities of the other in addition to its own. This often happens between two friends of the same sex, who are much associated in their daily life: and it would be a common, if not the commonest, case in marriage, did not the totally different bringing-up of the two sexes make it next to an impossibility to form a really well-assorted union. Were this remedied, whatsoever differences there might still be in individual tastes, there would at least be, as a general rule, complete unity and unanimity as to the great objects of life. When the two persons both care for great objects, and are a help and encouragement to each other in whatever regards these, the minor matters on which their tastes may differ are not all-important to them; and there is a foundation for solid friendship, of an enduring character, more likely than anything else to make it, through the whole of life, a greater pleasure to each to give pleasure to the other, than to receive it.

I have considered, thus far, the effects on the pleasures and benefits of the marriage union which depend on the mere unlikeness between the wife and the husband: but the evil tendency is prodigiously aggravated when the unlikeness is inferiority. Mere unlikeness, when it only means difference of good qualities, may be more a benefit in the way of mutual improvement, than a drawback from comfort. When each emulates, and desires and endeavours to acquire, the other's peculiar qualities, the difference does not produce diversity of interest, but increased identity of it, and makes each still more valuable to the other. But when one is much the inferior of the two in mental ability and cultivation, and is not actively attempting by the other's aid to rise to the other's level, the whole influence of the connection upon the development of the superior of the two is deteriorating: and still more so in a tolerably happy marriage than in an unhappy one. It is not with impunity that the superior in intellect shuts himself up with an inferior, and elects that inferior for his chosen, and sole completely intimate, associate. Any society which is not improving, is deteriorating: and the more so, the closer and more familiar it is. Even a really superior man almost always begins to deteriorate when he is habitually (as the phrase is) king of his company: and in his most habitual company the husband who has a wife inferior to him is always so. While his self-satisfaction is incessantly ministered to on the one hand, on the other he insensibly imbibes the modes of feeling, and of looking at things, which belong to a more vulgar or a more limited mind than his own. This evil differs from many of those which have hitherto been dwelt on, by being an increasing one. The association of men with women in daily life is much closer and more complete than it ever was before. Men's life is more domestic. Formerly, their pleasures and chosen occupations were among men, and in men's company: their wives had but a fragment of their lives. At the present time, the progress of civilization, and the turn of opinion against the rough amusements and convivial excesses which formerly occupied most men in their hours of relaxation—together with (it must be said) the improved tone of modern feeling as to the reciprocity of duty which binds the husband towards the wife—have thrown the man very much more upon home and its inmates, for his personal and social pleasures: while the kind and degree of improvement which has been made in women's education, has made them in some degree capable of being his companions in ideas and mental tastes, while leaving them, in most cases, still hopelessly inferior to him. His desire of mental communion is thus in general satisfied by a communion from which he learns nothing. An unimproving and unstimulating companionship is substituted for (what he might otherwise have been obliged to seek) the society of his equals in powers and his fellows in the higher pursuits. We see, accordingly, that young men of the greatest promise generally cease to improve as soon as they marry, and, not improving, inevitably degenerate. If the wife does not push the husband forward, she always holds him back. He ceases to care for what she does not care for; he no longer desires, and ends by disliking and shunning, society congenial to his former aspirations, and which would now shame his falling-off from them; his higher faculties both of mind and heart cease to be called into activity. And this change coinciding with the new and selfish interests which are created by the family, after a few years he differs in no material respect from those who have never had wishes for anything but the common vanities and the common pecuniary objects.

What marriage may be in the case of two persons of cultivated faculties, identical in opinions and purposes, between whom there exists that best kind of equality, similarity of powers and capacities with reciprocal superiority in them—so that each can enjoy the luxury of looking up to the other, and can have alternately the pleasure of leading and of being led in the path of development— I will not attempt to describe. To those who can conceive it, there is no need; to those who cannot, it would appear the dream of an enthusiast. But I maintain, with the profoundest conviction, that this, and this only, is the ideal of marriage; and that all opinions, customs, and institutions which favour any other notion of it, or turn the conceptions and aspirations connected with it into any other direction, by whatever pretences they may be coloured, are relics of primitive barbarism. The moral regeneration of mankind will only really commence, when the most fundamental of the social relations is placed under the rule of equal justice, and when human beings learn to cultivate their strongest sympathy with an equal in rights and in cultivation.

Thus far, the benefits which it has appeared that the world would gain by ceasing to make sex a disqualification for privileges and a badge of subjection, are social rather than individual; consisting in an increase of the general fund of thinking and acting power, and an improvement in the general conditions of the association of men with women. But it would be a grievous understatement of the case to omit the most direct benefit of all, the unspeakable gain in private happiness to the liberated half of the species; the difference to them between a life of subjection to the will of others, and a life of rational freedom. After the primary necessities of food and raiment, freedom is the first and strongest want of human nature. While mankind are lawless, their desire is for lawless freedom. When they have learnt to understand the meaning of duty and the value of reason, they incline more and more to be guided and restrained by these in the exercise of their freedom; but they do not therefore desire freedom less; they do not become disposed to accept the will of other people as the representative and interpreter of those guiding principles. On the contrary, the communities in which the reason has been most cultivated, and in which the idea of social duty has been most powerful, are those which have most strongly asserted the freedom of action of the individual—the liberty of each to govern his conduct by his own feelings of duty, and by such laws and social restraints as his own conscience can subscribe to.

He who would rightly appreciate the worth of personal independence as an element of happiness, should consider the value he himself puts upon it as an ingredient of his own. There is no subject on which there is a greater habitual difference of judgment between a man judging for himself, and the same man judging for other people. When he hears others complaining that they are not allowed freedom of action—that their own will has not sufficient influence in the regulation of their affairs—his inclination is, to ask, what are their grievances? what positive damage they sustain? and in what respect they consider their affairs to be mismanaged? and if they fail to make out, in answer to these questions, what appears to him a sufficient case, he turns a deaf ear, and regards their complaint as the fanciful querulousness of people whom nothing reasonable will satisfy. But he has a quite different standard of judgment when he is deciding for himself. Then, the most unexceptionable administration of his interests by a tutor set over him, does not satisfy his feelings: his personal exclusion from the deciding authority appears itself the greatest grievance of all, rendering it superfluous even to enter into the question of mismanagement. It is the same with nations. What citizen of a free country would listen to any offers of good and skilful administration, in return for the abdication of freedom? Even if he could believe that good and skilful administration can exist among a people ruled by a will not their own, would not the consciousness of working out their own destiny under their own moral responsibility be a compensation to his feelings for great rudeness and imperfection in the details of public affairs? Let him rest assured that whatever he feels on this point, women feel in a fully equal degree. Whatever has been said or written, from the time of Herodotus to the present, of the ennobling influence of free government—the nerve and spring which it gives to all the faculties, the larger and higher objects which it presents to the intellect and feelings, the more unselfish public spirit, and calmer and broader views of duty, that it engenders, and the generally loftier platform on which it elevates the individual as a moral, spiritual, and social being—is every particle as true of women as of men. Are these things no important part of individual happiness? Let any man call to mind what he himself felt on emerging from boyhood—from the tutelage and control of even loved and affectionate elders—and entering upon the responsibilities of manhood. Was it not like the physical effect of taking off a heavy weight, or releasing him from obstructive, even if not otherwise painful, bonds? Did he not feel twice as much alive, twice as much a human being, as before? And does he imagine that women have none of these feelings? But it is a striking fact, that the satisfactions and mortifications of personal pride, though all in all to most men when the case is their own, have less allowance made for them in the case of other people, and are less listened to as a ground or a justification of conduct, than any other natural human feelings; perhaps because men compliment them in their own case with the names of so many other qualities, that they are seldom conscious how mighty an influence these feelings exercise in their own lives. No less large and powerful is their part, we may assure ourselves, in the lives and feelings of women. Women are schooled into suppressing them in their most natural and most healthy direction, but the internal principle remains, in a different outward form. An active and energetic mind, if denied liberty, will seek for power: refused the command of itself, it will assert its personality by attempting to control others. To allow to any human beings no existence of their own but what depends on others, is giving far too high a premium on bending others to their purposes. Where liberty cannot be hoped for, and power can, power becomes the grand object of human desire; those to whom others will not leave the undisturbed management of their own affairs, will compensate themselves, if they can, by meddling for their own purposes with the affairs of others. Hence also women's passion for personal beauty, and dress and display; and all the evils that flow from it, in the way of mischievous luxury and social immorality. The love of power and the love of liberty are in eternal antagonism. Where there is least liberty, the passion for power is the most ardent and unscrupulous. The desire of power over others can only cease to be a depraving agency among mankind, when each of them individually is able to do without it: which can only be where respect for liberty in the personal concerns of each is an established principle.

But it is not only through the sentiment of personal dignity, that the free direction and disposal of their own faculties is a source of individual happiness, and to be fettered and restricted in it, a source of unhappiness, to human beings, and not least to women. There is nothing, after disease, indigence, and guilt, so fatal to the pleasurable enjoyment of life as the want of a worthy outlet for the active faculties. Women who have the cares of a family, and while they have the cares of a family, have this outlet, and it generally suffices for them: but what of the greatly increasing number of women, who have had no opportunity of exercising the vocation which they are mocked by telling them is their proper one? What of the women whose children have been lost to them by death or distance, or have grown up, married, and formed homes of their own? There are abundant examples of men who, after a life engrossed by business, retire with a competency to the enjoyment, as they hope, of rest, but to whom, as they are unable to acquire new interests and excitements that can replace the old, the change to a life of inactivity brings ennui, melancholy, and premature death. Yet no one thinks of the parallel case of so many worthy and devoted women, who, having paid what they are told is their debt to society—having brought up a family blamelessly to manhood and womanhood—having kept a house as long as they had a house needing to be kept—are deserted by the sole occupation for which they have fitted themselves; and remain with undiminished activity but with no employment for it, unless perhaps a daughter or daughter-in-law is willing to abdicate in their favour the discharge of the same functions in her younger household. Surely a hard lot for the old age of those who have worthily discharged, as long as it was given to them to discharge, what the world accounts their only social duty. Of such women, and of those others to whom this duty has not been committed at all—many of whom pine through life with the consciousness of thwarted vocations, and activities which are not suffered to expand—the only resources, speaking generally, are religion and charity. But their religion, though it may be one of feeling, and of ceremonial observance, cannot be a religion of action, unless in the form of charity. For charity many of them are by nature admirably fitted; but to practise it usefully, or even without doing mischief, requires the education, the manifold preparation, the knowledge and the thinking powers, of a skilful administrator. There are few of the administrative functions of government for which a person would not be fit, who is fit to bestow charity usefully. In this as in other cases (pre-eminently in that of the education of children), the duties permitted to women cannot be performed properly, without their being trained for duties which, to the great loss of society, are not permitted to them. And here let me notice the singular way in which the question of women's disabilities is frequently presented to view, by those who find it easier to draw a ludicrous picture of what they do not like, than to answer the arguments for it. When it is suggested that women's executive capacities and prudent counsels might sometimes be found valuable in affairs of state, these lovers of fun hold up to the ridicule of the world, as sitting in parliament or in the cabinet, girls in their teens, or young wives of two or three and twenty, transported bodily, exactly as they are, from the drawing-room to the House of Commons. They forget that males are not usually selected at this early age for a seat in Parliament, or for responsible political functions. Common sense would tell them that if such trusts were confided to women, it would be to such as having no special vocation for married life, or preferring another employment of their faculties (as many women even now prefer to marriage some of the few honourable occupations within their reach), have spent the best years of their youth in attempting to qualify themselves for the pursuits in which they desire to engage; or still more frequently perhaps, widows or wives of forty or fifty, by whom the knowledge of life and faculty of government which they have acquired in their families, could by the aid of appropriate studies be made available on a less contracted scale. There is no country of Europe in which the ablest men have not frequently experienced, and keenly appreciated, the value of the advice and help of clever and experienced women of the world, in the attainment both of private and of public objects; and there are important matters of public administration to which few men are equally competent with such women; among others, the detailed control of expenditure. But what we are now discussing is not the need which society has of the services of women in public business, but the dull and hopeless life to which it so often condemns them, by forbidding them to exercise the practical abilities which many of them are conscious of, in any wider field than one which to some of them never was, and to others is no longer, open. If there is anything vitally important to the happiness of human beings, it is that they should relish their habitual pursuit. This requisite of an enjoyable life is very imperfectly granted, or altogether denied, to a large part of mankind; and by its absence many a life is a failure, which is provided, in appearance, with every requisite of success. But if circumstances which society is not yet skilful enough to overcome, render such failures often for the present inevitable, society need not itself inflict them. The injudiciousness of parents, a youth's own inexperience, or the absence of external opportunities for the congenial vocation, and their presence for an uncongenial, condemn numbers of men to pass their lives in doing one thing reluctantly and ill, when there are other things which they could have done well and happily. But on women this sentence is imposed by actual law, and by customs equivalent to law. What, in unenlightened societies, colour, race, religion, or in the case of a conquered country, nationality, are to some men, sex is to all women; a peremptory exclusion from almost all honourable occupations, but either such as cannot be fulfilled by others, or such as those others do not think worthy of their acceptance. Sufferings arising from causes of this nature usually meet with so little sympathy, that few persons are aware of the great amount of unhappiness even now produced by the feeling of a wasted life. The case will be even more frequent, as increased cultivation creates a greater and greater disproportion between the ideas and faculties of women, and the scope which society allows to their activity.

When we consider the positive evil caused to the disqualified half of the human race by their disqualification—first in the loss of the most inspiriting and elevating kind of personal enjoyment, and next in the weariness, disappointment, and profound dissatisfaction with life, which are so often the substitute for it; one feels that among all the lessons which men require for carrying on the struggle against the inevitable imperfections of their lot on earth, there is no lesson which they more need, than not to add to the evils which nature inflicts, by their jealous and prejudiced restrictions on one another. Their vain fears only substitute other and worse evils for those which they are idly apprehensive of: while every restraint on the freedom of conduct of any of their human fellow creatures, (otherwise than by making them responsible for any evil actually caused by it), dries up *pro tanto* the principal fountain of human happiness, and leaves the species less rich, to an inappreciable degree, in all that makes life valuable to the individual human being.

❧ *Alice Rossi*

Alice Rossi, professor of sociology at the University of Massachusetts, has been widely acclaimed for her work on women's rights. She is joint editor of Academic Women on the Move *and editor of* The Feminist Papers: From Adams to Beauvoir *and* Essays on Sex Equality. *In the introduction to the latter, which is excerpted in the following pages, she stresses the relevance of Mill's* Subjection of Women *to contemporary society.*

From *Essays on Sex Equality*

SENTIMENT AND INTELLECT

. . .

There are several reasons why *The Subjection of Women* continues to be a powerfully effective essay, which people in the 1970s can find as stimulating as those who read it for the first time in the 1870s. It is grounded in basic libertarian values that ring as true today as then:

We have had the morality of submission and the morality of chivalry and generosity: the time is ripe for morality of justice. . . . The principle of the modern movement in morals and politics is that conduct and conduct alone entitles to respect: that not what men are but what they do constitutes their claim to deference. . . . It is totally out of keeping with modern values to have ascribed statuses; . . . human beings are no longer born to their place in life; . . . individual choice is our model now.

To the generations of the twentieth century who have seen tyranny and the suppression of human liberty in all forms of government—Fascist, Communist, and democratic—John Stuart Mill's invocation of the rights of men and women to liberty and justice has a strong, continuing appeal. And to the women of the twentieth century, who have seen very little difference in the actual condition, if not the formal rights, of women under any existing form of government, *The Subjection of Women* continues to serve as a resounding affirmation of their human right to full equality and a sophisticated analysis of the obstacles that bar their way to it.

A second basic reason for the continuing relevance of the Mill essay on women is that it is not burdened with the dead weight of any of the social and psychological theories that have emerged during the hundred years separating us from the Mills: no Darwinism to encourage an unthinking expectation of unilinear progress of mankind through "natural selection" or "selective breeding"; no Freudian theory to belittle women's sexuality and encourage their acceptance as the "second sex"; no functional anthropology or sociology to justify a conservative acceptance of the status quo; no Marxist theory to encourage a narrow concentration on economic variables. What the Mills had as their guide is what we have only begun to recapture in our counterpart efforts to expand the horizons of men and women to fuller realization of their human potential: a blend of compassion and logic and a commitment to the view that liberty cannot exist in the absence of the power to use it.

The closest analogy to Mill's intellectual style is the formal structure of what is known in the behavioral sciences as functional analysis, but with this difference: Mill attempted to probe beneath the surface of social forms to find the latent function served by that form, not, however, to pinpoint its "social utility" but to identify the root cause which must be changed to effect the release of women from their subjection. Thus in analyzing chivalry and its equivalent in modern times, "consideration for women," Mill characterized it as a mask hiding the idea of servitude, the notion that women need protection or help because they are "weak." So in a passage that anticipates Genet's analysis, Mill argued that society can never be organized on merit, or depart from its imposition of the power of the strong over the weak, so long as this right of the strong rules in the family, the heart of society:

The principle cannot get hold of men's inmost sentiments until this assumption of superiority of power merely on the ascribed grounds of sex, persists. The selfish propensities, self worship of men, have their source and root in the present constitution of the relation between men and women.

So, too, Mill had a terse and firm answer to the claim that there are "natural" differences between the sexes which preclude full equality for women (by our time amplified by the thousands of psychological and sociological studies which demonstrate differences between the sexes): "No one can know the nature of the sexes as long as they have only been seen in their present relation to each other; . . . what women are is what we have required them to be." Mill left open the possibility that women qua women may have some special type of originality to contribute, though cautious to point out we have no way to predict this until women have had the freedom to develop in an autonomous way, with time to emancipate themselves from the "influence of accepted male models," and strike out on their own.

From Mill's correspondence following the publication of the *Subjection* essay, we can gain some understanding of his reasons for developing the particular arguments he does in the volume, and for excluding certain other topics. There is, for example, little or nothing in the book on marriage and divorce laws. In a letter to Professor John Nichol of Glasgow, Mill wrote:

I thought it best not to discuss the questions of marriage and divorce along with that of the equality of women; not only from the obvious inexpediency of establishing a connection in people's minds between the equality and any particular opinions on the divorce question, but also because I do not think that the conditions of the dissolubility of marriage can be properly determined until women have an equal voice in determining them, nor until there has been experience of the marriage relation as it would exist between equals. Until then I should not like to commit myself to more than the general principle of relief from the contract in extreme cases.[1]

Mill's sense of political expediency and timing played a major role in what he felt was useful to discuss in the essay. At the time he wrote, women had no legal right to their own children, and one reader of his essay wrote to suggest that since there was an infinitely closer relationship of children to their mothers than to their fathers, the law should really reflect this reality, and if anything, give legal rights over children to women. Mill answered Mrs. Hooker:

What you so justly say respecting the infinitely closer relationship of a child to its mother than to its father, I have learned . . . to regard as full of important consequences with regard to the future legal position of parents and children. This, however, is a portion of the truth for which the human mind will not, for some time, be sufficiently prepared to make its discussion useful.[2]

The underlying intent behind Mill's argument in the essay comes out most clearly in a letter to his friend and biographer, Alexander Bain. Mill explained that the stress he gave to the capacities of women, which occupy so large a proportion of the essay, was done for two reasons. One was that the principal objection then offered against sex equality was that women were not "fit for or capable of this, that or the other mental achievement." The second reason is perhaps as cogent in 1970 as it was in John Mill's own time:

But there is still stronger reason. The most important thing women have to do is to stir up the zeal of women themselves. We have to stimulate their aspirations— to bid them not despair of anything, nor think anything beyond their reach, but try their faculties against all difficulties. In no other way can the verdict of experience be fairly collected, and in no other way can we excite the enthusiasm in women which is necessary to break down the old barriers. I believe the point has now been reached at which, the higher we pitch our claims, the more disposition there will be to concede part of them. . . . Everything I hear strengthens me in the belief, which I at first entertained with a slight mixture of misgiving, that the book has come out at the right time, and that no part of it is premature.[3]

It is fitting to note the reaction to the book by an American woman famous in the history of the women's movement, Elizabeth Cady Stanton. This *enfant terrible* of the suffrage cause wrote Mill after reading the *Subjection* essay in 1869:

I lay the book down with a peace and joy I never felt before, for it is the first response from any man to show he is capable of seeing and feeling all the nice shades and degrees of woman's wrongs and the central point of her weakness and degradation.[4]

[1] Hugh S. R. Elliot, ed., *The Letters of John Stuart Mill* (London: Secker and Warburg, 1954), vol. 2, p. 212.

[2] Ibid., p. 214.

[3] Ibid., p. 210.

[4] Alma Lutz, *Created Equal: A Biography of Elizabeth Cady Stanton* (New York: John Day Company, 1940), pp. 171–72.

That Mill was able to achieve this is a tribute to the remarkable blend of compassion and logic both Harriet and Mill himself brought to the analysis of women and the hope for a future equality of the sexes.

When Carrie Chapman Catt wrote her foreword to an American edition of Mill's *The Subjection of Women*, she closed with a few lines that are as relevant in 1970 as they were in 1911:

For some years the book has been out of print, and its pages have grown unfamiliar to those who should know them best. A new edition is a happy incident and its accessibility to the masses will prove of untold value to the movement.[5]

In 1911 the "movement" was the suffrage movement, still some nine years from its victory in securing the vote for American women. In 1970 the movement is much broader and its goals more diffuse, for the women's liberation movement seeks nothing short of full equality of the sexes. In this sense contemporary activists are closer to the perspective of John Mill and Harriet Taylor than of the majority of turn-of-century American suffragists. We can not tell how many years remain until our movement is victorious. The answer lies with those who read and study these pages: all the tens of thousands of women and men who seek to understand the political and ideological history of the movement to secure equality between the sexes. If these same readers carry their knowledge into a vigorous commitment to scholarship and to political action, at least one small corner of this whirling globe may know full sex equality by the close of the twentieth century.

---

[5] John Stuart Mill, *The Subjection of Women* (New York: Frederick A. Stokes, 1911), p. xv.

❧ 18 *Friedrich Engels*

Friedrich Engels was born in 1820 in Barmen, a village in the German Rhineland. His father, a cotton manufacturer, had intended to give the boy a liberal education, but financial reverses forced him to withdraw young Friedrich from preparatory school before his education was complete—although not before he had developed a taste for Hegelian dialectic. He took a position in one of his father's commercial firms in England, where he formed associations with various members of Britain's labor movement and began writing for the socialist press. In 1844 Engels returned to Germany by way of Paris, where he renewed his acquaintance with Karl Marx, whom he had met in Cologne two years before. The friendship of the two resulted in the Communist Manifesto, published in 1848. Shortly afterward, in 1850, Engels returned to Manchester, and Marx and his family moved to London. Twenty years later Engels and his Irish wife, Elizabeth Burns, joined Marx in London. During all those years Engels had been making substantial financial contributions toward the support of the Marx family. Karl Marx died in 1883, Friedrich Engels in 1895.

Marx and Engels not only devoted themselves to the theoretical development of the materialist conception of history; they also undertook to put theory into practice. In 1864 Marx founded the International Working Men's Association, in which Engels took an active part. By 1868 Marx had made clear that membership was open to women as well as men, and subsequently he submitted to the General Council a proposal that it encourage the establishment of special women's branches in addition to the already existing branches that consisted of members of both sexes. Under Marx's leadership, a woman, Harriet Law, was elected to the General Council during the first decade of its existence.

Friedrich Engels referred to The Origin of the Family, Private Property, and the State as a "bequest," a "debt I owe to Marx." In the winter of 1880–1881 Marx had read Lewis Henry Morgan's Ancient Society, or Researches in the Lines of Human Progress from Savagery through Barbarism to Civilization, and had been struck by its relevance to Marxist theory. But ill health had prevented his doing more than taking ninety-eight pages of notes on the book. In 1884, a year after Marx's death, Engels published the work that his friend had apparently wished to write.

Basing his ideas on Morgan, who in turn had found support for his theories in Bachofen's Mutterrecht, Engels took an anthropological approach to the problem of woman's status in modern society. Societies pass from savagery to barbarism to civilization, he asserted, and as they do so the sexual unions within them change from group marriage to pairing marriage to monogamy. A basic factor in the transition from barbarism to civilization, Engels went on, is the tilling of the soil and the domestication of animals. In much the same way that man asserts himself over the animal and the vegetable, he asserts himself over his fellow man through the institution of slavery. And wives are *essentially slaves, Engels believed, part of men's property, just as are land and cattle. Only under socialism, with the abolition of private property, would the relationship between men and women change, Engels predicted. Then wives would no longer belong to husbands. When marriage is determined by love, not economy, both marriage and divorce will become much simpler.*

From *The Origin of the Family, Private Property, and the State*

PREFACE

. . .

Up to the beginning of the sixties, a history of the family cannot be spoken of. This branch of historical science was then entirely under the influence of the decalogue. The patriarchal form of the family, described more exhaustively by Moses than by anybody else, was not only, without further comment, considered as the most ancient, but also as identical with the family of our times. No historical development of the family was even recognized. At best it was admitted that a period of sexual license might have existed in primeval times.

To be sure, aside from monogamy, oriental polygamy and Indo-Tibethan polyandry were known; but these three forms could not be arranged in any historical order and stood side by side without any connection. That some nations of ancient history and some savage tribes of the present day did not trace their descent to the father, but to the mother, hence considered the female lineage as alone valid; that many nations of our time prohibit intermarrying inside of certain large groups, the extent of which was not yet ascertained and that this custom is found in all parts of the globe—these facts were known, indeed, and more examples were continually collected. But nobody knew how to make use of them. Even in E. B. Taylor's "Researches into the Early History of Mankind," etc. (1865), they are only mentioned as "queer customs" together with the usage of some savage tribes to prohibit the touching of burning wood with iron tools, and similar religious absurdities.

This history of the family dates from 1861, the year of the publication of Bachofen's "Mutterrecht" (maternal law). Here the author makes the following propositions:

1. That in the beginning people lived in unrestricted sexual intercourse, which he dubs, not very felicitously, hetaerism.

2. That such an intercourse excludes any absolutely certain means of determining parentage; that consequently descent could only be traced by the female line in compliance with maternal law—and that this was universally practiced by all the nations of antiquity.

3. That consequently women as mothers, being the only well known parents of younger generations, received a high tribute of respect and deference,

amounting to a complete women's rule (gynaicocracy), according to Bachofen's idea.

4. That the transition to monogamy, reserving a certain woman exclusively to one man, implied the violation of a primeval religious law (i.e., practically a violation of the customary right of all other men to the same woman), which violation had to be atoned for or its permission purchased by the surrender of the women to the public for a limited time.

Bachofen finds the proofs of these propositions in numerous quotations from ancient classics, collected with unusual diligence. The transition from "hetaerism" to monogamy and from maternal to paternal law is accomplished according to him—especially by the Greeks—through the evolution of religious ideas. New gods, the representatives of the new ideas, are added to the traditional group of gods, the representatives of old ideas; the latter are forced to the background more and more by the former. According to Bachofen, therefore, it is not the development of the actual conditions of life that has effected the historical changes in the relative social positions of man and wife, but the religious reflection of these conditions in the minds of men. Hence Bachofen represents the Oresteia of Aeschylos as the dramatic description of the fight between the vanishing maternal and the paternal law, rising and victorious during the time of the heroes.

Klytemnaestra has killed her husband Agamemnon on his return from the Trojan war for the sake of her lover Aegisthos; but Orestes, her son by Agamemnon, avenges the death of his father by killing his mother. Therefore he is persecuted by the Erinyes, the demonic protectors of maternal law, according to which the murder of a mother is the most horrible, inexpiable crime. But Apollo, who has instigated Orestes to this act by his oracle, and Athene, who is invoked as arbitrator—the two deities representing the new paternal order of things—protect him. Athene gives a hearing to both parties. The whole question is summarized in the ensuing debate between Orestes and the Erinyes. Orestes claims that Klytemnaestra has committed a twofold crime: by killing her husband she killed his father. Why do the Erinyes persecute him and not her who is far more guilty?

The reply is striking:

"She was not related by blood to the man whom she slew."

The murder of a man not consanguineous, even though he be the husband of the murderess, is expiable, does not concern the Erinyes; it is only their duty to prosecute the murder of consanguineous relatives. According to maternal law, therefore, the murder of a mother is the most heinous and inexpiable crime. Now Apollo speaks in defense of Orestes. Athene then calls on the areopagites—the jurors of Athens—to vote; the votes are even for acquittal and for condemnation. Thereupon Athene as president of the jury casts her vote in favor of Orestes and acquits him. Paternal law has gained a victory over maternal law, the deities of the "younger generation," as the Erinyes call them, vanquish the latter. These are finally persuaded to accept a new office under the new order of things.

This new, but decidedly accurate interpretation of the Oresteia is one of the most beautiful and best passages in the whole book, but it proves at the same time that Bachofen himself believes as much in the Erinyes, in Apollo and in Athene, as Aeschylos did in his day. He really believes, that they performed the miracle of securing the downfall of maternal law through paternal law during the time of the Greek heroes. That a similar conception, representing religion as the main level of the world's history, must finally lead to sheer mysticism, is evident.

Therefore it is a troublesome and not always profitable task to work your way through the big volume of Bachofen. Still, all this does not curtail the value of his fundamental work. He was the first to replace the assumption of an unknown primeval condition of licentious sexual intercourse by the demonstration that ancient classical literature points out a multitude of traces proving the actual existence among Greeks and Asiatics of other sexual relations before monogamy. These relations not only permitted a man to have intercourse with several women, but also left a woman free to have sexual intercourse with several men without violating good morals. This custom did not disappear without leaving as a survival the form of a general surrender for a limited time by which women had to purchase the right of monogamy. Hence descent could originally only be traced by the female line, from mother to mother. The sole legality of the female line was preserved far into the time of monogamy with assured, or at least acknowledged, paternity. Consequently, the original position of the mothers as the sole absolutely certain parents of their children secured for them and for all other women a higher social level than they have ever enjoyed since. Although Bachofen, biased by his mystic conceptions, did not formulate these propositions so clearly, still he proved their correctness. This was equivalent to a complete revolution in 1861.

. . .

THE FAMILY

. . .

Bachofen . . . is perfectly right in contending that the transition from what he calls "hetaerism" or "incestuous generation" to monogamy was brought about mainly by women. The more in the course of economic development, undermining the old communism and increasing the density of population, the traditional sexual relations lost their innocent character suited to the primitive forest, the more debasing and oppressive they naturally appeared to women; and the more they consequently longed for relief by the right of chastity, of temporary or permanent marriage with one man. . . .

[The monogamous family] is founded on male supremacy for the pronounced purpose of breeding children of indisputable paternal lineage. The latter is required, because these children shall later on inherit the fortune of their father. The monogamous family is distinguished from the pairing family by the far greater durability of wedlock, which can no longer be dissolved at the pleasure of either party. As a rule, it is only the man who can still dissolve it and cast off his wife. The privilege of conjugal faithlessness remains sanctioned for men at least by custom (the Code Napoleon concedes it directly to them, as long as they do not bring their concubines into the houses of their wives). This privilege is more and more enjoyed with the increasing development of society. If the woman remembers the ancient sexual practices and attempts to revive them, she is punished more severely than ever.

. . .

Monogamy, then, does by no means enter history as a reconciliation of man and wife and still less as the highest form of marriage. On the contrary, it enters as the subjugation of one sex by the other, as the proclamation of an antagonism between the sexes unknown in all preceding history. In an old unpublished manuscript written by Marx and myself in 1846, I find the following passage: "The first division of labor is that of man and wife in breeding children." And to-day I may add: The first class antagonism appearing in history coincides with the development of the antagonism of man and wife in monogamy, and the first class oppression with that of the female by the male sex. Monogamy was a great historical progress. But by the side of slavery and private property it marks at the same time that epoch which, reaching down to our days, takes with all progress also a step backwards, relatively speaking, and develops the welfare and advancement of one by the woe and submission of the other. It is the cellular form of civilized society which enables us to study the nature of its now fully developed contrasts and contradictions.

The old relative freedom of sexual intercourse by no means disappeared with the victory . . . of the monogamous family. "The old conjugal system, now reduced to narrower limits by the gradual disappearance of the punaluan groups, still environed the advancing family, which it was to follow to the verge of civilization. . . . It finally disappeared in the new form of hetaerism, which still follows mankind in civilization as a dark shadow upon the family."[1]

By hetaerism Morgan designates sexual intercourse of men with unmarried women outside of the monogamous family, flourishing, as is well known, during the whole period of civilization in many different forms and tending more and more to open prostitution. This hetaerism is directly derived . . . from the sacrificial surrender of women for the purpose of obtaining the right to chastity. The surrender for money was at first a religious act; it took place in the temple of the goddess of love and the money flowed originally into the treasury of the temple. The hierodulae of Anaitis in Armenia, of Aphrodite in Corinth and the religious dancing girls of India attached to the temples, the so-called bajaderes (derived from the Portuguese "bailadera," dancing girl), were the first prostitutes. The surrender, originally the duty of every woman, was later on practiced by these priestesses alone in representation of all others. Among other nations, hetaerism is derived from the sexual freedom permitted to girls before marriage. . . . With the rise of different property relations . . . wage labor appears sporadically by the side of slavery, and at the same time its unavoidable companion, professional prostitution of free women by the side of the forced surrender of female slaves. It is the heirloom bequeathed . . . to civilization, a gift as ambiguous as everything else produced by ambiguous, double-faced,

[1] Morgan, *Ancient Society*, p. 504.

schismatic and contradictory civilization. Here monogamy, there hetaerism and its most extreme form, prostitution. Hetaerism is as much a social institution as all others. It continues the old sexual freedom—for the benefit of the men. In reality not only permitted, but also assiduously practised by the ruling class, it is denounced only nominally. Still in practice this denunciation strikes by no means the men who indulge in it, but only the women. These are ostracised and cast out by society, in order to proclaim once more the fundamental law of unconditional male supremacy over the female sex.

However, a second contradiction is thereby developed within monogamy itself. By the side of the husband, who is making his life pleasant by hetaerism, stands the neglected wife. And you cannot have one side of the contradiction without the other, just as you cannot have the whole apple after eating half of it. Nevertheless this seems to have been the idea of the men, until their wives taught them a lesson. Monogamy introduces two permanent social characters that were formerly unknown: the standing lover of the wife and the cuckold. The men had gained the victory over the women, but the vanquished magnanimously provided the coronation. In addition to monogamy and hetaerism, adultery became an unavoidable social institution—denounced, severely punished, but irrepressible. The certainty of paternal parentage rested as of old on moral conviction at best, and in order to solve the unreconcilable contradiction, the code Napoléon decreed in its article 312: "L'enfant conçu pendant le mariage a pour père le mari;" the child conceived during marriage has for its father—the husband. This is the last result of three thousand years of monogamy.

Thus we have in the monogamous family, at least in those cases that remain true to historical development and clearly express the conflict between man and wife created by the exclusive supremacy of men, a miniature picture of the contrasts and contradictions of society at large. Split by class-differences since the beginning of civilization, society has been unable to reconcile and overcome these antitheses.

.   .   .

The legal equality of man and woman in marriage is by no means better founded. Their legal inequality inherited from earlier stages of society is not the cause, but the effect of the economic oppression of women. In the ancient communistic household comprising many married couples and their children, the administration of the household entrusted to women was just as much a public function, a socially necessary industry, as the procuring of food by men. In the patriarchal and still more in the monogamous family this was changed. The administration of the household lost its public character. It was no longer a concern of society. It became a private service. The woman became the first servant of the house, excluded from participation in social production. Only by the great industries of our time the access to social production was again opened for women—for proletarian women alone, however. This is done in such a manner that they remain excluded from public production and cannot earn anything, if they fulfill their duties in the private service of the family; or that they are unable to attend to their family duties, if they wish to participate in public industries and earn a living independently. As in the factory, so women are situated in all business departments up to the medical and legal professions. The modern monogamous family is founded on the open or disguised domestic slavery of women, and modern society is a mass composed of molecules in the form of monogamous families. In the great majority of cases the man has to earn a living and to support his family, at least among the possessing classes. He thereby obtains a superior position that has no need of any legal special privilege. In the family, he is the bourgeois, the woman represents the proletariat. In the industrial world, however, the specific character of the economic oppression weighing on the proletariat appears in its sharpest outlines only after all special privileges of the capitalist class are abolished and the full legal equality of both classes is established. A democratic republic does not abolish the distinction between the two classes. On the contrary, it offers the battleground on which this distinction can be fought out. Likewise the peculiar character of man's rule over woman in the modern family, the necessity and the manner of accomplishing the real social equality of the two, will appear in broad daylight only then, when both of them will enjoy complete legal equality. It will then be seen that the emancipation of women is primarily dependent on the re-introduction of the whole female sex into the public industries. To accomplish this, the monogamous family must cease to be the industrial unit of society.

. . .

We are now approaching a social revolution, in which the old economic foundations of monogamy will disappear just as surely as those of its complement, prostitution. Monogamy arose through the concentration of considerable wealth in one hand—a man's hand—and from the endeavor to bequeath this wealth to the children of this man to the exclusion of all others. This necessitated monogamy on the woman's, but not on the man's part. Hence this monogamy of women in no way hindered open or secret polygamy of men. Now, the impending social revolution will reduce this whole care of inheritance to a minimum by changing at least the overwhelming part of permanent and inheritable wealth—the means of production—into social property. Since monogamy was caused by economic conditions, will it disappear when these causes are abolished?

One might reply, not without reason: not only will it not disappear, but it will rather be perfectly realized. For with the transformation of the means of production into collective property, wage labor will also disappear, and with it the proletariat and the necessity for a certain, statistically ascertainable number of women to surrender for money. Prostitution disappears and monogamy, instead of going out of existence, at last becomes a reality—for men also.

At all events, the situation will be very much changed for men. But also that of women, and of all women, will be considerably altered. With the transformation of the means of production into collective property the monogamous family ceases to be the economic unit of society. The private household changes to a social industry. The care and education of children becomes a public matter. Society cares equally well for all children, legal or illegal. This removes the care about the "consequences" which now forms the essential social factor—moral and economic—hindering a girl to surrender unconditionally to the beloved man. Will not this be sufficient cause for a gradual rise of a more unconventional intercourse of the sexes and a more lenient public opinion regarding virgin honor and female shame? And finally, did we not see that in the modern world monogamy and prostitution, though antitheses, are inseparable and poles of the same social condition? Can prostitution disappear without engulfing at the same time monogamy?

Here a new element becomes active, an element which at best existed only in the germ at the time when monogamy developed: individual sexlove.

. . .

Since sexlove is exclusive by its very nature—although this exclusiveness is at present realized for women alone—marriage founded on sexlove must be monogamous. . . . Remove the economic considerations that now force women to submit to the customary disloyalty of men, and you will place women on an equal footing with men. All present experiences prove that this will tend much more strongly to make men truly monogamous, than to make women polyandrous.

However, those peculiarities that were stamped upon the face of monogamy by its rise through property relations, will decidedly vanish, namely the supremacy of men and the indissolubility of marriage. The supremacy of man in marriage is simply the consequence of his economic superiority and will fall with the abolition of the latter.

The indissolubility of marriage is partly the consequence of economic conditions, under which monogamy arose, partly tradition from the time where the connection between this economic situation and monogamy, not yet clearly understood, was carried to extremes by religion. To-day, it has been perforated a thousand times. If marriage founded on love is alone moral, then it follows that marriage is moral only as long as love lasts. The duration of an attack of individual sexlove varies considerably according to individual disposition, especially in men. A positive cessation of fondness or its replacement by a new passionate love makes a separation a blessing for both parties and for society. But humanity will be spared the useless wading through the mire of a divorce case.

What we may anticipate about the adjustment of sexual relations after the impending downfall of capitalist production is mainly of a negative nature and mostly confined to elements that will disappear. But what will be added? That will be decided after a new generation has come to maturity: a race of men who never in their lives have had any occasion for buying with money or other economic means of power the surrender of a woman; a race of women who never had any occasion for surrendering to any man for any other reason but love, or for refusing to surrender to their lover from fear of economic consequences. Once such people are in the world, they will not give a moment's thought to what we to-day believe should be their course. They will follow their own practice and fashion their own public opinion about the individual practice of every person—only this and nothing more.

. . .

~§§~ *Eleanor Burke Leacock*

Eleanor Burke Leacock is professor of anthropology at the City College of the City University of New York. A scholar of great versatility, Professor Leacock has published books on topics as diverse as elementary and secondary education, poverty, and the American Indian. In the following pages, from the Introduction to her edition of Engels' Origin of the Family, Private Property, and the State, Professor Leacock emphasizes Engels' thesis that it is not the function of childbearing but the economic unity of the monogamous family that is responsible for women's subjugation.

From Introduction to Engels' *Origin of the Family, Private Property, and the State*

POLITICAL RAMIFICATIONS OF ENGELS' ARGUMENT ON WOMEN'S SUBJUGATION

Engels writes, "the peculiar character of the supremacy of the husband over the wife in the modern family . . . will only be seen in the clear light of day when both possess legally complete equality of rights," although, in itself, legal equity affords no solution. Just as the legal equality of capitalist and proletarian makes visible "the specific character of the economic oppression burdening the proletariat," so also will legal equality reveal the fundamental change that is necessary for the liberation of women. Engels goes on to say: "Then it will be plain that the first condition for the liberation of the wife is to bring the whole female sex back into public industry, and that this in turn demands that the characteristic of the monogamous family as the economic unit of society be abolished" (137–38).

Such a change is dependent on the abolition of private ownership. "With the transfer of the means of production into common ownership, the single family ceases to be the economic unit of society. Private housekeeping is transformed into a social industry. The care and education of the children becomes a public affair; society looks after all children alike" (139). Only when this is accomplished will a new generation of women grow up, Engels writes, who have never known "what it is to give themselves to a man from any other considerations than real love or to refuse to give themselves to their lover from fear of the economic consequences." Then men and women "will care precious little what anybody today thinks they ought to do; they will make their own practice and their corresponding public opinion about the practice of each individual—and that will be the end of it" (145). To which must be added today that the destruction of the family as an economic unit does not *automatically* follow with the establishment of socialism, but rather is one of the goals to be fought for as central to the transition to communism.

There has recently been much discussion about the extent to which women can achieve a measure of personal "liberation" by rejecting the sex-role definitions of the contemporary "monogamous" family, and about the relevance such rejection can have to the furthering of revolutionary aims and consciousness. There has also been considerable argument about the basis for women's inferior position, ranging from the extreme psychobiological view that it results from an innate masculine drive for domination and can be changed only through a single-minded "battle of the sexes," to the extreme economic determinist—and generally masculine—view that since all basic changes ultimately depend on the revolutionary restructuring of society, it is both illusory and diversionary to focus on ameliorating the special problems of women.

While there is still a great deal of abstract argument about the correct position on women's liberation, there is also a growing recognition that it is fruitless to debate the extent to which various parts of the women's movement can or cannot be linked with revolutionary goals, and there is a growing commitment to developing concrete tactics of program and organization around situations where women are in motion on basic issues. It might seem that Engels' discussion of family arrangements that have long ceased to exist in their pristine forms is somewhat esoteric and of little relevance today. However, it is crucial to the organization of women for their liberation to understand that it is the monogamous family as an economic unit, at the heart of class society, that is basic to their subjugation. Such understanding makes clear that child-bearing itself is not responsible for the low status of women, as has been the contention of some radical women's groups. And more important, it indicates the way in which working-class women, not only in their obviously basic fight on the job but also in their seemingly more conservative battles for their families around schools, housing and welfare, are actually posing a more basic challenge than that of the radicals. By demanding that society assume responsibility for their children, they are attacking the nature of the family as an economic unit, the basis of their own oppression and a central buttress of class exploitation. Therefore, while some of the activities of middle-class radical women's groups can be linked with the struggles of working-class women, such as the fight for free legalized abortion, others are so psychologically oriented as to be confusing and diversionary.

The self-declared women's movement in this country has historically been middle class and largely oriented toward a fight for the same options as middle-class men within the system, while the struggles of working-class women have not been conceived as fights for women's liberation as such. This has been true since the close of the Civil War, when the women's movement that had been closely concerned with the fight against slavery and for the rights of women factory workers broke away on its "feminist" course. Today there is more widespread awareness that all oppressive relations are interconnected and embedded in our system as a whole, and that only united effort can effect fundamental change. However, there has been little clear and consistent effort made to achieve such unity. For example, the committees formed by professional women to fight job discrimination are generally prepared to admit forthrightly that their battle is ultimately inseparable from that of working-class and especially Black working-class women, but they have done virtually nothing to find ways of linking the two. And it is commonplace to point out that, despite basic differences between the oppression of women and the oppression of Blacks, there are marked parallels of both an economic and a social-psychological nature—not to mention the fact that half of Black people are women. But again, there has been no solid commitment to building organizational ties between the two movements around specific issues. The theoretical differentiation between the symptoms and the causes of women's oppression can help clarify the issues around which united organization must be built, and can help remove the blocks hampering the enormous potential a women's movement could have for unifying sections of the middle and working classes and bridging some of the disastrous gap between white workers and Black, Puerto Rican, and Mexican American workers. However, in this effort it is important to be wary of a certain suspect quality of many white middle-class women (akin to that of their male counterparts) to be attracted and exhilarated by the assertiveness of the struggle for Black liberation, and to neglect their responsibility to find ways of also building an alliance with white working-class women and men.

Theoretical understanding is sorely needed to help combat the difficulties that will continue to beset the women's movement. Male supremacy, the enormous difficulty men have in facing up to their pathetic feelings of superiority and display of petty power over women, even when theoretically dedicated to revolutionary change, will continue to feed what is often a narrowly anti-men orientation among "movement women;" and the media will continue to exploit this as a gimmick that serves at the same time to sell cigarettes and shampoo, dissipate energies, and divide women from each other and from what should be allied struggles. As with the black-power movement, the sheer possibility of open confrontation will for some serve the need to express a great pent-up anger, and token victories will temporarily serve to give the illusion of some success. The overwhelming need is to keep this powerful anger from being dissipated— to find ways of building upon it through taking organizationally meaningful steps.

৵৶ 19 *Bertrand Russell*

Bertrand Arthur William Russell was born in 1872 in Trelleck, Wales. His mother, an active advocate of the franchise for women, chose to have him brought into the world by Garrett Anderson, who at that time was certified only as a midwife, but later became the world's first woman doctor. His father, Lord Amberly, an equally liberated thinker, stipulated in his will that in the event that his sons were orphaned, they were to be brought up as atheists under the guardianship of two of his freethinking friends. But upon his death, when Bertrand was three, the will was broken and the two boys were placed in the care of their paternal grandparents. Their grandfather, Lord John Russell, a former prime minister, died two years later, leaving Lady Russell to educate her grandsons in the best Victorian tradition, with private tutors at home. More or less balancing her conservatism was the liberal influence of John Stuart Mill, young Russell's godfather ("so far as it is possible in a non-religious sense"), whose works Bertrand had read eagerly even before his matriculation at Cambridge. At the university Russell, at first attracted to the English Hegelians, began to feel other influences as well: that of C. E. Moore, a year his junior, who was formulating his "common sense" philosophy; that of Alfred North Whitehead, who taught him mathematics and with whom he was to collaborate on Principia Mathematica; and later that of his brilliant pupil Ludwig Wittgenstein.

Meanwhile, despite rather strong objections from his family, Russell had married Alys Pearsall Smith, an American debutante of great intelligence and extraordinary beauty. Russell engaged in political as well as philosophical activity and even served a six-month prison term for the expression of pacifist views in an article in The Tribunal. In 1931, having been divorced by Alys Russell, he married Dora Black, with whom from 1927 to 1932 he operated a school for small children, including their own, John and Kate. In 1935 the two were divorced, and a year later Russell married Patricia Helen Spence, mother of his third child, Conrad, who was born a year later. From 1938 to 1944 Russell lectured in the United States at many of the country's leading universities. Notable by its absence from the group was the City College of New York, which canceled his contract because of, acceding to demands made in a taxpayer's lawsuit, his liberal views on sex and morality, expressed largely in Marriage and Morals, for which he had won a Nobel prize in 1930. With his fourth and last wife, Edith Finch, Russell finally found, according to his own testimony, the peace for which he had yearned through-out his life. He died in 1970 at the age of ninety-eight.

Throughout the nineteenth century, woman suffrage had been a hotly debated political issue in England. The emphasis of the Liberals had been on extending suffrage for men; they had considered women to be of secondary importance. The Conservatives, on the other hand, had advocated that the vote be ex-tended to upper-class women and denied to working-class men. The Liberals reacted by opposing the woman suffrage movement altogether.

As the century wore on, women began to organize. They were active in the British antislavery groups, which were organized in the 1830s. In the 1840s various women's rights groups were formed, and in 1865 the first women's suffrage committee was founded in Manchester.

As Emmeline Pankhurst and her daughters, Christabel and Sylvia, began their activities, the women's movement began to gain ground. In 1903 the Pankhursts formed the Women's Social and Political Union, a militant organization devoted to gaining publicity for the suffrage movement. Its tactics included protests and demonstrations of all kinds: breaking up meetings, throwing stones, heckling, parading in the streets, and hunger strikes.

Russell was one of the staunchest champions of the movement, and the first of his three unsuccessful bids for Parliament was backed by the National Union of Women's Suffrage Societies. Russell's liberal social theories—not only his advocacy of pacifism and women's suffrage but also his liberal views concerning education and sexual morality—might appear to be at variance with the subjectivistic ethics to which he subscribed. In his mature ethical works Russell regarded "good" and "bad" not as qualities of objects but as indications of the attitudes of those who used the words. Thus a statement such as "The suppression of women is bad" is not an assertion but the emotive expression of a wish cherished by the speaker (equivalent, perhaps, to "Would that women were not suppressed"). Russell distinguishes between "personal" and "impersonal" desires, however. The desire of a hungry man for food or of an ambitious man for fame is a desire of the former type, while moral judgments fall into the latter category and are held to be universal in character. If anything saves Russell from inconsistency as he holds to subjectivism while preaching reform, it is that the desires that prompt him to urge reform are not personal but universal.

Liberalism and Women's Suffrage

By Mr. Asquith's pronouncement of May 20th, women's suffrage, for the first time in this country, becomes likely to form part of a Bill intended by the House of Commons to pass into law. It now rests with the friends of women's suffrage in the House of Commons to introduce a suitable amendment into the promised Electoral Reform Bill, and with the friends of democracy in the country to use their utmost endeavours to force the acceptance of this Bill on the House of Lords. In spite of the continued opposition to Liberals on the part of the militant suffragists, the cause of women's suffrage is now, at any rate for the moment, bound up with the fortunes of Liberalism. As temporary circumstances have tended to cause an apparent divergence of interest between Suffragists and Liberals, it may be well now to remind ourselves of the permanent reasons which should lead the two to co-operate. The reasons in favour of women's suffrage are all such as ought to appeal with special force to Liberals. In the heat of political controversy reasons of principle are too often lost sight of; I shall therefore make an attempt to recall them, and to show that they are such as no consistent Liberal can fail to acknowledge.

The grounds in favour of women's suffrage are, in the main, the same as those in favour of democracy in general; but in some respects these grounds apply with special force to the case of women. It is plain that no man can call himself truly a democrat if he is in favour of excluding half the nation from all participation in public affairs. Yet we find that democracy now-a-days is usually conceded as no longer open to discussion, even by people who are strong opponents of the claims of women. Such people, it seems to me, have forgotten what the benefits of democracy really are: for if they remembered them they could hardly fail to see that these benefits are to be expected from the enfranchisement of women, just as much as from the enfranchisement of working men. I shall, therefore, make no apology for recalling some of the main arguments in favour of democracy.

The chief traditional argument in favour of democracy is that it is difficult for one class to judge of the interest of another, and rare for one class to care as much for the interest of another as for its own. The illustrations of this in history are too numerous to need citing: oligarchies have invariably been more or less ignorant of and indifferent to the interests of those whom they governed. It may be said that the relations of men and women are so close that this particular argument does not apply to the case of women. But I think this view is not borne out by the facts. There are, as every one knows, many respects in which the laws are unequal as between men and women. And there are many evils from which women suffer which are quietly accepted as inevitable, because those who have political power are not those who have to endure the evils. Is it just, for example, that a working woman and her children should, through no fault of her own, be reduced to destitution if her husband takes to drink? Yet no one regards this as a political question.

But perhaps a more important argument for democracy is its educational effect on the voter and its effect in improving the relations between different classes. To speak first of the educational effect: there is the direct education of being brought into contact with political questions, and there is the education of character resulting from responsibility and freedom. Of these two, the education of character seems to me the more important, but the other is by no means a small matter. Anyone who has watched an election must have been struck by the amount of knowledge on politics which the voters acquire from meetings and canvassers, and discussions among themselves. The diffusion of such knowledge throughout the population not only increases the stability of a civilisation, but also has the merit of making people aware of greater and more important matters than are to be found in their personal circumstances.

Closely connected with this purely political education is the education of character which I spoke of just now. It is good for people to feel that momentous questions depend in part upon their decision: it leads them to think responsibly and seriously, and it cultivates self-respect. One of the great arguments in favour of liberty is that those who have the direction of their own lives are in general intrinsically better than they would have been if others had regulated their lives for them. And this applies with at least as much force to the part of life which is political or affected by politics as it does to more private concerns. Therefore, when it is said that women should be politically educated first before being given the vote, it is forgotten that the vote itself is the great engine of political education. This has proved to be the case with working men, who very generally had hardly any political education before they got the vote; and that it will prove so with women seems not open to doubt.

Another of the arguments for democracy is that it improves the relations between classes. When one class has power and another has not, those who have the power are not likely to feel as much respect for those who have not as for those who have. We all know the aristocratic attitude in politics, the attitude which instinctively ignores all interests except those of its own class, and feels that other classes are comparatively of no account. This attitude has been rapidly dying out under the influence of popular election. But in relation to women all men are in the position of aristocrats, and a contempt for the opinions or interests of women receives no political punishment. Considering how much closer are the relations of men and women than the relations of different classes, and how much better for both parties are equal relations than unequal ones, this must be regarded as a powerful argument in favour of giving votes to women. For it seems certain that the political enfranchisement of women would react beneficially on private life, engendering greater liberty and greater mutual respect in the relations of the sexes.

The chief arguments of principle in favour of women's suffrage may, then, be summed up as follows. First, that from defect of imagination and good will no class can be trusted to care adequately for the interests of another class, and that, in fact, women's interests have been unduly neglected by men. Secondly, that participation in politics widens people's outlook, and improves character by cultivating self-respect and a sense of responsibility; and that these advantages are just as certain to accrue to women if they have the vote as they were to accrue to working men. Thirdly, that it is easier to give due respect to those who have the same legal powers as we have, and that a feeling of equality between men and women is of immense benefit, not only in politics, but in private life.

I ought to add among the arguments of principle the argument of abstract justice. This argument is sometimes supposed to rest upon an antiquated philosophy of natural right, and is, therefore, now rather discredited. But it does not seem to me to require any such fallacious foundation. To inflict a special disability upon any class of the community is in itself an evil, and is calculated to generate resentment on the one side and arrogance on the other. It may be admitted that this evil, in some cases, is more than balanced by compensating advantages; but it remains an evil, and any gain for the sake of which it is to be endured must be very great and very certain. In the case of the disabilities of women, no such gain is apparent, and the argument from justice must therefore be admitted.

Having now considered the main arguments in favour of giving votes to women, I will pass to some of the arguments on the other side.

(1) We are often told that women are unreasonable, that they are governed

by their emotions, and that they are unable to understand politics. I do not know that I need waste much time on this argument. "Reason," in the mouths of those men who advance this modest opinion, generally means "wanting what I want," and being "governed by emotions" means "wanting what I don't want." Queen Elizabeth considered the House of Commons incapable of understanding foreign politics, because their aims were not the same as hers. The House of Lords considers the House of Commons incapable of understanding the land question, because the House of Commons does not recognise the paramount necessity of increasing rents. I suspect that women's incapacity for politics is of the same kind, and that if they alone had the vote it would be men who would be incapable and emotional.

(2) We are told that women would be priest-ridden, that they would vote always at the dictation of their religious advisers. In Catholic countries there may be some truth in this as things stand, though in Great Britain there seems no reason whatever to think it would be the case. But if it were true, it would only mark the neglect of women's political education, which is due to their exclusion from the vote, and would presumably be remedied by their enfranchisement. If it were not remedied, that would mean that a minority are inflicting their policy upon the majority, and that those who fear priestly domination are nevertheless prepared to prolong their own domination because they are so certain that it is the better. But such a position is the negation of all democratic principles, and would, if logically carried out, be found to justify all degrees of intolerance, including religious persecution. This argument, therefore, even if it were not mistaken as to facts, would not be available for anyone who believes in popular government.

(3) Women, it is said, ought not to have the vote because they cannot fight. If this argument were pushed home we ought to disfranchise all men who are too old to fight, or are in any way physically incapable; and we ought to disfranchise Quakers because they will not fight. But it is hard to see why the vote should be confined to those who can fight. The idea seems to be that you will have all the men on one side and all the women on the other, and that then the action of the majority would be defeated by an appeal to arms. But the supposition is so fantastic that it is hard to take it seriously, especially as the same people who make it tell us that it is unnecessary to give votes to women, because they would always vote with their husbands. The notion that in such a country as England an appeal to arms could ever be made successfully against the decision of Parliament is obviously absurd; and if this idea is not entertained, the question whether women can fight is of no importance.

(4) I come now to a very favourite argument. Women's suffrage, we are told, would promote quarrels in families and destroy the happiness of home life. Those who advance this argument apparently think that it is impossible to discuss without quarrelling, that a man cannot be happy unless all his words are received as oracles by a dutiful family, and that the ideal of home life is to avoid all conversation on every important subject. A husband and wife who cannot get on together unless they confine themselves to trivialities had better, I should say, learn a little mutual forbearance; and I should count it among the

advantages of women's suffrage that it would tend to promote a reasonable discussion of things outside the home.

(5) It is often said that women ought not to have votes because they do not want them. Those who say this, by the way, are loudest in condemnation of those women who have taken steps to let us know that they do want votes. But that is natural, for no one is so annoying as a person who disproves one's favourite argument. Speaking seriously, the allegation that women do not want the vote is rapidly becoming untrue, although it is perhaps not yet untrue of the majority. But even if it is still true of the majority, it does not warrant the conclusion that women ought not to have the vote. In the first place, it does not warrant the exclusion of that large and increasing number of women who do want the vote. In the second place, all the arguments which we considered in favour of women's suffrage remain valid, even if women are indifferent, and when women have had the political education resulting from the franchise, they will see the advantage of the vote. The question, therefore, whether a majority of women desire the vote is not really relevant to the issue, though it does, of course, vitally affect the likelihood of their getting the vote.

(6) One bogey which is used to frighten timid people is the argument that there are more women than men in the United Kingdom, and that, therefore, we should be governed by women if we gave the vote to all women. Now, in the first place, very few advocates of women's suffrage demand the vote for *all* women. In the second place, if it is urged that any measure of women's suffrage would be merely a stage on the way to the enfranchisement of all women (which I should admit), it still does not follow that we should be governed by women. This assumes, like the argument that women cannot fight, that we shall have all women on one side and all men on the other; but I cannot think that either sex will make themselves so very obnoxious as to bring about such a result as that. And in the third place, even if we were governed by women, would it be so very terrible? At present we are governed by men, and the result, though perhaps not very admirable, is one which we all endure patiently. I fail to see why being governed by one sex should be any worse than being governed by the other. This argument, therefore, is peculiarly futile, for what it dreads would certainly not happen, and there is no reason to think it would matter if it did.

There remains one reason against the suffrage, which certainly has more force than all the others put together: I mean the instinctive love of dominion. Most men like to be cock-of-the-walk somewhere, and home is generally the only place where they get a chance. They dread that in an equal contest they might fail to maintain the lead, and they therefore insist that the matrimonial race shall continue to be a handicap. For this reason many men who are willing enough that spinsters and widows should have votes are most unwilling that married women should, because they do not wish to lose the one corner where they have mastery. Against this state of mind it is useless to bring mere arguments. It has been partially overcome among educated people by novelists and playwrights, but among the uneducated it is still rampant. While it is the most serious obstacle with which advocates of women's suffrage have to contend, it must also be said that one of the gains to be expected from women's suffrage is that it will tend to substitute for the somewhat brutal desire for mastery a co-operation which cannot fail to develop the intelligence and the good will of both parties.

I would appeal to Liberals, therefore, in the name of all their professed principles, to support the demand which women suffragists make, namely, the demand that women should have votes on the same terms as men. It is only through supporting this demand that we can hope to reach that complete democracy which ought to be our goal, and to resist such a demand from a section of the nation can only be justified by oligarchical principles, such as no Liberal has a right to hold. The gains to the community to be expected from granting it are very great. First, an immense advance in the political education of women and a broadening of their outlook on life. Secondly, a gain to liberty and an improvement in the attitude of men towards women. Thirdly, in the long run a greater care for questions of women's work, of the rearing and education of children, and of all those increasingly important problems upon which the biological future of the race depends. The rise of women to equality with men, which has been rapidly advancing during the past half-century, is one of those great social improvements of which only a few occur in a thousand years. To let prejudice or an uncertain party advantage stand in the way of our contributing to this improvement is unworthy of men who have liberty at heart, and I most earnestly hope that few Liberals will any longer be guilty of such a treachery to all their professions.

✒️ *Emma Goldman*

Emma Goldman, a Lithuanian-born anarchist, came to America in 1885. Early in this century she founded the anarchist journal Mother Earth, *which she edited for almost a dozen years. She also lent her support to the birth-control movement and other liberal causes. Woman suffrage, however, was not among them. Goldman stoutly denied that suffrage was the key to women's freedom. Were voting a privilege, she agreed, women should have the franchise. But as an anarchist, she denied that this was the case. Women's freedom, she concluded, could come only from women themselves.*

From *Anarchism and Other Essays*

WOMAN SUFFRAGE

We boast of the age of advancement, of science, and progress. Is it not strange, then, that we still believe in fetich worship? True, our fetiches have different form and substance, yet in their power over the human mind they are still as disastrous as were those of old.

Our modern fetich is universal suffrage. Those who have not yet achieved that goal fight bloody revolutions to obtain it, and those who have enjoyed its reign bring heavy sacrifice to the altar of this omnipotent deity. Woe to the heretic who dare question that divinity!

Woman, even more than man, is a fetich worshipper, and though her idols may change, she is ever on her knees, ever holding up her hands, ever blind to the fact that her god has feet of clay. Thus woman has been the greatest supporter of all deities from time immemorial. Thus, too, she has had to pay the price that only gods can exact,—her freedom, her heart's blood, her very life.

Nietzsche's memorable maxim, "When you go to woman, take the whip along," is considered very brutal, yet Nietzsche expressed in one sentence the attitude of woman towards her gods.

Religion, especially the Christian religion, has condemned woman to the life of an inferior, a slave. It has thwarted her nature and fettered her soul, yet the Christian religion has no greater supporter, none more devout, than woman. Indeed, it is safe to say that religion would have long ceased to be a factor in the lives of the people, if it were not for the support it receives from woman. The most ardent churchworkers, the most tireless missionaries the world over, are women, always sacrificing on the altar of the gods that have chained her spirit and enslaved her body.

The insatiable monster, war, robs woman of all that is dear and precious to her. It exacts her brothers, lovers, sons, and in return gives her a life of loneliness and despair. Yet the greatest supporter and worshiper of war is woman. She it is who instills the love of conquest and power into her children; she it is who whispers the glories of war into the ears of her little ones, and who rocks her baby to sleep with the tunes of trumpets and the noise of guns. It is woman, too, who crowns the victor on his return from the battlefield. Yes, it is woman who pays the highest price to that insatiable monster, war.

Then there is the home. What a terrible fetich it is! How it saps the very life-energy of woman,—this modern prison with golden bars. Its shining aspect blinds woman to the price she would have to pay as wife, mother, and housekeeper. Yet woman clings tenaciously to the home, to the power that holds her in bondage.

It may be said that because woman recognizes the awful toll she is made to pay to the Church, State, and the home, she wants suffrage to set herself free. That may be true of the few; the majority of suffragists repudiate utterly such blasphemy. On the contrary, they insist always that it is woman suffrage which will make her a better Christian and homekeeper, a staunch citizen of the State. Thus suffrage is only a means of strengthening the omnipotence of the very Gods that woman has served from time immemorial.

What wonder, then, that she should be just as devout, just as zealous, just as prostrate before the new idol, woman suffrage. As of old, she endures persecution, imprisonment, torture, and all forms of condemnation, with a smile on her face. As of old, the most enlightened, even, hope for a miracle from the twentieth-century deity,—suffrage. Life, happiness, joy, freedom, independence,—all that, and more, is to spring from suffrage. In her blind devotion woman does not see what people of intellect perceived fifty years ago: that suffrage is an evil, that it has only helped to enslave people, that it has but closed their eyes that they may not see how craftily they were made to submit.

Woman's demand for equal suffrage is based largely on the contention that woman must have the equal right in all affairs of society. No one could, possibly, refute that, if suffrage were a right. Alas, for the ignorance of the human mind, which can see a right in an imposition. Or is it not the most brutal imposition for one set of people to make laws that another set is coerced by force to obey? Yet woman clamors for that "golden opportunity" that has wrought so much misery in the world, and robbed man of his integrity and self-reliance; an imposition which has thoroughly corrupted the people, and made them absolute prey in the hands of unscrupulous politicians.

The poor, stupid, free American citizen! Free to starve, free to tramp the highways of this great country, he enjoys universal suffrage, and, by that right, he has forged chains about his limbs. The reward that he receives is stringent labor laws prohibiting the right of boycott, of picketing, in fact, of everything, except the right to be robbed of the fruits of his labor. Yet all these disastrous results of the twentieth-century fetich have taught woman nothing. But, then, woman will purify politics, we are assured.

Needless to say, I am not opposed to woman suffrage on the conventional ground that she is not equal to it. I see neither physical, psychological, nor mental reasons why woman should not have the equal right to vote with man. But that can not possibly blind me to the absurd notion that woman will accomplish that wherein man has failed. If she would not make things worse, she certainly could not make them better. To assume, therefore, that she would succeed in purifying something which is not susceptible of purification, is to credit her with supernatural powers. Since woman's greatest misfortune has been that she was looked upon as either angel or devil, her true salvation lies in being placed on earth; namely, in being considered human, and therefore subject to all human follies and mistakes. Are we, then, to believe that two errors will make a right? Are we to assume that the poison already inherent in politics will be decreased, if women were to enter the political arena? The most ardent suffragists would hardly maintain such a folly.

As a matter of fact, the most advanced students of universal suffrage have come to realize that all existing systems of political power are absurd, and are completely inadequate to meet the pressing issues of life. This view is also borne out by a statement of one who is herself an ardent believer in woman suffrage, Dr. Helen L. Sumner. In her able work on *Equal Suffrage*, she says: "In Colorado, we find that equal suffrage serves to show in the most striking way the essential rottenness and degrading character of the existing system." Of course, Dr. Sumner has in mind a particular system of voting, but the same applies with equal force to the entire machinery of the representative system. With such a basis, it is difficult to understand how woman, as a political factor, would benefit either herself or the rest of mankind.

But, say our suffrage devotees, look at the countries and States where female suffrage exists. See what woman has accomplished—in Australia, New Zealand,

Finland, the Scandinavian countries, and in our own four States, Idaho, Colorado, Wyoming, and Utah. Distance lends enchantment—or, to quote a Polish formula—"it is well where we are not." Thus one would assume that those countries and States are unlike other countries or States, that they have greater freedom, greater social and economic equality, a finer appreciation of human life, deeper understanding of the great social struggle, with all the vital questions it involves for the human race.

The women of Australia and New Zealand can vote, and help make the laws. Are the labor conditions better there than they are in England, where the suffragettes are making such a heroic struggle? Does there exist a greater motherhood, happier and freer children than in England? Is woman there no longer considered a mere sex commodity? Has she emancipated herself from the Puritanical double standard of morality for men and women? Certainly none but the ordinary female stump politician will dare answer these questions in the affirmative. If that be so, it seems ridiculous to point to Australia and New Zealand as the Mecca of equal suffrage accomplishments.

On the other hand, it is a fact to those who know the real political conditions in Australia, that politics have gagged labor by enacting the most stringent labor laws, making strikes without the sanction of an arbitration committee a crime equal to treason.

Not for a moment do I mean to imply that woman suffrage is responsible for this state of affairs. I do mean, however, that there is no reason to point to Australia as a wonder-worker of woman's accomplishment, since her influence has been unable to free labor from the thraldom of political bossism.

Finland has given woman equal suffrage; nay, even the right to sit in Parliament. Has that helped to develop a greater heroism, an intenser zeal than that of the women of Russia? Finland, like Russia, smarts under the terrible whip of the bloody Tsar. Where are the Finnish Perovskaias, Spiridonovas, Figners, Breshkovskaias? Where are the countless numbers of Finnish young girls who cheerfully go to Siberia for their cause? Finland is sadly in need of heroic liberators. Why has the ballot not created them? The only Finnish avenger of his people was a man, not a woman, and he used a more effective weapon than the ballot.

As to our own States where women vote, and which are constantly being pointed out as examples of marvels, what has been accomplished there through the ballot that women do not to a large extent enjoy in other States; or that they could not achieve through energetic efforts without the ballot?

True, in the suffrage States women are guaranteed equal rights to property; but of what avail is that right to the mass of women without property, the thousands of wage workers, who live from hand to mouth? That equal suffrage did not, and cannot, affect their condition is admitted even by Dr. Sumner, who certainly is in a position to know. As an ardent suffragist, and having been sent to Colorado by the Collegiate Equal Suffrage League of New York State to collect material in favor of suffrage, she would be the last to say anything derogatory; yet we are informed that "equal suffrage has but slightly affected the economic conditions of women. That women do not receive equal pay for equal work, and that, though woman in Colorado has enjoyed school suffrage since 1876, women teachers are paid less than in California." On the other hand, Miss Sumner fails to account for the fact that although women have had school suffrage for thirty-four years, and equal suffrage since 1894, the census in Denver alone a few months ago disclosed the fact of fifteen thousand defective school children. And that, too, with mostly women in the educational department, and also notwithstanding that women in Colorado have passed the "most stringent laws for child and animal protection." The women of Colorado "have taken great interest in the State institutions for the care of dependent, defective, and delinquent children." What a horrible indictment against woman's care and interest, if one city has fifteen thousand defective children. What about the glory of woman suffrage, since it has failed utterly in the most important social issue, the child? And where is the superior sense of justice that woman was to bring into the political field? Where was it in 1903, when the mine owners waged a guerilla war against the Western Miners' Union; when General Bell established a reign of terror, pulling men out of bed at night, kidnapping them across the border line, throwing them into bull pens, declaring "to hell with the Constitution, the club is the Constitution"? Where were the women politicians then, and why did they not exercise the power of their vote? But they did. They helped to defeat the most fair-minded and liberal man, Governor Waite. The latter had to make way for the tool of the mine kings, Governor Peabody, the enemy of labor, the Tsar of Colorado. "Certainly male suffrage could have done nothing worse." Granted. Wherein, then, are the advantages to woman and society from woman suffrage? The oft-repeated assertion that woman will purify politics is also but a myth. It is not borne out by the people who know the political conditions of Idaho, Colorado, Wyoming, and Utah.

Woman, essentially a purist, is naturally bigoted and relentless in her effort to make others as good as she thinks they ought to be. Thus, in Idaho, she has disfranchised her sister of the street, and declared all women of "lewd character" unfit to vote. "Lewd" not being interpreted, of course, as prostitution *in* marriage. It goes without saying that illegal prostitution and gambling have been prohibited. In this regard the law must needs be of feminine gender: it always prohibits. Therein all laws are wonderful. They go no further, but their very tendencies open all the floodgates of hell. Prostitution and gambling have never done a more flourishing business than since the law has been set against them.

In Colorado, the Puritanism of woman has expressed itself in a more drastic form. "Men of notoriously unclean lives, and men connected with saloons, have been dropped from politics since women have the vote."[1] Could Brother Comstock do more? Could all the Puritan fathers have done more? I wonder how many women realize the gravity of this would-be feat. I wonder if they understand that it is the very thing which, instead of elevating woman, has made her a political spy, a contemptible pry into the private affairs of people, not so much for the good of the cause, but because, as a Colorado woman said, "they like to get into houses they have never been in, and find out all they can,

[1] *Equal Suffrage*, Dr. Helen Sumner.

politically and otherwise."[2] Yes, and into the human soul and its minutest nooks and corners. For nothing satisfies the craving of most women so much as scandal. And when did she ever enjoy such opportunities as are hers, the politician's?

"Notoriously unclean lives, and men connected with the saloons." Certainly, the lady vote gatherers can not be accused of much sense of proportion. Granting even that these busybodies can decide whose lives are clean enough for that eminently clean atmosphere, politics, must it follow that saloon-keepers belong to the same category? Unless it be American hypocrisy and bigotry, so manifest in the principle of Prohibition, which sanctions the spread of drunkenness among men and women of the rich class, yet keeps vigilant watch on the only place left to the poor man. If for no other reason, woman's narrow and purist attitude toward life makes her a greater danger to liberty wherever she has political power. Man has long overcome the superstitions that still engulf woman. In the economic competitive field, man has been compelled to exercise efficiency, judgment, ability, competency. He therefore had neither time nor inclination to measure everyone's morality with a Puritanic yardstick. In his political activities, too, he has not gone about blindfolded. He knows that quantity and not quality is the material for the political grinding mill, and, unless he is a sentimental reformer or an old fossil, he knows that politics can never be anything but a swamp.

Women who are at all conversant with the process of politics, know the nature of the beast, but in their self-sufficiency and egotism they make themselves believe that they have but to pet the beast, and he will become as gentle as a lamb, sweet and pure. As if women have not sold their votes, as if women politicians cannot be bought! If her body can be bought in return for material consideration, why not her vote? That it is being done in Colorado and in other States, is not denied even by those in favor of woman suffrage.

As I have said before, woman's narrow view of human affairs is not the only argument against her as a politician superior to man. There are others. Her life-long economic parasitism has utterly blurred her conception of the meaning of equality. She clamors for equal rights with man, yet we learn that "few women care to canvas in undesirable districts."[3] How little equality means to them compared with the Russian women, who face hell itself for their ideal!

Woman demands the same rights as man, yet she is indignant that her presence does not strike him dead: he smokes, keeps his hat on, and does not jump from his seat like a flunkey. These may be trivial things, but they are nevertheless the key to the nature of American suffragists. To be sure, their English sisters have outgrown these silly notions. They have shown themselves equal to the greatest demands on their character and power of endurance. All honor to the heroism and sturdiness of the English suffragettes. Thanks to their energetic, aggressive methods, they have proved an inspiration to some of our own lifeless and spineless ladies. But after all, the suffragettes, too, are still lacking in appreciation of real equality. Else how is one to account for the

[2] *Equal Suffrage.*
[3] Dr. Helen A. Sumner.

tremendous, truly gigantic effort set in motion by those valiant fighters for a wretched little bill which will benefit a handful of propertied ladies, with absolutely no provision for the vast mass of workingwomen? True, as politicians they must be opportunists, must take half-measures if they can not get all. But as intelligent and liberal women they ought to realize that if the ballot is a weapon, the disinherited need it more than the economically superior class, and that the latter already enjoy too much power by virtue of their economic superiority.

The brilliant leader of the English suffragettes, Mrs. Emmeline Pankhurst, herself admitted, when on her American lecture tour, that there can be no equality between political superiors and inferiors. If so, how will the working-women of England, already inferior economically to the ladies who are benefited by the Shackleton bill,[4] be able to work with their political superiors, should the bill pass? Is it not probable that the class of Annie Keeney, so full of zeal, devotion, and martyrdom, will be compelled to carry on their backs their female political bosses, even as they are carrying their economic masters? They would still have to do it, were universal suffrage for men and women established in England. No matter what the workers do, they are made to pay, always. Still, those who believe in the power of the vote show little sense of justice when they concern themselves not at all with those whom, as they claim, it might serve most.

The American suffrage movement has been, until very recently, altogether a parlor affair, absolutely detached from the economic needs of the people. Thus Susan B. Anthony, no doubt an exceptional type of woman, was not only in-different but antagonistic to labor; nor did she hesitate to manifest her antag-onism when, in 1869, she advised women to take the places of striking printers in New York.[5] I do not know whether her attitude had changed before her death.

There are, of course, some suffragists who are affiliated with working-women—the Women's Trade Union League, for instance; but they are a small minority, and their activities are essentially economic. The rest look upon toil as a just provision of Providence. What would become of the rich, if not for the poor? What would become of these idle, parasitic ladies, who squander more in a week than their victims earn in a year, if not for the eighty million wage-workers? Equality, who ever heard of such a thing?

Few countries have produced such arrogance and snobbishness as America. Particularly is this true of the American woman of the middle class. She not only considers herself the equal of man, but his superior, especially in her purity, goodness, and morality. Small wonder that the American suffragist claims for her vote the most miraculous powers. In her exalted conceit she does not see how truly enslaved she is, not so much by man, as by her own silly notions and

[4] Mr. Shackleton was a labor leader. It is therefore self-evident that he should introduce a bill excluding his own constituents. The English Parliament is full of such Judases.

[5] *Equal Suffrage*, Dr. Helen A. Sumner.

traditions. Suffrage can not ameliorate that sad fact; it can only accentuate it, as indeed it does.

One of the great American women leaders claims that woman is entitled not only to equal pay, but that she ought to be legally entitled even to the pay of her husband. Failing to support her, he should be put in convict stripes, and his earnings in prison be collected by his equal wife. Does not another brilliant exponent of the cause claim for woman that her vote will abolish the social evil, which has been fought in vain by the collective efforts of the most illustrious minds the world over? It is indeed to be regretted that the alleged creator of the universe has already presented us with his wonderful scheme of things, else woman suffrage would surely enable woman to outdo him completely.

Nothing is so dangerous as the dissection of a fetich. If we have outlived the time when such heresy was punishable by the stake, we have not outlived the narrow spirit of condemnation of those who dare differ with accepted notions. Therefore I shall probably be put down as an opponent of woman. But that can not deter me from looking the question squarely in the face. I repeat what I have said in the beginning: I do not believe that woman will make politics worse; nor can I believe that she could make it better. If, then, she cannot improve on man's mistakes, why perpetrate the latter?

History may be a compilation of lies; nevertheless, it contains a few truths, and they are the only guide we have for the future. The history of the political activities of man proves that they have given him absolutely nothing that he could not have achieved in a more direct, less costly, and more lasting manner. As a matter of fact, every inch of ground he has gained has been through a constant fight, a ceaseless struggle for self-assertion, and not through suffrage. There is no reason whatever to assume that woman, in her climb to emancipation, has been, or will be, helped by the ballot.

In the darkest of all countries, Russia, with her absolute despotism, woman has become man's equal, not through the ballot, but by her will to be and to do. Not only has she conquered for herself every avenue of learning and vocation, but she has won man's esteem, his respect, his comradeship; aye, even more than that: she has gained the admiration, the respect of the whole world. That, too, not through suffrage, but by her wonderful heroism, her fortitude, her ability, willpower, and her endurance in her struggle for liberty. Where are the women in any suffrage country or State that can lay claim to such a victory? When we consider the accomplishments of woman in America, we find also that something deeper and more powerful than suffrage has helped her in the march to emancipation.

It is just sixty-two years ago since a handful of women at the Seneca Falls Convention set forth a few demands for their right to equal education with men, and access to the various professions, trades, etc. What wonderful accomplishments, what wonderful triumphs! Who but the most ignorant dare speak of woman as a mere domestic drudge? Who dare suggest that this or that profession should not be open to her? For over sixty years she has molded a new atmosphere and a new life for herself. She has become a world-power in every domain of human thought and activity. And all that without suffrage, without the right to make laws, without the "privilege" of becoming a judge, a jailer, or an executioner.

Yes, I may be considered an enemy of woman; but if I can help her see the light, I shall not complain.

The misfortune of woman is not that she is unable to do the work of a man, but that she is wasting her life-force to outdo him, with a tradition of centuries which has left her physically incapable of keeping pace with him. Oh, I know some have succeeded, but at what cost, at what terrific cost! The import is not the kind of work woman does, but rather the quality of the work she furnishes. She can give suffrage or the ballot no new quality, nor can she receive anything from it that will enhance her own quality. Her development, her freedom, her independence, must come from and through herself. First, by asserting herself as a personality, and not as a sex commodity. Second, by refusing the right to anyone over her body; by refusing to bear children, unless she wants them; by refusing to be a servant to God, the State, society, the husband, the family, etc.; by making her life simpler, but deeper and richer. That is, by trying to learn the meaning and substance of life in all its complexities, by freeing herself from the fear of public opinion and public condemnation. Only that, and not the ballot, will set woman free, will make her a force hitherto unknown in the world, a force for real love, for peace, for harmony; a force of divine fire, of life-giving; a creator of free men and women.

part seven: THE IMPACT OF EXISTEN- TIALISM

In herself woman appeals to a strange flesh which is to transform her into a fullness of being by penetration and dissolution.
    —Jean-Paul Sartre

{Sartre} insists repeatedly that there is no established, immutable human nature, yet in both his philosophy and his literary works he associates a fixed nature with the female.
    —Margery L. Collins and
      Christine Pierce

An existent is nothing other than what he does; . . . if one considers a woman in her immanent presence, her inward self, one can say absolutely nothing about her, she falls short of having any qualifications.
    —Simone de Beauvoir

Of all feminist theorists de Beauvoir is the most comprehensive and far-reaching, relating feminism to the best ideas in our culture.
    —Shulamith Firestone

To the existentialist it is not institutions that matter but the individuals of whom those institutions are comprised. And individuals fit no preconceived mold. They are what they make of themselves as they commit themselves to whatever causes they may select in the world in which they exist. Regarding the human situation from a man's point of view, Jean-Paul Sartre sees feminine nature as a part of the fixed world with which the male is faced. Thus, while man's nature may be defined by man himself, woman's nature, in Sartre's view, is

313

always the same—a thesis that Margery L. Collins and Christine Pierce find not only surprising but disappointing.

Simone de Beauvoir finds woman's nature to be no more pre-determined than man's: woman, too, is what she makes of herself. While Shulamith Firestone attests to the breadth and depth of Beauvoir's views, she questions the attempt to ground feminism in existentialist theory, suggesting that sexual dualism is more funda-mental than the dichotomy that Beauvoir finds between self and others.

ᴥᵍᵎᵉ᭢20 *Jean-Paul Sartre*

Jean-Paul Sartre was born in Paris in 1905 and was brought up primarily in the family of his mother, an aunt of Albert Schweitzer, the famous humanitarian. Sartre received his early education largely from his maternal grandfather, the founder of the Berlitz system of teaching modern languages. In 1924 he matriculated at the École Normale Supérièure. Upon passing his aggrégation in 1929, he spent a decade teaching at various French lycées, with a two-year interlude studying philosophy in Germany. In 1939, a year after the publication of a philosophical novel, Nausea, he was inducted into the French army. He was captured by the Germans and put into a Nazi prison camp, but was soon released because of ill health. Upon his return to Paris he resumed teaching, wrote his major philosophical work, Being and Nothingness, and became active in the French resistance movement. After the war he became a prolific writer of novels, stories, plays, and essays, and founded (together with former classmates Maurice Merleau-Ponty and Simone de Beauvoir) an existentialist literary and political review, Les temps modernes. Sartre has come to be recognized as the foremost existentialist of France.

At the beginning of the twentieth century the position of women in France was still quite traditional. Although normally girls were sent to school until the age of sixteen or eighteen, they were chiefly concerned with preparation for marriage. To this end they carefully cultivated the arts of conversation and flirtation and acquired such skills as drawing, sewing, painting, and playing musical instruments. They rarely went out unchaperoned, and the associations they formed were carefully scrutinized.

Upon the acquisition of a husband, the Frenchwoman devoted herself exclusively to managing his household, caring for his children, and entertaining his friends and business associates. By way of amusement she went to shops and tea salons, and she paid and received social calls. The unmarried woman was an object of pity or contempt.

Certain changes were introduced into the life of the Frenchwoman as a result of World War I. The death of a million and a half Frenchmen left almost as many women unmarried and unmarriageable. Careers had to be provided for them, and they had to be educated for those careers. Gradually women began to attain a degree of emancipation. By 1938 they had achieved independent legal status, and in 1944 they were enfranchised.

In Sartre's works, however, women never emerge as full-fledged human beings. His phenomenological analysis of experience into consciousness (the For-itself) and what it appears to be (the In-itself) is completely male-oriented. He appears quite unable to place woman in the former category. In his view she is being in-itself, part of man's world—and an obscene, frightening part, at that.

As an existentialist Sartre is committed to an emphasis on action. His

315

predecessors, he argues, were wrong in trying to penetrate human essence and then prescribe actions on the basis of it. This was the approach of Aristotle, for example, who, convinced that it was reason that set the human being apart from other members of the animal kingdom, defined man as a rational animal and measured human virtue in terms of the use people made of their rational faculty. Even Kierkegaard bemoaned the gap between the existential human situation and essential human nature. But according to Sartre, "Existence precedes essence." Human beings are free. In fact, they are condemned to be free. And every action is the result of a choice consciously or unconsciously made—even if occasionally the decision has been made by indecision. As one freely adopts projects, one forges an essence for oneself— and for all other people as well. Each project adopted determines the world in which one will live. If a man becomes a drunkard, beats his wife and neglects his children, for example, he does so not because he had an under-privileged childhood, as the determinist would have us believe, but because he chooses to be a drunkard; once that choice is made, he must live in a drunkard's world, which includes wife-beating and child-neglect. But one may renounce that world at any time by choosing to live in a new one. One has but to give up the bottle, and a new world will appear in the old one's stead. And such action is always well within the realm of possibility. Such a statement as "Oh, I could never do such-and-such" is never true. Human freedom is unlimited.

Sartre's version of existentialism would appear to provide fertile soil in which to sow the seeds of feminism. If existence precedes essence, there can be no essential difference between man and woman, who presumably creates her own essence just as man does. But Sartre does not plant those seeds. True, he exemplifies his distinction between acting in good faith and exhibiting bad faith with references to women as well as to men, but he speaks metaphorically as if woman's very physical nature had endowed her with the essence that is absent from man. And it is not a very pretty essence, for he depicts woman as a hole, a voracious mouth, ready to devour man.

From *Being and Nothingness*

DOING AND HAVING

... [T]o the extent that the *this* which I wish to appropriate, represents the entire world, the slimy, from my first intuitive contact, appears to me rich with a host of obscure meanings and references which surpass it. The slimy is revealed in itself as "much more than the slimy." From the moment of its appearance it transcends all distinctions between psychic and physical, between the brute existent and the meanings of the world; it is a possible meaning of being. The first experience which the infant can have with the slimy enriches him psychologically and morally; he will not need to reach adulthood to discover the kind of sticky baseness which we figuratively name "slimy"; it is there near him in the very sliminess of honey or of glue. What we say concerning the slimy is valid for all the objects which surround the child. The simple revelation of their matter extends his horizon to the extreme limits of being and bestows upon him at the same stroke a collection of clues for deciphering the being of all human facts. This certainly does not mean that he *knows* from the start the "ugliness," the "characteristics," or the "beauties" of existence. He is merely in possession of all the *meanings of being* of which ugliness and beauty, attitudes, psychic traits, sexual relations, *etc.*, will never be more than particular exemplifications. The gluey, the sticky, the hazy, *etc.*, holes in the sand and in the earth, caves, the light, the night, *etc.*—all reveal to him modes of pre-psychic and pre-sexual being which he will spend the rest of his life explaining. There is no such thing as an "innocent" child. We will gladly recognize along with the Freudians the innumerable relations existing between sexuality and certain matter and forms in the child's environment. But we do not understand by this that a sexual instinct already constituted has charged them with a sexual significance. On the contrary it seems to us that this matter and these forms are apprehended in themselves, and they reveal to the child the For-itself's modes of being and relations to being which will illuminate and shape his sexuality.

To cite only one example—many psychoanalysts have been struck by the attraction which all kinds of holes exert on the child (whether holes in the sand or in the ground, crypts, caves, hollows, or whatever), and they have explained this attraction either by the anal character of infant sexuality, or by prenatal shock, or by a presentiment of the adult sexual act. But we can not accept any of these explanations. The idea of "birth trauma" is highly fantastic. The comparison of the hole to the feminine sexual organ supposes in the child an experience which he can not possibly have had or a presentiment which we can not justify. As for the child's anal sexuality, we would not think of denying it; but if it is going to illuminate the holes which he encounters in the perceptual field and charge them with symbolism, then it is necessary that the child apprehend his anus as a hole. To put it more clearly, the child would have to apprehend the essence of the hole, of the orifice, as corresponding to the sensation which he receives from his anus. But we have demonstrated sufficiently the subjective character of "my relation with my body" so that we can understand the impossibility of saying that the child apprehends a particular part of his body as an objective structure of the universe. It is only to another person that the anus appears as an orifice. The child himself can never have experienced it as such; even the intimate care which the mother gives the child could not reveal the anus in this aspect, since the anus as an erogenous zone, or a zone of pain is not provided with tactile nerve endings. On the contrary it is only through another—through the words which the mother uses to designate the child's body—that he learns that his anus is a *hole*. It is therefore the objective nature of the hole perceived in the world which is going to illuminate for him the objective structure and the meaning of the anal zone and which will give a transcendent meaning to the erogenous sensations which hitherto he was limited to merely "existing." In itself then the *hole* is the symbol of a mode of being which existential psychoanalysis must elucidate.

We can not make such a detailed study here. One can see at once, however, that the hole is originally presented as a nothingness "to be filled" with my own flesh; the child can not restrain himself from putting his finger or his whole arm into the hole. It presents itself to me as the empty image of myself. I have only to crawl into it in order to make myself exist in the world which awaits me. The ideal of the hole is then an excavation which can be carefully moulded about my flesh in such a manner that by squeezing myself into it and fitting myself tightly inside it, I shall contribute to making a fullness of being exist in the world. Thus to plug up a hole means originally to make a sacrifice of my body in order that the plenitude of being may exist; that is, to subject the passion of the For-itself so as to shape, to perfect, and to preserve the totality of the In-itself.[1]

Here at its origin we grasp one of the most fundamental tendencies of human reality—the tendency to fill. We shall meet with this tendency again in the adolescent and in the adult. A good part of our life is passed in plugging up holes, in filling empty places, in realizing and symbolically establishing a plenitude. The child recognizes as the results of his first experiences that he himself has holes. When he puts his fingers in his mouth, he tries to wall up the holes in his face; he expects that his finger will merge with his lips and the roof of his mouth and block up the buccal orifice as one fills the crack in a wall with cement; he seeks again the density, the uniform and spherical plenitude of Parmenidean being; if he sucks his thumb, it is precisely in order to dissolve it, to transform it into a sticky paste which will seal the hole of his mouth. This tendency is certainly one of the most fundamental among those which serve as the basis for the act of eating; nourishment is the "cement" which will seal the mouth; to eat is among other things to be filled up.

It is only from this standpoint that we can pass on to sexuality. The obscenity of the feminine sex is that of everything which "gapes open." It is *an appeal to being* as all holes are. In herself woman appeals to a strange flesh which is to transform her into a fullness of being by penetration and dissolution. Conversely woman senses her condition as an appeal precisely because she is "in the form of a hole." This is the true origin of Adler's complex. Beyond any doubt her sex is a mouth and a voracious mouth which devours the penis—a fact which can easily lead to the idea of castration. The amorous act is the castration of the man; but this is above all because sex is a hole. We have to do here with a *pre-sexual* contribution which will become one of the components of sexuality as an empirical, complex, human attitude but which far from deriving its origin from the sexed being has nothing in common with basic sexuality . . . Nevertheless the experience with the hole, when the infant sees the reality, includes the ontological presentiment of sexual experience in general; it is with his flesh that the child stops up the hole and the hole, before all sexual specification, is an obscene expectation, an appeal to the flesh.

· · ·

---

[1] We should note as well the importance of the opposite tendency, to poke through holes, which in itself demands an existential analysis.

❧ *Margery L. Collins and Christine Pierce*

Margery L. Collins, a specialist in the eighteenth- and nineteenth-century British novel, is an instructor in English at the Westminster Choir College in Princeton, New Jersey.

Christine Pierce, a specialist in ethics and the philosophy of law, is an associate professor in the Department of Philosophy at the State University of New York College at Oswego. Author of an essay in Women in Sexist Society, *edited by Vivian Gornick and Barbara K. Moran, and of articles that have appeared in* Analysis, *Professor Pierce has addressed the issue of Plato's egalitarianism in the* Monist. *In the following pages Collins and Pierce contend that there is a basic inconsistency between Sartre's existentialism and his statements about woman.*

Holes and Slime: Sexism in Sartre's Psychoanalysis

Freudian psychology has been extensively examined and castigated for its sexist assumptions, but Jean-Paul Sartre's existential psychoanalysis has rarely been investigated for evidence of sexism; indeed Sartre's view of human nature and relationships would seem, on the face of things, to preclude such sexist bias. Moreover, one suspects that the vigilance of Simone de Beauvoir might have prevented such a disaster. Nonetheless, Sartre's theory of human nature implies a systematic inconsistency in his treatment of women: he insists repeatedly that there is no established, immutable human nature, yet in both his philosophy and his literary works he associates a fixed nature with the female. This nature, in the psychology, is labelled feminine. . . .

In brief, Sartre claims that human beings are entirely what they make of themselves:

As a For-itself one is not man first in order to be oneself subsequently and one does not constitute oneself as oneself in terms of a human essence given *a priori*. Quite the contrary, it is in its effort to choose itself as a personal self that the For-itself sustains in existence certain social and abstract characteristics which make of it a man (or a woman).[1]

Nevertheless, people want to believe that they have a fixed nature because such a belief relieves them of the responsibility for defining themselves and provides them with a measure of psychological comfort. A For-itself tries to discard its freedom and gain security by becoming "serious," i.e., by treating values or roles

---

[1] Jean-Paul Sartre, *Being and Nothingness*, trans. Hazel Barnes (New York: Washington Square Press, 1972), p. 666.

as "transcendent givens independent of human subjectivity."[2] Hence, individuals die for an "honorable peace" without realizing that the abstraction is of their own making, and are loyal to their roles of "soldier," "mother," or "church-member" because such roles are viewed as given rather than chosen.[3]

Sartre, however, endorses the Nietzschean insight that if God is dead, we must ourselves become gods and must be responsible for creating ourselves and our values. To rely on God as an external source of values, then, is an instance of bad faith, or self-deception. Albeit, Nietzsche advocates the pursuit of power on grounds that this propensity is "natural." Sartre sees the contradiction inherent in this position, and contends that refusing to take the responsibility for our values and our existence by excusing ourselves with an appeal to what is "natural" is as inauthentic as claiming that values come from God. Both are metaphysical props; Sartre diagnoses the effort to derive values from either nature or God as self-deception, an inability to assume our human freedom.

We see, consequently, that one would not expect to find sexism in Sartrean psychology because Sartre denies the concept of human nature and therefore its legitimacy as a source of human values. Such a view disallows the argument that roles are natural as a basis for assigning particular roles to women. Indeed, anyone who uses such arguments would be guilty of bad faith.

. . .

[Nevertheless] Sartre's existential psychoanalysis . . . offer[s] instances in which the In-itself is associated with distinctly feminine, or female, qualities,[4] thereby implying that a typical female nature does exist and function. Moreover, this female essence is invested with an utterly negative value, making Sartre guilty of blatant sexism.

This specific feminine nature, with its negative value and behavior, is particularly evident in Sartre's discussion of holes and slime in *Being and Nothingness*. In his analysis of slime, Sartre insists that it is a horrifying image, soft, clinging, leech-like, and, regardless of its docility, threatening. Normally, the phenomenon of possession is characterized by the For-itself asserting its primacy, yet the slimy reverses these terms:

The For-itself is suddenly compromised. I open my hands, I want to let go of the slimy and it sticks to me, it draws me, it sucks at me . . . It is a soft, yielding action, a moist and feminine sucking . . . I cannot slide on this slime, all its suction cups

---

[2] *Ibid.*, p. 796.

[3] Simone de Beauvoir suggests that even such qualities as vitality and sensitivity are not "ready-made" parts of our nature, but are ways of casting ourselves into the world, a matter of generosity.

[4] While we are familiar with the semantic difference between female and feminine as terms referring, respectively, to physical and cultural concepts, sexual anatomy and sexual role, there is no evidence, linguistic or otherwise, that Sartre employs or implies such a distinction. He consistently uses the word *feminin*, which translates interchangeably as female or feminine. Thus, females may or may not possess feminine characteristics, and insofar as one discourages "feminine" behavior in females (or males), one may be anti-feminine without being anti-female or sexist. To escape a charge of sexism, one needs to make such a differentiation, and Sartre does not do so.

hold me back . . . it is a trap . . . Slime is the revenge of the In-itself. A sickly-sweet feminine revenge which may be symbolized on another level by the quality sugary.[5]

The sugary, furthermore, poses an ultimate threat: "A sugary sliminess is the ideal of the slimy; it symbolizes the sugary death of the For-itself (like that of the wasp which sinks into the jam and drowns in it)."[6]

Sartre's analysis of slime leaves him in an ambiguous position at best, for what emerges here is a traditional concept of the feminine, a sweet, clinging, dependent threat to male freedom. Like his predecessors Nietzsche and Schopenhauer, Sartre identifies his concept of femininity with female and rails against these qualities in women as if they were natural characteristics, evidence of a given nature. In the discussion of holes, however, it becomes clear that it is not culturally acquired or chosen qualities, but actual female anatomy which constitutes the threatening In-itself. Here, the translation "feminine sexual organ" undoubtedly denotes female.

One of the strongest sources of nausea is the human body, through its perpetual revelation of contingency. Nonetheless, in his remarks on sexual organs only the female, corresponding obviously to the hole, is labelled obscene: "The obscenity of the feminine sex is that of everything which gapes open."[7] This gaping obscenity prompts Sartre to conclude:

In herself woman appeals to a strange flesh which is to transform her into a fullness of being by penetration and dissolution. Conversely, woman senses her condition as an appeal precisely because she is "in the form of a hole." This is the true origin of Adler's complex. Beyond any doubt her sex is a mouth and a voracious mouth which devours the penis . . . The amorous act is the castration of the man; but this is above all because sex is a hole.[8]

Clearly, Sartre suggests here that Adler's complex in women, their inferiority feeling, is caused by inferior and obscene anatomy; something is missing. The "masculine protest," for Sartre, is not against the feminine role, as Adler argued, but against being female. The conventional piece of wisdom this quotation expresses is derived from the view that all holes are obscene, and that filling holes is a fundamental human tendency. Sartre is careful to distinguish his view from Freudianism. He does not explain holes in terms of sexuality, but rather explains sexuality in terms of the ontological meaning of holes: ". . . the hole, before all sexual specifications, is an obscene expectation, an appeal to the flesh."[9] Apparently, all holes are appeals to the flesh, i.e., the objective nature of a hole is a nothingness which we fill with flesh. Hence, children crawl into holes, put fingers in their mouths, etc. If we take seriously the view that all holes are obscene, then we should by extension view these activities as obscene. Con-

---

[5] *Being and Nothingness*, pp. 776–777.

[6] *Loc. cit.*

[7] *Ibid.*, p. 782.

[8] *Loc. cit.*

[9] *Loc. cit.*

sequently, we should also recognize that such items as Swiss cheese and bowling balls are obscene. Filling holes, Sartre claims, is a fundamental human tendency, but the opposite tendency, to poke holes, is also of considerable importance. From this type of vacuous psychological statement, it is difficult to ascertain anything at all.

Even if there is a fundamental Parmenidean urge to fill holes, we need not deduce that the female sexual organ will be filled by a penis. Notwithstanding, Sartre does draw this conclusion and significantly, characterizes the plugger as For-itself and the plugee as In-itself. ". . . to plug up a hole means originally to make a sacrifice of my body in order that the plentitude of being may exist; that is, to subject the passion of the For-itself so as to shape, to perfect, and to preserve the totality of the In-itself."[10] Thus, we see that holes and slime are obscene qualities of the In-itself which are identified, in anatomy and behavior, with the female.[11]

. . .

Thus, in . . . his psychology . . . Sartre associates essence and roles with women, which both violates his theory and makes of him a traditional sexist. Women possess a fixed nature, determined by their unfortunate sexual anatomy, which limits them to roles approximating the non-conscious, unliberated Being-in-itself. Female attempts at freedom and self-creation are . . . doomed to ignominious failure; women are forever enmeshed in their physical necessities and established functions.

The philosophical acceptance of human nature that Sartre supposedly repudiates has done enormous moral, political, and psychological damage to women. Women have been denied entrance to the professions because of their nature, yet if they refuse to conform to their nature, they have been declared insane, or at best, neurotic. It is gravely disappointing that a major contemporary effort to refute the existence of human nature and its legitimacy as a source of human values fails to encompass women, one of the groups of human beings to suffer most from essentialist views.

[10] *Ibid.*, p. 781.

[11] A sexual interpretation of the For-itself and In-itself changes Sartre's view of intimate relationships from a theory about the way human beings relate to each other to a theory about the way men and women relate to each other. Intimate relationships, according to Sartre, must be characterized in terms of the alienation of a subject from an object, so that a partner as subject tries to possess or entrap the liberty of the Other, thus making the Other an object. Love is impossible, for love would be the meeting of subject with subject, but there can never be a mutual recognition of freedom. In other words, one of the partners is always an object, but it seems that people can at least take turns. If men are subjects and women are objects, even these limited options are unavailable.

⋘⋙21 *Simone de Beauvoir*

Simone de Beauvoir was born in Paris on January 9, 1908, the elder of the two daughters of Georges de Beauvoir, lawyer and amateur actor. Her parents held conventional views on the relationship between the sexes, especially between husband and wife: that a woman is largely what her husband makes of her and that she should be completely obedient to his wishes. Belief in the superiority of men and the inferiority of women was instilled in Simone from childhood. Yet soon she came to consider herself an exception to the general rule. "Simone has a man's brain," her father used to announce proudly; "she thinks like a man; she is a man." Nevertheless, M. de Beauvoir continued to believe that a woman's place was in the home, and was deeply disturbed when his financial condition became such that he could not provide dowries for his daughters and each had to be educated for a profession.

Not so Simone. Dissatisfied with her parents' double moral standard and leaning toward a single moral code, she found the quest for truth to her liking and discovered her sex to be an advantage rather than a disadvantage in the pursuit of it. Since she was a woman, she was not expected to perform well. When her performance surpassed all expectations, her successes shone all the more brightly. And her successes have come to shine brightly in many skies, for Simone de Beauvoir has attained eminence as a novelist, as a journalist, as an autobiographer, as an existentialist philosopher.

Yet looking back on her early life Beauvoir claims to find herself haunted by a recurring question: "Do men marry women like me?"—a question she later thought to have been badly phrased owing to her youthful failure to discriminate between love and marriage. The answer to the original question turned out to be, in her case, no. The answer to the rephrased query appeared to her when she was twenty in the form of Jean-Paul Sartre, with whom she was to share a "comradeship that welded [their] lives together." And they have been together for close to half a century.

Although The Second Sex has been called the "classic manifesto of the liberated woman," Beauvoir did not lend her support to the feminist cause until the 1970s. Before that she had regarded feminist activity as unnecessary, believing that the attainment of women's goals would be a natural product of the growth of society. In the most recent volume of her autobiography, Beauvoir dubbed her earlier optimism "premature." "I declare myself a feminist," she announced. And her activities during the preceding few years anticipated that announcement. She participated in the march for abortion in Paris in 1970, and she became involved in an exposé of the undesirable conditions in a school for unwed mothers. In All Said and Done she noted with pride that American feminists cite her work as their authority.

In her philosophy of woman Simone de Beauvoir achieves the consistency that Sartre's views lack. She extends Sartrean existentialism to include woman in her own right. Is woman's nature inferior to man's? equal to man's? so *different as to be incomparable to man's? The question is meaningless to Beauvoir. Existence, she agrees with Sartre, precedes essence. Man is what he does—but so is woman. A female worker may be said to work well or badly. An actress may be said to demonstrate talent or not. Only individuals exist. Of woman qua woman one can say nothing whatever. She has no attributes. Nor, of course, does man qua man. The difference between the two, as Beauvoir sees it, is that women are less likely to be engaged in meaningful activity than are men. One is what one makes of oneself, according to Beauvoir. And what does woman make of herself? In most cases very little.*

The human being, in Beauvoir's estimation, has a primordial habit of dichotomizing the world into Self and Other. The standards of one's own community are unassailable; those of the rest of the world are suspect. The behavior of one's own compatriots constitutes the norm; that of foreigners deviates from it. Gentiles look down on Jews, whites on blacks, colonists on natives, men on women. But the last case is slightly different from the others. The rest of the relationships are reciprocal, according to Beauvoir. One crosses the boundary of one's own country, and one is no longer a native; one is a foreigner. Jews and American blacks are minority groups, subjugated to majorities as the result of historical occurrence. But women are not a minority, nor is their subjugation the result of historical events. They have always been regarded by men as the Other, and since they have always lived in a manmade world, they have come to regard themselves as the Other. This orientation is reflected even in speech patterns. Men say, "We think so-and-so, but women disagree." But do women say, "We believe so-and-so, while men embrace contrary views"? No. They say of themselves, "Women have the following beliefs." They regard themselves as the Other, and until they have ceased alienating themselves from themselves, they will be unable to live the full and meaningful lives wherein lies their freedom. But a change, Beauvoir thinks, is at hand. When it is effected, the world will be populated not by men and women, but by human beings.

From *The Second Sex*

MYTH AND REALITY

The myth of woman plays a considerable part in literature; but what is its importance in daily life? To what extent does it affect the customs and conduct of individuals? In replying to this question it will be necessary to state precisely the relations this myth bears to reality.

There are different kinds of myths. This one, the myth of woman, sublimating an immutable aspect of the human condition—namely, the "division" of humanity into two classes of individuals—is a static myth. It projects into the realm of Platonic ideas a reality that is directly experienced or is conceptualized on a basis of experience; in place of fact, value, significance, knowledge, empirical law, it substitutes a transcendental Idea, timeless, unchangeable, necessary. This idea is indisputable because it is beyond the given: it is endowed with absolute truth. Thus, as against the dispersed, contingent, and multiple existences of actual women, mythical thought opposes the Eternal Feminine, unique and changeless. If the definition provided for this concept is contradicted by the behavior of flesh-and-blood women, it is the latter who are wrong: we are told not that Femininity is a false entity, but that the women concerned are not feminine. The contrary facts of experience are impotent against the myth. In a way, however, its source is in experience. Thus it is quite true that woman is other than man, and this alterity is directly felt in desire, the embrace, love; but the real relation is one of reciprocity; as such it gives rise to authentic drama. Through eroticism, love, friendship, and their alternatives, deception, hate, rivalry, the relation is a struggle between conscious beings each of whom wishes to be essential, it is the mutual recognition of free beings who confirm one another's freedom, it is the vague transition from aversion to participation. To pose Woman is to pose the absolute Other, without reciprocity, denying against all experience that she is a subject, a fellow human being.

In actuality, of course, women appear under various aspects; but each of the myths built up around the subject of woman is intended to sum her up *in toto*; each aspires to be unique. In consequence, a number of incompatible myths exist, and men tarry musing before the strange incoherencies manifested by the idea of Femininity. As every woman has a share in a majority of these archetypes—each of which lays claim to containing the sole Truth of woman— men of today also are moved again in the presence of their female companions to an astonishment like that of the old sophists who failed to understand how man could be blond and dark at the same time! Transition toward the absolute was indicated long ago in social phenomena: relations are easily congealed in classes, functions in types, just as relations, to the childish mentality, are fixed in things. Patriarchal society, for example, being centered upon the conservation of the patrimony, implies necessarily, along with those who own and transmit wealth, the existence of men and women who take property away from its owners and put it into circulation. The men—adventurers, swindlers, thieves, speculators—are generally repudiated by the group; the women, employing their erotic attraction, can induce young men and even fathers of families to scatter their patrimonies, without ceasing to be within the law. Some of these women appropriate their victims' fortunes or obtain legacies by using undue influence; this role being regarded as evil, those who play it are called "bad women." But the fact is that quite to the contrary they are able to appear in some other setting—at home with their fathers, brothers, husbands, or lovers— as guardian angels; and the courtesan who "plucks" rich financiers is, for painters and writers, a generous patroness. It is easy to understand in actual experience the ambiguous personality of Aspasia or Mme de Pompadour. But if woman is depicted as the Praying Mantis, the Mandrake, the Demon, then it is most confusing to find in woman also the Muse, the Goddess Mother, Beatrice.

As group symbols and social types are generally defined by means of antonyms in pairs, ambivalence will seem to be an intrinsic quality of the Eternal Feminine. The saintly mother has for correlative the cruel stepmother, the angelic young girl has the perverse virgin: thus it will be said sometimes that Mother equals Life, sometimes that Mother equals Death, that every virgin is pure spirit or flesh dedicated to the devil.

Evidently it is not reality that dictates to society or to individuals their choice between the two opposed basic categories; in every period, in each case, society and the individual decide in accordance with their needs. Very often they project into the myth adopted the institutions and values to which they adhere. Thus the paternalism that claims woman for hearth and home defines her as sentiment, inwardness, immanence. In fact every existent is at once immanence and transcendence; when one offers the existent no aim, or prevents him from attaining any, or robs him of his victory, then his transcendence falls vainly into the past—that is to say, falls back into immanence. This is the lot assigned to woman in the patriarchate; but it is in no way a vocation, any more than slavery is the vocation of the slave. The development of this mythology is to be clearly seen in Auguste Comte. To identify Woman with Altruism is to guarantee to man absolute rights in her devotion, it is to impose on women a categorical imperative.

The myth must not be confused with the recognition of significance; significance is immanent in the object; it is revealed to the mind through a living experience; whereas the myth is a transcendent Idea that escapes the mental grasp entirely. When in *L'Age d'homme* Michel Leiris describes his vision of the feminine organs, he tells us things of significance and elaborates no myth. Wonder at the feminine body, dislike for menstrual blood, come from perceptions of a concrete reality. There is nothing mythical in the experience that reveals the voluptuous qualities of feminine flesh, and it is not an excursion into myth if one attempts to describe them through comparisons with flowers or pebbles. But to say that Woman is Flesh, to say that the Flesh is Night and Death, or that it is the splendor of the Cosmos, is to abandon terrestrial truth and soar into an empty sky. For man also is flesh for woman; and woman is not merely a carnal object; and the flesh is clothed in special significance for each person and in each experience. And likewise it is quite true that woman—like man—is a being rooted in nature; she is more enslaved to the species than is the male, her animality is more manifest; but in her as in him the given traits are taken on through the fact of existence, she belongs also to the human realm. To assimilate her to Nature is simply to act from prejudice.

Few myths have been more advantageous to the ruling caste than the myth of woman: it justifies all privileges and even authorizes their abuse. Men need not bother themselves with alleviating the pains and the burdens that physiologically are women's lot, since these are "intended by Nature"; men use them as a pretext for increasing the misery of the feminine lot still further, for instance by refusing to grant to woman any right to sexual pleasure, by making her work like a beast of burden.[1]

---

[1] Cf. Balzac: *Physiology of Marriage:* "Pay no attention to her murmurs, her cries, her pains; *nature has made her for our use* and for bearing everything: children, sorrows, blows and pains inflicted by man. Do not accuse yourself of hardness. In all the codes of so-called civilized nations, man has written the laws that ranged woman's destiny under this bloody epigraph: *'Væ victis!* Woe to the weak!'"

Of all these myths, none is more firmly anchored in masculine hearts than that of the feminine "mystery." It has numerous advantages. And first of all it permits an easy explanation of all that appears inexplicable; the man who "does not understand" a woman is happy to substitute an objective resistance for a subjective deficiency of mind; instead of admitting his ignorance, he perceives the presence of a "mystery" outside himself: an alibi, indeed, that, flatters laziness and vanity at once. A heart smitten with love thus avoids many disappointments: if the loved one's behavior is capricious, her remarks stupid, then the mystery serves to excuse it all. And finally, thanks again to the mystery, that negative relation is perpetuated which seemed to Kierkegaard infinitely preferable to positive possession; in the company of a living enigma man remains alone—alone with his dreams, his hopes, his fears, his love, his vanity. This subjective game, which can go all the way from vice to mystical ecstasy, is for many a more attractive experience than an authentic relation with a human being. What foundations exist for such a profitable illusion?

Surely woman is, in a sense, mysterious, "mysterious as is all the world," according to Maeterlinck. Each is *subject* only for himself; each can grasp in immanence only himself, alone: from this point of view the *other* is always a mystery. To men's eyes the opacity of the self-knowing self, of the *pour-soi*, is denser in the *other* who is feminine; men are unable to penetrate her special experience through any working of sympathy: they are condemned to ignorance of the quality of woman's erotic pleasure, the discomfort of menstruation, and the pains of childbirth. The truth is that there is mystery on both sides: as the *other* who is of masculine sex, every man, also, has within him a presence, an inner self impenetrable to woman; she in turn is in ignorance of the male's erotic feeling. But in accordance with the universal rule I have stated, the categories in which men think of the world are established *from their point of view, as absolute*: they misconceive reciprocity, here as everywhere. A mystery for man, woman is considered to be mysterious in essence.

To tell the truth, her situation makes woman very liable to such a view. Her physiological nature is very complex; she herself submits to it as to some rigmarole from outside; her body does not seem to her to be a clear expression of herself; within it she feels herself a stranger. Indeed, the bond that in every individual connects the physiological life and the psychic life—or better the relation existing between the contingence of an individual and the free spirit that assumes it—is the deepest enigma implied in the condition of being human, and this enigma is presented in its most disturbing form in woman.

But what is commonly referred to as the mystery is not the subjective solitude of the conscious self, nor the secret organic life. It is on the level of communication that the word has its true meaning: it is not a reduction to pure silence, to darkness, to absence; it implies a stammering presence that fails to make itself manifest and clear. To say that woman is mystery is to say, not that she is silent, but that her language is not understood; she is there, but hidden behind veils; she exists beyond these uncertain appearances. What is she? Angel, demon, one inspired, an actress? It may be supposed either that there are answers to these questions which are impossible to discover, or, rather, that no answer is adequate because a fundamental ambiguity marks the feminine being; and perhaps in her heart she is even for herself quite indefinable: a sphinx.

The fact is that she would be quite embarrassed to decide *what* she *is*; but this not because the hidden truth is too vague to be discerned: it is because in this domain there is no truth. An existent *is* nothing other than what he does; the possible does not extend beyond the real, essence does not precede existence: in pure subjectivity, the human being *is not anything*. He is to be measured by his acts. Of a peasant woman one can say that she is a good or a bad worker, of an actress that she has or does not have talent; but if one considers a woman in her immanent presence, her inward self, one can say absolutely nothing about her, she falls short of having any qualifications. Now, in amorous or conjugal relations, in all relations where the woman is the vassal, the other, she is being dealt with in her immanence. It is noteworthy that the feminine comrade, colleague, and associate are without mystery; on the other hand, if the vassal is male, if, in the eyes of a man or a woman who is older, or richer, a young fellow, for example, plays the role of the inessential object, then he too becomes shrouded in mystery. And this uncovers for us a substructure under the feminine mystery which is economic in nature.

A sentiment cannot be supposed to *be* anything. "In the domain of sentiments," writes Gide, "the real is not distinguished from the imaginary. And if to imagine one loves is enough to be in love, then also to tell oneself that one imagines oneself to be in love when one is in love is enough to make one forthwith love a little less." Discrimination between the imaginary and the real can be made only through behavior. Since man occupies a privileged situation in this world, he is in a position to show his love actively; very often he supports the woman or at least helps her; in marrying her he gives her social standing; he makes her presents; his independent economic and social position allows him to take the initiative and think up contrivances: it was M. de Norpois who, when separated from Mme de Villeparisis, made twenty-four-hour trips to visit her. Very often the man is busy, the woman idle: he *gives* her the time he passes with her; she takes it: is it with pleasure, passionately, or only for amusement? Does she accept these benefits through love or through self-interest? Does she love her husband or her marriage? Of course, even the man's evidence is ambiguous: is such and such a gift granted through love or out of pity? But while normally a woman finds numerous advantages in her relations with man, his relations with a woman are profitable to a man only in so far as he loves her. And so one can almost judge the degree of his affection by the total picture of his attitude.

But a woman hardly has means for sounding her own heart; according to her moods she will view her own sentiments in different lights, and as she submits to them passively, one interpretation will be no truer than another. In those rare instances in which she holds the position of economic and social privilege, the mystery is reversed, showing that it does not pertain to *one* sex rather than the other, but to the situation. For a great many women the roads to transcendence are blocked: because they *do* nothing, they fail to *make themselves* anything. They wonder indefinitely what they *could have* become, which sets them to asking about what they *are*. It is a vain question. If man fails to discover that secret essence of femininity, it is simply because it does not exist. Kept on the fringe of the world, woman cannot be objectively defined through this world, and her mystery conceals nothing but emptiness.

Furthermore, like all the oppressed, woman deliberately dissembles her objective actuality; the slave, the servant, the indigent, all who depend upon the caprices of a master, have learned to turn toward him a changeless smile or an enigmatic impassivity; their real sentiments, their actual behavior, are carefully hidden. And moreover woman is taught from adolescence to lie to men, to scheme, to be wily. In speaking to them she wears an artificial expression on her face; she is cautious, hypocritical, play-acting.

But the Feminine Mystery as recognized in mythical thought is a more profound matter. In fact, it is immediately implied in the mythology of the absolute Other. If it be admitted that the inessential conscious being, too, is a clear subjectivity, capable of performing the *Cogito*, then it is also admitted that this being is in truth sovereign and returns to being essential; in order that all reciprocity may appear quite impossible, it is necessary for the Other to be for itself an other, for its very subjectivity to be affected by its otherness; this consciousness which would be alienated as a consciousness, in its pure immanent presence, would evidently be Mystery. It would be Mystery in itself from the fact that it would be Mystery for itself; it would be absolute Mystery.

In the same way it is true that, beyond the secrecy created by their dissembling, there is mystery in the Black, the Yellow, in so far as they are considered absolutely as the inessential Other. It should be noted that the American citizen, who profoundly baffles the average European, is not, however, considered as being "mysterious": one states more modestly that one does not understand him. And similarly woman does not always "understand" man; but there is no such thing as a masculine mystery. The point is that rich America, and the male, are on the Master side and that Mystery belongs to the slave.

To be sure, we can only muse in the twilight byways of bad faith upon the positive reality of the Mystery; like certain marginal hallucinations, it dissolves under the attempt to view it fixedly. Literature always fails in attempting to portray "mysterious" women; they can appear only at the beginning of a novel as strange, enigmatic figures; but unless the story remains unfinished they give up their secret in the end and they are then simply consistent and transparent persons. The heroes in Peter Cheyney's books, for example, never cease to be astonished at the unpredictable caprices of women: no one can ever guess how they will act, they upset all calculations. The fact is that once the springs of their action are revealed to the reader, they are seen to be very simple mechanisms: this woman was a spy, that one a thief; however clever the plot, there is always a key; and it could not be otherwise, had the author all the talent and imagination in the world. Mystery is never more than a mirage that vanishes as we draw near to look at it.

We can see now that the myth is in large part explained by its usefulness to man. The myth of woman is a luxury. It can appear only if man escapes from the urgent demands of his needs; the more relationships are concretely lived, the less they are idealized. The fellah of ancient Egypt, the Bedouin peasant, the artisan of the Middle Ages, the worker of today has in the requirements of work and poverty relations with his particular woman companion which are too definite for her to be embellished with an aura either auspicious or inauspicious. The epochs and the social classes that have been marked by the leisure to dream have been the ones to set up the images, black and white, of femininity. But along with luxury there was utility; these dreams were irresistibly guided by interests. Surely most of the myths had roots in the spontaneous attitude of man toward his own existence and toward the world around him. But going beyond experience toward the transcendent Idea was deliberately used by patriarchal society for purposes of self-justification; through the myths this society imposed its laws and customs upon individuals in a picturesque, effective manner; it is under a mythical form that the group-imperative is indoctrinated into each conscience. Through such intermediaries as religions, traditions, language, tales, songs, movies, the myths penetrate even into such existences as are most harshly enslaved to material realities. Here everyone can find sublimation of his drab experiences: deceived by the woman he loves, one declares that she is a Crazy Womb; another, obsessed by his impotence, calls her a Praying Mantis; still another enjoys his wife's company: behold, she is Harmony, Rest, the Good Earth! The taste for eternity at a bargain, for a pocket-sized absolute, which is shared by a majority of men, is satisfied by myths. The smallest emotion, a slight annoyance, becomes the reflection of a timeless Idea—an illusion agreeably flattering to the vanity.

The myth is one of those snares of false objectivity into which the man who depends on ready-made valuations rushes headlong. Here again we have to do with the substitution of a set idol for actual experience and the free judgments it requires. For an authentic relation with an autonomous existent, the myth of Woman substitutes the fixed contemplation of a mirage. "Mirage! Mirage!" cries Laforgue. "We should kill them since we cannot comprehend them; or better tranquilize them, instruct them, make them give up their taste for jewels, make them our genuinely equal comrades, our intimate friends, real associates here below, dress them differently, cut their hair short, say anything and everything to them." Man would have nothing to lose, quite the contrary, if he gave up disguising woman as a symbol. When dreams are official community affairs, clichés, they are poor and monotonous indeed beside the living reality; for the true dreamer, for the poet, woman is a more generous fount than is any down-at-heel marvel. The times that have most sincerely treasured women are not the period of feudal chivalry nor yet the gallant nineteenth century. They are the times—like the eighteenth century—when men have regarded women as fellow creatures; then it is that women seem truly romantic, as the reading of *Liaisons dangereuses, Le Rouge et le noir, Farewell to Arms,* is sufficient to show. The heroines of Laclos, Stendhal, Hemingway are without mystery, and they are not the less engaging for that. To recognize in woman a human being is not to impoverish man's experience: this would lose none of its diversity, its richness, or its intensity if it were to occur between two subjectivities. To discard the myths is not to destroy all dramatic relation between the sexes, it is not to deny the significance authentically revealed to man through feminine reality; it is not to do away with poetry, love, adventure, happiness, dreaming. It is simply to ask that behavior, sentiment, passion be founded upon the truth.[2]

"Woman is lost. Where are the women? The women of today are not women at all!" We have seen what these mysterious slogans mean. In men's eyes—and for the legion of women who see through men's eyes—it is not enough to have a woman's body nor to assume the female function as mistress or mother in order to be a "true woman." In sexuality and maternity woman as subject can claim autonomy; but to be a "true woman" she must accept herself as the Other. The men of today show a certain duplicity of attitude which is painfully lacerating to women; they are willing on the whole to accept woman as a fellow being, an equal; but they still require her to remain the inessential. For her these two destinies are incompatible; she hesitates between one and the other without being exactly adapted to either, and from this comes her lack of equilibrium. With man there is no break between public and private life: the more he confirms his grasp on the world in action and in work, the more virile he seems to be; human and vital values are combined in him. Whereas woman's independent successes are in contradiction with her femininity, since the "true woman" is required to make herself object, to be the Other.

It is quite possible that in this matter man's sensibility and sexuality are being modified. A new aesthetics has already been born. If the fashion of flat chests and narrow hips—the boyish form—has had its brief season, at least the overopulent ideal of past centuries has not returned. The feminine body is asked to be flesh, but with discretion; it is to be slender and not loaded with fat; muscular, supple, strong, it is bound to suggest transcendence; it must not be pale like a too shaded hothouse plant, but preferably tanned like a workman's torso from being bared to the open sun. Woman's dress in becoming practical need not make her appear sexless: on the contrary, short skirts made the most of legs and thighs as never before. There is no reason why working should take away woman's sex appeal.[3] It may be disturbing to contemplate woman as at once a social personage and carnal prey: in a recent series of drawings by Peynet (1948), we see a young man break his engagement because he was seduced by the pretty mayoress who was getting ready to officiate at his marriage. For a woman to hold some "man's position" and be desirable at the same time has long been a subject for more or less ribald joking; but

[2] Laforgue goes on to say regarding woman: "Since she has been left in slavery, idleness, without occupation or weapon other than her sex, she has overdeveloped this aspect and has become the Feminine. . . . We have permitted this hypertrophy; she is here in the world for our benefit. . . . Well! that is all wrong. . . . Up to now we have played with woman as if she were a doll. This has lasted altogether too long! . . ."

[3] A point that hardly needs to be made in America, where even cursory acquaintance with any well-staffed business office will afford confirmatory evidence.—TR.

gradually the impropriety and the irony have become blunted, and it would seem that a new form of eroticism is coming into being—perhaps it will give rise to new myths.

What is certain is that today it is very difficult for women to accept at the same time their status as autonomous individuals and their womanly destiny; this is the source of the blundering and restlessness which sometimes cause them to be considered a "lost sex." And no doubt it is more comfortable to submit to a blind enslavement than to work for liberation: the dead, for that matter, are better adapted to the earth than are the living. In all respects a return to the past is no more possible than it is desirable. What must be hoped for is that the men for their part will unreservedly accept the situation that is coming into existence; only then will women be able to live in that situation without anguish. Then Laforgue's prayer will be answered: "Ah, young women, when will you be our brothers, our brothers in intimacy without ulterior thought of exploitation? When shall we clasp hands truly?" Then Breton's "Mélusine, no longer under the weight of the calamity let loose upon her by man alone, Mélusine set free . . ." will regain "her place in humanity." Then she will be a full human being, "when," to quote a letter of Rimbaud, "the infinite bondage of woman is broken, when she will live in and for herself, man—hitherto detestable—having let her go free."

❧ Shulamith Firestone

Shulamith Firestone, one of the founders of the New York Radical Feminists and its offshoot the Redstockings, is the only radical feminist who has developed a comprehensive theory to account for woman's oppression. Although The Dialectic of Sex is dedicated to Simone de Beauvoir, Firestone takes exception to Beauvoir's basically existential approach to women's liberation. Sexual distinction is far more fundamental than Beauvoir would have one believe, Firestone maintains; she grounds her own radical feminism in biological rather than economic dualism.

From *The Dialectic of Sex: The Case for Feminist Revolution*

THE DIALECTIC OF SEX

. . .

The early feminist theorists were to a materialist view of sex what Fourier, Bebel, and Owen were to a materialist view of class. By and large, feminist theory has been as inadequate as were the early feminist attempts to correct sexism. This was to be expected. The problem is so immense that, at first try, only the surface could be skimmed, the most blatant inequalities described. Simone de Beauvoir was the only one who came close to—who perhaps has done—the definitive analysis. Her profound work *The Second Sex*—which appeared as recently as the early fifties to a world convinced that feminism was dead—for the first time attempted to ground feminism in its historical base. Of all feminist theorists De Beauvoir is the most comprehensive and far-reaching, relating feminism to the best ideas in our culture.

It may be this virtue is also her one failing: she is almost too sophisticated, too knowledgeable. Where this becomes a weakness—and this is still certainly debatable—is in her rigidly existentialist interpretation of feminism (one wonders how much Sartre had to do with this). This in view of the fact that all cultural systems, including existentialism, are themselves determined by the sex dualism. She says:

Man never thinks of himself without thinking of the Other; he views the world under the sign of duality *which is not in the first place sexual in character*. But being different from man, who sets himself up as the Same, it is naturally to the category of the Other that woman is consigned; the Other includes woman. [Italics mine.]

Perhaps she has overshot her mark: Why postulate a fundamental Hegelian concept of Otherness as the final explanation—and then carefully document the biological and historical circumstances that have pushed the class "women" into such a category—when one has never seriously considered the much simpler and more likely possibility that the fundamental dualism sprang from sex itself? To posit *a priori* categories of thought and existence—Otherness, Transcendence, Immanence—into which history then falls may not be necessary. Marx and Engels had discovered that these philosophical categories themselves grew out of history.

Before assuming such categories, let us first try to develop an analysis in which biology itself—procreation—is at the origin of the dualism. The immediate assumption of the layman that the unequal division of the sexes is "natural" may be well-founded. We need not immediately look beyond this. Unlike economic class, sex class sprang directly from a biological reality: men and women were created different, and not equally privileged. Although, as De Beauvoir points out, this difference of itself did not necessitate the development of a class system—the domination of one group by another—the reproductive *functions* of these differences did. The biological family is an inherently unequal power distribution. The need for power leading to the development of classes arises from the psychosexual formation of each individual according to this basic imbalance, rather than, as Freud, Norman O. Brown, and others have, once again overshooting their mark, postulated, some irreducible conflict of Life against Death, Eros vs. Thanatos.

The *biological family*—the basic reproductive unit of male/female/infant, in whatever form of social organization—is characterized by these fundamental—if not immutable—facts:

1) That women throughout history before the advent of birth control were

at the continual mercy of their biology—menstruation, menopause, and "female ills," constant painful childbirth, wetnursing and care of infants, all of which made them dependent on males (whether brother, father, husband, lover, or clan, government, community-at-large) for physical survival.

2) That human infants take an even longer time to grow up than animals, and thus are helpless and, for some short period at least, dependent on adults for physical survival.

3) That a basic mother/child interdependency has existed in some form in every society, past or present, and thus has shaped the psychology of every mature female and every infant.

4) That the natural reproductive difference between the sexes led directly to the first division of labor based on sex, which is at the origins of all further division into economic and cultural classes and is possibly even at the root of all caste (discrimination based on sex and other biologically determined characteristics such as race, age, etc.).

These biological contingencies of the human family cannot be covered over with anthropological sophistries. Anyone observing animals mating, reproducing, and caring for their young will have a hard time accepting the "cultural relativity" line. For no matter how many tribes in Oceania you can find where the connection of the father to fertility is not known, no matter how many matrilineages, no matter how many cases of sex-role reversal, male housewifery, or even empathic labor pains, these facts prove only one thing: the amazing flexibility of human nature. But human nature is adaptable *to* something, it is, yes, determined by its environmental conditions. And the biological family that we have described has existed everywhere throughout time. Even in matriarchies where woman's fertility is worshipped, and the father's role is unknown or unimportant, though perhaps not the genetic father, there is still some dependence of the female and the infant on the male. And though it is true that the nuclear family is only a recent development, one which . . . only intensifies the psychological penalties of the biological family, though it is true that throughout history there have been many variations on this biological family, the contingencies I have described existed in all of them, causing specific psychosexual distortions in the human personality.

But to grant that the sexual imbalance of power is biologically based is not to lose our case. We are no longer just animals. And the Kingdom of Nature does not reign absolute. As Simone de Beauvoir herself says:

The theory of historical materialism has brought to light some important truths. Humanity is not an animal species, it is a historical reality. Human society is an antiphysis—in a sense it is against nature; it does not passively submit to the presence of nature but rather takes over the control of nature on its own behalf. This arrogation is not an inward, subjective operation; it is accomplished objectively in practical action.

Thus, the "natural" is not necessarily a "human" value. Humanity has begun to outgrow nature: we can no longer justify the maintenance of a discriminatory sex class system on grounds of its origins in Nature. Indeed, for pragmatic reasons alone it is beginning to look as if we *must* get rid of it.

Suggestions for Further Reading

Works excerpted in *Woman in Western Thought* are not included in the following selected bibliography. Bibliographical information about them may be found in the Acknowledgments.

BIOGRAPHY

ADAMSON, ROBERT. *Fichte.* Edinburgh and London: W. Blackwood & Sons, 1901.

ALGREN, NELSON. "The Question of Simone de Beauvoir." *Harper's*, May 1965.

ANSCHUTZ, RICHARD PAUL. "J. S. Mill, Carlyle, and Mrs. Taylor." *Political Science* 7 (September 1955), 65–75.

AUGUSTINE, ST. *Confessions.* Trans. E. B. Pusey. New York: Modern Library, 1949.

BEAUVOIR, SIMONE DE. *All Said and Done.* Trans. Patrick O'Brian. New York: Putnam; London: André Deutsch and Weidenfeld & Nicholson, 1974.

———. *Force of Circumstance.* Trans. Richard Howard. 2 vols. New York: Putnam, 1965.

———. *Memoirs of a Dutiful Daughter.* Trans. James Kirkup. Cleveland: World, 1959.

———. *The Prime of Life.* Trans. Peter Green. Cleveland: World, 1962; London: André Deutsch and Weidenfeld & Nicholson, 1963.

———. *A Very Easy Death.* Trans. Patrick O'Brian. London: André Deutsch and Weidenfeld & Nicholson, 1965.

BLUCK, RICHARD STANLEY HAROLD. *Plato's Life and Thought.* London: Routledge and Kegan Paul, 1949.

BOURNE, H. R. FOX. *The Life of John Locke.* New York: Harper, 1876.

CAIRD, EDWARD. *Hegel.* Hamden, Conn.: Anchor Books, 1968.

CHEVIGNY, BELL GALE. *The Woman and the Myth: Margaret Fuller's Life and Writings.* New York: Feminist Press, 1977.

———. "Growing out of New England: the Emergence of Margaret Fuller's Radicalism." *Women's Studies* 5 (1977), 65–100.

COURTNEY, WILLIAM LEONARD. *Life of John Stuart Mill.* London: Walter Scott, 1889.

CRANSTON, MAURICE W. *John Locke: A Biography.* Mystic, Conn.: Lawrence Verry, 1957.

DETRE, JEAN. *A Most Extraordinary Pair: Mary Wollstonecraft and William Godwin.* New York: Doubleday, 1975.

DIOGENES LAERTIUS. *Lives of the Philosophers.* Trans. and ed. A. Robert Caponigri. Chicago: Henry Regnery, 1969.

DURING, INGMAR. *Aristotle in the Ancient Biographical Tradition.* Gothenburg (distr.: Almquist & Wiksell, Stockholm), 1957.

FLEXNER, ELEANOR. *Mary Wollstonecraft.* New York: Coward, McCann, & Geoghegan, 1972.

FRENZEL, IVO. *Friedrich Nietzsche: An Illustrated Biography.* New York: Pegasus, 1967.

GENNARI, GENEVIEVE. *Simone de Beauvoir.* Paris: Editions universitaires, 1958.

GOUHIER, HENRI. *La Vie d'Auguste Comte.* Rev. ed. Paris: J. Vrin, 1965.

GREEN, F. C. *Jean-Jacques Rousseau: A Critical Study of His Life and Writings.* Cambridge: Cambridge University Press, 1955.

GRIBBLE, FRANCIS. *Rousseau and the Women He Loved.* New York: Scribner's, 1908.

HAMILTON, MARY AGNES. *John Stuart Mill.* London: Hamish Hamilton, 1933.

HAYEK, FRIEDRICH A. *John Stuart Mill and Harriet Taylor: Their Friendship and Subsequent Marriage.* Chicago: University of Chicago Press, 1951.

HOHLENBERG, J. E. *Søren Kierkegaard.* Trans. T. H. Croxall. New York: Pantheon Books, 1954.

HOLLINGDALE, R. G.: *Nietzsche: The Man and His Philosophy.* Baton Rouge: Louisiana State University Press, 1965.

KING, LORD PETER. *The Life and Letters of John Locke.* London: G. Bell & Sons, 1884.

KNIGHT, A. H. J. *Some Aspects of the Life and Work of Nietzsche.* Cambridge: Cambridge University Press, 1933.

LEGGETT, H. W. *Bertrand Russell.* New York: Philosophical Library, 1950; London: Lincolns-Prager, 1959.

LOWRIE, WALTER. *Kierkegaard.* New York: Harper & Row, 1962.

———. *A Short Life of Kierkegaard.* Princeton: Princeton University Press, 1942.

MACDONALD, FREDERIKA. *Jean Jacques Rousseau.* London: Chapman & Hall, 1906.

MADSEN, AXEL. *Hearts and Minds: The Common Journey of Simone de Beauvoir and Jean-Paul Sartre.* New York: Morrow, 1977.

MARITAIN, JACQUES. *St. Thomas Aquinas.* Trans. Joseph W. Evans and Peter O'Reilly. New York: Meridian Books, 1958.

MARROU, HENRI IRENÉ. *St. Augustine and His Influence through the Ages.* Trans. Patrick Hepburne-Scott. New York: Harper Torchbooks; London: Longmans, 1957.

MARSTON, MANSFIELD. *The Life of J. S. Mill.* London: F. Farrah, 1873.

MILL, JOHN STUART. *Autobiography* (with an appendix of hitherto unpublished speeches and a preface by Harold J. Lasky). London and New York: H. Milford, Oxford University Press, 1924.

MILLER, PERRY, ED. *Margaret Fuller, American Romantic: A Selection from Her Writings and Correspondence.* Garden City, N.Y.: Doubleday, 1963; reissued Ithaca: Cornell University Press, 1970.

MORLEY, JOHN, VISCOUNT OF BLACKBURN. *Rousseau.* 2 vols. London: Chapman & Hall, 1873; Macmillan, 1886.

PACKE, MICHAEL ST. JOHN. *The Life of John Mill.* London: Secker & Warburg; New York: Macmillan, 1954.

PAPPE, H. O. *John Stuart Mill and the Harriet Taylor Myth.* Parkville: Melbourne University Press, 1960.

———. "The Mills and Harriet Taylor." *Political Science* 8 (March 1956), 19–30.

POLLOCK, SIR FREDERICK. *Spinoza: His Life and Philosophy.* London: Kegan Paul, 1880.

ROUSSEAU, JEAN-JACQUES. *Confessions.* Trans. Maurice Leloir. Philadelphia and London: J. B. Lippincott, 1901(?).

RUSSELL, BERTRAND. *The Autobiography of Bertrand Russell.* London: Allen & Unwin; Boston: Little, Brown, 1967.

———. *Fact and Fiction.* New York: Simon & Schuster, 1962.

————. "My Mental Development." In *The Philosophy of Bertrand Russell*, ed. P. A. Schilpp. Evanston and Chicago: Northwestern University Press, 1944.

————. *My Philosophical Development*. London: Allen & Unwin; New York: Simon & Schuster, 1959.

————. "My Religious Reminiscences." *Rationalist Annual* 55 (1938), 3–8.

————. *Portraits from Memory and Other Essays*. London: Allen & Unwin; New York: Simon & Schuster, 1962.

————. *Selected Papers of Bertrand Russell*. New York: Modern Library, 1927.

SARTRE, JEAN-PAUL. *The Words*. Trans. Bernard Frechtman. New York: George Braziller, 1964.

SUNSTEIN, EMILY W. *A Different Face: The Life of Mary Wollstonecraft*. Boston and Toronto: Little, Brown, 1975.

SWENSON, DAVID FERDINAND. *Something about Kierkegaard*. Minneapolis: Augsburg, 1941.

TAYLOR, ALFRED EDWARD. *Plato: The Man and His Work*. London: Methuen, 1926.

TOMALIN, CLAIRE. *The Life and Death of Mary Wollstonecraft*. New York: New American Library, 1974.

WALLACE, WILLIAM. *Life of Schopenhauer*. London: Walter Scott, 1890.

WOOD, ALAN. *Bertrand Russell: The Passionate Sceptic*. London: Allen & Unwin; New York: Simon & Schuster, 1957.

ZIMMERN, HELEN. *Arthur Schopenhauer: His Life and Philosophy*. Rev. ed. London: Allen & Unwin, 1932.

BACKGROUND STUDIES

ANTHONY, KATHARINE. *Feminism in Germany and Scandinavia*. New York: Henry Holt, 1915.

BEARD, MARY R. *Woman as a Force in History*. New York: Collier Books, 1962.

BEBEL, AUGUST. *Women and Socialism*. Trans. H. B. Adams Walther. New York: AMS Press, 1976.

BLEASE, W. LYON. *The Emancipation of English Women*. London: Constable, 1910; reissued New York: Benjamin Blom, 1971.

BLUMNER, HUGO. *The Home Life of the Ancient Greeks*. Trans. Alice Zimmern. Rev. ed. London and Paris: Cassell, 1895.

BRIGGS, ASA. *The Age of Improvement, 1783–1867*. London and New York: Longmans, Green, 1959.

————. *Victorian People: A Reassessment of Persons and Themes, 1851–1867*. Chicago: University of Chicago Press, 1970.

BUCKLEY, JEROME H. *The Victorian Temper*. New York: Vintage Books, 1964.

BURN, WILLIAM LAURENCE. *The Age of Equipoise*. New York: Norton; London: Allen & Unwin, 1964.

DECKARD, BARBARA SINCLAIR. *The Women's Movement*. New York: Harper & Row, 1975.

DONALDSON, JAMES. *Woman: Her Position and Influence in Ancient Greece and Rome, and Among the Early Christians*. New York: Longmans, Green, 1907.

ECKENSTEIN, LIMA. *Woman Under Monasticism*. Cambridge: Cambridge University Press, 1896.

FLEXNER, ELEANOR. *Century of Struggle: The Woman's Rights Movement in the United States*. Cambridge: Harvard University Press, 1959.

GARDINER, DOROTHY. *English Girlhood at School.* London: Oxford University Press, 1929.

GOMME, ARNOLD WYCOMBE. *Essays in Greek History and Literature.* London: Basil Blackwell, 1937.

GONCOURT, EDMOND DE, and JULES DE GONCOURT. *The Woman of the Eighteenth Century.* Trans. J. LeClercq and R. Roeder. New York: Minton, Balch, 1927.

GUETTEL, CHARNIE. *Marxism and Feminism.* Toronto: Women's Press, 1974.

GULICK, CHARLES BURTON. *The Life of the Ancient Greeks.* New York: D. Appleton, 1905.

HARRISON, A. R. W. *The Law of Athens.* 2 vols. Oxford: Oxford University Press, 1968.

HECKER, EUGENE A. *A Short History of Women's Rights.* Westport, Conn.: Greenwood Press, 1914.

HOUGHTON, WALTER E. *The Victorian Frame of Mind: 1830–1870.* New Haven: Published for Wellesley College by Yale University Press, 1957.

JERNESS, LINDA, ed. *Feminism and Socialism.* New York: Pathfinder Press, 1972.

KELSO, RUTH. *Doctrine for the Lady of the Renaissance.* Urbana: University of Illinois Press, 1956.

KITTO, HUMPHERY DAVY FINDLEY. *The Greeks.* Rev. ed. Baltimore: Penguin Books, 1957.

LEWIS, C. S. *The Allegory of Love.* Oxford: Clarendon Press, 1936.

MILLER, KATE. *Sexual Politics.* New York: Doubleday, 1969.

MORLEY, JOHN, VISCOUNT OF BLACKBURN. *Rousseau and His Era.* London: Macmillan, 1923.

PATAI, RAPHAEL. *Women in the Modern World.* New York: Free Press, 1967.

POMEROY, SARAH B. *Goddesses, Whores, Wives, and Slaves: Women in Classical Antiquity.* New York: Schocken Books, 1975.

POWER, EILEEN E. *Medieval English Nunneries.* Cambridge: Cambridge University Press, 1922.

———. *Medieval Women.* Ed. M. M. Postan. Cambridge: Cambridge University Press, 1975.

———. "The Position of Women." In *The Legacy of the Middle Ages,* ed. C. G. Grump and E. F. Jacob. Oxford: Clarendon Press, 1926.

PUCKETT, HUGH WILEY. *Germany's Women Go Forward.* New York: AMS Press, 1967.

ROBINSON, CYRIL EDWARD. *Everyday Life in Ancient Greece.* Oxford: Clarendon Press, 1933.

ROVER, CONSTANCE. *Women's Suffrage and Party Politics in Britain: 1866–1914.* London: Routledge & Kegan Paul; Toronto: Toronto University Press, 1967.

SACHS, HANNELORE. *The Renaissance Woman.* Trans. Marianne Herzfeld. New York: McGraw-Hill, 1971.

SCHIRMACHER, KAETHE. *The Modern Woman's Rights Movement.* Trans. Carl Conrad Eckhardt. New York: Macmillan, 1912.

SCOTT, HILDA. *Does Socialism Liberate Women?* Boston: Beacon Press, 1974.

TROTSKY, LEON. *Women and the Family.* New York: Pathfinder Press, 1970.

VICINUS, MARTHA, ed. *Suffer and Be Still: Women in the Victorian Age.* Bloomington: Indiana University Press, 1972.

YOUNG, GEORGE MALCOLM, ed. *Early Victorian England: 1830–1865.* 2 vols. London: Oxford University Press, 1934.

PHILOSOPHY AND PHILOSOPHICAL CRITICISM

ALEXANDER, WILLIAM K. "Sex and Philosophy in Augustine." *Augustinian Studies* 5 (1974), 197–208.

ALLEN, CHRISTINE GARSIDE. "Plato on Women." *Feminist Studies* 2, 2–3 (1975), 131–138.

ANNAS, JULIA. "Mill and the Subjection of Women." *Philosophy* 52 (April 1977), 179–194.

AUGUSTINUS, AURELIUS. *Continence. Fathers of the Church,* ed. R. J. Deferrari et al. New York: Fathers of the Church, Inc., 1948–1960; Washington: Catholic University of America Press, 1960–1962. Vol. 14.

———. *The Excellence of Widowhood. Fathers of the Church,* ed. R. J. Deferrari et al. New York: Fathers of the Church, Inc., 1948–1960; Washington: Catholic University of America Press, 1960–1962. Vol. 14.

———. *The Good of Marriage. Fathers of the Church,* ed. R. J. Deferrari et al. New York: Fathers of the Church, Inc., 1948–1960; Washington: Catholic University of America Press, 1960–1962. Vol. 15.

———. *Holy Virginity. Fathers of the Church,* ed. R. J. Deferrari et al. New York: Fathers of the Church, Inc., 1948–1960; Washington: Catholic University of America Press, 1960–1962. Vol. 15.

———. *To Pollentius on Adulterous Marriages. Fathers of the Church,* ed. R. J. Deferrari et al. New York: Fathers of the Church, Inc., 1948–1960; Washington: Catholic University of America Press, 1960–1962. Vol. 15.

BLUM, LARRY, MARCIA HOMIAK, JUDY HOUSMAN, and NAOMI SCHEMAN. "Altruism and Women's Oppression." *Philosophical Forum* 5 (Fall 1973– Winter 1974), 222–247.

CALVERT, BRIAN. "Plato and the Equality of Women." *Phoenix* 29 (Autumn 1975), 231–243.

CLARK, STEPHEN B. *Aristotle's Man.* Oxford: Clarendon Press, 1975.

CUMMING, ALAN. "Pauline Christianity and Greek Philosophy: A Study of the Status of Women." *Journal of the History of Ideas* 34 (Fall 1973), 517–528.

DALY, MARY. *Beyond God the Father.* Boston: Beacon Press, 1973.

———. *The Church and the Second Sex.* 2d ed. New York: Harper & Row, 1975.

DICKASON, ANNE. "Anatomy and Destiny: The Role of Biology in Plato's Views of Woman." *The Philosophical Forum* 5 (Fall 1973—Winter 1974), 45–53.

DURANT, WILL. "Bertrand Russell on Marriage and Morals." In *Adventures in Genius.* New York: Simon & Schuster, 1931.

——— and ARIEL DURANT. *The Story of Civilization.* New York: Simon & Schuster, 1935–1975.

FORTENBAUGH, W. W. "On Plato's Feminism in *Republic* V." *Apeiron* 9 (November 1975), 1–4.

FRISBE, SANDRA. "Women and the Will to Power." *Gnosis* 1 (Spring 1975), 1–10.

FULLER, MARGARET. "The Great Lawsuit: Man *versus* Men, Woman *versus* Women." *Dial* 4 (July 1843), 1–47.

HEGEL, GEORG WILHELM FRIEDRICH. *The Philosophy of Right.* Trans. T. M. Knox. Oxford: Oxford University Press, 1952.

HELD, VIRGINIA. "Marx, Sex, and the Transformation of Society." *The Philosophical Forum* 5 (Fall 1973–Winter 1974), 168–184.

HILL, THOMAS E. "Servility and Self-Respect." *Monist* 57 (January 1973), 87–104.

KANT, IMMANUEL. *Anthropology from a Pragmatic Point of View.* Trans. Mary J. Gregor. The Hague: Martinus Nijhoff, 1974.

KIERKEGAARD, SØREN. *Either/Or.* Vol. I, trans. David F. Swenson and Lillian Marvin Swenson. Vol. II, trans. Walter Lowrie. Princeton: Princeton University Press, 1944.

———. *Repetition.* Trans. Walter Lowrie. Princeton: Princeton University Press, 1941.

———. *Stages on Life's Way.* Trans. Walter Lowrie. New York: Schocken Books, 1967.

LEIGHTON, JEAN. *Simone de Beauvoir on Woman.* Cranbury, N.J., and London: Associated University Presses, 1975.

MARCUSE, HERBERT. "Marxism and Feminism," *Women's Studies* 2 3 (1974), 279–288.

MARX, KARL. *On Education, Women, and Children.* Trans. Saul K. Padover. The Karl Marx Library, vol. 5. New York: McGraw-Hill, 1975.

MATHERON, ALEXANDRE. "Femmes et serviteurs dans le démocratie spinoziste." *Revue Philosophique de la France et de l'etranger* 167, (1977), 181–200.

MILL, JOHN STUART. "Enfranchisement of Women." *Westminster Review* (July 1851).

MITCHELL, JULIET. "Marxism and Women's Liberation." *Social Praxis* 1 (1973), 23–33.

———. *Woman's Estate.* New York: Random House, 1971.

NIETZSCHE, FRIEDRICH. *The Gay Science.* Trans. Walter Kaufmann. New York: Random House, 1974.

OKIN, SUSAN MOLLETT. "Philosopher Queens and Private Wives: Plato on Woman and the Family." *Philosophy and Public Affairs,* 6 (Summer 1977), 345–369.

OSBORNE, MARTHA LEE. "Plato's Unchanging View of Woman: A Denial that Anatomy Spells Destiny." *The Philosophical Forum* 6 (Summer 1975), 447–452.

OSTHEIMER, ANTHONY. *The Family: A Thomistic Study in Social Philosophy.* Washington, D.C.: Catholic University of America Press, 1939.

PETIT, ANNE, and BERNADETTE BENSAUDE. "Le Féminisme militant d'un auguste phallocrate (Auguste Comte, *Système de politique positive*)." *Revue philosophique de la France et de l'étranger* 166 (July–September 1976), 293–311.

PIERCE, CHRISTINE. "Equality: *Republic* V." *Monist* 57 (January 1973), 1–11.

POMEROY, SARAH. "Feminism in Book V of Plato's *Republic.*" *Apeiron* 8 (May 1974), 33–35.

RUSSELL, BERTRAND. *Marriage and Morals.* New York: Horace Liveright, 1929.

———. "The Status of Women." *Journal of the Bertrand Russell Archives,* Summer 1974, 3–12.

SAXONHOUSE, ARLENE W. "The Philosopher and the Female in the Political Thought of Plato." *Political Theory* 4 (May 1976), 195–212.

SCHOPENHAUER, ARTHUR. *The Basis of Morality.* Trans. Arthur Brodrick Bullock. London: Allen & Unwin, 1903.

———. *The World as Will and Idea.* Trans. R. B. Haldane and J. Kemp. 3 vols. London: Trubner, 1883.

STEPHEN, LESLIE. *English Utilitarians.* London: London School of Economics and Political Science, 1900.

STERN, BERNHARD J. "Engels on the Family." In *A Centenary of Marxism,* ed. Samuel Bernstein. New York: Science and Society, 1948.

STERN, KARL. *The Flight from Woman.* New York: Farrar, Straus & Giroux, 1965.

WHITBECK, CAROLINE. "Theories of Sex Difference." *The Philosophical Forum* 5 (Fall 1973–Winter 1974), 54–80.

WILLIFORD, MARIAM. "Bentham on the Rights of Women." *Journal of the History of Ideas* 36 (January–March 1975), 167–176.

REVIEWS OF RECENT RESEARCH

ENGLISH, JANE. "Review Essay: Philosophy." *Signs: Journal of Women in Culture and Society* 3 (Summer 1978), 823–831.

MOULTON, JANICE. "Review Essay: Philosophy." *Signs: Journal of Women in Culture and Society* 2 (Winter 1976), 422–433.

PIERCE, CHRISTINE. "Review Essay: Philosophy." *Signs: Journal of Women in Culture and Society* 1 (Winter 1975), 487–501.

About the Editor

Martha Lee Osborne, a graduate of The University of Kentucky and Bryn Mawr College, has been teaching at The University of Tennessee in Knoxville since 1954. She is a member of the Department of Philosophy and also serves on the women's studies faculty. Professor Osborne has contributed articles on Plato to such journals as *The Philosophical Forum* and *The Southern Journal of Philosophy*.

80-1056   301.412
                       W844

Woman in western thought.

Mount Mary College

Library

Milwaukee, Wisconsin 53222

DEMCO